Guidance of Young Children

Sixth Edition

Marian Marion

University of Wisconsin–Stout

Merrill
Prentice Hall

Upper Saddle River, New Jersey
Columbus, Ohio

Library of Congress Cataloging in Publication Data

Marion, Marian
    Guidance of young children / Marian Marion.—6th ed.
      p. cm.
    Includes bibliographical references and indexes.
    ISBN 0-13-097621-0
     1. Child psychology. 2. Child rearing. I. Title.

    HQ772 .M255 2003
    649'.1—dc21

                         2002025063

Vice President and Publisher: Jeffery W. Johnston
Executive Editor: Kevin M. Davis
Associate Editor: Christina M. Tawney
Editorial Assistant: Autumn Crisp
Production Editor: Sheryl Glicker Langner
Production Coordination: Clarinda Publication Services
Design Coordinator: Diane C. Lorenzo
Photo Coordinator: Cynthia Cassidy
Cover Designer: Thomas Borah
Cover Photo: Corbis Stock Market
Production Manager: Laura Messerly
Director of Marketing: Ann Castel Davis
Marketing Manager: Amy June
Marketing Coordinator: Tyra Cooper

This book was set in Fruitiger by The Clarinda Company. It was printed and bound by Maple Vail Book Manufacturing Group. The cover was printed by The Lehigh Press, Inc.

Photo Credits: Scott Cunningham/Merrill: pp. 43, 132; Kevin Fitzsimons/Merrill: p. 356; Dan Floss/Merrill: pp. 32, 279; Ken Karp/PH College: p. 277; Lloyd Lemmerman/Merrill: p. 255; Anthony Magnacca/Merrill: pp. 97, 298, 303; Gail Meese/Merrill: p. 264; Barbara Schwartz/Merrill: pp. 70, 73, 88, 116, 328, 352; Silver Burdett Gin; p. 202; Anne Vega/Merrill: pp. 2, 23, 66, 82, 115, 176, 206, 242, 246, 270, 335, 345, 359; Todd Yarrington/Merrill: p. 193; Shirley Zeiberg/PH College: 189, 234.

Pearson Education Ltd
Pearson Education Australia Pty. Limited
Pearson Education Singapore Pte. Ltd.
Pearson Education North Asia Ltd.
Pearson Education Canada, Ltd
Pearson Educacion de Mexico, S.A. de C.V.
Pearson Education—Japan
Pearson Education Malaysia Pte. Ltd.
Pearson Education, *Upper Saddle River, New Jersey*

Merrill
Prentice Hall

10 9 8 7 6 5 4 3 2
ISBN: 0–13–097621–0

For Bill and Lucy Ann

For Roxie and Bekka, my canine companions,
now very old, who have sat under the computer table
as I have written three editions of this text

Preface

Welcome to the sixth edition of *Guidance of Young Children*. The first edition of *Guidance of Young Children* was published in 1981, the second in 1987, the third in 1991, the fourth in 1995, and the fifth in 1999. My purpose in writing the sixth edition is exactly the same as for earlier editions—to give students a book grounded in solid theory and research, a book that will help them understand the process of child guidance.

I have designed this edition so that it continues to reflect my beliefs about children and child guidance; it is these beliefs that I want to pass on to students.

- **I believe that protecting children is our most important role.** Students reading this text should understand that we teach and protect children most effectively by making active, conscious decisions about positive strategies. We protect children when we refuse to use strategies that are degrading or hurtful or have the potential to harm or humiliate children. Some strategies denigrate and dishonor children and should never be used, such as shaking, hitting, and other forms of physically hurtful interaction, as well as hostile humor, embarrassment, ridicule, sarcasm, judging, manipulation, mind games, hurtful punishment, ignoring, terrorizing, isolating, and boundary violations. These are personality-numbing horrors. They are abusive and have no place in our lives with children.

  The National Association for the Education of Young Children (NAEYC), in its Code of Ethics, notes that the most important part of the Code is that early childhood professionals never engage in any practice that hurts or degrades a child. Therefore, this textbook takes quite seriously the Latin phrase *primum non nocere,* or "First of all, do no harm." Students who use this textbook will learn **only** positive strategies and a respectful approach to guiding children.

- **I believe that we have a choice about how we think about and behave with children.** John Steinbeck, in *East of Eden,* said that the beauty of being human is our ability to make choices. Students need to know that what they choose to think about children, how they act with them, and the discipline strategies they use *do* matter. Using a positive, constructivist approach on a daily basis has a long-term impact on children—helping them become self-responsible, competent, independent, cooperative people who like themselves and who have a strong core of values.

- **I believe that an adult's "style" of guiding children does affect children.** It affects several parts of their personality and their approach to life—for example, their moral compass and their level of self-esteem, how they manage anger and aggression, how they handle stress, their willingness to cooperate with others, whether they can take another person's perspective, and their social skills.

Therefore, the organizing force for this text is the concept of styles of caregiving—a concept presented right away in Chapter 1. Students should come away from that chapter with a clear idea of the authoritarian, authoritative, and permissive styles. They will learn about adult beliefs and behavior in each style and about the likely effect of that style on children. They will then encounter the concept of caregiving style woven into almost every chapter.

- **I believe that constructivist, positive, and effective child guidance is based on solid knowledge of child development.** Without this knowledge, adults might well have unrealistic expectations of children. Having this knowledge gives professionals a firm foundation on which to build child guidance skills.

  Chapter 2 examines several aspects of child development. Students will quickly see that this chapter is not merely a review of child development. They will understand that knowing about specific areas of child development enables them to guide children more effectively.

- **I believe that there is no one right way to deal with any issue, but that there are many good ways.** This is not a cookbook in which students will find nice, neat answers. I will not give them a set of tricks to use with children. However, students will find numerous exercises and questions designed to help them understand basic concepts of child guidance. My hope is that they will enjoy thinking critically about guidance issues and making active decisions about child guidance.

- **I believe that we should each develop a personal approach to guiding children, one built on theoretical eclecticism.** In this text, students will study and use the Decision-Making Model of Child Guidance, a model that evolves from understanding various theoretical approaches to child guidance. Students will use four main theories—those of Piaget, Vygotsky, Rogers, and Adler—in constructing positive child guidance decisions. Chapter 11 stresses the common themes in these four theories when applied to child guidance.

SPECIAL FEATURES OF *GUIDANCE OF YOUNG CHILDREN,* SIXTH EDITION

I am, first of all, a teacher, and it was my goal to write a *student-friendly* book that actively engages students in the learning process. Therefore, I've retained certain features from other editions that have worked, and I have added specific features designed to help students learn this material even more effectively. Here are some of these features:

- *Four main teachers from the same school* (**new feature**). Mrs. Vargas (preschool), Mr. Claiborne (first grade), Mr. Nellis (K–2), and Mr. Lee (grades 3 and 4). These teachers appear in examples throughout the text and deal with guidance problems faced in classrooms every day.

- *Case study approach.* Case studies at the beginning of every chapter focus on children and teachers in early childhood classrooms. I intended that case studies illustrate the major points in each chapter. I have developed several new cases for this edition.
- *Case study analysis* in every chapter. Students apply newly acquired knowledge to the chapter's case study.
- A chapter summary, entitled *Reflecting on Key Content,* helps students reflect on what they have learned rather than just on listing main points. The objectives, expanded table of contents, and Reflection on Key Content, all *advance organizers,* should help students get an overall picture of the chapter content before they begin studying it.
- *Working with Parents* boxes in selected chapters will help students use the chapter's information with parents of the children that they teach.
- *Apply Your Knowledge* activities. Students will have an opportunity to apply the information that they have learned to real situations.
- Real-life examples gleaned from observing in classrooms for infants, toddlers, and preschool, kindergarten, and primary grade children.
- An *appendix* that summarizes the major positive discipline strategies in outline form.
- Liberal use of **bold** to highlight definitions and other important terms.
- A *writing style* that is conversational yet informative.
- *Web sites* for each chapter.
- *An instructor's guide.* I have refined this guide to support busy instructors as they teach from this textbook. You will find teaching objectives, descriptions of videos, suggestions for teaching each section, evaluation questions, and transparency masters.

STRUCTURE OF THE SIXTH EDITION

This edition is organized by chapters within four parts. Here is a brief table of contents.

Part One: Guidance of Young Children: Three Essential Elements

Part One of the text has three chapters, each explaining an essential element in guiding children. The first major element in guidance is an adult's "style" of interacting with children—one's "caregiving" style. The second essential element is one's knowledge of child development and willingness to learn how to make wise guidance decisions. The third major element is the ability to observe children.

Chapter 1, DAP Child Guidance, comes first in order to emphasize caregiving styles as the organizing principle of the text. It also presents the Decision-Making Model of child guidance. Chapter 2, Construct Child Guidance Decisions, presents child development as the foundation for developmentally appropriate child guidance. Chapter 3, Observing Behavior in Child Guidance, is a **completely new**

chapter added to emphasize the importance of observing children as the basis of any and all guidance decisions.

Part Two: "Direct" and "Indirect" Child Guidance

Part Two of the text will help students understand that they can guide children directly with specific guidance and discipline strategies. They will also learn about the concept of "indirect" guidance through setting up a classroom well.

Chapter 4, Positive Guidance and Discipline Strategies, offers **new** positive guidance and discipline strategies, augmenting the list presented in previous editions. Chapter 5, Early Childhood Classroom Management, deals with developing a DAP early childhood classroom as an important "indirect" way to guide children.

Part Three: Special Topics in Child Guidance

Part Three has as its purpose illustrating how authoritative caregivers deal with each of several special topics. The chapter on preventing violent behavior, for example, will help students understand how violence grows and what they can do to prevent violent, aggressive behavior.

Chapter 6, Authentic Self-Esteem and Moral Identity, describes how moral identity and authentic self-esteem evolve and describes practices that help children develop them. Chapter 7, Resilience and Stress in Childhood, has been **expanded** to include information on the biology of stress as well as different types of stress. It offers suggestions on helping children cope with stress in general as well as the specific stressor of moving. Chapter 8, Emotional Intelligence and Anger Management, has been **updated** to emphasize emotional intelligence. It includes specific suggestions on helping young children learn to manage the emotion of anger.

Chapter 9, Preventing Violent Behavior and Understanding Aggression in Children, presents **new information** on school violence and bullying. Chapter 10, Guiding the Devlopment of Prosocial Behavior, describes and explains the development of prosocial behavior, e.g., compassion, cooperativeness, helpfulness. I also offer specific suggestions adults can use to help children become kind, compassionate people.

Part Four: Develop an "Eclectic" Approach to Child Guidance

Part Four will help students understand how helpful good theory is in building guidance skills. This part of the text encourages students to make wise guidance decisions.

Chapter 11, Theories, has **changed significantly** since the last edition. I have dropped behaviorist theory completely and now emphasize the common themes in the theories of Vygotsky, Rogers, and Adler. Chapter 12, Apply Your Knowledge, is an **expanded** chapter describing the Decision-Making Model and showing how it can be used in everyday discipline encounters, and with different behaviors, to change the context of a classroom.

ACKNOWLEDGMENTS

Some of the major changes for this edition of the text grew out of my reading the work of Alfie Kohn. I have used one of his books, *Beyond Discipline*, in our senior seminar. This book, which urges teachers to adopt a problem-solving approach to discipline issues, has helped me refine the Decision-Making Model of Child Guidance. Another of his books, *Punished by Rewards*, and a recent article in *Young Children*, "Five Reasons to Stop Saying 'Good Job!,'" encouraged me to rewrite Chapter 11, the theories chapter, to exclude the behavioral approach.

A special note of thanks to my child guidance and advanced child guidance classes of 1999, 2000, and 2001 for field-testing the new case studies, the case study analyses, and the *Apply Your Knowledge* sections of each chapter. My students do an excellent job with the decision-making model of child guidance, and I believe their developing skill will carry over into their teaching.

Several colleagues from around the country who have used the other editions reviewed material for the sixth edition: Elaine Goldsmith, Texas Woman's University, Denton; Herman Walston, Kentucky State University; Susan Christian, Patrick Henry Community College; and Pamela O. Fleege, University of South Florida. They gave positive comments and helpful suggestions for change. Their comments were especially useful as I refined the book's content and structure. I am grateful for every one of their suggestions about reorganizing the text, incorporating information on school violence, additional research, and adding additional cases to the last chapter.

Several years ago, the chancellor of my university, Charles Sorenson, requested a review of and then supported a major change in the sabbatical leave policy. This made it possible for faculty carrying a full teaching load to engage even more intensely in scholarly activity. I remain grateful to him for his continued support of sabbatical leaves and of scholarly activity in general.

Finally, my early childhood colleagues have been generous with discussions about children and suggestions and comments about this text and about how they teach child guidance. Many thanks!

Marian Marion
Email: *Marionm@uwstout.edu*

Discover the Companion Website
Accompanying This Book

THE PRENTICE HALL COMPANION WEBSITE:
A VIRTUAL LEARNING ENVIRONMENT

Technology is a constantly growing and changing aspect of our field that is creating a need for content and resources. To address this emerging need, Prentice Hall has developed an online learning environment for students and professors alike—Companion Websites—to support our textbooks.

In creating a Companion Website, our goal is to build on and enhance what the textbook already offers. For this reason, the content for each user-friendly website is organized by topic and provides the professor and student with a variety of meaningful resources. Common features of a Companion Website include:

For the Professor—
Every Companion Website integrates **Syllabus Manager™**, an online syllabus creation and management utility.

- **Syllabus Manager™** provides you, the instructor, with an easy, step-by-step process to create and revise syllabi, with direct links into Companion Website and other online content without having to learn HTML.
- Students may logon to your syllabus during any study session. All they need to know is the web address for the Companion Website and the password you've assigned to your syllabus.
- After you have created a syllabus using **Syllabus Manager™**, students may enter the syllabus for their course section from any point in the Companion Website.
- Clicking on a date, the student is shown the list of activities for the assignment. The activities for each assignment are linked directly to actual content, saving time for students.
- Adding assignments consists of clicking on the desired due date, then filling in the details of the assignment—name of the assignment, instructions, and whether or not it is a one-time or repeating assignment.
- In addition, links to other activities can be created easily. If the activity is online, a URL can be entered in the space provided, and it will be linked automatically in the final syllabus.
- Your completed syllabus is hosted on our servers, allowing convenient updates from any computer on the Internet. Changes you make to your syllabus are immediately available to your students at their next logon.

For the Student—

- **Topic Overviews**—outline key concepts in topic areas
- **Web Links**—General websites related to topic areas as well as associations and professional organizations.
- **Read About It**—Timely articles that enable you to become more aware of important issues in early childhood education.
- **Learn by Doing**—Put concepts into action, participate in activities, complete lesson plans, examine strategies, and more.
- **For Teachers**—Access information that you will need to know as an in-service teacher, including information on materials, activities, lessons, curriculum, and state standards.
- **Visit a School**—Visit a school's website to see concepts, theories, and strategies in action.
- **Electronic Bluebook**—send homework or essays directly to your instructor's email with this paperless form
- **Message Board**—serves as a virtual bulletin board to post—or respond to—questions or comments to/from a national audience
- **Chat**—real time chat with anyone who is using the text anywhere in the country—ideal for discussion and study groups, class projects, etc.

To take advantages of these and other resources, please visit the *Guidance of Young Children,* Sixth Edition, Companion Website at

www.prenhall.com/marion

Contents

2   Construct Child Guidance Decisions: Apply Knowledge of Child Development   32

3 Observing Behavior in Child Guidance   66

Part Two "Direct" and "Indirect" Child Guidance   87

4 Positive Guidance and Discipline Strategies: Direct Guidance   88

Part Three   Special Topics in Child Guidance   173

6   Authentic Self-Esteem and Moral Identity   176

7 Resilience and Stress in Childhood   202

8 Emotional Intelligence and Anger Management   234

9   Preventing Violent Behavior and Understanding Aggression in Children   264

10   Guiding the Development of Prosocial Behavior   298

Note: Every effort has been made to provide accurate and current Internet information in this book. However, the Internet and information posted on it are constantly changing, so it is inevitable that some of the Internet addresses listed in this textbook will change.

Guidance of Young Children: Three Essential Elements

Chapter 1 DAP Child Guidance: Authoritative Style and Decision-Making Model. Authoritarian, authoritative, and permissive. This chapter describes each of these adult **caregiving styles**—adults' behavior and impact on children's personality and behavior. It explains the concept of developmentally appropriate practices (DAP) as a part of the authoritative style and introduces the Decision-Making Model of Child Guidance. This model will help you learn how to construct wise decisions about discipline encounters.

Chapter 2 Construct Child Guidance Decisions: Apply Knowledge of Child Development. Chapter 2 is not just a review of child development. The chapter does describe selected facets of child development, such as memory and perception, but explains how child development knowledge can help professionals construct appropriate guidance decisions. With this chapter, you will use your existing knowledge base in child development to build a working knowledge of child development. You will be able to make informed decisions about child guidance issues.

Chapter 3 Observing Behavior in Child Guidance. Children tell us what they need in so many ways—charming, downright funny, and on occasion, aggressive ways. Their behavior alone can communicate curiosity, excitement, happiness, or even heavy sadness or great anger. Behavior is a code, and only a person who knows the code can read it. Chapter 3 will help you understand the value of observation as the first step in **cracking the code** of children's behavior. This is the first step in figuring out how to help them get what they need.

PART 1

DAP Child Guidance: Authoritative Style and Decision-Making Model

"... children of authoritative parents have proved to be more competent than the children of either authoritarian or permissive parents."

(Maccoby & Martin, 1983, p. 46)

Case Studies: Styles of Caregiving

Responsiveness: Major Dimension of Caregiving
Warmth
Child Development Knowledge
Partners in Interaction
Communication Style
Giving Explanations

Demandingness: Major Dimension of Caregiving
Boundaries, Limits, and Expectations
Monitoring and Supervising
Discipline Strategies
Styles of Confrontation

Authoritative Caregiving Style
High Demandingness, High Responsiveness
Positive and Powerful Effect on Young Children's Development

Authoritarian Caregiving Style
High Demandingness, Low Responsiveness
Negative Effect on Young Children's Development

Permissive Caregiving Style
Low Demandingness
Low Demandingness Plus High Responsiveness
Low Demandingness Plus Low Responsiveness
How Permissiveness Affects Young Children

Case Study Analysis: Styles of Caregiving

Basic Processes Adults Use to Influence Children
Modeling
Direct Instruction
Practicing with Coaching
Giving Feedback
Managing the Child's Environment
Stating Expectations of Desired Behaviors
Encouraging Children to Modify Attitudes and Understanding

Decision-Making Model of Child Guidance
Authoritative Caregivers Use the Decision-Making Model
Steps in the Decision-Making Model

After reading and studying this chapter, you will be able to:

❑ **Name and describe** the two major dimensions of caregiving.

❑ **Name, describe, and explain** the three styles of caregiving.

❑ **Explain** the major similarities and differences between the two types of permissiveness.

❑ **Explain** how each caregiving style tends to affect children's development.

❑ **Name and explain** basic processes through which adults influence children.

❑ **Name** the steps in the decision-making model of child guidance. **Use** the decision-making model to deal with a specific guidance issue.

Case Studies: Styles of Caregiving

Nathan

Nathan left his scooter in the middle of the living room. His mother called out to him, "Put the scooter outside, Nathan." Nathan heard but ignored her as he walked away. "Nathan, did you hear me? Put that scooter outside this instant. I mean it. No water park for you this afternoon if you don't put that scooter outside!" Nathan shuffled down the hall to his room and Mom continued in an exasperated tone, "Nathan, get back here. I want that scooter put away."

Finally, Mom just turned back to the kitchen. "That boy never listens to me." Nathan pays little attention to his mother's limits. He also knows that she hardly ever follows up on her threats. That afternoon, for example, Mom took Nathan to the water park, after saying, "Next time, Nathan, you'd better listen to me when I tell you to do something." Nathan turned his head away from Mom and rolled his eyes.

Harley

At 18 months, Harley, when visiting a friend with his mother, banged on the friend's television screen and pushed at the door screen. His mom said nothing until the friend expressed concern for her property. Then she said, "Harley, do you think you should be doing that?" To the friend she said, "You know, I don't think I should order him around." When he was 4 years old, Harley stayed up until 11:30 when company was over. To the friend who inquired about his bedtime Mom replied, "Oh, I let Harley make decisions on his own." Harley fell asleep in the book corner at his preschool the next day. At 6 years of age, Harley pushed ahead of others at a zoo exhibition and Mom ignored them and she said, "Go ahead. Can you see? Move up closer."

Ryan

Ryan's father is irritable around his children. His sister-in-law has watched him for years and now thinks that he really dislikes being a father. He tells his three children, including Ryan, what he wants them to do by cursing at them and barking and snapping orders. He expects his children to obey immediately despite anything else they might be doing. He laughed when he recited his "motto" to one of the other men at work: "My kids know that I mean business! When I say jump, they know that they'd better say, 'how high?'" Ryan has watched as Dad used a belt on an older brother.

When Ryan was a toddler and learning how to use the toilet, Dad spanked him when he had an accident. When Ryan was 4 years old Dad grabbed one of his arms and yanked him to make Ryan move along at the store, saying, "#%&*#$#. (curse word). I'm sick of you holding us up all the time." At preschool Ryan had trouble with other children because he hit them when he was angry and the other children started to leave him out of activities. Then he met Mr. Claiborne, his first-grade teacher. You will read about how Mr. Claiborne helped Ryan in spite of Ryan's background.

Megan

Megan's mother is a home care provider for Megan, 18 months old, and her friend's two children, Robert, aged 24 months, and Steven, aged 9 months. Steven's mother asked Megan's mom what to do when Steven bites her during feeding. "Quickly tell him NO and pull his mouth off your breast. Don't make a joke of it, either, or he'll think you're playing a game." Megan wanted a toy that Robert had but didn't seem to have the words for asking. She grew more agitated and then, even to her own surprise, she bit him! Megan's mother, also surprised, immediately took care of the bite on Robert's arm. Then, to her daughter, she said, "No, Megan. Biting is a no-no. Biting hurts Robert. If you need help, come to Mommy and I will help you get a toy."

This entire textbook focuses on positive, authoritative child guidance, based on principles of developmentally appropriate practice, or DAP[1]. Many adults, like Megan's mother and many teachers, use developmentally appropriate, authoritative child guidance. They are warm, very responsive, and supportive while they also have high expectations of children. Their beliefs about discipline and guidance are developmentally appropriate. Their practices are also developmentally appropriate; i.e., their beliefs and practices are "in sync." This first chapter describes DAP, or authoritative child guidance and the decision-making process that authoritative caregivers use when working with young children.

Other adults, like Ryan's father, use the developmentally inappropriate practices (hereinafter called DIP) of the authoritarian. Still others, like Harley and Nathan's parents, use the DIP style of caregiving and guidance called permissiveness. You will read about the authoritarian and permissive styles in this chapter as well, but the emphasis is on positive authoritative caregiving and guidance.

RESPONSIVENESS AND DEMANDINGNESS: TWO MAJOR CAREGIVING DIMENSIONS

Researchers have long been interested in how one parent or teacher differs from others. Researchers have also been interested in how these differences affect children. For example, it has been almost 50 years since Becker (1954) analyzed several studies and classified a parent's style by looking at whether the parent was (a) hostile or warm and (b) restrictive or permissive. Then and now, we know that **warmth** is probably the single most important factor in an adult's relationship with a child.

This text concentrates on describing the work of Diana Baumrind (Baumrind, 1967, 1971, 1977, 1979, 1996; Baumrind & Black, 1967) who built on the foundation of the earlier research. She has found that two major factors—**responsiveness and demandingness**—determine an adult's **style of caregiving.** Some adults are highly responsive to children while others are not very responsive. Some adults are high in demandingness while others make very few demands. See Figure 1.1.

---

[1]DAP was described by Bredekamp (1987).

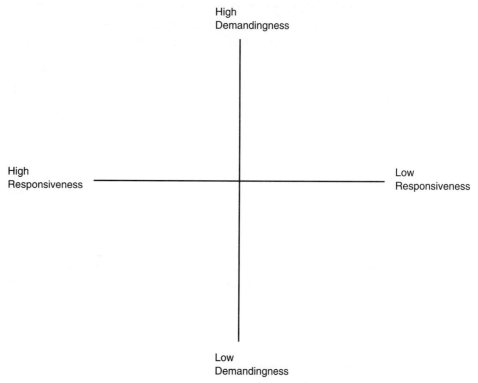

Figure 1.1 Two major dimensions—demandingness and responsiveness—form the basis of a caregiver's style.

RESPONSIVENESS

Responsiveness: one of two major caregiving dimensions; refers to degree of adult supportiveness, degree to which adult is tuned in to a child's developmental level, and whether adult meets a child's needs. Figure 1.1 shows that responsiveness is on a continuum; i.e., a person can exist anywhere along the continuum. Some adults are highly responsive to children while others are not.

This section and Figure 1.2 describes several important aspects of responsiveness: warmth, whether an adult knows child development, whether he views children and adults as partners in interaction, communication style, and whether an adult uses good explanations along with guidance strategies (Baumrind, 1996).

Warmth

Warmth: the emotional expression of liking or love.

Observe a group of adults, either parents or teachers, as they interact with young children. You will observe differences in how warm they are toward children. Some teachers and parents are highly responsive in that they show a high degree of

What Is Responsiveness? What Is Demandingness?	
Responsiveness	Demandingness
• **Warmth** Do I show that I like children? Do I show appropriate affection and support? Are my expressions of warmth sincere? • **Child development knowledge** Do I have a good knowledge base in child development? Do I understand how families affect children? Do I understand how a child's culture affects him or her? • **Children and adults as partners in interaction** Do I really understand that both adults and children have a part in any interaction? Do I also understand that my adult role carries greater responsibility? • **Communication style** Do I communicate in an open and direct way? How do I send messages, especially limits? • **Giving explanations** Do I use a reason along with a guidance strategy? Do I know how to state reasons well?	• **Boundaries, limits, and expectations** Do I have age- and individually appropriate expectations for behavior? Do I clearly state appropriate limits? • **Monitoring and supervising** Do I know how to create an orderly, consistent environment? Do I monitor children and supervise them well? • **Discipline strategies** Are my discipline strategies positive, age appropriate, individual appropriate, and culturally sensitive? • **Style of confrontation** Am I willing to confront children when necessary? Do I confront in a firm yet kind way?

Figure 1.2

sincere warmth, but others are low in responsiveness and do not express affection or love at all or do not express it appropriately.

There are many ways to shows warmth; no one way is best because we each have our own approach. However, whatever our culture or personal manner, the common thread in warmth is making it clear to a child through our interactions that we genuinely like or love him. Our warmth shows a genuine concern for that child's welfare.

Example. Lev's father is a quiet man who loves his son deeply, but is not given to extravagant expressions of emotion. When Lev said before dinner, "Can I feed Samson (the cat) before we sit down to eat? He looks hungry," Dad thought that Lev had done a good thing but said little. He expressed his warmth in his own way, however, during the prayer before eating: "I am also thankful for a son who thinks about his cat first." Lev kept his head down but shifted his eyes to look quickly at his Dad and then back at his plate. Lev is secure in his father's love and affection.

Example. Jake's mother also loves her son but expresses her warmth differently, in a more unrestrained way. She tells Jake every night before he goes to sleep to remember that she "... loves him right up to the moon and back again" (a statement from his favorite children's book). Jake always says, "A-w-w, Ma," but looks forward to hearing this affectionate close to his day.

Example. Mr. Claiborne said to his first-graders who were sitting in a circle, "When I was driving to school this morning, I thought about how happy I was that I would see all the children in my class again." He then looked at each child, saying his or her name. "Susan, Tom, Vinnie, Sam, Reese ... let's hold hands and make a circle of friends. This circle of friends is going to help each other to have a good week at school."

Warmth is an exceedingly important part of responsiveness. Children are often quite aggressive when their parents are not warm; when they are negative and irritable (Grusec & Lytton, 1988). These children act out in school when their parents are angry, nonaccepting, and disapproving (Anderson, Hinshaw, & Simmel, 1994). Baumrind (1996) cautions that warmth should be sincere. She believes that false expressions of affection prevent parents and teachers from appropriately managing discipline encounters when limits are necessary.

Child Development Knowledge

Teachers using DAP child guidance have usually taken formal course work in child development. Parents, too, can take formal course work, or they can acquire child development knowledge by reading and attending parent education classes. This knowledge base allows adults to have realistic expectations of children of different ages in terms of motor, physical, cognitive, social, and emotional development. It also enables adults to understand the role that families play in a young child's development.

Example. Mr. Claiborne, a first-grade teacher, realizes that his children feel emotions such as anger and that they express their angry feelings. He also knows that 5½-year old children do not understand anger. Nor can they manage their feelings on their own. So, he helps them label feelings and he gives them the words to use for expressing feelings.

Partners in Interaction

Researchers started to think about this concept in the late 1960s (Bell, 1968; Bell & Harper, 1977). We know that children are active partners in every interaction with other children or with adults. Adults who use DAP child guidance believe that children have an important part in any interaction, but at the same time, they know that adults always have a greater responsibility (Maccoby & Martin, 1983).

Example. Mr. Claiborne has a right to expect his class to put things away after using them. The teacher also realizes that he has a greater responsibility in that he has to make the clean-up limit clear. He also has to teach children how to put things away, and has to manage the classroom so that clean-up is simple. In addition, he has to pay attention to the children when they do put things away and acknowledge their efforts.

Communication Style

Communication style of highly responsive adults

Highly responsive adults communicate in an open, congruent, validating, and direct way. They deliver messages simply, kindly, firmly, and consistently. Children tend to readily accept this type of communication because it relies on persuasion, not force, to get an adult's point across. Children are socialized most effectively by adults who use this type of communication and who enforce their directives (Baumrind, 1993, 1996; Dunn, Brown, & Beardsall, 1991). Such a positive way of communicating indicates that they also see children as competent, as having choices, and worthy of respect (Bishop & Rothbaum, 1992).

Example. Vinnie and Sam scooted off to the computer, leaving their library books on the table even though the classroom limit is that people put things away before they start a new activity. Mr. Claiborne, responsive in this discipline encounter, used a direct and validating style of communication: "I know that you've been waiting for your turn at the computer and I'll save your spot for you. First, though, I want you to put your library books in your cubbies." Then he grinned, clapped his hands together very softly, and said, "Hurry, scurry," and away went the boys to get the books.

Giving Explanations

Giving explanations to children is good for both children and adults. We all, and that includes children, tend to be more cooperative when we know why somebody wants us to do something or even to stop doing something. It is a sign of respect to give an explanation and children deserve to know why we ask them to do something.[2]

Giving explanations benefits adults, too. Already using positive guidance strategies, highly responsive adults are even more effective because they state a reason along with the guidance strategy. Discipline encounters usually deal with one specific act; e.g., a child who leaves books strewn about the library. A good strategy (simply reminding the child to put the books away) helps a child understand what is appropriate for that incident. However, giving a reason along with the strategy paints a broader picture for the child. It tells him that the appropriate behavior would apply in many other cases as well (Baumrind, 1996).

Example. Mr. Claiborne says to Reese, one his first-graders, "Reese, I noticed that you left the library books on the floor near the beanbag chair. Please stand the books back up on the shelf. Then the other children can see them easily and the books won't get stepped on."

---

[2]Chapter 4 explains how to give reasons to children when you are stating a limit.

DEMANDINGNESS

Demandingness: the other major caregiving dimension; refers to a person's understanding and setting boundaries, limits, and expectations; how one monitors and supervises, the type of discipline strategies used, and an adult's style of confrontation. Demandingness, an off-putting word to some, is merely the word indicating how an adult makes requests or suggestions, how he asks that children do something (Baumrind, 1996).

Adults differ in how demanding they are with children. Figure 1.1 shows that demandingness, like responsiveness, is on a continuum; i.e., a person can exist anywhere along the demandingness continuum. Some adults are on the higher end while others tend to be at the lower end of the continuum—some are high, some lower in making demands of children.

This section and Figure 1.2 explain the elements of demandingness.

Boundaries, Limits, and Expectations

Adults differ in their ability and willingness to help children understand that there are boundaries, or limits, on behavior. They differ in how they state expectations for (how they request or ask for) cooperative, helpful, appropriately self-controlled behavior from children. Demanding *and* responsive adults understand the importance of proper boundaries and appropriate limits in guiding young children. They develop and clearly communicate appropriate limits.[3] The key is to combine high demandingness with warmth, understanding child development, and giving explanations, (high responsiveness).

Monitoring and Supervising

One part of demandingness is whether adults monitor and supervise children's activities and behavior and whether they provide an orderly and consistent physical environment and time schedule. Authoritative adults steadfastly believe that monitoring and supervising children is essential. Their actions or practices are in sync with their beliefs because they are willing to commit themselves to the time necessary to monitor children in a classroom or at home. They fully understand that continuous but not annoying monitoring, combined with appropriate supervision, prevents or ends some inappropriate behavior in children (Baumrind, 1996; Patterson, 1986). Early childhood students learn quickly that, when in a classroom with young children, they must be aware of the entire room or playground and what is going on. They learn that they must monitor all activities. It also takes time, effort, and skill to develop a responsive physical environment and time schedule (Haupt, Larsen, Robinson, & Hart, 1995).[4]

---

[3]Chapter 4 will help you learn about specific ways of stating limits with children.
[4]Chapter 5 explains how to set up a developmentally appropriate physical environment in a classroom.

Discipline Strategies

Adults believe in and use a variety of discipline strategies. Some adults use discipline strategies that are age, individually, and culturally appropriate. Other adults use strategies that are not appropriate for the age or individual needs of a child and very often focus on punishing a child. There is another set of adults that uses unhelpful discipline strategies; the strategies do not hurt children physically and might not punish, but neither do they help children. The strategies are simply confusing.

Age-appropriate discipline strategies are suitable for the general age group of the children they teach. For example, it would be **age appropriate** to teach all the children in a group of 3-year-olds to label feelings.

An **individually appropriate** strategy is suitable for a specific child, regardless of the child's age. It would, for instance, be individually appropriate to teach Harley, one of the case study children who is now 8 years old, how to put labels on his feeling of frustration when his dog does not sit on command. Why? Harley did not learn how to label feelings when he was a preschooler and he needs to learn the lesson now.

Style of Confrontation

Confrontation: to meet head on, to cope with, to face. In child guidance, confrontation deals with how an adult confronts, faces, copes with, behavior that is clearly hurtful or inappropriate; e.g., name-calling, physical aggression. Adults differ in how they confront children. Some adults are firm yet kind and willing to take a stand even if doing so provokes a conflict.

Example. Mr. Claiborne heard Jack say to a child in a wheelchair, "We don't want you to play with us. Get that stupid chair out of here." He quietly asked Jack to come with him so that he could talk to (confront) him in private. Mr. Claiborne did not accuse him but dealt with this discipline encounter by using a discipline strategy called an I-message: "I heard you say . . . to Pippin. I was surprised to hear you say that because we have talked about kindness in our room and I know that you are usually very kind."

This teacher statement started a short conversation that gave Jack an opportunity to tell Mr. Claiborne that he was afraid of the wheelchair. He was also afraid that Pippin would fall out of the wheelchair. Jack did not think that Pippin would be able to work very well with the science equipment while seated in the wheelchair. Mr. Claiborne then realized that Jack needed to know more about Pippin's wheelchair and that Pippin could do all the class activities but that she had to do them sitting down.

STYLES OF CAREGIVING: AUTHORITATIVE, AUTHORITARIAN, PERMISSIVE

Baumrind's longitudinal study is called the Family Socialization and Competence Project (FSP). The focus of this research begun in the 1960s is on the relation between adult authority and normal children's development. Over time she has

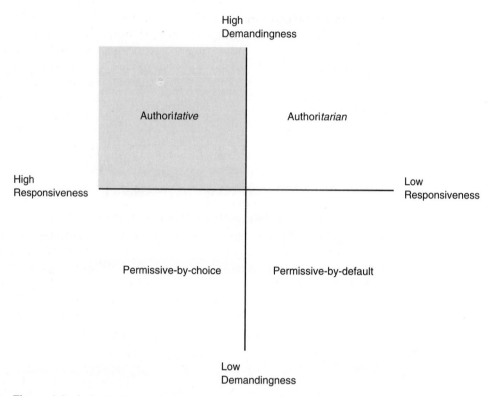

Figure 1.3 Authori*tative* caregivers combine high responsiveness with high demanding-ness. They use the Decision-Making Model of child guidance.

studied the effects of demandingness and responsiveness on the same children's development at three ages—preschool, school age, and adolescence. She assessed parents' specific discipline strategies but focused most pointedly on their overall levels of demandingness and responsiveness (Baumrind, 1996).

Baumrind identified and labeled several styles of parenting or caregiving based on the adult's level of demandingness and responsiveness, as shown in Figure 1.3. These caregiving styles are the **authoritative, authoritarian, and permissive** styles. For each style, you will read about an adult's level of demandingness and responsiveness and the impact of the style on children. I will emphasize, though, the positive authoritative style.

THE AUTHORITATIVE STYLE

High Demandingness, High Responsiveness

Figures 1.1 and 1.3 show that **authoritative** caregivers are high in both demanding-ness and responsiveness. In terms of demandingness, they expect developmentally appropriate mature behavior. They set and maintain reasonable, fair limits and closely supervise and monitor children's activities. They are willing to confront a child when necessary but confront in a respectful, kind way. In terms of responsiveness, authoritative adults are warm and nurturing. They understand child development, and tend to have realistic expectations from children of different ages.

Authoritative adults have a clear communication style. They deliver messages simply, kindly, firmly, and consistently. They use persuasion, not force, to help children understand things. They use positive, developmentally appropriate discipline strategies. The strategies, described and explained in detail in Chapter 4, focus on teaching and not on punishment. Authoritative adults believe in giving simple and clear reasons and explanations in discipline encounters.

Positive and Powerful Effect on Young Children's Development

The authoritative style helps children feel safe and secure

One of a child's most basic needs is for safety and security. Authoritative caregivers help children feel both psychologically and physically safe. They clearly communicate rules that say, "I will never hurt you and I expect you to treat others with respect." Adults who use positive discipline speak to children respectfully and refuse to degrade or demean children. Authoritative adults know that children control their own behavior best when they feel safe and secure (Baumrind, 1993; Dekovic & Janssens, 1992).

The authoritative style encourages self-responsibility

Children learn to take responsibility for their own actions when they have good models of self-responsible behavior. Authoritative caregivers use positive discipline strategies such as I-messages that model self-responsible behavior. They accept responsibility for their actions and do not blame others for how they themselves feel or act. They are nonjudgmental as they explain the consequences of a child's choice of safe behaviors. They model self-responsible behavior.

The authoritative style fosters competence and healthy self-control

Authoritative caregiving helps children become competent. Children of authoritative parents tended to be socially responsible and independent when first observed in preschool. When these same children were 8 and 9 years old, both boys and girls from authoritative families were still quite competent in the cognitive and social spheres (Baumrind, 1996; Baumrind & Black, 1967).

Our long-range goal in guiding children is to help them achieve healthy self-control. We want children to be able to regulate their own behavior and to **want** to behave appropriately in school as well as 5, 10, or 20 years from now. Children develop the ability to regulate or control their behavior when they interact with warm and supportive adults who use positive discipline (Hart, DeWolf, Wozniak, & Burts, 1992). Authoritative teachers and parents help children become self-controlled because they:

- model self-control.
- clearly communicate their expectation that children will show the level of self-control that they are capable of showing.

- give specific information on how children can control themselves.
- recognize and encourage children who act in an age-appropriate, self-controlled way.

The authoritative style helps children to develop empathy.

Piaget (1983) believed that there are certain **classical factors of development**—maturation, social interaction, physical activity. He noted that social interaction helps children gradually become less egocentric and more empathic because contact with other children and adults exposes children to ideas different from their own. The ability to see things from somebody else's perspective—**perspective taking**—is a cognitive developmental skill that begins to develop in early childhood but does not develop automatically (Selman, 1976). Authoritative adults are themselves more empathic (Brems & Sohl, 1995). They model empathy and encourage children to look at things from someone else's perspective. Adults can guide children's understanding of that other viewpoint by taking the time to explain the other person's perspective.

Example. Mr. Claiborne had playground duty and observed that one of the first-graders hit a kindergarten child. Mr. Claiborne, after first helping the kindergarten child, said to the first-grader, "I think that you hurt Cody when you hit him. I can tell because he is crying."

Mr. Claiborne's discipline strategy was developmentally appropriate. It will help the child understand how Cody seems to feel. The teacher has actually told the child how Cody feels and has avoided simply asking, "How do you think Cody feels?"

The authoritative style builds authentic self-esteem and a strong core of personal values.

Competence, confidence, and a sense of worthiness are the cornerstones of positive self-esteem. One of our goals as early childhood educators is to help each child develop authentic self-esteem. Along with authentic self-esteem we want to help children develop a strong core of personal values that guides them to believe in the rights of others to dignified, fair treatment.

Children are motivated by a need to be competent and to have confidence in their ability to do things well, whether it is identifying birds, finger painting, making and keeping friends, doing math problems, or taking care of a horse. The authoritative style helps children feel competent and confident enough to behave appropriately (Bishop & Rothbaum, 1992).

It takes time, effort, and creativity to use positive discipline strategies well, and children who experience positive discipline view themselves as worthy of an adult's time and effort. Adults who rely on positive discipline strategies also model, expect, teach, and encourage fair, dignified treatment of other people and animals.

Example. Mr. Claiborne quietly and calmly introduced the gerbils to his first-graders during morning large group. With the teacher's guidance, the entire group developed the **kindness rules** for dealing with the gerbils. They printed the kindness rules and posted them near the gerbil house. Mr. Claiborne reminded the children about the kindness rules at other group times and he pointed to the rule about being quiet around the gerbils when Jessie and Lee started talking too loudly near the gerbil's house.

THE AUTHORITARIAN STYLE

High Demandingness, Low Responsiveness

Figure 1.3 shows the authoritarian style in the upper right quadrant, where high demandingness meets low responsiveness—not a good combination.

Demandingness

Think about the differences between the high demandingness of an authoritative and an authoritarian caregiver. Both set limits, but authoritarians develop arbitrary limits and then state them poorly. Authoritarian caregivers do not monitor or supervise children's activities very well; then they punish when a child does something of which they disapprove. When authoritarians confront children, they tend to do so in an inconsiderate, inept, or mean-spirited way. They try to exert a great deal of psychological control.

Example. Ryan and his family were eating at a buffet-style restaurant. Six-year-old Ryan ran to the serving area by himself, despite the rule requiring an adult to accompany children to the buffet. His father just kept on eating. After about 5 minutes, however, Dad sighed, got up, and went to the buffet to get Ryan. They came back, Dad belittling Ryan and Ryan carrying a dish overflowing with ice cream. Dad was furious because Ryan had slopped ice cream on the counter, himself, and the floor. (Ryan's father could easily have prevented this whole episode by monitoring his son's activity and by setting some limits.)

Authoritarian adults like Ryan's father rely on negative discipline strategies and equate discipline with punishment (Trickett & Kuczynski, 1986). Ryan's father does not just use one negative discipline strategy. He uses a **combination of negative discipline strategies** such as harsh corporal punishment, threats, lies, shame or ridicule or sarcasm, hostile humor, love withdrawal, and refusal or inability to teach a different way to behave. These negative discipline strategies reflect his need to control and blame.

Most of the time, his discipline strategies seem arbitrary and don't appear to be connected to Ryan's behavior (they are **noncontingent**). These inconsistent noncontingent discipline strategies are harmful, and in Ryan's case, will likely lead him to think that his family environment is not responsive to its members' behavior (Baumrind, 1996). Ryan's father gets very frustrated and angry after his negative discipline strategies do not "work" (Herrenkohl, Herrenkohl, & Egolf, 1983).

Responsiveness

Ryan's father is like many authoritarian parents—not very responsive to his children. He is often irritable and angry. He does not like being a parent and really does not know how to deal with the role of parent. He is rigid in his interactions with his children, and speaks negatively about them, especially Ryan (Trickett & Susman, 1988). Parents who are unresponsive and who emotionally neglect their children set their children up for acting out types of problem behavior (Simons, Johnson, & Conger, 1994).

Ryan's father knows very little about child development. Consequently, he has unrealistic expectations of Ryan.

Example. Dad expects 6-year-old Ryan to sit quietly in a doctor's office or other public place, no matter how long they are there. Dad makes no attempt to help Ryan find something to read or to do while he waits. He does not know that young children have great difficulty with self-control. He does not attempt to talk to Ryan except to scold him.

Like many authoritarian adults, Ryan's dad rarely even thinks about how Ryan might feel, what Ryan might try to tell him, or what Ryan needs. He uses force (**coercion**) and places great value on unquestioning obedience. He punishes any attempt from his children at verbal give-and-take and suppresses any attempt at independence or autonomy.

Ryan's father also communicates in an unhelpful, hurtful way. He **orders:** "I said to get over here. Do it now." He **blames:** "I hope you're satisfied. You made a real mess at the ice cream machine." He **distracts;** i.e., he avoids issues and occasionally makes completely irrelevant statements: when Ryan complained that his brother had pinched him, Dad only said, "Ryan, pass the mustard." Dad **criticizes** by focusing on the negative. He criticizes even when Ryan does something Dad asked him to do: "Yeah, I see. You raked the leaves but you missed that whole pile!"

Ryan's father never thinks about the long-term effects of his authoritarian style; he is concerned only about short-term control. He does not know any good child guidance skills (Aragona, 1983). He rarely gives a good reason to help Ryan understand a limit. The few reasons that he does give tend to be related to his adult power.

Example. When Ryan asked his father why his brother never had to empty the trash, Dad said, "I don't have to explain myself to you, boy. You hear me?"

Over the years, all of these negative interactions add up, making it difficult for children like Ryan to believe that their parents love them (see Figure 1.4).

Authoritarian Caregiving Has a Negative Effect on Young Children's Development

Authori*tarian* caregiving sets the stage for harm to children (Baumrind, 1996). Authoritarian caregiving:

Fosters negative self-esteem

Ryan experiences negative discipline and has developed negative self-esteem. He has not developed the competence, confidence, or sense of worthiness on which self-esteem is built. Instead, he mirrors the lack of trust that his parents communicate. He feels degraded by their authoritarian tactics.

Green Jelly Beans: Authoritarian Caregivers Make It Difficult for Children to Behave Well

Hurtful discipline strategies are a lot like green jelly beans. Yell at a child; drop a green jelly bean in his memory jar. Make fun of him; green jelly bean. Slap him; several green jelly beans. So it goes. Some children end up with a memory jar chock full of green jelly beans.

The children with whom you work, from different backgrounds, will be affected by their culture's views on discipline and their family's caregiving style. Children who come from authoritarian homes will have hundreds or thousands of bad experiences with discipline. They will have experienced some or all of the situations listed below. Knowing this might help you understand that those children, when confronted with a problem, often reach into that jar of jelly beans and come up with a green jelly bean, a hurtful, unhelpful strategy, which they themselves then use.

Authoritarian adults often use:

- **Harsh physical punishment.** They use physical force to try to change a behavior. They do not understand or refuse to take a child's perspective and defend their right to use harsh punishment. They minimize the real harm that they do.
- **Threats.** Threats create fear and anxiety and are negative and harmful. Some children are terrorized through threats, a form of psychological abuse (Garbarino, Guttmen, & Seeley, 1986).
- **Lies.** We are talking here about a nasty pattern of lying to children, a form of manipulation aimed at changing or controlling a child's behavior.
- **Shaming, ridicule, sarcasm, humiliation.** Such strategies foster a negative view of the self and make unpleasant feelings and moods fester.
- **Hostile humor.** Ryan's father often cloaks his aggression as humor, but it is still aggression and is always disrespectful. **Example:** When Ryan had his first ice-skating lesson he was afraid of falling down. His dad called him a sissy and made him get moving. At home that night, Dad cruelly imitated what he called "sissy-boy Ryan's" fearful approach to the ice and his wobbly start on skates. Ryan burned with embarrassment.
- **Love withdrawal.** They refuse to talk or listen to, threaten to leave or abandon, or glare at a child (Hoffman, 1970). **Example:** Ryan was slow in getting into Mom's car after Little League practice. Mom was angry and Ryan sensed it when she refused to talk to him and stared straight ahead. She looked at him a few times but only shook her head.

Figure 1.4

Results in poor self-control

Ryan's father, like many authoritarian adults, aims to control his children. He believes that he has to control Ryan (external control) and does not help Ryan learn to control himself (self- or internal control). He does not teach Ryan about how his behavior affects others. Therefore, it is difficult for Ryan to act in a self-controlled way in school or anywhere.

Teaches and encourages aggression

Children who experience negative discipline tend to be more aggressive than children whose parents and teachers use more positive discipline. They either aim their aggression toward the adult who hurt them (Patterson, 1982) or they recycle their anger and use the same degrading behavior with people or animals who had nothing to do with hurting the child.

Example. Dad, angry with 6-year-old Ryan for crying, said "Cut the crying or you'll really get something to cry about." Ryan stopped crying and walked outside. His dog barked a greeting to him but Ryan threw a rock that smashed against his dog's kennel.

Does not stop unacceptable behavior

Researchers have known for decades now that high levels of punishment can restrain behavior only for a short time and, surprisingly, can make the undesired behavior even worse (Church, 1963; Rollins & Thomas, 1979). Undesired behavior seems to occur at a more intense level than it did before the punishment. This is a phenomenon called **response recovery.** After the punishment is meted out, the behavior appears to cease. However, when the adult stops punishing, the behavior often reoccurs and is more intense.

Negatively reinforces adults for using harsh discipline

Authoritarian adults who rely on negative discipline strategies wrongly believe that this sort of discipline works because they have been **reinforced** for using it. For example, when Ryan was a toddler and kicked his high chair, his teacher slapped Ryan's legs and Ryan stopped kicking. The teacher was reinforced for using slapping. The sequence goes like this:

- Ryan kicked his high chair (a behavior that annoyed the teacher).
- Teacher slapped Ryan's legs (negative discipline strategy).
- Ryan was surprised and stopped kicking—but only for the moment.
- Teacher thought, "Hmm, that worked." (Teacher was reinforced because the negative discipline strategy of hitting seemed to work to stop an annoying behavior.)
- The next day, Ryan kicked his high chair again. (Response recovery is operating. The negative discipline strategy only stopped the behavior temporarily).
- Teacher slapped Ryan again. (Remember, slapping **seemed** to work yesterday.)

The real problem here is that hitting Ryan became firmly entrenched in this caregiver's repertoire of disciplinary strategies. She has begun to believe that hitting was effective (Patterson, 1982). It becomes easy for adults to rely on an ineffective discipline strategy, especially when they do not know or do not practice more effective strategies or when they rationalize their harsh behavior. Note also that Ryan's teacher has used negative, hurtful discipline. She has violated the NAEYC Code of Ethics.

In its extreme form, is child abuse

First, we live in a society accepting of violent conflict resolution. Many parents reflect this idea by using violence to solve family problems; they use physical or psychological force as discipline and such discipline can easily injure a child (Marion, 1983). Second, negative discipline **seems** to work but really does not. Negative discipline is very ineffective. Third, adults are reinforced for using negative discipline and will tend to use the same method again. Finally, an adult who relies on harsh negative discipline strategies soon discovers that he must increase the intensity of the punishment in order for it to be "effective." She must yell more loudly or hit harder, intensifying the strategy until it becomes abusive.

THE PERMISSIVE STYLE

Low Demandingness

Figure 1.3 shows that all permissive adults are low in demandingness. They allow children to regulate their own behavior and to make their own decisions. They establish very few guidelines, even about when children eat, watch television, or go to bed. They make few demands for mature behavior, such as showing good manners or carrying out tasks. They avoid imposing any controls or restrictions and have a tolerant, accepting attitude toward the child's impulses, even aggressive ones.

Permissive adults are alike because they are all low in demandingness; they differ, however, in their degree of responsiveness. Some permissive adults are highly responsive to children, but others are quite low in responsiveness (Figure 1.3). Thus, there are two types of permissive adults.

Low Demandingness Plus High Responsiveness

The first type of permissiveness is called **permissive-by-choice**—low in demandingness and high in responsiveness. Members of this group are permissive because they choose to be permissive. Their view is a part of their belief system about how to treat children. They firmly believe that children have rights that ought not to be interfered with by adults (Sears, Maccoby, & Levin, 1957). These parents do not demand much from their children but they are highly responsive. They are warm and understand child development. They give their child much of what he needs, except for good limits.

Low Demandingness Plus Low Responsiveness

The second type of permissiveness is **permissive-by-default** (Baumrind calls them *unengaged*). These adults are also low in demandingness as well as in responsiveness. Members of this group have drifted into being permissive. They are permissive not because of a strong philosophical belief in a child's rights but because their method of discipline has been so ineffective (Patterson, 1982). They would like to be able to set and maintain limits, but have been so ineffective in getting compliance from children that they have given up trying. They might even begin to see some behaviors, such as aggression, as normal. Once on the slippery slope of permissiveness, these adults could not get off and have become unresponsive and indifferent toward children—they have become permissive by default. Think about this way: If you forget to set the margins on your word processor, the computer sets the margins by default. Similarly, a parent who does not consciously decide on and choose a style of caregiving has his style set by default.

Permissive adults tend to use ineffective discipline. They do not hurt children, but they are not very helpful, either. For example, permissive adults often fail to set appropriate limits, and even when they do set a limit, they frequently fail to maintain it.

Example. Liza's mother told Liza to clean up her space at the table. When Liza left the table without cleaning her space, Mom just shrugged her shoulders and walked away.

We guide children effectively by giving them enough of the right type of information so that they will be able to act appropriately under different conditions. Liza's mother did not follow through with her legitimate limit.

Permissive-by-default adults tend to natter and nag. These adults have tried to set limits but have been very ineffective. On occasion, they still try to set limits, but they tend to talk so much that the child ignores their limits.

Some permissive adults use inconsistent discipline. One way of being inconsistent is for a person to deal differently with the same situation each time it occurs. Take biting as an example. Jared's father was inconsistent when he ignored Jared's biting one day and the next day told him, "No, no, Jared. Biting hurts." The third time he bit another child, Dad ignored him. This is called **intra**agent inconsistency, inconsistency within the same individual.

Another way of being inconsistent is for two adults to deal with a behavior differently. Inconsistency between two different adults is **inter**agent inconsistency. Parents might disagree about how they will deal with any number of issues. Ryan's parents, for example, inconsistently dealt with Ryan's biting when Ryan was a toddler. Dad hit him and Mom ignored the biting. Both techniques are **in**effective and negative (Greenberg, 1991).

How Permissiveness Affects Young Children

Both children and adults pay a heavy price when adults refuse to make or give up making demands for maturity or to set clear, firm standards of behavior. Children from permissive systems tend to be low in impulse control. They are not very self-reliant or self-responsible. They tend to be dependent and are not very competent, either socially or cognitively. These results held when the children were 8 and 9 years old (Baumrind, 1967, 1971).

Case Study Analysis: Styles of Caregiving

Analyze the case studies at the beginning of the chapter by answering the following questions.

1. Both Nathan's and Harley's parents are permissive.
   a. Which boy has the **permissive-by-choice** parent? Name at least two things that led you to this conclusion.
   b. In what way are the parents of the two boys alike? In what major way do they differ?
2. Ryan's father is an authori**tarian** caregiver.
   a. Cite at least three pieces of data that you could use to support this statement. In your response, be sure to talk about Dad's demandingness and responsiveness.
   b. Then, from information in the chapter, name at least three ways in which this authoritarian father has affected his son.
   c. What do you think is the greatest obstacle standing in the way of Ryan's father making any significant changes in his style?
3. Megan's mother is an authori**tative** caregiver. Explain why her way of dealing with Megan's biting another child so clearly illustrates the authoritative style.

BASIC PROCESSES ADULTS USE TO INFLUENCE CHILDREN

Modeling, direct instruction and coaching, using reinforcement and comments, managing the environment, stating expectations, and encouraging children to modify their attitudes and understanding, all can influence children. All adults, authoritarian, authoritative, or permissive use these **basic processes to directly and indirectly influence children.** In this section, you will read about each of the basic processes that are used by adults, whatever the caregiving style, to influence children. For example, all adults use the basic process of modeling, but an authoritarian adult demonstrates behavior that is very different from that modeled by an authoritative adult. The process is the same, but the content is different.

Modeling

Much human behavior is learned simply by watching someone else perform the behavior. The other person is the model, and the basic process is **modeling.** Perhaps the best-known researcher to give us information about this process is Albert Bandura. His research (1971) demonstrates that children can effectively learn a behavior just by watching it. Although children can learn from several types of models (e.g., cartoon characters, pictures in books, and movie or video characters), Bandura's group demonstrated just how powerful adult models are in demonstrating aggression.

Children learn undesirable behaviors—such as aggression or abusiveness—by observing models. An authoritarian parent or teacher who disciplines by hitting or with sarcasm actually models (demonstrates) aggressive behavior. You will also see evidence throughout this book that children just as effectively learn more desirable and positive behaviors—such as generosity, cooperation, kindness, and helpfulness—through the same basic process. An authoritative adult who uses positive discipline teaches a different lesson than does the authoritarian adult.

Imitation is different from modeling. A child might learn, for example, how to be kind to animals by observing his teacher model the behavior. The child learns the behavior. There is no guarantee, though, that the child will also perform the behavior that he has learned. When he does perform a behavior learned via modeling, then he has **imitated** the behavior. Children in this country observe thousands of acts of violence on television and in video games before they enter first grade. They have, then, several thousand sessions of modeling of aggression and violence. They learn the violence. Whether they imitate what they have observed is another story. Avoid saying, "He modeled after the television violence." Instead, consider saying, "He imitated the violence modeled in the television show."

Direct Instruction

Direct instruction: involves intentional and explicit teaching. There are many examples of adults influencing children through direct instruction. Teacher education students take curriculum courses so that they can learn developmentally appropriate methods of giving instruction in math, science, social studies, and language arts. Adults also instruct children in physical safety, such as traffic safety, safe use of toys, and how to recognize "good" and "bad" touches. We instruct children about so many things: the correct way to hold a baseball bat, build a campfire, ride a horse, or execute a figure eight on skates.

Consider the benefits of instructing children in social skills—how to make and keep friends, how to take another person's perspective, how to work cooperatively with friends, and how to resolve conflicts (King & Kirschenbaum, 1992). Figure 9.1 in Chapter 9 gives suggestions for teaching specific social skills.

Practicing with Coaching

The next step, after giving direct instruction, is to encourage a child to practice a new skill. It is very helpful to give on-the-spot guidance or coaching as the child practices.

Example. Mr. Claiborne had taught Ryan how to wait for his turn at the computer (he is working on helping Ryan be more observant about approaching activities and other children because Ryan just barges right on in). The teacher believes that Ryan will make changes, but is going to do so gradually. Now, he is at the computer with Ryan. He encourages Ryan to go through the steps that he has modeled and taught.

- First, check the list of names to see who is next.
- Second, put his name on the list if necessary.
- Third, find something else to do while he waits for his turn and ask for help if he needs it.

Adults influence children through direct instruction. Sean's father and their neighbor are teaching Sean about cars.

The teacher coaches Ryan through each step. "What's the first thing to do, Ryan? Right! Look at the list." He continues this coaching.

Mr. Claiborne believes that this is a much better approach than punishing Ryan for pushing ahead of others on the list to use the computer. It actually teaches something positive.

Giving Feedback

Adults influence children by giving them feedback. Information from adults about how a child has done something or what a child knows is an important source of information about the child's competence. Feedback is critical to constructing skills and competencies as well as for making changes.

Giving good feedback means that teachers give positive feedback as well as suggestions for change, when appropriate.

Positive, unconditional feedback

This is positive information independent of anything that the child has done; the child does **not** have to earn the feedback. For example, "I love you," or "I like being your teacher" (teacher to class).

Positive, conditional feedback

Positive comments expressed after a child has done a specific task. For example, "Thank you, Reese, for showing Sam how to feed the gerbils without disturbing them," or "The fire alarm was very loud but everybody listened so carefully to my instructions." This is positive, meaningful feedback, not empty flattery, and should help children build a healthy view of their competence.

Feedback that helps children construct more helpful skills or competencies

Adults, with their expert knowledge and skills, can help children construct positive and satisfying interaction skills.[5] For example, Mrs. Vargas, a preschool teacher, said to Jackie, "You look upset. Is that right?" Jackie told her yes and that Ralph would not give him the wagon. Mrs. Vargas had observed Jackie capture the wagon, pushing Ralph in the process. He needed to learn a better way to get what was rightfully his. "I see. Now, everybody is upset. Let's figure out how to use words to tell Ralph that it's your turn." The teacher expanded her feedback to include specific words: "You can say, 'It's my turn now, Jackie.'"

Managing the Child's Environment

Adults manage a child's environment by providing physical materials, the setting in which the child exists, and a time schedule. Researchers have examined the effects of a child's physical or temporal environment on several areas of development. For example, a well-designed and well-managed physical environment helps children become independent and to take initiative (Howes, 1991; Jones & Prescott, NAEYC Film #806; King, Oberlin, & Swank, 1990). A child's physical environment affects the development of several other social behaviors such as sharing (Caplan, 1991), expressing emotions (Honig & Wittmer, 1992), and managing anger (Denham, Zoller, & Couchoud, 1994; Marion, 1997).

Stating Expectations of Desired Behaviors

Example. "Ryan," called Mr. Claiborne, "wash your hands and then you can join the group and help us cut up the fruit for our snack."

Mr. Claiborne makes a conscious effort to define cooperative, helpful behavior. Authoritative adults like Ryan's teacher develop good rules or limits and then communicate them clearly to children. Authoritarian adults, on the other hand, tend to set too many arbitrary limits, and permissive adults may fail to communicate expectations at all.

---

[5]Chapter 11 expands on this concept.

Encouraging Children to Modify Attitudes and Understanding

Infants, toddlers, and young children have a central nervous system that enables them to process information and make sense of the world. Children can act cooperatively when someone takes the time to present them with additional or different information in a way that is appropriate to the child's particular level of development. Focus on teaching children to understand why they should or should not do certain things. Be gently firm about the need for the children to act more appropriately, and make it clear that there is a **reason** for acting more appropriately. Be kind at the same time, though. Authoritative caregivers are firm and kind.

An effective way to do this is to **help a child become more empathic.** The goal is to help a child to understand gradually how his actions affect others and to be able to take somebody else's perspective. Like most learning, this occurs gradually over a period of years and begins in infancy. The goal here is **not** to induce excessive guilt or to shame a child. A good way to arouse empathy is to describe another's situation in an open, direct way that still validates the other person and that does not accuse him.

Examples. Mrs. Vargas said to Ralph, "I see from the job chart that it's your day to feed the gerbils. I'll bet that they're hungry. So get the gerbil food and I'll help you put it in their house."

Mr. Lee, the third-grade teacher, said to Rory, "Name calling hurts feelings, Rory. Remember our class rules? That's right. Treat each other with respect."

Each adult avoided sarcasm, threats, and accusations while focusing on how the other person or animal might have felt. Arousing a child's empathy—having him "walk a mile in somebody else's shoes or tracks"—is a powerful technique because it encourages the child to examine and begin to understand how her behavior might well have affected someone else.

A common thread linking different forms of antisocial behavior, including child abuse, is the perpetrator's inability to take another person's perspective (Chalmers & Townsend, 1990). Preventing abuse involves helping abusive adults learn social perspective taking. Helping children become empathic, to take the perspective of others, then, is an important task for teachers and parents during a child's first 8 years.

DECISION-MAKING MODEL OF CHILD GUIDANCE

Authoritative Caregivers Use the Decision-Making Model

Authoritative caregivers use the **decision-making model** of child guidance. They actively make decisions when interacting with children, including during discipline encounters. The decision-making model is a way of examining any discipline encounter and thinking about how to handle it in a DAP way. Authoritative caregivers make DAP guidance plans in a logical and clearheaded manner. They avoid the quicksand of emotional reactions to a discipline encounter. Authoritative caregivers think clearly and purposefully about a problem and then make a decision about discipline encounters—the typical ones as well as those that are more challenging.

Authoritative caregivers consciously think about each child in their care. They know that any child from infancy to 9 years has a basic style or temperament and a rich personal history of interactions. They understand the impact of families and culture on children. For instance, authoritative caregivers understand that each child's family has its own scripts and rules, its own communication style, its own cultural history, its own view of how children should behave, and its own style of discipline. They know that some parents feel secure, understand children and children's needs, know how to communicate legitimate rules and limits, know how to help children live within limits, and know how to demonstrate their love and respect to their children.

Authoritative caregivers also understand that other parents have not had their own needs for nurturance met and cannot now, as adults, meet their children's needs for nurturance and security. They know that these parents do not understand how infants and children develop, are angry, and do not know how or refuse to take their children's perspective. They lack empathy for their children. These parents have very poor and ineffective child guidance skills; for example, they do not know how to set limits effectively or how to help children accept limits. Unfortunately, many of them do not know how to demonstrate the love that they feel for their children.

Authoritative adults practice what they believe, no matter what a child's background has been. This is a difficult thing to do when children who come from widely different backgrounds are in the same classroom. Nevertheless, authoritative caregivers are committed to practicing the decision-making model of child guidance. They do not just use the first strategy that pops into their heads. They work at finding a solution. Authoritative caregivers deliberately walk through the systematic process of choosing a strategy.

Steps in the Decision-Making Model

There are specific steps in the decision-making model, which include

- observing,
- deciding,
- taking action, and
- reflecting.

These steps are relatively easy to learn and use. See Figure 1.5.

Authoritative adults realize that the children with whom they work truly are individuals. That is the best reason for adopting as flexible as possible an approach to guiding children. The decision-making model is an individualized, personal model that allows you to determine the course of action most beneficial for a specific child in specific circumstances. The decision-making model is **eclectic** (flexible) in that it draws from many different ideas about children and guidance. The decision-making model provides the means for you to combine your knowledge and personal strengths to deal more effectively with issues facing individual children. You will be using the decision-making model throughout this text and especially in Chapter 12.

Four Steps in the Decision-Making Model of Child Guidance[6]

✓ Observe

Observe the child's behavior.
Focus on the encounter as a problem to be solved.
Clearly identify the problem. Decide whether the child or the adult "owns the problem." Focus on solving a problem, not on blaming a child.
Examine the "context" of the problem.
Ask yourself how the child's age might be affecting her behavior. Ask how the child's family, culture, or the classroom physical environment, activities, or materials have contributed to the problem. Ask how your way of talking with a child might be contributing to the problem. The idea is not to place blame but simply to get a better picture of the context or setting in which the behavior has evolved.

✓ Decide

Your observation will tell you what to change. For example, you might need to:
Choose a guidance strategy.
Use **only** positive, developmentally appropriate strategies, not punishment. Consult your list of guidance strategies in the Appendix and in Chapter 4. Say why the chosen strategy is appropriate for this child at this time
Change the context.
You might decide that you have to change the classroom physical environment or the time schedule. You might decide that you should choose more DAP activities, or that materials need to be organized better.
Change your own practices.
You might decide that you want to change something that you are doing. For instance, you decide that you want to talk with children about playground rules after you realize that you have never done this.

✓ Take Action

Take action. Carry out the guidance strategy, make the contextual change, or change the practice that you want to change.

✓ Reflect

Figure 1.5

REFLECTING ON KEY CONCEPTS

1. Take another look at the case study on Nathan at the beginning of the chapter. Use the steps in the decision-making model of child guidance (Figure 1.4) to come up with a developmentally appropriate, authori**tative** way of dealing with the scooter issue. Be prepared to describe each of the four steps that you take.

---

[6]This figure also appears in Chapter 12 in more detail.

2. Think about an authori**tarian** caregiver you have observed. Avoid using his name or any identifying information about him. Describe the adult's behavior toward a child. Say how the adult's behavior was high in demand-ingness but low in responsiveness. Be specific and refer to elements of each (Figure 1.2).

3. Think back on your childhood and try to figure out the style of caregiving used by the people who were your main caregivers. Use the information from the text, including Figure 1.2 and Figure 1.3 to do your analysis. The idea here is to identify and describe, not judge, the style of caregiving used by your parents or caregivers.

4. Again, think about your past. Recall a couple of examples of when adults influenced you by modeling something. Recall a time when an adult gave you specific and direct instruction about something and then had you practice that skill. Did the adult do any coaching? Please describe it if he did. Recall the feedback that you received from adults. What was it like?

APPLY YOUR KNOWLEDGE

1. You have read several examples of Mr. Claiborne's **authoritative** style in this chapter. One morning, this is what happened. He had invited the director of the local Humane Society to talk with the children about kind treatment of animals. The director brought along Hannah, a mellow golden retriever who was accustomed to such presentations. Ryan, happy about the dog, grew increasingly excited, causing Hannah to step away from Ryan and go to sit on the other side of the director.

   Role-play how you think Mr. Claiborne would guide Ryan in this dis-cipline encounter, using information from the chapter on how he man-ages his classroom and deals with Ryan. He will not punish Ryan because you know already that he does not believe in punishment. What is he very likely to do instead?

2. Accentuate the positive! Do a real-world observation and find examples of positive authori**tative** caregiving. You should be able to see lots of good examples by visiting a variety of places in which you can observe adults and children interacting; for example, a grocery store, park, family reunion, Laundromat, place of worship, or school. Briefly describe the setting and record the approximate age of the child(ren). Write a description of each interaction. Describe why you think this was an example of authoritative caregiving.

3. You are the leader of a parent education group. A frustrated parent of a 5-year-old child asks you what she should do to get her child to put her tricy-cle away and not leave it in the driveway. Use one or two of the **basic processes of influence** (modeling, direct instruction, practice with coach-ing, and others described in the chapter) as you offer this mother some simple, practical, and realistic suggestions for guiding her child. Be pre-pared to present your suggestions to your class.

REFERENCES

Anderson, C. A., Hinshaw, S. P., & Simmel, C. (1994). Mother-child interactions in ADHD and comparison boys: Relationships with overt and covert externalizing behavior. *Journal of Abnormal Child Psychology, 22,* 247–265.

Aragona, J. A. (1983). Physical child abuse: An interactional analysis (Doctoral dissertation, University of South Florida). *Dissertation Abstracts International, 44,* 125B.

Bandura, A. (1971). Analysis of modeling processes. In A. Bandura (Ed.), *Psychological modeling.* Chicago: Aldine-Asherton.

Baumrind, D. (1967). Child care practices anteceding three patterns of preschool behavior. *Genetic Psychology Monographs, 75,* 43–88.

Baumrind, D. (1971). Current patterns of parental authority. *Developmental Psychology Monograph, 4*(1, Pt. 2).

Baumrind, D. (1977, March). *Socialization determinants of personal agency.* Paper presented at the meeting of the Society for Research in Child Development, New Orleans, LA.

Baumrind, D. (1979). *Sex-related socialization effects.* Paper presented at the meeting of the Society for Research in Child Development, San Francisco, CA.

Baumrind, D. (1993). The average expectable environment is not good enough: A response to Scarr. *Child Development,64,* 1299–1317.

Baumrind, D. (1996). Parenting: The discipline controversy revisited. *Family Relations, 45,* 405–414.

Baumrind, D., & Black, A. E. (1967). Socialization practices associated with dimensions of competence in preschool boys and girls. *Child Development, 38,* 291–327.

Becker, W. C. (1954). Consequences of different kinds of parental discipline. In M. L. Hoffman & L. S. Hoffman (Eds.), *Review of child development research* (Vol. 1). New York: Russell Sage Foundation.

Bell, R. Q. (1968). A reinterpretation of the direction of effect in studies of socialization. *Psychological Review, 75,* 81–95.

Bell, R. Q., & Harper, L. V. (Eds.) (1977). *Child effects on adults.* Hillsdale, NJ: Erlbaum.

Bishop, S., & Rothbaum, F. (1992). Parents' acceptance of control needs and preschoolers' social behaviour: A longitudinal study. *Canadian Journal of Behavioural Science, 24*(2), 171–185.

Bredekamp, S. (1987). *Developmentally appropriate practice in early childhood programs serving children from birth through age 8, expanded edition.* Washington, DC: NAEYC.

Brems, C., & Sohl, M. A. (1995). The role of empathy in parenting strategy choices. *Family Relations, 44,* 189–194.

Caplan, M. (1991). Conflict and its resolution in small groups of 1- and 2-year-olds. *Child Development, 62* (6), 1513–1524.

Chalmers, J. B., & Townsend, M. A. R. (1990). The effects of training in social perspective-taking on socially maladjusted girls. *Child Development, 61,* 178–190.

Church, R. M. (1963). The varied effects of punishment on behavior. *Psychological Review, 70,* 369–402.

Dekovic, M., & Janssens, J. (1992). Parents' child-rearing style and child's sociometric status. *Developmental Psychology, 28*(5), 925–932.

Denham, S. A., Zoller, D., & Couchoud, E. A. (1994). Socialization of preschoolers' emotion understanding. *Developmental Psychology, 30*(6), 928–937.

Dunn, J., Brown, J., & Beardsall, L. (1991). Family talk about feeling states and children's later understanding of others' emotions. *Developmental Psychology, 27,* 448–455.

Garbarino, J., Guttman, E., & Seeley, J. W. (1986). *The psychologically battered child.* San Francisco: Jossey-Bass.

Greenberg, P. (1991). *Character development: Encouraging self-esteem and self-discipline in infants, toddlers, and two-year-olds.* Washington, DC: NAEYC.

Grusec, J. E., & Lytton, H. (1988). *Social development: History, theory, and research.* New York: Springer-Verlag.

Hart, C., DeWolf, M., Wozniak, P., & Burts, D. (1992). Maternal and paternal disciplinary styles: Relations with preschoolers' playground behavioral orientations and peer status. *Child Development, 63,* 879–892.

Haupt, J. J., Larsen, J. M., Robinson, C. C., & Hart, C. H. (1995). The impact of DAP Inservice training on the beliefs and practices of kindergarten teachers. *Journal of Early Childhood Teacher Education, 16*(2), 12–18.

Herrenkohl, R., Herrenkohl, E., & Egolf, B. P. (1983). Circumstances surrounding the occurrence of child maltreatment. *Journal of Consulting and Clinical Psychology, 51,* 424–431.

Hoffman, M. L. (1970). Moral development. In P. Mussen (Ed.), *Carmichael's manual of child psychology* (Vol. 2). New York: Wiley.

Honig, A., & Wittmer, D. (1992). *Prosocial development in children: Caring, sharing, and cooperation: A bibliographic resource guide.* New York: Garland Press.

Howes, C. (1991). Caregiving environments and their consequences for children: The experience in the United States. In E. Melhuish & P. Moss (Eds.), *Day care for young children.* New York: Routledge.

Jones, E., & Prescott, E. *Environments for young children.* Washington, DC: NAEYC, Film # 806.

King, C., & Kirschenbaum, D. (1992). *Helping young children develop social skills.* Pacific Grove, CA: Brooks/Cole Publishing Company.

King, M., Oberlin, A., & Swank, T. (1990). Supporting the activity choices of 2-year-olds. *Day Care and Early Education, 17*(2), 9–13 and 67–70.

Maccoby, E., & Martin, J. A. (1983). Socialization in the context of the family: Parent-child interaction. In P. Mussen (Ed.), *Handbook of child psychology* (Vol. 4). New York: Wiley.

Marion, M. (1983). Child compliance: A review of the literature with implications for family life education. *Family Relations, 32,* 545–555.

Marion, M. (1997). Research in review: Guiding young children's understanding and management of anger. *Young Children, 52*(7), 62–68.

Patterson, G. R. (1982). *Coercive family process.* Eugene, OR: Castalia Press.

Piaget, J. (1983). Piaget's theory. In P. Mussen (Ed.), *Handbook of child psychology* (Vol. 1). New York: Wiley.

Rollins, B. C., & Thomas, D. L. (1979). Parental support, power, and control techniques in the socialization of children. In W. R. Burr, R. Hill, F. Nye, & I. Reiss (Eds.), *Contemporary theories about the family* (Vol. 1). New York: Free Press.

Sears, R. R., Maccoby, E. E., & Levin, H. (1957). *Patterns of child rearing.* Evanston, IL: Row Peterson.

Selman, R. L. (1976). Social-cognitive understanding: A guide to educational and clinical practice. In T. Lickona (Ed.), *Moral development and behavior.* New York: Holt, Rinehart, & Winston.

Simons, R. L., Johnson, C., & Conger, R. D. (1994). Harsh corporal punishment versus quality of parental involvement as an explanation of adolescent maladjustment. *Journal of Marriage and Family, 56,* 591–607.

Trickett, P., & Kuczynski, L. (1986). Children's misbehaviors and parental discipline strategies in abusive and nonabusive families. *Developmental Psychology, 22,* 115–123.

Trickett, P., & Susman, E. (1988). Parental perceptions of child-rearing practices in physically abusive and nonabusive families. *Developmental Psychology, 24*(2), 270–276.

✓ CHECK OUT THE WEB SITES RELATED TO THIS CHAPTER

✓ **About: The Human Internet.** Large number of topics in its own site. Look at the site for childhood stress, anger, anxiety. Links to related sites. *http://about.com.* Main page.

✓ **Center for Effective Parenting.** A collaborative project of the University of Arkansas for Medical Science, the Arkansas Children's Hospital, and the Jones Family Center. This site has numerous links for parent education information. *www.parenting-ed.org.* The homepage for the Center for Effective Parenting. The following is one of the many good links. *www.parenting-ed.org/handouts.htm.* Look for handouts/information on parenting and discipline.

✓ **ERIC Clearinghouse on Elementary and Early Childhood Education,** University of Illinois at Urbana-Champaign. A valuable resource on many topics, including styles of discipline and effects of discipline on children. *www.ericps.crc.uiuc.edu/eece.* Main page. *www.ericps.crc.uiuc.edu/eece/pubs/digests.* Page for a set of publications called ERIC DIGESTS.

✓ **Extension Divisions of Land Grant Universities.** Each state has a university with an extension division, charged with providing information and education for people throughout that state. Extensions produce written documents on many topics, including parenting. Check the extension division in your own state, either on the Internet or at your county's extension office (check the Yellow Pages).

www.urbanext.uiuc.edu. University of Illinois Extension. Look for the publications link and then for information on parenting and discipline.

www.unce.unr.edu/. University of Nevada Reno. Look for the publications link and then for information on parenting and discipline.

✓ **Internet address for my state's land grant university:**

www._____

Construct Child Guidance Decisions: Apply Knowledge of Child Development

"According to Vygotsky, the role of education is to provide experiences that are in the child's zone of proximal development—activities challenging for the child but achievable with sensitive adult guidance."

(Berk & Winsler, 1995)

Case Studies: DAP Child Guidance in Action

Cognitive Development
Preoperational Stage
Concrete Operational Stage
Sensorimotor Stage
Knowing About Cognitive Development: What It
Means for Guiding Children

Perception During Early Childhood
Problems Affecting How Children Pay Attention
Changes in Perception: Children Pay Attention Better
As They Get Older
Knowing About Perception: What It Means for
Guiding Children

Memory
Definitions
Milestones in the Development of Memory
Explaining Changes in Memory
Knowing About Memory: What It Means for Guiding
Children

Temperament
Definition
Three Basic Temperamental Styles
Knowing About Temperament: What It Means for
Guiding Children

Social Cognition
How Children Describe Other People and Their
Behavior
How Children Understand Intentional Versus
Accidental Behavior
How Children View Friendship
Conflict Resolution
Knowing About Social Cognition: What It Means for
Guiding Children

Self-Control
What Is Self-Control?
How Children Demonstrate Self-Control
How Self-Control Emerges
Milestones in the Development of Self-Control
Knowing About Self-Control: What It Means for
Guiding Children

After reading and studying this chapter, you will
be able to:

❏ **Explain in your own words** how a child's
level of cognitive development affects how you
are able to guide him or her.

❏ **Explain** why good perspective-taking skills are
so important to both adults and children.

❏ **Describe** a young child's memory capacity,
memory skills, and perceptual problems, and
list and describe specific guidance strategies
for helping children remember things and for
dealing with the perceptual limitations of
preschoolers.

❏ **Define** *temperament* and **describe** different
temperament styles. **Explain** how temperament style affects how a young child deals with
others.

❏ **Describe** a young child's view of the behavior
of others, of friendship, and of conflict resolution.

❏ **Outline** the development of self-control.

❏ **Analyze** case studies on developmentally
appropriate child guidance.

Case Studies: Developmentally Appropriate Child Guidance in Action

Mr. Thompson, Teacher, Infant Room

Mr. Thompson planned some "memory" games for 6-month-old Ray. Mr. Thompson showed Ray a plastic block and then slowly covered it with a cloth. Ray grabbed the cover and pulled it off. Mr. Thompson encouraged his effort by saying, "You found the toy!"

On another day, Ray smiled when his teacher showed him his favorite stuffed bear, which had been lost for about two weeks. Then Mr. Thompson turned Ray away so he couldn't see it. When Ray turned his head back to look for the bear, the teacher praised his effort and helped him retrieve the toy.

Seventeen-month-old Ernesto waddled out the door as the aide opened it; then he started down the corridor. Mr. Thompson called, "Ernesto, stop." Ernesto turned and looked at his teacher, who had stooped and held out his arms. "Come on, Ernesto." Ernesto walked toward his teacher, who said, "You came when I called you, Ernesto!"

Mrs. Vargas's Preschool Classroom

Selected Observations

Monday: The children seemed happy that the first snow had fallen overnight. "Look, it's snowing on my tray!" said Tahisha, as she made delicate small dots on the clear plastic tray with white finger paint. "Well, my snow is really deep," replied Ralph, his palms swirling two globs of white paint onto his tray. Next to him, Justine announced, "My Dad said that we might have a blizzard tonight. He said that the wind blows snow around and we will stay inside." With that, she quietly made "wind noises" and intensified her white finger-paint swirls.

Tuesday: Mrs. Vargas's group of 4-year-olds dictated a story about the heavy snowfall that had indeed taken place on Monday evening. Ralph, Justine, and Tahisha all worked at the playdough table where they pummeled white dough into "snow." Ralph plunked down a small plastic wolf in the "snow."

Wednesday: Throughout the morning, several children at the sand table poured sand from one unbreakable container into others. The children in the dramatic play area used a plastic snow shovel to clear imaginary snow from the front of the play space so, as Nellie said, "I can get my car out of the garage."

Thursday: Mrs. Vargas observed as Ralph ran into the classroom and zoomed right into the crowded puzzle area. There was no room for him. She quietly called Ralph aside and said, "Ralph, you are really eager to work in this area! But it looks like there might be too many people here right now. The sign says '4.' Now, count the children." (Ralph counts.) "That's right, five children. Let's go hang up your coat and then find something else to do. You can come back here just as soon as somebody leaves."

Mr. Nellis's K–2 Grade Classroom

Willis and Michael, second-graders, had worked on a social studies project together for several days—planning and making a model of a farm with the unit blocks. After they built the road leading to the farm, the boys put a large building off to the right. Willis said that it was the tractor shed but Michael wanted it to be the garage for the farm's trucks and cars. Mr. Nellis heard the discussion escalate into an argument, with Willis getting a tractor to place in the shed and Michael insisting that he wanted to put the trucks and cars in the enclosure. Mr. Nellis was approaching the boys when Michael angrily grabbed the tractor and threw it on the floor, then punched Willis on the arm. Willis retaliated by hitting Michael.

"Whoa, there! You both know the main rule in our classroom—keeping everybody safe—and that means no hurting other people or animals. I want each of you to sit here next to me and take some slow breaths. Willis started to explain. "We'll talk in a minute, Willis. For now, just take slow breaths." (Both boys sat glaring at each other but did the deep breathing.) "Good. Now, let's talk about what happened, OK?" Both boys nodded.

"It sure looks like we have a problem here. You worked together on the farm and finished the road. What happened next?"

Willis: "I want the building to be the tractor shed!"
Michael: "But I want it to be the garage for cars and trucks!"

"You each want the shed to be something different," said the teacher, "so let's figure out how to solve this problem. You have one big building and two different ideas. What do you think you could do?"

Michael: "But it's not really big enough for all the trucks, cars, and tractors" (he demonstrates by trying to put all the vehicles in the building).

"Maybe," said Willis, "we could build one of those 'lean-to' buildings that we learned about and put it on the shed. Then we'd have a lot more room."

"H-m-m. Do you mean that you could add more space and then use it for all of the cars, trucks, and tractors?" asked Mr. Nellis. "Yeah," said both children. Mr. Nellis asked if they had the material for building the lean-to and had them agree on a time to get started on their work. Then he said to them, "I like the way you thought this out and solved the problem. Let's try your idea and then see if it's working for both of you. We'll talk after you finish the lean-to." (You will read a similar scenario when you learn about teaching conflict resolution.)

Mr. Nellis, Mrs. Vargas, and Mr. Thompson use principles of DAP (developmentally appropriate practice) when they guide children. They are all authoritative caregivers[7]—warm, highly responsive, and supportive—but they also have high expectations of children.

Example. Mrs. Vargas, on Thursday, spoke with Ralph privately when he burst into a crowded activity area. She acted in a sensitive way by not talking in front of the other children. Still, she demonstrated her expectation that Ralph could indeed comply with the classroom limit by restating the limit appropriately. She has been both responsive and demanding, the two hallmarks of the authoritative style.

There is a good match between what these three teachers believe about child guidance and what they practice. For instance, all three believe that adults should treat children with respect (their belief). All three actually do treat children with respect when guiding them.

Example. Describe how Mr. Nellis and Mr. Thompson demonstrated respect for a child or children when guiding them.

Skillful and compassionate teachers such as Vargas, Thompson, and Nellis did not just pull their guidance strategies out of a hat. They did not do the first thing that popped into their heads. Instead, they made decisions about their guidance

---

[7]Chapter 1 in this text describes the authoritative style of caregiving.

strategies in each and every case. One of the major reasons they can use DAP child guidance so effectively is that they have a solid foundation in child development. Their child development knowledge helps them make wise guidance decisions.

This chapter is **not** just a review of child development. Instead, you will read about selected topics in child development and then about what this development means for you as you guide children. You will employ what you learn to develop a working knowledge of child development.

COGNITIVE DEVELOPMENT

There is a strong link between a child's cognitive and social development. You will be most effective with children when you keep in mind how a specific child thinks, whether he can understand what you say, whether he can take somebody else's perspective, and whether he can even remember what is said. This section describes cognitive development in early childhood. Children in the preoperational stage are described first, followed by the concrete operations stage, and finally the sensorimotor stage (infancy). The emphasis is on ages 2 to 6 in Piaget's framework (Piaget, 1952, 1965, 1968, 1976a, 1976b, 1983).

Two- to 6-year-old children are usually in the second of Piaget's stages of cognitive development, the preoperational stage. The early childhood years are a time of positive intellectual accomplishment, but preoperational thinkers also have some major limitations on their ability to think. This section focuses on the major positive features and describes some of the cognitive limitations of preoperational thinking. These cognitive abilities and limitations influence the child's interactions with adults and the child's capacity for self-control.

Preoperational Stage

Major Cognitive Ability: 2-to-6-Year-Olds Can "Represent" Experiences

Two- to 6-year-old children **can use symbols to represent (stand for) their experiences.** Observe any group of young children and you will quickly see that they represent their experiences, both good and bad,

- through deferred imitation,
- with language, and by
- using a variety of art media or technology.

Deferred imitation. Young children learn from all sorts of models. The models can be real people (adults or other children). Children also learn from real people on any type of screen (movie, video, computer). They learn from models in audio recordings or on computers. Additionally, children learn from models in reading material such as books, pamphlets, or even billboards, whether the book is one from Sunday School or a Boy Scout guide.

Children observe an event, form and hold a visual image of the event, and then often defer, or put off, imitating the action until some later time. Each of the children in the following examples has observed models and imitates them now for the first time.

Examples. Six-year-old Samuel was outside playing when his neighbor got out of her car. She dropped a bag of groceries, spilling cherries all over the driveway. Samuel ran over and helped her pick them up. (The model: a *Mr. Rogers* television episode. One neighbor helped another.)

Joseph swung his foot up in a martial arts arc and kicked another child on the legs. (The model: an adult cartoon character in a video game.)

Sarah softly sang, "Hush, little baby" as she cradled her doll in her arms. (The models: Sarah's father and mother, who both sing to Sarah's new baby brother.)

Language. One of the major ways that children relate their experiences is talking about them. The major cognitive accomplishment of this stage is that children can use a symbol to represent something else; words are the symbols through which children represent experiences.

Example. Justine used words to tell Mrs. Vargas that she and her family had gotten a new aquarium.

Andy used words to tell his mother that he and his dog played ball.

Use of art media or technology. Children also record their experiences through art media such as painting, drawing, or playdough. They use chalk, paint, playdough, markers, pencils, computers, and other media or technology to create an artistic expression that symbolizes, represents, or stands for an experience that they have had. Mrs. Vargas's 4-year-olds (in the case study at the beginning of this chapter) represented their "snow" experience with white finger paint and playdough.

Limitations of preoperational thinking

A 4-year-old's cognitive skills seem so much more advanced than the skills of an 18-month-old because the older child can represent experiences. Nevertheless, a 4-year-old preoperational thinker still has a limited ability to think logically. Preoperational thinkers tend to:

- view things from a somewhat egocentric perspective.
- judge things by how they look.
- focus on the before and after and ignore how things change (transformations).
- have trouble reversing a process.

Preoperational thinkers tend to be somewhat egocentric. Listen to a preschool child for a short time and you will smile at some of the things he says and the charm with which he says them. You may also be slightly puzzled, as I was in the following conversation with my 5-year-old niece, who wanted me to take her to get ice cream.

Marian (adult): "Lisa, tell me how to get to the ice cream store."
Lisa: "You go to the corner and then turn."
Marian: "Which corner?"
Lisa: "You know, the one with the trees."

At the time of our conversation, Lisa was somewhat egocentric and not very good at perspective taking. She did not give me all the necessary information, largely because she did not understand exactly what I needed to know. She, like others in the preoperational stage, probably also thought I had the same information she did.

Preoperational thinkers have difficulty with perspective taking. Egocentric thinkers center on themselves and what they want, but this is **not** the same thing as being selfish. A selfish person understands somebody else's perspective and chooses to ignore it, but an egocentric thinker cannot take the other person's perspective; there is a blurring of his or her own viewpoint with the perspective of the other person. A preoperational thinker, such as Lisa in the example above, believes that everyone thinks the same way she does.

Levels in Perspective Taking[8]		
Age in Years	**Level**	**Perspective-Taking Ability**
3 to 6	Level 0	• Egocentric perspective. • No distinction between own and another's perspective.
6–8	Level 1	• Still not able to take another's perspective. • Believes that another, if in the same situation, will respond just as the target child would respond.
8–10	Level 2	• Can take another's perspective. • Sees self as others do. • Not everyone reaches this level.
10–12	Level 3	• Can take another's perspective but in a more sophisticated way than at Level 2. • Now aware of recursive nature of different perspectives: "Mom thinks that I think she wants me to." Not everybody reaches this level.
Adolescence and Adulthood	Level 4	• Very sophisticated in perspective-taking ability. • Believes that different perspectives form a network. • Has conceptualized society's viewpoints on legal and moral issues. • Not everybody reaches this level.

Figure 2.1

[8]Selman R. L. (1976).Social-cognitive understanding. In T. Lickona (Ed.) *Moral development and behavior.* New York: Holt, Rinehart, & Winston.

Perspective taking: a cognitive developmental skill; the ability to understand how another person views a situation; takes several years to develop; first evident at the end of early childhood (Dixon & Soto, 1990). Selman (1976) described an orderly series of "levels" in perspective taking (Figure 2.1). As with any other area of development, children progress through the levels at different rates, so the ages in the chart are approximate.

A child must get older before perspective taking can ever happen. However, getting older is, by itself, not enough to get better at taking another's perspective. Some people never go beyond Levels 0 or 1; they never learn to take the perspective of others and have a great deal of trouble in their lives because of this deficiency. Many (but not all) abusive parents, for example, cannot take their child's perspective. See Figure 2.2.

Preoperational thinkers tend to judge things by how they look. Figure 2.3b shows two containers, one short and one tall, each holding an equal volume of water. Preoperational thinkers typically assert that the tall container has more water in it "because it looks like it has more." Appearances deceive them because they tend to judge something by how it appears on the surface.

**Q & A: Why Are Social
Perspective-Taking Skills Important?**

Question: What is social perspective taking?
Answer: It is the ability to control one's viewpoint when making judgments of others.
Question: Why is social perspective taking such an important cognitive developmental skill?
Answer: The foundation of effective social interaction is the ability to take another person's perspective (Chalmers & Townsend, 1990; Selman, 1980). A person who can take someone else's perspective can anticipate what others might be thinking, making interactions more predictable (Dixon & Soto, 1990). We can actually see ourselves as others see us if we can take their perspective. If, for example, one of the reactions that you get from others is that they smile and say hello, then you will begin to use this information as you define yourself.
Question: What types of problems do people with poor perspective-taking skills have?
Answer: They systematically misread or misinterpret the actions and intentions of others. They act in ways judged to be callous and disrespectful of the rights of others (Chalmers & Townsend, 1990). Parents with these tendencies use harsh discipline (Marion, 2000), and adults who cannot take a child's perspective are at risk for becoming child abusers (Milner, Robertson, & Rogers, 1990).
Question: How does a child with good social perspective-taking skills benefit?
Answer: Children who are good at perspective taking are better at persuading others and are better able to regulate aggressive impulses (Jones, 1985). Older children with good perspective-taking skills tend to be generous, helpful, and cooperative.

Figure 2.2

Figure 2.3a. *Step 1:* Child agrees that each container holds an equivalent volume of water. Child watches adult pour liquid from container B into container C (Figure 2.3b). A preoperational thinker will say that container C contains more than container A. His reason: he will say that it *looks* like more.

Figure 2.3b. The *pouring* of the liquid is the *transformation*.

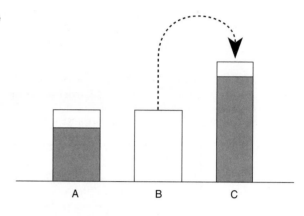

Figure 2.3c. Preoperational thinkers have difficulty reversing a thought. They will *not* say that you could prove that the two containers hold an equivalent volume by simply pouring the contents of container C back into container B.

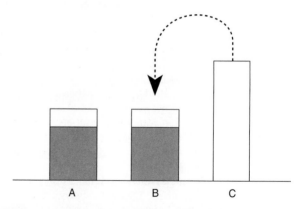

Preoperational thinkers focus on the before and after, ignoring how things change. Preoperational thinkers ignore the process through which something is transformed or changed. As shown in Figure 2.3a, a preoperational thinker focuses first on the water in the two short glasses (the "before" state). Then he focuses on the water in one short glass and one tall glass (the "after" state). He tends to ignore the pouring of the water from the short glass to the tall glass (the transformation) (Figure 2.3b). An older child, adolescent, or adult, aware of the pouring, would explain things by saying, "All you did was pour water from one container to another."

This cognitive limitation affects how young children operate in their social world, as the following examples demonstrate.

Example. Three-year-old Jeff watched as his older brother, Erik, transformed himself into a Halloween monster. Jeff cried and ran to Dad when he saw the finished product, and Dad made the mistake of trying to explain the transformation: "Oh, Jeff that's just Erik." Jeff was *not* convinced, having focused on plain old Erik (the "before" state) and then on the monster (the "after" state). In spite of having intently observed the whole makeup and costuming process, Jeff seems to have ignored it completely.

Preoperational thinkers have difficulty reversing a process. Preoperational thinkers focus on one thing at a time, either the "before" or the "after" in any action. An older child, who can think about a couple of things at once, is not deceived by how things look. Adults and older children realize that they could quickly show that the volume of liquid in the tall glass is equivalent to that in the short glass. They would simply pour the contents of the tall glass back into the short glass (Figure 2.3c). They can reverse the process; young children, however, do not think so logically.

Concrete Operational Stage

Children in this stage of cognitive development are usually between the ages of about 6 and 11 and in primary (first, second, or third grade) or elementary school (grades four, five, and six). Some of the cognitive skills of the concrete operational child include the ability to:

- distinguish reality from appearances.
- more easily detect apparent changes. They pay attention consistently to both relevant dimensions (height and width) in the standard conservation task. A concrete operational thinker uses this information about dimensions to arrive at an understanding of conservation.
- pay attention to how things change—transformations—even in standard conservation experiments.

These changes represent a qualitative shift in the type of thinking that a child this age can do. A primary or elementary school child shows evidence of the further development of skills that emerged during the preschool years.

Sensorimotor Stage

Piaget called the first stage of cognitive development (birth to approximately 24 months) the **sensorimotor stage** because infants are equipped with sensory actions (looking, listening, touching) and motor actions (grasping, head turning, hitting, etc.). They use sensorimotor actions or schemes to acquire information about and impose order on their world. Infants do not think or reflect on problems as older children or adults do.

Piaget divided the sensorimotor stage into six substages to describe an infant's cognitive skills. An infant spends most of his first few months of life practicing those sensory and motor (sensorimotor) schemes, but by 24 months, he will start to use symbols. Progress through the six substages occurs partly because of an infant's ability to imitate, which is evident quite early in life and improves as the infant gets older. Infants also acquire knowledge about object permanence as they progress through the sensorimotor stage.

Human infants are competent, active, information-processing creatures. A baby's perceptual skills are good enough, even at birth, to allow him to explore and discover his world, but perceptual skills change in several ways as infants grow older (Gibson & Spelke, 1983). Young infants seem to prefer some patterns to others and are able to perceive depth and color in their surroundings. The visual and nervous systems undergo continual development during a child's first year, making more sophisticated perception possible.

An infant's sensorimotor and perceptual skills affect his learning and remembering. Sensory, perceptual, and attention skills develop rapidly from birth to 12 months. Infants use all of their skills to acquire and retain a knowledge base.

Knowing About COGNITIVE DEVELOPMENT: What This Means for Guiding Children

- **Representing experience.** Expect children to describe their experiences in many ways—in words, by actions, through art, by singing, and in play. They will represent both happy and unhappy experiences. Observe carefully, record observations, and use the child's descriptions for clues about how to help him or her.
- **Play with peers.** Give children opportunities to play with other children to expose them to challenging ideas from others. They will find out that others have ideas, too, and that they have to learn how to deal with different perspectives.
- **Perspective taking.** Expect that, during early childhood, children will **not** be able to take another person's or animal's perspective.

    Example. Twenty-seven-month-old Josh pinched another child. His dad, surprised by the pinching, understood that his son does not understand how he hurt the other child. Josh cannot take the other child's perspective. Dad also knew that he had to tell his son how the other child felt. Dad said, "Oh, no, Josh! Ouch! Pinching hurts Sara. Use words to tell her to move."

    Dad's discipline was positive. He was firm but kind in dealing with the hurtful behavior. He made it clear that pinching was not allowed. He understands his egocentric son's need for information along with limit setting: "Use words to tell her to move."
- **Encourage children to do "transformations."** Avoid explaining transformations because preschool children simply do not pay attention to the process of transforming things. For example, a child will squash a ball of playdough into a pancake but ignore the process, focusing on the ball of playdough (the before) and then on the pancake (the after).

    Instead, give children many chances to **perform** many types of transformations. Manage a classroom or playground so that preschool children can pour water and sand into different containers, roll playdough into different shapes, and take on different roles in dramatic play. Performing many transformations eventually helps preschool children focus on the process or transformation.

Figure 2.4

Charlie and David are performing transformations by pouring water from one type of container to another.

Profound cognitive changes occur between 12 and 24 months. We see the result of all of these changes when they converge in the development of **symbolic thought.** By age 2, a child does several things to show us that he is able to use symbols. She pictures things in her mind, imitates things seen earlier, and understands and uses language.

PERCEPTION DURING EARLY CHILDHOOD

Infancy is a time of remarkable perceptual development, as you know from your study of child development, and children continue to develop perceptual skills as they get older. At 2 years old he has many perceptual skills, and by age 5 has skills that are even better than when he was a toddler. However, young children still have problems directing their attention and these problems fall into four areas. These issues affect your guidance.

Problems Affecting How Children Pay Attention

Young children do not search or scan very well

Young children can search for something, but they are not systematic in their search. Their search is not as accurate or efficient as an older child's, and some children do not seem to realize that they should stop searching at some point.

Example. Robert watched Mrs. Vargas write Robert's name on a name tag. Robert easily recognized his when the teacher showed Robert his name tag along with three others. The next day, however, Robert's name tag was on the chart with 22 others. Robert looked for a long time, but became frustrated when he could not find his name tag.

Young children have difficulty "tuning out" irrelevant information

Young children are not able to control their attention. They have difficulty tuning out (ignoring) meaningless information or stimulation. Their attention wanders when they hear or see some sudden, intense stimulus.

Example. A new student teacher was frustrated when he read a story to a small group of 3-year-olds. A squealing sound from the parking lot and the squeaking from wheels on the lunch cart easily distracted them. Older children might also have noticed the noise, but would have been better able to "get back" to listening to the story (provided the story was developmentally appropriate and interesting).

Young children tend to focus on only one thing at a time

This was evident in the section on limitations of preoperational thinking. Figure 2.3 shows that preoperational thinkers focus on either the height or the width of the liquid in the glasses but they cannot focus on both at the same time. This inability makes it difficult for young children to focus on their own viewpoint and on somebody else's viewpoint at the same time.

Example. Two of Mrs. Vargas's preschool children were playing at the sand table, constructing a tunnel. Then they had an argument about which way the tunnel should turn. Each child's focus was his own idea and neither could deal with the other child's suggestion.

Impulsiveness affects perception

Reflective children tend to be more accurate in their work because they proceed slowly enough to avoid major mistakes. Impulsive children, however, tend to work too quickly, thereby missing important information and making unnecessary mistakes. Ralph, in the case study at the beginning of this chapter, is an example. Younger children tend to be impulsive, making it difficult for them to stop, look around, and think about choices.

Changes in Perception Help Children Pay Attention Better As They Get Older

More mature reasoning skills, more efficient memory, more mature language abilities, abstract concepts, and more experiences to draw on are some of the things that go along with changing perceptual abilities as children get older. Here are some of the ways in which perception changes during the early childhood period.

Children get better at selecting things they ignore or to which they pay attention

Child development researchers have known for over 30 years that even infants select—and seem to prefer—certain patterns (Fantz, 1966). A 2-year-old has the ability to attend selectively to stimuli, but this ability improves during childhood as he eventually learns to ignore distracting stimuli. Older children are much better than are younger children at selecting the things to which they prefer to attend or which they ignore.

Example. Preschoolers in Mrs. Vargas's class looked up in surprise when they heard a helicopter flying over the school. Many jumped up from the group and ran to the window. The fourth-graders in another part of the building heard the same noise. Several fourth-graders simply said, "Helicopter," and went right on with their work. The older children chose to ignore the intense, intrusive sound.

Children spend more time "on task" as they get older

Older children tend to stay with a task for a longer period than do younger children. Children spend less time in an activity that they think is boring or uninteresting.

Knowing About PERCEPTION:
What This Means for Guiding Children

- **Screen for sensory impairments.** Make sure that each child has had a vision and hearing check. A child who has a hearing problem might appear to ignore a signal for cleanup when, in fact, she has a hearing problem.
- **Disruptions.** Children acquire self-control slowly and gradually. Sudden noises, flashing lights, and people who interrupt a class make it difficult for young children to concentrate on work and play. Manage the classroom and time schedule to minimize disruptions from noise, people interrupting the group, and sudden light changes. Be calm and help children adjust to the necessary or unavoidable disruptions.

    Mr. Nellis noticed that several of his children seemed anxious during the fire drill. After it was over, instead of marching right back to the room, he said, "I want all of us to just stand here (on the playground) quietly for a minute. Be very quiet and take one slow breath. Good. Now close your eyes and take one more s-l-o-w breath." They then walked back to the classroom and the teacher calmly said that they should resume their work.
- **Systematic scanning.** Teach children to scan systematically. For example, Mrs. Vargas knew that Ralph could read his name but could not pick out his name tag when all the name tags were hanging on the chart—the collection of name tags was simply too large. Mrs. Vargas observed that Ralph was haphazard and unsystematic when he searched.

    She taught him a simple scanning technique. "Ralph, look at only one row—this one. Your name begins with R. Look for the first letter. Look for R." She encouraged Ralph to ignore names beginning with other letters.
- **Calmly encourage impulsive children to slow their reaction time.** Ralph usually worked very quickly and impulsively. When a small group was doing a counting activity, Ralph hurried through and missed several things to be counted. Mrs. Vargas helped him slow down by telling him to touch each item that he was to count.

Figure 2.5

Children are more likely to start an activity in the first place if it is captures their interest in some way.

Example. Mrs. Vargas set out small plastic tubs filled with wet sand on a table. Larry walked around the room that day and looked in each center. When he saw the wet sand and things for making impressions in the sand, Larry sat at that table for 30 minutes, working industriously at smoothing sand, making impressions, then smoothing sand again.

Children are better able to redirect their attention as they get older

Older children can more easily redirect their attention than can younger children. When a task has a number of parts, the older child has an advantage because she is able to shift her focus from one aspect to another quickly. These children are better able to say, for example, "OK, I'm done with that part. I can start on the next part and then I can finish with the third part. Whoops! I forgot something in part one."

Example. Almost all of Mr. Nellis's second-graders worked with several specialists at different times each week. This resulted in many interruptions to classwork for individuals. Mr. Nellis has made anecdotal records of which children could or could not quickly get back to their work when they returned to the classroom. Several of his 7-year-olds could not shift gears and redirect their attention to classroom work when they returned.

MEMORY

Definitions

Memory: basic cognitive process by which we store information and then later retrieve it.

Long-term memory: storage for the information that we perceive and then make an effort to learn. We collect such information and then store it as a permanent record. Most of us can call up information from long-term memory because we often have stored the memory as a strong sensory image of places and events, sometimes from years or even decades ago. For instance, I remember one sunny afternoon in my grandfather's garden whenever I smell basil because he crushed some of the fragrant herb that day and let me sniff it. Unpleasant or frightening events are also stored. For example, people who were in New York City on September 11, 2001, or in Oklahoma City on April 19, 1995, will probably never forget the sounds of the World Trade Center or the Murrah Federal Building as they crashed to the ground.

Short-term memory or "working" memory: storage site for temporarily storing new information or well-known information to which we need access. A child's space for short-term memory increases with age, allowing him to work with and process more information and do so for longer periods (Case, 1992).

Example. Willis, in Mr. Nellis's mixed-age class, is working on a classification activity that the teacher developed—classifying fruits as citrus or noncitrus. Mr. Nellis defined a citrus fruit and then Willis had to take his memory of names of different fruits out of long-term memory and place them in his short-term memory while he worked on the activity.

Recognition memory: the realization that we have seen or experienced some information that we now encounter (Shaffer, 1996). Ask a child, for example, to pick out pictures of her dog and the cat who lives next door from a small group of photos of cats and dogs. She probably will easily recognize her pet and the pet from next door. Recognition tasks are easier than recall, described next.

Recall memory: used when a person has to retrieve or call up some information. There are different types of recall memory and these are important when we look at the memory capacity of infants and young children.

"Cued" recall memory: memory prompted by a cue or reminder.

Example. Mr. Nellis made a list of the names of trees that the children have studied. He posted the list (the cue) at the children's level in the area where they worked on the tree project.

"Pure" recall memory: a memory that does not require prompting with any cue or reminder. A child actively retrieves information from memory with no cues involved, as Willis did with names of fruits in the classification activity.

Metamemory: a person's overall knowledge about memory. Adults, for example, understand that they have different types of memory. Adults also know that they can use memory strategies and they understand why memory strategies work.

Milestones in the Development of Memory

Birth to 5 Months

Recognition memory: Infants are well equipped even at birth to recognize familiar objects. Observe an infant's recognition memory when the baby **habituates to—** becomes accustomed to or bored with—a stimulus; for example, a toy that is put in front of him several times. This boredom indicates that a baby remembers or **recognizes** the object.

Recall memory, cued recall: Very young infants can recall a memory but need to be reminded about a familiar event or experience; they rely on getting a **cue or reminder.** An adult can encourage a 2- to 3-month-old infant to kick a mobile, then remind the infant several days later about the mobile by moving it while she watches. The infant will recall having kicked the mobile. However, notice that the adult had to give the baby a **cue;** the baby could not actively recall kicking the mobile on his own.

5 months to 1 year

Recognition memory: improved. Infants can recognize objects after seeing them only a few times. They also seem to be able to remember the object for several weeks (Fagan, 1984).

Figure 2.6. Show these pictures to a young child and let her look at them for a few minutes. Then mix them in with a larger number of pictures. The child will probably *recognize* all the items in the figure. Later, ask the child to *recall* as many of the 12 pictures as possible. She will remember some but not all, because pure recall memory is not very good in early childhood.

Recall memory: also improved. After about six months, infants can actively recall events from the recent past; they do not need cues as often.

1 year to 3 years

Recall memory: improves even more (Howe & Courage, 1993; Perlmutter, 1986). After about age 2, children can recall exciting events that happened quite some time before and occasionally even tell about the memory in the form of a story. By the time a child is 3 years old, he might be able to recall something that happened to him 1 or 2 years previously.

4 years to 12 years

Memory improves remarkably during the preschool and middle childhood years.

Pure recall memory: 4-year-olds can do pure recall but 8-year-olds are even better at remembering something without a reminder. Here is an example:

Show Figure 2.6 to preschoolers. They will **recognize** almost all items but they would not be able simply to recall more than three or four of them. Third-graders, on the other hand, would be able to recall about eight of the items (Baker-Ward, Gordon, Ornstein, Larus, & Clubb, 1993).

Explaining Changes in Memory

Shaffer (1996) points to four reasons for the dramatic improvement in memory from ages 3 to 12:

There are changes in basic capacities

Older children process information more quickly and manipulate information better than younger children because they have more "working" memory (short-term memory) space in their brains. Third-graders, therefore, can keep more infor-
...ds and can perform mental operations much more rapidly than

```
            SALE RECEIPT
Store #/481    tko  06/30/05 14:57:00
  SUBWAY
1296 N. Kinzie Ave.
Bradley                    IL 60915
(815)939-3331
Trans# 234 Clerk 53  Dwr 1 TRDT 063005
Receipt # 0000247174 Reg-ID REG-MAIN
-- ITEM --- QTY      PRICE MEMO  PLU
RK-16oz      1  T $   1.09         1
COOKIE       1  T $   0.45        11
                     ---------
    SUBTOTAL $        1.54
    Sales Tx $        0.10
                     ---------
TAKE-OUT **TOTAL $    1.64
ash   AMT TEND $      2.00
                     ---------
    CHANGE DUE$       0.36
   Stamps earned this sale:     +.

Thank you for making Subway
The World's Best Sandwich!
```

...trategies used for remembering things

...e learned a greater number of and more effective methods ...into their long-term memory and then for retrieving it later. ...ly use **memory strategies** once they have learned a strategy ...ng a memory strategy is helpful.
...ear-olds use the strategy called **rehearsal;** they will rehearse ...ntil they remember it. Preschool children generally do not ...mary children use it but not very effectively—adults have to ...e things. Older elementary school children rehearse lists or ...mbered very effectively (Flavell, Miller, & Miller, 1993) if ...i rehearsal or other strategies.
...so use another memory strategy called **organization** more ...unger children. Figure 2.6 can be organized into four ...als, food, and clothing. Researchers have shown us that ...i organize groups of items in order to make recalling the ...dren do make these logical groupings and are therefore ...i such lists (Hasselhorn, 1992).

...ledge about memory

...stand how and why memory strategies work and therefore ...more effectively. This overall understanding of memory is ...iildren who are at least 10 years old seem to understand ...e younger children do not (Schneider & Pressley, 1989). ...lerstand why a memory strategy is helpful are much more ...ies in everyday life and in schoolwork (Brown & Campione,

...nowledge about the world

...i simply have been on the earth for a shorter time than older children and have not had the opportunity to acquire the wealth of knowledge that an older child has. Older children have learned more and therefore are more familiar with a greater amount of knowledge, which makes remembering things much easier (Schneider & Bjorklund, 1992).

Knowing About MEMORY:
What This Means for Guiding Children

When children use memory strategies, they do much better on tests of recall memory (Moely, Hart, Leal, Santulli, Rao, Johnson, & Hamilton, 1992). Similarly, preschool and kindergarten teachers have opportunities every day to focus on memory development.

- **Encourage children to use memory strategies.** Rehearse or repeat something that children need to remember. Rehearse by singing a name song at the beginning of the year to help children learn names. Repeat the schedule so that children remember what comes next. Group things into logical groups; e.g., red, yellow, and pink flowers.
- **Teach children why memory strategies are so useful.** Tell children why a memory strategy is useful and tell them when to use a strategy. Mr. Nellis helped his children understand that they could remember the names of eight trees more easily by placing the trees into smaller groups; e.g., trees that lose or do not lose leaves.
- **Use familiar pictures, sounds, and objects.** Mr. Nellis used digital photos of their trip to the zoo to help the children retrieve information from long-term memory. He placed the disk with the photos in the computer and the children eagerly identified each animal. He also played a tape of sounds made by the new animals that the children had seen. In addition, the children also scanned, printed, and posted pictures of each of the eight trees.
- **Plan activities and lessons with fewer steps.** Mrs. Vargas arranged an obstacle course with only four parts so that the children could easily remember it: **over** the rope, **through** the tire, **up** the ladder, and **down** the slide.
- **Present only a few bits of new information.** Mrs. Vargas introduced the names of six birds in one lesson and discovered that the children could not handle this much new information. However, they easily remembered the names of the birds when she focused on only three.
- **Think of different and creative ways to repeat things.** Mrs. Vargas showed the pictures of the three birds at several group times and repeated their names with the children. Remembering that a square is a rectangle with four equal sides was easier when she repeated the information in creative ways over several days using computer models, transparencies, Styrofoam models, a construction paper mural, and square cookie cutters.
- **Actively involve children with things to be remembered.** Active involvement enhances memory. The preschool children in Mrs. Vargas's class learned about squares by forming one themselves at group time with four children on each side of the square. During Fire Safety Week, Mr. Nellis helped his class remember the emergency fire escape route by having them walk it a number of times and then drawing the route on pieces of paper and on the computer.
- **Label objects and experiences.** Labeling things helps children remember them. Before the trip to the zoo, Mr. Nellis showed pictures of animals he thought might be unfamiliar and named them for the children. At the zoo, he repeated the names and the class wrote the names on a chart when they returned to school. The children also printed labels for each of the eight trees.

Figure 2.7

TEMPERAMENT

Description

Temperament: the predictable, characteristic way that any person—infant, child, or adult—responds to events or expresses emotion; a person's behavioral style (Kagan, Reznick, Snidman, Gibbons, & Johnson, 1988). Researchers who have examined temperament usually look at several different elements of an infant's behavioral style (Buss & Plomin, 1984; Goldsmith et al., 1987) including:

- **activity level** (whether activity level is fast paced, slow paced, vigorous, not so vigorous)
- **irritability level** (how negative events affect a child; i.e., how upset does he get?)
- **soothability** (whether and how easily a child can be soothed)
- **levels of fearfulness**
- **sociability** (whether a child is receptive to social stimulation)

Three Basic Temperament Styles

Some of the earliest research on temperament found that infants seemed to fall into one of three general or broad categories of temperament style. The temperament qualities listed above tended to group together to form an overall style for each infant. This longitudinal research (Thomas & Chess, 1986) described three basic temperament styles. An infant's temperament affects her development (Buss & Plomin, 1984).

Easy temperament

Children with easy temperaments:

- have predominantly positive moods
- adapt easily
- have a positive approach to new situations
- express emotions in a mild way
- have predictable and regular eating and sleeping patterns

Example. Sasha, 8 months old, has an easy temperament. He spends very little time crying and spends a great deal of time watching, listening to, and playing with things and people. This allows him to take in information and he has more time to accommodate to that information and to learn than a baby who cries a lot.

Slow-to-warm-up temperament

Children who are slow to warm up:

- express emotion mildly
- are cautious
- are somewhat moody
- are slow to adapt to change

- withdraw from or are passively resistant to new objects and people
- are reluctant to try new things; this might cause others to ignore them

Difficult temperament

Difficult children:

- express emotion in highly intense way; i.e., show happiness energetically and demonstrate anger or sadness equally vigorously
- might be perceived as having predominantly negative dispositions if adults do not understand how to deal with this temperament
- are quite slow to adapt to change
- might even stubbornly resist change if adults try to force them to accept a change too quickly
- withdraw from new stimuli
- have irregular bodily functions

A child's temperament and her parents' caregiving style affect the child's social skills. Specifically, the **goodness of fit** of a child in her home strongly predicts her social skills. A "good fit" occurs when a child's temperament characteristics enable her to cope well with the demands and expectations of her family's environment (Paterson & Sanson, 1999). A child also needs a "good fit" between her temperament characteristics and her classroom.

Knowing About TEMPERAMENT:
What This Means for Guiding Children

- **Identify temperaments.** Identify your own temperament as well as that of the children in your class. This is the starting point.
- **Temperamental styles often clash!** Accept the idea that children will very likely have a temperament different from your own. For example, you are easygoing, and you are working with a child who has strong reactions to most things. He practically bursts with joy when he is happy but is equally strongly negative when unhappy. Acknowledge that you will feel irritated or even angry when your mellow outlook hits his hard-driving, often negative approach head-on.
- **Positive guidance strategies.** Consciously and consistently, choose positive guidance strategies. Mr. Nellis, for example, realized that Michael had a difficult temperament and that he had strong negative reactions to many things. In the chapter-opening case study, Michael grabbed the tractor, threw it on the floor, and punched Willis. Think about how Mr. Nellis was calm and used positive guidance strategies.
- **Maintain perspective and manage stress.** Keep your long-term goal in mind, to guide children effectively, whatever their temperament. Learn to manage the stress of dealing with children with temperaments that cause them problems. Rely on your patience, sensitivity, and goodwill. They will help you maintain the calm attitude you need to deal with different temperaments.

Figure 2.8

SOCIAL COGNITION

Social cognition: how children think about the behavior, motives, feelings, or intentions of others (Shaffer, 1996). How do children describe how other people behave? Will they understand the difference between another person's accidental and intentional behavior? How will they view friendship? How will they think about resolving conflict? Your knowledge about these developmental issues will give you a firm foundation for making developmentally appropriate child guidance decisions.

How Children Describe Other People and Their Behavior

Teachers spend a lot of time thinking about children's social development and are justifiably concerned about helping children interact with others in friendly and amicable ways. We adults also want children to be able to deal with conflicts in a nonaggressive manner. Our social interactions are more likely to be friendly if we perceive others accurately and if we can predict what they might be feeling (Shaffer, 1996).

You will be able to guide children more effectively if you comprehend that their interactions are often affected by how they understand the behavior of other people. Researchers have given us a lot information about what children of different ages pay attention to in others, what they remember, and how they describe other people and their behavior.

Younger than 7 or 8 years

During early childhood, children tend to use concrete terms to describe another person, such as "My mommy is pretty. She smells good. She likes dogs." They rarely describe abstract qualities, such as trustworthiness or honesty. Occasionally, a young child will describe someone by using what seems to be an abstract term, such as "He's *mean!*" Here, though, the child usually is describing something the other person has recently done, such as yelling at the child for running onto the lawn, rather than identifying a major psychological characteristic (Rholes, Jones, & Wade, 1988).

Show a video to young children and ask them to describe what they saw. They will concentrate on describing concrete, observable actions: "She opened the gate and the kitten got out." They might describe obvious emotional reactions, ". . . and the girl cried." However, young children will not try to interpret feelings. Children viewing this video would very likely not try to tell you why the girl was crying.

After Age 8

Children at this age use fewer concrete terms and begin using broad psychological terms to describe other people (Damon, 1999). A child in first, second, or third grades, for example, might describe his friends by **comparing** their behaviors in some way: "Carl **draws better** than anybody in our class," or "Cecil **spells better** than most of the class." Children usually use fewer and fewer such behavioral comparisons as they get older. When our primary children are in the fifth grade—10 years-old—and describe Carl and Cecil, they are likely to use broader psychological constructs in their descriptions (Shaffer, 1996): "Carl is very **artistic**"; "Cecil is one of the **smartest** people in class."

Eight- to 10-year-olds are also much better able to describe another person's behavior. Show a video to this group and you will hear interpretations of some of the feelings and intentions of other people, but only in familiar situations; for example, "She cried when the kitten got out of the yard. She's probably feeling sad and afraid that her kitten will get hurt."

How Children Understand Intentional Versus Accidental Behavior

Children are better able to control themselves when they can look at another's behavior and decide whether the person acted intentionally or whether the behavior was accidental. Children can distinguish between accidental and intentional behavior as their cognitive skills develop and if the adults in their lives help them understand what others intended to do. Four-year-olds tend not to differentiate between intentional and accidental behavior, but by 5½ years, many children can make this distinction.

How Children View Friendship

You have already read about how important it is to be able to take another person's perspective. Perspective-taking ability changes as a child gets older and affects how children view friendship. At first, young children are rather self-centered or egocentric about who their friends are because a friend is viewed as somebody who simply plays with the child (Hartup, 1992) or who can help a child. In late childhood and early adolescence, children view friends as people who understand each other and who provide emotional support (Furman & Buhrmester, 1992).

Friendship becomes important during the early childhood years for three reasons (Damon, 1983). First, children have a blossoming sense of moral obligation, a willingness to share or to take turns. Although indications of sharing or turn taking were evident earlier, they now occur with regularity. Second, children begin to view peers as friends as well as momentary playmates. Social interactions are seen for the first time as part of a system of relationships that go beyond the present moment. Third, a wide range of possibilities for social interaction arise because of a young child's development of symbolic awareness.

Children need social skills to interact effectively

Good peer relationships are necessary for a child's healthy development (Asher & Rose, 1997; Bullock, 1997). Teachers can help children develop the skills they need to experience pleasant and rewarding peer relationships. Some of the competencies, or social skills, required for effective interaction with peers are the ability to initiate interaction with peers, the ability to maintain a relationship, and the ability to deal with conflict.

Popular and unpopular children initiate contact with peers differently. Observe a preschool child who has good social skills and who wants to join a group activity with other children that she knows. She is most likely to be admitted to the group if she approaches the group, watches the ongoing activity, and then engages in the same behavior without disrupting the group.

A child who has initiated contact with peers must be able to maintain the relationship. Children who are cooperative and friendly when interacting with peers are generally successful in maintaining relationships. Children who are unfriendly to, make fun of, or interfere with other children have great difficulty maintaining relationships. Other children often reject them (Bullock, 1991).

Conflict Resolution

The capacity to resolve conflict peaceably is an important social skill that rests on a child's ability to take another person's perspective and whether a child has been taught how to perform conflict resolution. Resolving conflicts is an important part of social cognition. By the age of 5, children realize that they can defend their rights (e.g., not allow somebody to take a toy with which they are playing), but their skill in resolving conflict varies considerably.

Knowing About SOCIAL COGNITION:
What This Means for Guiding Children

- **When a young child has hurt someone or an animal.** Resist the urge to ask how the other person or animal feels (young children really do not know). Tell the child how the person or animal feels.

  Example. Mr. Nellis to one of his kindergartners: "Sonny was really angry with you. I could tell because he screamed at you."

- **Understanding another person's purpose.** Help young children distinguish between accidental and intentional behavior. Some aggressive or abused children often attribute hostile intent when there was none. Help them understand that there was no mean-spirited motivation on the other person's part, if this is truly the case.

  Example. Mr. Nellis to one of his second-graders: "Sometimes people aren't very careful, and I think Sam ran into you by accident. I was watching him and he really wasn't looking at where he was going. He didn't mean to hurt you." Mr. Nellis then talked with Sam about looking where he was going.

- **Teach specific social skills** (Asher & Rose, 1997). All children need to learn social skills. Aggressive, abused, or unpopular children need this instruction to a greater degree (Bullock, 1997; Carlyon, 1997). Model, directly teach, and then coach a behavior that a child needs; e.g., how to enter a play or work group. Then provide helpful information on how the child can use the new skill.

  Example. Mrs. Vargas used a puppet play (modeling) with Larry to demonstrate how to ask to join a group. After watching the puppets, the teacher gave specific verbal instructions to Larry on how to join a group. "OK, Larry, go over to the table and pick a spot where you won't be in somebody's way. Then use a toy that nobody else is using. Remember the water table rules? That's right. No splashing and no grabbing!" Mrs. Vargas nodded encouragingly (nonverbal feedback) at Larry as he took a place at an unoccupied side of the water table and played with an unclaimed toy.

- **Teach conflict resolution skills.** Children will easily learn the steps in settling disputes if you demonstrate the steps in everyday situations.

Figure 2.9

Successful conflict resolution requires that a child be able to think of more than one thing at a time. She has to think about alternative ways of solving problems. She must know how the other person might view the problem. Finally, she has to know how another person is likely to respond to different solutions and to understand how her actions will affect another person. These steps involve focusing on a conflict as a problem to be solved and not as an argument. Steps in teaching conflict resolution include the following:

- **Identify and define the conflict.** Avoid accusing the other person. Approach it like this: "We have a problem."
- **Invite children to participate in solving the problem.**
- **Work together to generate possible solutions.** Accept a variety of solutions and do not evaluate solutions during this brainstorming phase.
- **Examine each idea for how well it might work.** Decide which one to try. Thank the children for coming up with ideas.
- **Help children with plans to implement the solution.** Young children will not know how to put the plan into action unless you teach them how to get started.
- **Follow up to evaluate how well the solution worked.** If the solution worked, thank the children for their help in cooperating to solve the problem. If the solution did not work, ask the children to try to figure out why and to fine-tune the solution or to try another one.

SELF-CONTROL

What Is Self-Control?

Self-control: voluntary, internal regulation of behavior. First, children actually construct their concept of self as their cognitive system develops. Second, they observe and then evaluate the self, deciding whether they like the self that they see (these two facets are described more fully in Chapter 6). Third, the self must learn to regulate its own behavior (Harter, 1983).

Self-control, or self-regulation, may well be one of the most significant changes taking place during early childhood. Self-control is an essential part of how children learn, is important in a child's growth and development, and is fundamental in preserving social and moral order (Harter, 1983; Shaffer, 1996).

How Children Demonstrate Self-Control

Children demonstrate self-control when they do the following.

Control impulses, wait, and suspend action

Children show self-control when they step back, examine a situation, and then decide how to act. They resist reacting impulsively.

Example. Things went smoothly in the block corner until Larry joined the group and took a block from Jordan's structure. Jordan's usual reaction has been an aggressive one, such as slugging or screaming at the other child. However, Mrs.

Vargas has been teaching him to be self-controlled and verbally assertive. So he **used words** as his teacher suggested: "Larry, I was using that block. Give it back!"

Tolerate frustration

A child demonstrates self-control when she can refrain from doing something that is either forbidden or inappropriate to the situation.

Example. While on a Christmas shopping trip, Jordan was attracted to a huge tree with hundreds of glass ornaments. He stood and looked, raised his hand to touch one, and then withdrew his hand, showing self-control.

Postpone immediate gratification

Adults demonstrate self-control when they carry through with some important task and only when it is completed engage in some gratifying (pleasurable) activity; for example, studying before meeting a friend for coffee. Children are simply not as good at delaying gratification as are adults. Use modeling, direct instruction, and all the other methods of influence to teach delay of gratification. Even older children need help figuring out when it is important to put off until later something that they want right now.

Example. Danny, 6 years old, popped several chocolate chips into his mouth as he and his brother helped Dad make chocolate chip cookies. Dad said, "Hey, Danny. Remember the ad on TV where that man sings 'Please don't eat all the morsels—or your cookies will look like this' [a chipless chocolate chip cookie]? You can have three more chips now but put the rest into the mix, not your mouth." Danny said, "O-OK!" as he added chips to the batter.

Initiate a plan and carry it out over time

Willis and Michael, two second-grade boys in the chapter-opening case study, planned how to build a model of a farm, drew the plans, and then set about building their model. It took them several days to complete their project.

How Self-Control Evolves

Self-control emerges "from the outside to the inside," slowly and haltingly.

Self-control evolves "from the outside to the inside"

Responsible adults actually perform most of an infant's or toddler's ego functions (e.g., remembering things for the infant, reminding a toddler to hold the kitten gently), thereby regulating the young child's behavior for her. In this case, the adult greatly controls the very young child's actions. The control is outside the infant; it is external. The infant cannot control herself.

Nevertheless, responsible adults who understand child development realize that a child can, and should, take on more responsibility for controlling herself as she grows older and acquires greater cognitive skills. They expect children to begin to internalize the control taught by the adult. Responsible adults communicate this expectation when they gradually transfer executive control to children (Brown, Bransford, Ferrara, & Campione, 1983). The adult might expect, for example, a child to try solving a problem with the adult observing and offering advice or help only when necessary.

Pulkkinen (1982) noted that child-rearing practices affect a child's level of self-control. She found that parents of adolescents with strong self-control used positive guidance strategies. These parents employed strategies that helped adolescents understand why control was necessary and did it in a way that avoided demonstrating raw power. Parents of adolescents with weak self-control used selfish, negative guidance strategies. They tried to use raw power and thought it unnecessary to explain their adult actions.

Self-control develops slowly

Children are not born with self-control, but begin to develop it around the age of 2. It takes several more years before this emerging ability fully develops. Children are better able to control themselves as they get older for a number of reasons. First, their cognitive, perceptual, and linguistic systems have developed, allowing them to understand things from a different perspective and giving them access to better skills for dealing with impulses. Control of the self also implies that a child realizes that a self exists; this knowledge develops during late infancy and early childhood.

Self-control evolves haltingly

Preschool children often astonish adults with remarkable self-control, but demonstrate considerable lack of control at other times. Jackie controlled himself in the block corner, but on the same day, he shoved someone out of the way while rushing to the swimming pool. Young children have to practice self-control, just as musicians have to practice their skills. It is reasonable to expect some measure of self-control in young children, but it is usually a mistake to expect perfect control.

Milestones in the Development of Self-Control

Birth to approximately 12 months

- Infants are not capable of self-control (Kopp, 1981). The reflex movements of the first several months of life give way to voluntary motor acts such as reaching and grasping, but Kopp notes that infants do not consciously control these movements. Infancy is a time to learn that the self is separate from other people, the very first step on the road to self-control.

Between age 1 and age 2

- Not yet capable of self-control.
- Begin to be able to start, stop, change, or maintain motor acts or emotional signals.
- Demonstrate an emerging awareness of the demands made on children by caregivers. Communication skills become more sophisticated, enabling a child to understand another person's instructions and modeling.
- Caregivers usually discover that children this age are ready to follow an adult's lead.

At approximately 24 months: Transition to self-control
- Can recall what someone has said or done.
- Can represent experiences.
- These new abilities help children make the transition to beginning self-control.
- At this stage, however, children have only a limited ability to control themselves; that is, to wait for their turn or to delay gratification.

At about 3 years: Self-control emerges
- Children are now able to use certain strategies that help them delay gratification, and this sets the stage for better self-control. Kopp (1981) did research with groups of 18-, 24-, and 36-month-old children to find out how they differ in their use of strategies to better tolerate delay. Raisins were hidden under a cup, and the child being tested was told not to eat them. The older children spontaneously did things to distract themselves, such as singing, talking, sitting on their hands, or looking away. Younger children could be instructed to use delaying strategies, but they did not use them automatically.

Knowing About SELF-CONTROL:
What This Means for Guiding Children

- **Acknowledge a child's frustration.** A child is more likely to tolerate frustration when we acknowledge her frustration; for example, "It must be frustrating, Jordan, to have to wait for a turn when you want to get to the computer."
- **Teach about "first things first."** It is entirely normal to want to engage in pleasure. Teach children when and how to postpone immediate gratification. Mrs. Vargas, for example, said to Jordan, "While you wait for your turn at the computer, take your library books back to the shelf and clean up your spot at the playdough table." Do this in a friendly, matter-of-fact way.
- **Teach project control.** Lead children in outlining steps in a project and then in choosing realistic chunks of work for specific periods. Start with small projects when dealing with children who lack self-control. For example, Mr. Nellis said to Ned, a kindergarten child, "OK, you want to write a story about the rabbit we saw. What is the first thing you need to do to write the story? Good, a marker. What's another thing you need? (Paper.) When you get those two things, where would you like to sit?"
- **Realize that you will have to perform most of an infant's or young toddler's ego functions.** For example, Mr. Thompson, the infant teacher, fully realizes that he has to remember things for the infants. Some samples: "Let's wipe your face with your napkin, Ernesto." "Now . . . let's wash your hands." He helps Ernesto.
- **Gradually—slowly—transfer control to children as they get older.** Two steps forward. . . . Expect children who are beginning to show self-control to forget and to act impulsively at times. None of us shows perfect self-control all the time. Stay calm, restate limits, and reteach.

Figure 2.10

Middle childhood to late adolescence

Pulkkinen (1982) carried out a longitudinal study of 8-year-olds and examined individual differences in behavior again when the children were 14 and 20 years old. Individual tendencies noted in the children at age 8 in how they coped with impulses endured through adolescence.

Case Study Analysis: Using Child Development in Child Guidance Decisions

The three teachers in the chapter-opening case studies rely on child development knowledge to make good child guidance decisions. Use information from the chapter to analyze the case studies.

Mr. Thompson's Infant Room

- The memory games that Mr. Thompson planned for 6-month-old Ray were appropriate for a 6-month-old infant because _____.
- Ernesto, 17 months old, is in the _____ stage in the development of self-control.
- He is in this stage because _____.
- Mr. Thompson's guidance with Ernesto was appropriate for a child this age because _____.

Mrs. Vargas's Preschool Classroom

- Activities that Mrs. Vargas planned for Monday and Tuesday—dictation of a story, white playdough, and white finger paint—were an appropriate way to help the children recall and tell about their experiences. What is it that children **can** do at this age that makes these activities age appropriate?
- Preschool children have some cognitive limitations. On which limitation does pouring sand from one container to another focus?
- On Thursday of that week, Mrs. Vargas used appropriate guidance with Ralph. The other children seemed to understand the classroom rule, but Ralph did not. Explain why her guidance was so appropriate for Ralph as an individual.

Mr. Nellis's K–2 Classroom

- One reason that Mr. Nellis's approach to Willis and Michael's conflict was so effective was _____.
- Another reason the teacher was effective was _____.

REFLECTING ON KEY CONCEPTS

1. Mrs. Vargas uses limit setting with all of her 4-year-olds.
   a. Setting limits is an appropriate thing to do with this age group (or any age group), (it is age appropriate) because _____.

   b. Larry's parents do not set limits for him. It is doubly important for Mrs. Vargas to set limits for Larry when he is in school because _____.

2. Each child in the situations below is representing some experience. Is that child using deferred imitation, language, or art media, or a combination to describe the experience? Give the reason for your choice.

   a. Robert, in the dramatic play area, has taken the role of nurse and says, just as he gives a make-believe injection to another child, "This will only hurt for a second. You'll feel a teensy, weensy little jab in your arm."

   b. Larry dictated a story about his hospital stay.

   c. Willis, wearing a firefighter's hat out on the playground, said in a commanding tone to Michael and Ned, "Over here! Over here! Aim the water over here."

   d. Tears streaming down her red and angry face, 8-year-old Samantha cried, "Tim broke my sculpture. Look at all the pieces!"

   e. Jordan flattened playdough and then started cutting away pieces. He picked up his creation and said, "A fish! He got away from the fishhook. Swim away, fish!"

3. Many people believe the following statement: "Children have short attention spans." Name at least three issues with children's perceptual problems that seem to affect how well a young child can pay attention. Focus on one of the three and state how it affects a child's attention span.

4. Mrs. Vargas's class had used the obstacle course during the morning activity period. During group time, she wanted the children to remember the steps in the course. She said, "First, you went over the block [she made one of her hands go "over" the other]. Then, you stepped into the middle of the tire [she made a circle with one arm and put the other arm into the circle]. Last, you went under the bar [one hand under the other] and around the table [one hand circled the other]."

   Mrs. Vargas was encouraging _____ memory. Give the reason for your response.

5. Look over the list in Figure 2.7, Knowing About MEMORY: What This Means for Guiding Children. Describe a time when someone used one of these strategies to help you with your memory.

6. Using information from the text as a guide, describe the biggest problem that a child with a difficult temperament might have if his teacher also had a difficult temperament. The teacher has never learned how to moderate his strong negative responses.

7. Two children, ages 4 years and 8½ years, watch a video. They observe a child in the video looking at a donation container in a fast-food restaurant. The lid to the container is loose. The child tells one of the workers about the lid.

   How would the 4-year-old viewer describe the video child's behavior? How would the 8½-year-old describe the video child's behavior? The major difference in how younger and older children describe behavior is _____.

APPLY YOUR KNOWLEDGE

1. **Planning Activities for Memory Development.** Students in Mrs. Vargas's preschool class viewed a large recipe sheet with pictures when they made a heart-shaped cake for Valentine's Day. They learned about the ingredients and the process for making their cake. Mrs. Vargas then used the recipe sheet in group time as an activity to call forth their memory of making the cake. She focused on **cued recall** (the recipe sheet was the cue).

    Now, three weeks later, the teacher wants to work on **recall memory** with the children. The children will bake another cake but will not use the recipe sheet (the teacher wants to focus on **pure recall**—no cues allowed if focusing on pure recall). They will use the same cake ingredients and the same process for mixing, and will even use the heart-shaped pan. Here is how she started. She sat at a small table with six children, and nothing on the table. She had all the equipment on the counter right next to the table.

    Mrs. Vargas: "We baked a _____ for Valentine's Day."
    The children answered, ". . . a cake!"

    "Good memories," said the teacher. "Tell me the shape of the cake and the color of the frosting."

    "It was a heart," Nellie said. "Red frosting," added Tahisha.

    "Yes, a red, heart-shaped cake. You have remembered it correctly," Mrs. Vargas told the class.

    Finish writing a list of short, simple questions that Mrs. Vargas can ask the children to help them focus on the specific ingredients in the cake. Suppose that the children remember eggs, honey, oil, and milk. What could the teacher say about their good, pure recall of the facts?

    The children could not remember that they used flour, baking soda, and baking powder. Use a **cue** to jog their memories. What would be the easiest cue to use, and how would you introduce it so that the children do not feel embarrassed?

2. **Transferring Control to Children.** Observe how adults seem to behave in terms of expectations for self-control for children of three different ages.

    Infants: Observe an adult/infant interaction. Look for evidence that the adult actually performs the infant's ego functions. Find evidence that the adult does not expect the infant to control himself (does not expect the infant to remember things, to manage his emotions, or to complete tasks on his own). Describe specific things an adult does **for** the infant (rocks him to sleep, calms him down, burps him, wipes his mouth, and changes his diaper).

    Toddlers, Younger Preschoolers, and Older Preschoolers: Now look for evidence that the adult is beginning to expect these children to show some measure of self-control. Gather several examples that indicate that this adult is indeed transferring control to children. For example, does the teacher expect the children to remember to wash their hands after using the bathroom, or does the teacher expect the children to begin to manage feelings by saying, "Use words to say that you are upset"?

Kindergarten and Primary School Children: What evidence do you find in a classroom for 5- to 8-year-olds that teachers really do expect older early childhood children to be better able to control themselves?

REFERENCES

Asher, S., & Rose, A. (1997). Promoting children's social-emotional adjustment with peers. In P. Salovey & D. Sluyter (Eds.), *Emotional development and emotional intelligence: Educational implications,* pp. 196–230. New York: Basic Books, Inc.

Baker-Ward, L., Gordon, B. N., Ornstein, P. A., Larus, D. M., & Clubb, P. A. (1993). Young children's long-term retention of a pediatric examination. *Child Development, 64,* 1519–1533.

Berk, L., & Winsler, A. (1995). *Scaffolding children's learning: Vygotsky and early education.* Washington, DC: NAEYC.

Brown, A. L., Bransford, J. D., Ferrara, R. A., & Campione, J. C. (1983). Learning, remembering and understanding. In P. Mussen (Ed.), *Handbook of child psychology* (Vol. 3). New York: Wiley.

Brown, A. L., & Campione, J. C. (1990). Communities of learning and thinking, or a context by any other name. In D. Kuhn (Ed.), *Developmental perspectives on teaching learning and thinking skills.* Basel: Karger.

Bullock, J. (1991). Supporting the development of socially rejected children. *Early Child Development and Care, 66,* 15–23.

Bullock, J. (1997). Children without friends: Who are they and how can teachers help? *Annual Editions/ Child Growth and Development.* Guilford, Connecticut: Duskin/McGraw-Hill, pp. 121–125 (reprinted from *Childhood Education, Winter,* 1992, 92–96).

Buss, A. H., & Plomin, R. A. (1984). *Temperament: Early developing personality traits.* Hillsdale, NJ: Erlbaum.

Carlyon, W. (1997). Attribution retraining: Implications for its integration into prescriptive social skills training. *School Psychology Review, 26*(1), 61–73.

Case, R. (1992). *The mind's staircase: Exploring the conceptual underpinnings of children's thought and knowledge.* Hillsdale, NJ: Erlbaum.

Chalmers, J. B., & Townsend, M. A. (1990). The effects of training in social perspective taking on socially maladjusted girls. *Child Development, 61,* 178–190.

Damon, W. (1983). *Social and personality development.* New York: W. W. Norton.

Damon, W. (1999). The moral development of children. *Scientific American,* August, 72–79.

Dixon, J. A., & Soto, C. F. (1990). The development of perspective taking: Understanding differences in information and weighting. *Child Development, 61,* 1502–1513.

Fagan, J. F. (1984). Infant memory: History, current trends, and relations to cognitive psychology. In M. Moscovitch (Ed.), *Infant memory: Its relation to normal and pathological memory in humans and other animals.* New York: Plenum.

Fantz, R. L. (1966). Pattern discrimination and selective attention as determinants of perceptual development from birth. In A. H. Kidd & J. L. Rivoire (Eds.), *Perceptual development in children.* New York: International Universities Press.

Flavell, J. H., Miller, P. H., & Miller, S. A. (1993). *Cognitive development* (3rd ed.). Upper Saddle River, NJ: Prentice Hall.

Furman, W., & Buhrmester, D. (1992). Age and sex differences in perceptions of networks of personal relationships. *Child Development, 63,* 103–115.

Gibson, E. J., & Spelke, E. S. (1983). The development of perception. In P. Mussen (Ed.), *Handbook of child psychology* (Vol. 3). New York: Wiley.

Goldsmith, H., Buss, A., Plomin, R., Rothbart, M., Thomas, A., Chess, S., Hinde, R., & McCall, R. (1987). Roundtable: What is temperament? Four approaches. *Child Development, 58,* 505–529.

Harter, S. (1983). Developmental perspectives on the self-system. In P. Mussen (Ed.), *Handbook of child psychology* (Vol. 4). New York: Wiley.

Hartup, W. W. (1992). Friendships and their developmental significance. In H. McGurk (Ed.), *Childhood social development: Contemporary perspectives.* Hove, England: Erlbaum.

Hasselhorn, M. (1992). Task dependency and the role of category typicality and metamemory in the development of an organizational strategy. *Child Development, 63,* 202–214.

Howe, M. L., & Courage, M. L. (1993). On resolving the enigma of infantile amnesia. *Psychological Bulletin, 113,* 305–326.

Jones, D. C. (1985). Persuasive appeals and responses to appeals among friends and acquaintances. *Child Development, 56,* 757–763.

Kagan, J., Reznick, J., Snidman, N., Gibbons, J., & Johnson, M. D. (1988). Childhood derivatives of inhibition and lack of inhibition to the familiar. *Child Development, 59,* 1580–1589.

Kopp, C. B. (1981). *The antecedents of self-regulation: A developmental perspective.* Unpublished manuscript, University of California, Los Angeles.

Marion, M. (2000). Keynote Address, Delaware AEYC, October.

Milner, J. S., Robertson, K. R., & Rogers, D. L. (1990). Childhood history of abuse and adult child abuse potential. *Journal of Family Violence, 5*(1), 15–34.

Moely, B. E., Hart, S. S., Leal, L., Santulli, K. A., Rao, N., Johnson, T., & Hamilton, L. B. (1992). The teacher's role in facilitating memory and study strategy development in the elementary school classroom. *Child Development, 63,* 653–672.

Paterson, G., & Sanson, A. (1999). The association of behavioural adjustment to temperament, parenting, and family characteristics among 5-year-old children. *Social Development, 8*(3), 293–309.

Perlmutter, M. (1986). A life-span view of memory. In P. B. Baltes, D. L. Featherman, & R. M. Lerner (Eds.), *Life-span development and behavior* (Vol. 7). Hillsdale, NJ: Erlbaum.

Piaget, J. (1952). *The origins of intelligence in children.* New York: W. W. Norton.

Piaget, J. (1965). *The moral judgment of the child* (M. Gabain, translator). New York: Free Press.

Piaget, J. (1968). *Six psychological studies.* New York: Random House.

Piaget, J. (1976a). *The grasp of consciousness: Action and concept in the young child.* Cambridge: Harvard University Press.

Piaget, J. (1976b). The stages of intellectual development of the child. In N. Endler, L. Boulter, & H. Osser (Eds.), *Contemporary issues in developmental psychology* (2nd ed.). New York: Holt, Rinehart, & Winston.

Piaget, J. (1983). Piaget's theory. In P. Mussen (Ed.), *Handbook of child psychology* (Vol. 1). New York: Wiley.

Pulkkinen, L. (1982). Self-control and continuity from childhood to late adolescence. In P. Bates and O. Brim (Eds.), *Life-span development and behavior* (Vol. 4). New York: Academic Press.

Rholes, W. S., Jones, M., & Wade, C. (1988). Children's understanding of personal disposition and its relationship to behavior. *Journal of Experimental Child Psychology, 45,* 1–17.

Schneider, W., & Bjorklund, D. F. (1992). Expertise, aptitude, and strategic remembering. *Child Development, 63,* 461–471.

Schneider, W., & Pressley, M. (1989). *Memory development between 2 and 20.* New York: Springer-Verlag.

Selman, R. L. (1976). Social-cognitive understanding. In T. Lickona (Ed.), *Moral development and behavior.* New York: Holt, Rinehart, & Winston.

Selman, R. L. (1980). *The growth of interpersonal understanding: Developmental and clinical analysis.* New York: Academic Press.

Shaffer, D. R. (1996). *Developmental psychology* (4th ed.). Pacific Grove, CA: Brooks/Cole.

Thomas, A., & Chess, S. (1986). The New York longitudinal study: From infancy to early adult life. In R. Plomin & J. Dunn (Eds.), *The study of temperament: Changes, continuities, and challenges.* Hillsdale, NJ: Erlbaum.

✓ CHECK OUT THE WEB SITES RELATED TO THIS CHAPTER

✓ **Cornell University Extension**

www.cce.cornell.edu/publications/children.cfm. Resources on children. For example, "Terrific and Terrible 2-Year-Olds" or "The World of the 5-Year-Old" are inexpensive and useful fact sheets with information on child development.

✓ **University of Wisconsin Extension.** In cooperation with other state university extension divisions, the UW Extension has produced newsletters on child development and parenting for the early childhood years. Research based, reader friendly, well-written. The newsletters are widely available.

Hard copy available from addresses listed on the Web site. Full text of every newsletter on the Web site. Superb resources.

www.uwex.edu/ces/pubs/. The publication page for the extension division. Click on "home and family" and then on "human development and family issues." Scroll to "Parenting Infants and Toddlers." You will see "Parenting the First Year," a series of multipage newsletters on infant development and parenting issues. See also "Parenting the Second and Third Years," a series of multipage newsletters on toddler development. Publications about older children also available.

www.uwex.edu/ces/cty/oconto/family.html. Find "Parenting the Preschooler," a series of multipage newsletters on preschool development. This site is the Oconto County Extension Web page.

Observing Behavior in Child Guidance

Observe: to see through directed careful analytic attention.

Websters New Collegiate Dictionary

After reading and studying this chapter, you will be able to

❑ **Summarize** the role of observation in authoritative caregiving and teaching.

❑ **List, explain, and give examples of** several reasons for observing children's behavior.

❑ **Identify** behavioral indicators of stress, ADHD, and child abuse and neglect.

❑ **Explain** the usefulness of asking specific questions about a child's behavior.

❑ **Summarize** the process for teaching children how to observe their own behavior. **Explain** how self-observation can help children older than 2 years develop self-control.

Case Studies: Observing Behavior

"Withdrawn. That's what I'd call it," concluded the assistant teacher. Mrs. Vargas, the lead teacher, later reflected on that conclusion about the behavior of Jordan, Chelsea, and Calvin, three of the 4-year-olds in the class. She agreed that their behavior did seem to show that they are all withdrawn; their behaviors, however, indicate that they are "withdrawn" in very different ways.[9]

Calvin

Calvin played alone most of the time and did not appear to be anxious about not playing with others. In fact, he seemed comfortable playing by himself. He usually chose an activity quickly and worked on it industriously. He looked around occasionally while he worked quietly. He was not aggressive toward the other children and did not object if they played near him, but he did not initiate conversations or play with others.

Chelsea

Chelsea participated, very quietly, in group activities. During individual choice times, however, Chelsea usually stood at the edge of a playgroup or at an area's entrance, often biting her lip or clenching her fists as she surveyed the activity. Mrs. Vargas observed that a sad and downcast sweep of her eyes generally replaced her once-hopeful facial expression as she turned away from a group. Chelsea's mother also reported that the child was exceptionally nervous whenever she had to meet new people, such as at a summer playgroup, on the playground, or a ballet class.

Jordan

Right away at the beginning of the school year, the teachers had noticed that Jordan responded aggressively to other children; the aggression most often seemed unprovoked. He barged into playgroups, seeming not to pay attention to what others were doing. He had a very difficult time in either large or small groups because he so frequently blurted out questions or comments. The other children had already begun to stop playing with or talking to Jordan.

AUTHORITATIVE CAREGIVING AND OBSERVATION

Mrs. Vargas is committed to helping each of these children. As described in Chapter 1, she is an **authoritative** early childhood professional—**highly responsive** to children (high degree of warmth and genuinely likes children, understands child development, and delivers messages simply, kindly, firmly, and consistently). She is also **highly demanding** (uses positive discipline strategies, sets reasonable fair limits, monitors and supervises children well, gives reasons for limits, and is not afraid to confront a child who has done something hurtful). The combination of high

---

[9]See Fujiki, Brinton, Morgan, & Hart (1999) for a review of research on "withdrawn" behavior.

responsiveness and high demandingness is the key to the positive, powerful, long-lasting effect of authoritative caregiving and teaching on children's behavior and development (Baumrind, 1993, 1996; Dekovic & Janssens, 1992).

Authoritative caregivers, who monitor and supervise children well, tend to understand the significance of observing behavior. Their proficiency at observation and willingness to observe children's behavior does not provide easy answers, but does yield information they can use for making sound decisions about how to support children. The assistant teacher's conclusion was correct: All three children do seem to be withdrawn, but it is up to the teachers to pinpoint the differences in the "withdrawn" behavior among the these children. Mrs. Vargas's willingness to try to "crack the code"—to unravel the meaning of Calvin's, Jordan's, and Chelsea's withdrawn behavior—will make it possible for both teachers to help these children.

REASONS FOR OBSERVING CHILDREN'S BEHAVIOR

Many factors motivate authoritative early childhood professionals to observe children's behavior. Among these factors are:

- Children communicate with behavior.
- Children demonstrate their strengths through behavior.
- Children's behavior often highlights a special need.
- Children's behavior gives clues about "challenging" behavior.
- Children's behavior expresses feelings and signs of stress and child abuse and neglect.
- We can help children construct their own solutions to child guidance issues if we teach them to observe their own behavior.

Children Communicate with Behavior

A 3-year-old whirls with delight, trying to catch snowflakes. Another child's face turns red with anger as he strikes out at a classmate. A 5-year-old twirls her hair tightly around her finger as she sits hunched over a workbook page. A boy in the same class lowers his head until it nearly touches his workbook and turns his head from side to side, eyes darting to the other children's pages. Finally, a tear drops onto his page. A first-grader, head thrust forward slightly, one hand scratching his head, eyes open wide in wonder and mouth making a little "O" shape, stares at the gorilla mother and her baby in the zoo.

Head scratching, wide eyes, worried looks, tears, twirling, smiling, a red face, and a fist that smashes. Not one of these children uttered a word, but they all communicated eloquently. Their hands, feet, facial expressions, and body movements communicated just as well as words could. Of course, young children *do* communicate with words. They are just as likely, though, to tell us what they are experiencing, how they feel, and what they think through their behavior.

Perceptive teachers know that behavior has meaning and that observing behavior is an essential skill in teaching.

Example. Mrs. Zimmer, Paul's teacher, observed that the toddler reached over and touched Alissa's curly red hair very gently with one finger, much like a person who gingerly touches wet paint. Paul pulled his hand back and looked at his finger, eyebrows and forehead knitted in puzzlement.

Example. Mrs. Vargas, the preschool teacher, observed Ralph motion to his dad to bend down. Ralph then spoke very softly into his dad's ear while Dad helped him take his coat off at arrival. He smiled and then gave his dad a "high five" before going off to play. Dad turned to the teacher: "Birthday party for his older brother this afternoon. Looks like he's a little excited."

Example. Philip, a 7-year-old in Mr. Nellis's class, had moved to this new school in September and had become good friends with two other boys. He usually approached school enthusiastically, but one Monday morning in March Mr. Nellis watched Philip walk slowly into the classroom. The second-grader moved listlessly and hung his head. He said nothing and responded with an uncharacteristically quiet "Hi" to greetings from other children. The teacher asked if something was wrong. Philip slowly lifted his eyes, looked at his teacher, and then looked away. "We're going to move—again," he whispered.

Paul, Ralph, and Philip all communicated mainly with their bodies and behavior. Paul seemed to be curious, but certainly not malicious, about Alissa's red

Mrs. Vargas has observed Chelsea (middle child) crying when another child has something that she wants. The teacher concluded after several such observations that Chelsea, a withdrawn, shy child, cries out of frustration over not knowing how to get what she wants.

hair. Ralph's behavior and facial expression told us that he was excited and happy; he did not have to use words. Philip's behavior and body language spoke of heavy sadness.

Behavior is a code, much like the code used to send secret messages that can only be read by someone who knows and understands it. A person who wants to decipher the coded message must understand the code to know what the signals mean. A child's behavior is his way of communicating what he needs or wants.

Teachers have a far greater share of the responsibility in any interaction with children, which encourages teachers to acknowledge and learn to decipher a child's code of using behavior to communicate feelings and thoughts. Authoritative teachers believe that it is an adult's job to observe a child's behavioral code and then to decode it as accurately as possible.

Observe Behavior to Discover and Build on Children's Strengths

One goal in observing, decoding, and then interpreting behavior should be to discover and build on children's strengths—always. It is unethical to observe with the intention of manipulating any child's behavior. Ethical authoritative professionals observe behavior to discover what children like to do or can do with success. This is especially important to keep in mind when observing challenging behavior or behavior brought on by stress.

Example. Mr. Lee, the third- and fourth-grade teacher, documented third-grader Jim's difficulty concentrating during large-group instruction in class. Mr. Lee also documented Jim's ability to concentrate much better when working either alone or in small groups. He also noticed that Jim seemed to be a natural leader in the small groups. Having identified two strengths—the ability to concentrate in small groups and the ability to lead—the teacher developed a plan to build on Jim's strengths.

Mr. Lee had used the anecdotal record method.[10] Figure 3.1 illustrates the anecdotal record format with one of Mr. Lee's observations of Jim's behavior. Part 1 is context; part 2 the anecdote; part 3 the interpretation.

Example. Sandi's teacher identified one of Sandi's (6½ years old) major strengths as her ability to deal in a positive way with almost any child in the class. She seems to have very good social skills. For instance, Mr. Nellis observed as Sandi prevented an argument in a small reading group. Bert finished reading, Sara started her turn, and Dave yelled, "It's my turn!" Sandi looked at each child in the group as if figuring something out and then said, pointing at Bert, "Uh-oh! Dave, look at Bert. He just read. Sara is sitting next to Bert, so Sara goes next." Then Sandi beamed at Dave and chirped," You go right after Sara!" Dave nodded and simply said, "Oh, yeah. OK."

---

[10]See Marion, M. (2004). *Using observation in early childhood.* Upper Saddle River, NJ: Merrill/Prentice Hall. Chapters 3, 4, and 5 describe, explain, and give examples of different methods of observing.

Format for Anecdotal Records

<u>Goal for this observation</u>: Document Jim's ability to concentrate in small groups
<u>Setting</u>: Round table in library area; area bounded by bookshelves on two sides, a wall on third side
<u>Date/day</u>: Tuesday, October 8
<u>Time of day</u>: 9:15 to 9:35 A.M.
<u>Basic activity</u>: Writing a summary of the group's "trees" project
<u>Focus child</u>: **Jim**
<u>Others involved</u>: Tracy, Xai [pronounced "sigh"], Bobbi Jo

<u>The Anecdote</u>: I had given brief instructions to the children to write a brief summary of the "trees" project on which they had worked; they had to decide how to proceed with the writing. After I left I noticed that Jim said, "We need some paper. Which paper should we use?" "OK, Xai, a big piece would work. Then we can show it to the whole class. Who wants to write?" "Tracy wants to write. Should we use a pencil or a pen?" "OK, a BIG FAT marking pen [the whole group giggled]. What's the first thing we want to say about the project?"

<u>Reflection/Comment</u>[11]: This is the third time that I have seen Jim assume leadership for a small group. He does it naturally and the children seem to accept his leadership cheerfully. They seem to look to him to lead them. He demonstrates a nice sense of humor, appreciated by the others. Additionally, I've noticed that Jim concentrates very well in groups of up to about four children. He also does well when the group is in an area somewhat separated from the hubbub of a larger group.

Figure 3.1

Observe Behavior to Assess Special Needs

Observing behavior plays a major role in assessing special needs children might have. For example, Landau & McAninch (1997) advocate a multidimensional approach to assessing ADHD (attention-deficit hyperactivity disorder) including systematic **observation of a child's behavior** in the classroom or play setting (assessment in a naturalistic setting). The teacher's assessment of a child's time spent engaged in on-task or in off-task behaviors yields direct information about how a child functions. See Figure 3.2 for behavioral indicators of ADHD.

Observing behavior in the naturalistic setting of a classroom is an excellent way to obtain data on current behavior and then combine that information with data from other sources, such as parent reports. The authors also advocate observing the behavior of the child's same-gender classmates. For example, "Joe [with symptoms of ADHD] spends 20% of the time in on-task behavior during math while the other boys spend almost 90% of the time in on-task behavior during math."

---

[11]It is not always necessary to interpret every observation. A hasty interpretation is often inaccurate. Gather enough good data and you will be better able to reflect. You will stand a better chance of making a more accurate comment with enough data (Marion, 2004).

Mr. Nellis has observed that Sandi (child on right) has good social skills. Today she invited Lisa to read books with her. Sandi knew how to approach Lisa and she knew how to issue an invitation.

Behavioral Indicators of ADHD

ADHD is seen in 3 to 5% of school-age children. The following are some of the behaviors that children with ADHD typically display. Many young children have difficulty paying attention or are easily distracted. Children with ADHD, however, show these behaviors **much more frequently and much more severely than do other children of the same age and developmental level.**

- Blurts out answers
- Very easily distracted
- Fidgets or squirms
- Talks too much and has difficulty playing quietly
- Has trouble paying attention
- Makes careless mistakes; does not pay attention to details
- Has trouble listening and following directions
- Interrupts others or intrudes on others
- Impatient

Source: Based upon material developed by the AACAP.

Figure 3.2

Observe Behavior as the First Step in Dealing with Challenging Behavior

Early childhood professionals deal with normal **discipline encounters** on a daily basis. They also confront what they classify as difficult or challenging behavior (Kaiser & Rasminsky, 1999; Marion & Swim, 2001). If challenging behavior involves hurting others or damaging property, a teacher is clearly responsible for stopping the behavior and ending the threat. Therefore, a short-term goal with challenging behavior is to protect children, animals, and property, and to communicate expectations.

Authoritative teachers also have a long-term goal to help children with challenging behavior learn a more positive way of interacting with others. Teachers observe a child with challenging behavior, as Mrs. Vargas did with Jordan, as the starting point in supporting that child.

Such teachers understand that challenging behavior is complex and puzzling, and has no easy solutions. They do not engage in "knee-jerk" reactions to misbehavior, such as automatically using some sort of punishment at the first sign of a challenging behavior. Instead, they observe challenging or difficult behavior carefully to determine factors contributing to the misbehavior. They realize that challenging behavior is the child's voice, his way of telling us what he needs or wants so desperately. Listen carefully to the voice of challenging or difficult behavior and it will tell how you can help a child. Challenging behavior might well say one of the following three things (Educational Productions, 1998; Kohn, 1996):

- "I have an unmet need. Please help me meet this need."
- "There is a skill that I need but don't have. Please teach this skill to me."
- "There is a mismatch between me and something in our classroom or in the schedule or in the curriculum. Can you please fix things to help me?"

Example of a mismatch between a child and the environment

Mr. Lee had realized that there was a mismatch between some of the children and the schedule in his classroom. The teacher had then examined his own instructional practices and rearranged the schedule and adjusted his instructional methods (Kohn, 1996).

Mr. Lee's new schedule enabled his children to do their work at their own pace. The children realized that they had to complete a menu of curriculum assignments within a specified time, but they chose the order in which they completed their work and where to work in the classroom (Pelander, 1997).[12] This method seemed to Mr. Lee to be more developmentally appropriate, and helped a number of children, including Jim, who concentrated poorly when the teacher had had the entire class doing the same tasks at the same time.

---

[12]Chapter 5 in this text shows a floor plan of Mr. Pelander's third-grade classroom. You can also read about how he schedules each morning.

Example of a child lacking a specific skill

In spite of a developmentally appropriate new schedule, Mr. Lee realized that one of the boys had a problem connected to the new arrangement. Rory, a very capable and bright third-grader, zoomed through his work. Rory got along well with the other children, engaging in friendly interaction while working and causing no disruptions. Mr. Lee quickly noticed, however, that Rory did not seem to know what to do after completing an assignment. Instead of just going on to choose the next thing, Rory darted around the classroom, good-naturedly creating chaos.

Mr. Lee decided, after observing Rory's behavior, that this child lacked a specific skill. Rory did not seem to know how to stop, look at his menu of choices, and then choose the next thing to do. Mr. Lee decided to simply teach this skill to Rory. He taught him how to **stop** (and cross off what he has just finished), **look** (at the choices remaining), and **choose** (the next activity, either another curriculum activity or a brief relaxation activity before commencing with the next curriculum activity). Mr. Lee coached Rory through this process the first few times that Rory used it.

Example of a child's unmet need

It had been raining all day and Mrs. Vargas's preschool children had not been able to get out to the playground. Because the children seemed unusually restless in large group, the teacher changed the group time to include some marching, jumping in place, and running in place. Then Mrs. Vargas moved her group time to the library so that the children had a chance to get a short walk. Still later that day, the children did four simple yoga stretches to soft music.

The teacher realized that her children had an **unmet** need for exercise. Adding well-supervised physical activity to the group time, going on a walk in the building, and yoga stretches helped to meet that need. Children have many basic needs—for rest, food, security, acceptance, love, and exercise. Authoritative (highly responsive) adults make a real effort to tune into those needs by observing a child's behavior. Then, as much as is possible, an authoritative adult supports a child in meeting the need.

Observe Behavior to Recognize Children's Feelings and Signs of Stress or Child Abuse and Neglect

Use observation to become aware of children's feelings

Authoritative adults understand child development and realize that even young infants have emotions and that the list of emotions children experience grows during early childhood. Not only that, but teachers who observe behavior will quickly see that different children express the same emotion in different ways (Fabes & Eisenberg, 1992).

Example. Mrs. Vargas observed several different reactions to one child's frequent grabbing of things from others. Ralph, for example, expressed anger when he **actively resisted** by asserting himself nonaggressively and simply demanding that Nellie return his Magic Marker. Justine's behavior, **venting**, expressed a greater degree of anger when she twisted her face into a frustrated expression, sank to the floor, and cried. Justine also revealed anger by **expressing her dislike** of Nellie; "You're mean, Nellie! You can't come to my birthday party!"

Observe behavior for signs of stress

Figure 3.3 lists several behaviors indicating that a child is probably experiencing stress. Often, we suspect that something is bothering a child but do not know the source of the worry. What teachers do see, however, is the child's clearly stressed behavior. For instance, Mr. Nellis has observed that one of the boys clenches his jaws together and at the same time squeezes pencils tightly when doing any type of written work. This child also repeatedly rubs one hand with his other hand during large-group instruction. Mrs. Vargas has noticed that Chelsea bites her lip when she stands on the edge of playgroups looking in.

The important thing to remember about a child's stress-induced behavior is that the behavior is a symptom of a problem, a problem that the child did not create. The child who is under stress needs help, not judgment, and certainly not punishment. Some teachers observe behaviors such as aggression (often a sign of stress) and then simply punish the child for behaving aggressively. They tend to punish the behavior but forget to acknowledge the stress that begets anger that begets aggression.

Other teachers prefer to avoid punishment and instead to take a problem-solving approach with such behavior (Kohn, 1996). Arriving at a problem-solving approach and avoiding punishment requires examining behavior, which might

---

Behavioral Indicators of Stress in Young Children

Children show us that they are experiencing stress in a number of ways:
1. **Reactions to stress might be passive.**
   - Excessive fatigue
   - Withdrawing and putting head on table or desk
   - Excessive fears
2. **Reactions to stress might be more active, with behaviors that involve only the child.**
   - Nail biting
   - Manipulating one's hands or mouth
   - Repetitive body movements
3. **Reactions to stress might show up when children interact with others.**
   - Stuttering
   - Bullying, threatening, or hurting others (See Seth in Chapter 9)
   - Nervous, inappropriate laughter
4. **Reactions to stress might show up as children work with objects.**
   - Excessive squeezing or tapping of pencils, markers, crayons
   - Clumsy or fumbling behavior

Sources: Hart, Burts, Durland, & Charlesworth, DeWolf, & Fleege (1998); Honig (1986); Brodeur & Monteleone (1994); Selye (1978).

Figure 3.3

appear, for example, to be defiant or aggressive. You have read about the Decision-Making Model of child guidance, a problem-solving approach, in Chapter 1.

Behaviors such as bullying or aggression often indicate that a child is under great stress. As usual, authoritative teachers deal with such behaviors by being highly demanding and highly responsive. They do confront an aggressive child, but use positive discipline strategies. They also respond to an aggressive child's needs by recognizing, acknowledging, and dealing with the stress running like an underground river below the behavior.[13]

Observe children for behaviors signaling abuse or neglect

Finally, conscientious observation can even help teachers identify behavioral indicators of child abuse or neglect. Because there are several forms of child abuse and neglect, there are also many different behavioral indicators, depending on the specific type and severity of the abuse or neglect. Figure 3.4 lists major behavioral

---

Some Child Behaviors Indicating Abuse or Neglect

Infants
- Shrill, high-pitched cry
- Passive watchfulness (excessive amount of lying quietly in crib and observing surroundings intently)
- Show little interest in toys
- Accept losses with little reaction

Beyond infancy
- Seems old for her age
- Lack of ability to play
- Temper tantrums beyond what would be expected for age and stage of development
- Low self-esteem—behaves in a way that tells us that he does not feel competent or in control or that he is not worthy of the attention of others
- Withdrawal—can, but does not always, indicate abuse
- Chronic aggression or overt hostility against peers, animals, adults, self
- Passive watchfulness
- Compulsivity or efforts to control some small aspect of his life
- Fear of failure
- Difficulty listening to or carrying out instructions
- Difficulty organizing thoughts, conceptualizing, and verbalizing
- Regression to an earlier stage of development—bed-wetting, thumb-sucking, baby talk
- Poor social skills
- Extreme shyness
- Steals or hoards food
- Little or no empathy for others

Sources: Brodeur & Monteleone (1994); Tower (1999).

Figure 3.4

---

[13]Chapter 7 in this book explains how to guide children who are experiencing stress.

indicators of child abuse and neglect. Any one indicator does not conclusively indicate abuse or neglect; however, teachers who observe a pattern of behavior, an abrupt change of behavior, or behavioral indicators combined with physical indicators of abuse or neglect (Tower, 1999) might well be dealing with an abused or neglected child.

Help Children Construct Solutions to Child Guidance Issues by Teaching Them to Observe Their Own Behavior

Chapter 2 described the development of self-control and social skills. With kindergarten or primary children, teachers can prevent many problems by helping children develop healthy self-control and good social skills. Observant adults should certainly give information to children about their behavior, but it is equally important for children to learn how to gather information about their own behavior. Gathering information about oneself is called **self-observation or self-monitoring** and is an essential part of developing self-control and good social skills.

Teachers can use their observations to help teach older early-childhood children to observe and record their own behavior. A good way to teach this skill is help the child learn to observe (to be "on the lookout for" or to "track down") and record specific behaviors (King and Kirschenbaum, 1992). For example, Mr. Nellis taught Willis, a second-grader, to track down a more helpful behavior, asking for things, instead of a behavior—grabbing things—which was causing Willis great trouble. Willis understood the concept of tracking because the children had learned about different animal tracks as part of a project.

- **Model the helpful behavior** (asking for things, not grabbing) **for the child.** "I need a marble, Willis. May I use one of yours?"
- **Model self-observation.** "H-m-m. I asked you for the marble."
- **Model remembering your self-observation.** "I want to remember that I asked."
- **Encourage the child to imitate you and coach him.** "Your turn, Willis. You ask me for a marble . . . great! Tell me what you did. That's right, you asked for the marble and you said that you asked."
- **Encourage the child to use this behavior with another child.** Set up a highly attractive activity in which he has to ask another, easily approachable child for something. Mr. Nellis set up an art activity, sprinkling shimmering golden glitter from shakers onto glue and paints, and said, "We have only one shaker of golden glitter for two children. If Sandi is using the shaker and you want it, say, 'I need some glitter, Sandi. Please pass it to me when you are done.'"
- **Observe and encourage the child.** It is good to remind a child to observe himself and then to record what he observed. Remind verbally. When he asks for glitter say, "I heard you ask for the glitter."
- **Review and encourage.** Mr. Nellis said to Willis as Willis was getting ready to go home, "You asked for something two times. That's good remembering!"

WHO, WHAT, WHEN, WHERE, WHY: FIVE QUESTIONS ABOUT BEHAVIOR

Background and Summary of Mitchell's Behavior

Background

Mitchell, a first-grader in Mr. Nellis's K–2 class, has always been a happy and well cared for child who has lived with his aunt and uncle, his foster parents, since the age of 2 months. Mitchell has had regular visits with his biological mother, who was released from a residential mental health treatment facility three months ago. One month ago, with the permission of the court, she had taken Mitchell back to live with her. Mr. Nellis fully expected a period of adjustment but was startled by some of Mitchell's specific behaviors that he observed after Mitchell had lived with his mom for two weeks. The teacher made a series of brief anecdotal records over the two-week period.

Summary

After moving to live with his mother 1 month ago, Mitchell continued to eat breakfast at school along with all the other children. Mr. Nellis first observed a change in Mitchell's behavior when Mitchell had begun, in the last 2 weeks, to ask for second helpings of breakfast, something he had never done in the past. At lunch, Mitchell had secretively begun to take whatever food he could off his tray, stuff it in his pockets, and then transfer it to his backpack after returning to the classroom after lunch. Just last Friday, Mitchell requested seconds at lunch, also cramming what he could of the extra food in his pocket.

The gradual change in Mitchell's behavior, at first surprising and confusing to the teacher, changed to alarm that Friday. Mr. Nellis was justifiably concerned about the sudden changes in Mitchell's behavior, hoarding food. His careful observations, documented in anecdotal records, allowed him to answer five questions about Mitchell's behavior: Who, what, when, where, and why? These five questions can help authoritative teachers begin to understand any behavior.

Who Was Involved in This Behavior?

Was only the one child involved, or were others also involved? If others were involved, were they adults, children, or both? Even if the child had been the only person involved, did the behavior ever involve animals? If this is a recurring behavior, are the same children, adults, or animals generally involved?

Who was involved in Mitchell's behavior? Mitchell was the only child involved. He never asked others to help him and he took only his own food. However, he did trade food with other children, food such as applesauce for things like cookies or fruit.

What Happened?

Carefully note the precise nature of the behavior. If possible, record what occurred before the behavior and then what happened after the behavior. It is also helpful to note if this behavior is new, or if it is part of a pattern of behavior. Note how long the behavior went on.

What happened with Mitchell's behavior? Mitchell asked for seconds at breakfast several times and ate the extra food. He ate very little at lunch and only those things that he could not take home or could not trade, such as milk or soup. He traded what he could at lunch for things that he could take with him. He did not ever bully the other children into trading and accepted "no" for an answer. On Friday he even asked for seconds at lunch and took that food with him, too.

When Did the Behavior Occur?

Does it occur at the same times during the day or at different times? Does it occur only on certain days of the week or throughout the week? What type of activity is going on at the time? Does it always happen when the child arrives at school, during naptime, during large group, at transitions? Does the behavior seem to occur during a variety of activities throughout the day? Be specific. If it occurred during large group, state whether it occurred at every group time or just some of them. If the behavior happens at arrival time, does it occur, for example, every morning or perhaps on the same two or three days each week?

Answering this question gives an observer helpful clues. If a behavior occurs at transitions, give specific information. State whether it happens with every transition during the day, only with transitions out of large group, only when specific adults are present, only when specific children are present, or usually after one specific specialist has led the group time. Jordan, for example, the 4-year-old in the chapter opener case study, behaved in an extremely impulsive way every day. He blurted things out during large and small group, when he talked with almost any adult, when he talked with other children, and when he played in a variety of centers.

When did Mitchell's behavior occur? Mr. Nellis had observed food gathering and hiding at all lunches for the past nine days. Later, on Friday afternoon, Mitchell had eaten only one bite of his piece of another child's birthday cake, carefully wrapping the rest of his portion and placing it in his backpack.

Where Does the Behavior Typically Take Place?

Does it happen only in certain areas of the classroom or school, or is the behavior likely to occur just about anywhere? For example, a teacher noticed that one of the girls in his class behaved in an extremely agitated way but only in one place—standing in the line waiting for the school bus at the end of the day. Her father, he discovered, had sexually abused this child for a number of years. School was a safe place for her and she acted in an agitated way only while she waited to leave her place of safety.

Where did Mitchell's behavior occur? Mitchell's behavior occurred mainly in the lunchroom, in his locker as he stored his food, and once in the classroom (with the birthday cake).

Cracking the Code:
Children Speak to Us With Behavior

A young child's behavior, translated into words, might say:

Behavior $\longrightarrow$	**What this behavior might be saying**
• Twirling in the snow, smiling	"I'm so happy that it's snowing!"
• Arms folded on chest, mouth closed tightly, chin down	"I think that I am powerless and I'll get some power by being stubborn with you."
• Talking quietly to the gerbil	"I think that loud noise scares the gerbil."
• Stands at edge of playgroup, looks at different children	"I'd like to play."
• Disrupts group time that lasts 40 minutes	"This group time has gone on way too long. Stop!"
• Interrupts frequently	"I have poor social skills."
• Waves at friends when leaving school for the day. Smiles.	"Tom and Kendra are my friends!"

Figure 3.5

Why Does the Child Behave This Way?

Answering this question requires that the observer interpret the child's behavior, which might be difficult in many cases. It helps to look at the answers to the other four questions and then to arrive at some conclusions based on this information. A child's behavior reveals a range of things—some happy, joyful, or curious, others sad, angry, or anxious. Figure 3.5 displays just a few of the things that asking "who, what, when, where, and why" might reveal.

Why did Mitchell's behavior occur? Mitchell's situation is complicated. His aunt came to see Mr. Nellis because she, too, was worried about Mitchell but said that the social worker had dismissed her concerns. She indicated that Mitchell's mom seemed unable to take care of him. She had stopped taking her medication, never really cooked regular meals, bought the few meals they did eat at fast-food restaurants, and kept only snack food in the house. Mr. Nellis accurately concluded that Mitchell had an unmet need for food. The first-grader's behavior (hoarding food) that had originally stirred the teacher's curiosity was this child's attempt to meet this need.

The teacher also guessed correctly that Mitchell had spent the whole weekend with little food other than what he had gathered from school. Mitchell's aunt had been out of town that weekend and figured out that Mitchell must have been on his own since dinner with his relatives on Thursday. The teacher called Social Services and, using his anecdotal records and notes from his conversation with the aunt, reported his suspicion of the behavioral indicators of possible child neglect.

Mr. Nellis acted properly in reporting suspected child neglect. As a teacher, he is a mandated reporter (is required to report). He does not make a decision about

The teachers have concluded after many observations that Paul (second child from left) concentrates remarkably well under almost any condition. He is *not* easily distracted.

whether Mitchell's mom is neglecting him but he is required to report indicators that a child's well-being is seriously threatened. A parent's mental illness often impairs the adult's ability to parent, thus placing children at risk for harm (American Academy of Child & Adolescent Psychiatry [AACAP], 2000), as Mitchell's mom possibly placed him at risk by not providing the food that he needed.

Some teachers would merely have stopped a child like Mitchell the minute they saw him stuff food in his pockets. Some might even have punished him. Mr. Nellis was curious at first and, to his credit, decided to observe, not to stop, this behavior. His observations gave him just the right information that he needed to begin to help both Mitchell and his mom.

There are several protective or positive factors that seem to decrease, but certainly not eliminate, the risk of harm to children who have mentally ill parents (AACAP, 2000):

- help and support from family members
- a naturally stable and happy personality in the child
- positive self-esteem
- inner strength and good coping skills in the child
- a strong relationship with a healthy adult
- friendships and positive peer relationships
- interest in and success at school

- help from outside the family to improve the family environment, such as, parenting classes.

Which of these factors seem to be present in Mitchell's life?

Case Study Analysis: Calvin, Chelsea, and Jordan

Calvin, Chelsea, and Jordan are three children whose behavior could be called **withdrawn** but in different ways. The common thread tying the three together is that they do not play with or play only rarely with other children.

1. In spite of the common thread, how do Calvin's and Chelsea's withdrawn behavior differ? Calvin's and Jordan's?
2. What did each child's behavior convey about that child's **feelings** about being alone in the midst of so many other children?
3. Name one social skill that, if acquired, would most help each child (e.g., how to join a group, how to invite another child to play, how to listen to what others say before speaking, how to say hello to someone, or other skills not listed here). Explain your choices. Why do you think that each child needs to learn the specific skill that you identified?

Calvin:

Chelsea:

Jordan:

REFLECTING ON KEY CONCEPTS

1. True or false? Observing a child's behavior always gives an authoritative caregiver the answer to a discipline dilemma or a child guidance issue. Explain your reasoning.
2. For you, what is the most important reason listed in this chapter for observing children's behavior? Why?
3. "Behavior does not occur in a vacuum" is a brief speech that you will give to a new group of teacher's aides. They have not been educated about observation. What are two essential concepts that you want them to learn from your speech about looking at behavior, including the concept of **misbehavior,** and really seeing beyond what appears on the surface? For example, a child daydreams a lot and hardly ever finishes his work.
4. You are having a parent conference with one of the parents of your K–1 children. Please explain to this parent why you are teaching her child to observe her own behavior; specifically, when she listens quietly at story time.

APPLY YOUR KNOWLEDGE

Practice teaching a social skill to a child. Choose one of the case study children—Calvin, Chelsea, or Jordan. In your case study analysis, you identified one thing that would help that child improve interaction with others. Now, teach that skill to him or her. Be specific and describe the steps and script you would use. Use information from the chapter to help you.

Observation. Observe behaviors that express anger by two children in the early childhood age range (birth to age 9). Ask questions about the angry behavior that you observe. Look for answers to the five "W" questions about each child's behavior: **Who** was involved? **What** happened? **When** did the behavior occur? **Where** did it happen? **Why** did it happen?

REFERENCES

American Academy of Child & Adolescent Psychiatry (AACAP) (1999). Children who cannot pay attention. *AACAP Facts for Families,* No. 6 Washington, DC: author.

AACAP (2000). Children of parents with mental illness. *AACAP Facts for Families,* No. 39. Washington, D.C.: author. (See the Web site listed at end of this chapter.)

Baumrind, D. (1993). The average expectable environment is not good enough: A response to Scarr. *Child Development, 64,* 1299–1317.

Baumrind, D. (1996). Parenting: The discipline controversy revisited. *Family Relations, 45,* 405–414.

Brodeur, A., & Monteleone, J. (1994). *Child maltreatment: A clinical guide and reference.* St. Louis: G.W. Medical Publishing, Inc.

Dekovic, M., & Janssens, J. (1992). Parents' child-rearing style and child's sociometric status. *Developmental Psychology, 28*(5), 925–932.

Educational Productions (1998). *Reframing discipline: Dealing with difficult behavior.* Portland, Oregon: Author.

Fabes, R., & Eisenberg, N. (1992). Young children's coping with interpersonal anger. *Child Development, 63,* 116–128.

Fujiki, M., Brinton, B., Morgan, M., & Hart, C. (1999). Withdrawn and sociable children with language impairment. *Language, Speech, & Hearing Services in Schools, 30,* 183–195.

Hart, C., Burts, D., Durland, M. A., Charlesworth, R., DeWolf, M., & Fleege, P. (1998). Stress behaviors and activity type participation of preschoolers in more and less developmentally appropriate classrooms: SES and sex differences. *Journal of Research in Childhood Education, 12*(2), 176–196.

Kaiser, B., & Rasminsky, J. (1999). *Meeting the challenge.* Ottawa, Ontario: Canadian Child Care Federation.

King, C. A., & Kirschenbaum, D. S. (1992). *Helping young children develop social skills.* Pacific Grove, CA: Brooks/Cole Publishing Company.

Kohn, A. (1996). *Beyond discipline.* Alexandria, VA: ASCD, Association for Supervision and Curriculum Development.

Landau, S., & McAninch, C. (1997). Young children with attention deficits. In E. Junn & C. Boyatzis (Eds.), *Child growth and development,* pp. 232–238. (Reprinted from *Young Children,* May, 1993, 49–58).

Marion, M. (2004). *Using observation in early childhood.* Upper Saddle River, NJ: Merrill/Prentice Hall.

Marion, M., & Swim, T. (2001). No quick fixes: Meeting the challenge of challenging behavior. Seminar presented at the National Conference of the National Association for the Education of Young Children, November, Anaheim, CA.

Pelander, J. (1997). My transition from conventional to more developmentally appropriate practices in the primary grades. *Young Children, 52*(7), 19–25.

Selye, H. (1978). *The stress of life* (Rev. ed.). New York: McGraw-Hill.

Tower, C. (1999). *Understanding child abuse and neglect.* Boston: Allyn & Bacon.

✓ CHECK OUT THE WEB SITES RELATED TO THIS CHAPTER

✓ **AACAP** (American Academy of Child and Adolescent Psychiatry). Check out the "Facts for Families Fact Sheets." They are excellent, are free, and may be reproduced (but not included in a document for sale). Go to the link for "fact sheets" to view the index for the entire list of fact sheets. *http://www.aacap.org*

✓ **CHADD** (Children and Adults with Attention-Deficit/Hyperactivity Disorder) *http://www.chadd.org.* Go the link "Frequently Asked Questions" for information about AD/HD or about the organization.

✓ **High Scope** (High Scope Foundation). Several good links. See especially the link for the Child Observation Record, the COR. An excellent observational assessment tool that charts a child's development and progress over time. Combines rating scales with anecdotal records. Highly recommended. *http://www.highscope.org*

✓ **New York University Child Study Center.** Provides timely tips and articles on a variety of children's behaviors. *http://www.aboutourkids.org*

"Direct" and "Indirect" Child Guidance

This book describes positive ways of guiding children, *only* positive approaches. NAEYC's Code of Ethics states that the most important part of the Code is that we do nothing to harm a child. To help you learn a positive constructivist approach, you will study how to guide children directly with positive guidance strategies. Then you will be shown how valuable good classroom management is in indirectly guiding children.

Chapter 4. Positive Guidance and Discipline Strategies: Direct Guidance. Setting good limits, redirecting behavior, delivering an I-message: these are just a few examples of **direct guidance** in this chapter. These strategies involve a child or group of children directly. Your confidence in dealing with day-to-day discipline encounters will grow as you learn about, practice, and experience success in using these and other **positive discipline strategies.** After reading this chapter, you will know exactly how to use a great many positive, specific, and practical discipline strategies.

Chapter 5. Early Childhood Classroom Management: Indirect Guidance. This chapter explains the concept of **indirect guidance.** This can be any of a number of things an adult does to indirectly influence a child. The adult might actually say little to the child; for example, hanging a poster on how to wash hands over the sink to remind children about proper handwashing technique. A classroom's physical layout and time schedule also indirectly and profoundly affect children's behavior.

You will read about the major indirect guidance strategies of designing and managing the physical environment effectively. You can minimize or even prevent problems by setting up your room well, by developing an appropriate curriculum and activities, and by competently managing materials. This chapter gives several examples of practical ideas for indirect guidance that can be adapted for any early childhood setting.

PART 2

Positive Guidance and Discipline Strategies: Direct Guidance

"Above all, we shall not harm children. We shall not participate in practices that are disrespectful, degrading, dangerous, exploitative, intimidating, psychologically damaging, or physically harmful to children. **This principle has precedence over all others in this code.**"

(Code of Ethical Conduct, 1998, NAEYC)

Case Studies: Positive Guidance Strategies

Concept of Discipline
Discipline and Socialization
Discipline Encounters
Discipline Strategies
Discipline: Positive or Negative?

Positive Guidance and Discipline Strategies: Description and Explanation
Develop Reasonable and Fair Limits and State Limits
Effectively
Help Children Accept Limits
Teach Helpful or Appropriate Behavior
Set Up Practice Sessions and Give "On-the-Spot"
Guidance
Give Signals or Cues for Appropriate Behavior
Encourage Children's Efforts to Accept Limits and to
Be Cooperative
Change Something About a Context or Setting
Ignore Behavior (Only When It Is Appropriate to Do
So)
Redirect Children's Behavior: Divert and Distract the
Youngest Children
Redirect Children's Behavior: Make Substitutions
When Dealing with
Listen Actively
Deliver I-Messages
Teach Conflict Resolution to Children
Recognize Signs of Stress, Anxiety, and Strong
Emotion, Prevent Overstimulation, and Teach
Calming Techniques
Help Children Save Face and Preserve Their Dignity

Your Beliefs About Discipline Influence You When You Choose Discipline Strategies
Beliefs Versus Practices
An Opportunity: Examine Your Own Beliefs
About Discipline

Working with Parents: Bring Parents into the Guidance Circle

After reading and studying this chapter, you will be able to:

❑ **List and explain** the several positive guidance and discipline strategies.

❑ **Explain** why each is a positive strategy.

❑ **Demonstrate** how to use specific positive guidance and discipline strategies.

❑ **Summarize and explain** methods for talking with parents about positive guidance and discipline strategies.

❑ **Analyze** a case study by **determining** how positive discipline strategies could be used.

Case Studies: Positive Guidance Strategies

Infants and Toddlers

In the infant room of a preschool, 11-month-old Pete grabbed the hair of Mr. Thompson, the teacher. He removed Pete's hand, picked him up, and turning to the window, said, "O-o-o-h! Look at the birds, Pete." Pete brightened when he saw birds at the feeder.

Fifteen-month-old Julianne scooted across the room toward the kitchen, and Mr. Thompson scooped her up and carried her back to a small table, singing, "Julianne, Julianne, lunchtime, lunchtime. Let's have lunch." "Lunch, lunch" returned Julianne, in singsong style.

Georgio, 2 years old, banged his hands on the playdough table while his teacher turned around to get the dough. The teacher placed his hands lightly on Georgio's small hands, showed him two lumps of playdough, and said, "Listen carefully, Georgio. Tell me whether you want white playdough or blue playdough." Georgio piped up cheerfully, "I want BLUE!"

Jordan, 4 Years Old

In the same preschool, 4-year-old Jordan stood at the sand table and scooped up a handful of sand. He looked at the sand and then at the floor. He then slowly drizzled sand onto the floor next to the sand table. He bent over to examine the little pile of sand on the floor. Mrs. Vargas watched for a few seconds and then decided that Jordan seemed to be doing an experiment with the sand. She said, "You're dropping the sand very carefully." Jordan replied, "Yeah. It goes straight down and doesn't fly around like snow." Mrs. Vargas said, "Well, I want you to continue your experiment but it's dangerous to put sand on the floor. I have an idea. Here is a towel to put on the floor to catch the sand. Then you can just lift the towel and put the sand right back in the sand table when you're done."

Sarah, 6 Years Old

Sarah and Mom went to the store to buy a backpack for Sarah. They were in a hurry, and had just enough time to pick out the backpack and still get to a doctor's appointment. Mom could afford to buy a backpack but nothing else before she received her next paycheck. She forgot to tell Sarah that they would have to hurry along and she did not know how to say that she had so little money. At the store, Sarah started the "Look-Mommy-I-want-that-WHY-can't-I-have-it" game. "Mom, can I get the lunchbox, too?" "No, Sarah. No lunchbox." "But Mom, I want the lunchbox. It has Mickey Mouse on it, just like my new backpack!" "Sarah, stop it. No lunchbox." "Why, Mom?"

At this point, Sarah increased her whining, and her mother, covering embarrassment with anger, exploded, "Shut up, Sarah!" Sarah then lost control and cried uncontrollably. Mom grabbed her wrist, yanked her around, got close to Sarah's face, and hissed, "You listen to me, young lady! Shut up this instant or I'll really give you something to cry about." (Sarah's mother typically uses corporal punishment when she is very angry.)

THE CONCEPT OF DISCIPLINE

Discipline and Socialization

Socialization: a process through which children acquire their culture and the values and habits that will help them adapt to that culture. Children acquire their culture's values through education, modeling by and imitation of teachers and parents using a process called **scaffolding** to gradually lead a child to accept certain behaviors and values (Bukatko & Daehler, 1992). **Discipline** is only one part of the process of socialization.

Discipline Encounters

Discipline encounter: an interaction between an adult and child in which the adult attempts to help a child to alter her behavior in some way; for example, the adult can help a child to stop doing something harmful or destructive, to treat someone with respect, to take responsibility for cleaning up. Discipline encounters occur frequently during the early childhood period, even in classrooms and homes where adults are warm and supportive. They occur as we help children understand that their obligation is to respect the rights of others. Discipline encounters take place as we help children comply with **legitimate authority** (Baumrind, 1996). Each of the adults in the following examples faced a discipline encounter.

Examples. Mrs. Vargas, the preschool teacher, watched as Calvin threw sand onto the trike path. She also heard Nellie and Justine arguing mildly over the jar of paste at the collage table. She turned quickly when she heard Jordan banging on the hamster's house.

Mr. Claiborne, the first-grade teacher, saw Ryan grab a marker from Reese.

Several of the second-graders in Mr. Nellis's class left their backpacks on the floor instead of putting them in lockers.

Mr. Lee, the third-grade teacher, noticed that two boys were bouncing their basketball on the wall right next to a classroom window.

Teachers deal with numerous discipline encounters every day. Some discipline encounters deal with everyday concerns (disturbing group time or not putting things away after using them). Others deal with more serious issues (e.g., a child's mean-spirited treatment of animals or other children). All, however, are discipline encounters.

Teachers and parents spend quite a bit of time managing discipline encounters and are justifiably concerned about such encounters for a couple of reasons. First, adults have to help children learn to control their short-term behavior; for example, to stop banging on the hamster's house. Second, adults want to influence attitudes, values, and long-term behavior, such as developing a humane attitude toward and kind, compassionate treatment of animals. They know, though, that they cannot fully determine attitudes or long-term behavior. They can only influence them.

Example. Mrs. Vargas has noticed that Jordan shows a considerable amount of aggression. She faces several discipline encounters with him each week over aggressive behavior. She is responsible for the safety of all the children in her class and therefore has to help Jordan control his aggression for the short term. She must stop him from hurting other children and the classroom animals. In addition, she is concerned about Jordan's long-term attitude and behavior. She knows that he will have an increasingly difficult time getting along with other children if he continues to hurt them, so she wants to help him willingly learn a more positive, less aggressive way of interacting with others.

Discipline Strategies

Discipline strategies: specific actions that adults use in managing discipline encounters (Marion, 1999). This chapter explains a large number of positive guidance and discipline strategies. Authoritative adults use positive strategies, focusing on teaching and not on punishment. For example, authoritative adults explain limits, redirect behavior, and teach behaviors that are more helpful. They give information that children need for learning and practicing behavior beneficial to the child (Clark, 1999; Eaton, 1997).

Other adults use negative strategies, focusing more on punishment. They isolate children, use physical punishment, are sarcastic, or even refuse to speak to a child (love withdrawal). Still other adults use strategies that are simply unhelpful, such as nattering and nagging.

Discipline: Positive or Negative?

Discipline: A word derived from the Latin **disciplina,** teaching, learning, and **discipulus,** a pupil (Webster's Dictionary).

Discipline can be either positive or negative. The word **discipline,** in itself, has no positive or negative meaning. The actions or discipline strategies that you choose give your discipline its positive or negative quality. Some discipline strategies are neither positive nor negative, but instead are simply not helpful.

Example. Mr. Lee managed the discipline encounter with the boys who were bouncing the basketball on the wall near the window by reminding them firmly but kindly to throw it only at the basketball backboard. His action, restating about a limit, was a positive one; his overall discipline style is a positive one.

Example. At home, Ryan, from Mr. Claiborne's class, forgot to feed his cat. His father managed this discipline encounter by yelling at Ryan and calling him a name. Dad's actions, yelling and name calling, were degrading and therefore negative.

There is a lot of confusion in the field of early childhood about whether discipline is positive or negative. Adults who use positive discipline strategies think of discipline as teaching, and believe in treating children with respect in any discipline encounter. Adults who primarily use negative discipline strategies tend to link the word *discipline* with punishment.

Some early childhood professionals abhor even thinking about negative or harsh discipline strategies because they know that negative discipline harms children. However, our goal is to guide children effectively. This requires that we acknowledge that many children come from families that use negative, harsh discipline. Acknowledging that some children experience harsh discipline at home will help us understand their behavior and develop appropriate guidance plans for them. All children benefit from positive discipline strategies, but children who have experienced harsh discipline at home need these strategies most desperately.

POSITIVE GUIDANCE AND DISCIPLINE STRATEGIES: DESCRIPTION AND EXPLANATION

This chapter describes and explains several positive guidance and discipline strategies (Figure 4.1). Learning how to use these strategies makes it possible for you to meet the needs of individual children. You will be able to choose the most effective strategy in a variety of discipline encounters. The Appendix also lists these strategies and outlines how to use each.

Positive discipline strategies begin with adult behaviors: good limit setting, clearly communicating limits. They include teaching more appropriate behavior, giving cues for the new behavior, giving choices, and supporting children in their new behavior. Positive guidance and discipline also include changing something about a situation, and ignoring behavior when it is appropriate to do so.

Positive guidance and discipline continue when adults manage typical discipline encounters with positive, helpful strategies: redirection, active listening, I-messages, conflict resolution, and recognizing and dealing with strong emotions.

Finally, helpful adults learn to recognize signs of stress, anxiety, and strong emotion. They try to prevent overstimulation and they teach calming techniques. The core of positive discipline strategies, however, is the last section in this chapter. Helping children save face and preserve their dignity in discipline encounters is the most important and essential element in child guidance.

DEVELOP REASONABLE AND FAIR LIMITS

Adults influence children by stating their expectations for desired behavior and helping children understand that there are boundaries, or limits, on behavior. Authoritative caregivers understand the importance of proper boundaries in relationships in general, and appropriate limits in an adult-child relationship in particular. They figure out and clearly communicate limits that will be most helpful in encouraging children to behave appropriately. They understand what a good limit is and what benefits appropriate limits have for children (Marion, Swim, & Jenner, 2000).

Authoritative adults work with children in developing some, but not all, limits. For example, Mr. Claiborne, the first-grade teacher, led a discussion about classroom limits at the beginning of the school year.

Example. He started by stating first, "The most important rule in our classroom is that we treat each other and our animals with respect," as he wrote on a large sheet of paper. He then described what that might mean and elicited the children's contributions; for example, "The gerbils get scared when they hear loud noises. What would be a good rule about noise around the gerbils?" He printed limits and posted them as a reminder. His children are much more likely to take ownership of limits because they have helped to develop them.

Good Limits Focus on Important Things

Highly responsive, authoritative adults set and maintain reasonable, fair, developmentally appropriate limits. Their limits focus on important, not trivial, things. The

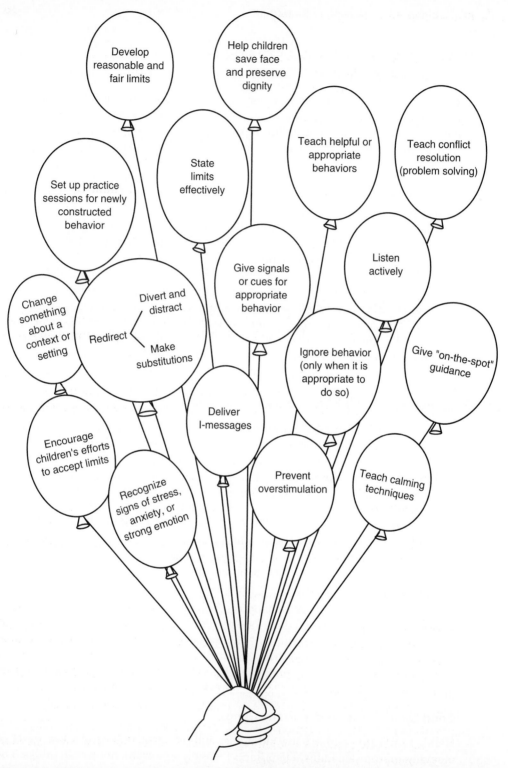

Figure 4.1. Authoritative adults know how to use many positive guidance and discipline strategies.

limits protect children's and adult's health and safety and encourage the development of healthy self-control. Their limits also transmit values of dignified, fair, humane treatment of people and animals to children.

Encourage healthy self-control through limits

Self-control develops slowly in children. Reasonable, fair limits can help children to achieve internal control gradually because limits clearly communicate appropriate behavior and reasons for that behavior.

Examples. "Scoot back to your spot on the carpet, Jack. Vinnie can't see if you sit in front of him."

"Let's tiptoe past the crib room because the babies are sleeping."

Mr. Nellis to second-grader Willis: "I see that you've finished your story. Please choose the next thing that you need to do now because the other children are also still working."

Rules protecting physical health

One set of important limits deals with health issues. Disease can spread exceptionally quickly in group settings for children. Design and communicate rules that protect the physical health of both adults and children. Some examples:

- Thorough hand washing by adults. All adults who work in a classroom or elsewhere should be required to demonstrate that they know proper handwashing techniques. All adults should also demonstrate the willingness to wash their hands at specific times.
- Thorough hand washing by children. A checklist would be useful.
- Proper handling of food.
- Washing and sanitizing toys and other equipment.
- Labeling and storing toothbrushes properly.
- Using tissues when sneezing.
- Proper toileting and diapering routines, including approved cleanup.

Figure 4.2 is a checklist used by a school district's "infection control officer." It documents the hand washing in Mrs. Vargas's preschool classroom.

Rules protecting everyone's safety

Appropriate limits ensure safety. Think about safety on different levels. One level governs the safe use of toys, equipment, and space. Typical limits include "You pour and dump sand in the sand box, but not on the trike path," or "You must stay inside the fenced area of our playground."

A child's inner feeling of safety and security calls for another level of safety rules. Children feel secure when they know that they will not be hurt; therefore, a good environment for children has rules that keep children and adults safe.

Examples. Mr. Claiborne to Vinnie: "Yes, you **are** angry, and that's OK, but I want you to **tell** Ryan that you are upset. Use words to tell him that you want your book back. Say, 'I want my book back.'"

Hand-Washing Checklist for Teachers Mrs. Vargas's Preschool Class: Oaklawn School					
	Lead Teacher	Assistant Teacher	Student Teacher	High School #1	Co-op Students #2
Proper hand washing technique	x	x	No	No	No
Washes hands before preparing food	x	x	x	No	No
Washes hands before eating	x	x	x	x	x
Washes hands after using tissue	n/c	x	No	No	n/c
Washes hands after helping children in bathroom	x	x	x	No	No
Washes hands at other appropriate times; e.g., after painting	x	x	x	x	No

(n/c: no chance to observe this)
Comments: The school must institute a method for teaching all volunteer teachers about proper hand-washing techniques. Although the student teacher washes his hands at appropriate times, he does not use proper technique. The high school co-op students do not know proper hand-washing technique and they make few attempts to wash their hands at necessary times. They need immediate instruction.

Figure 4.2.

Mr. Nellis to kindergarten child Louie, who had asked what day it was several times in one morning: "Today is Thursday. You go home with your dad on Thursdays. He always comes to get you right on time." Louie goes through many transitions (Mom's house to school, school to baby-sitter, baby-sitter's to Mom's house, school to Dad's house, Dad's house to Mom's house). His mother does not prepare him very well for transitions, but his father does a better job. Mr. Nellis does whatever he can to help Louie feel secure.

Encourage respectful treatment of others with limits

Responsible adults set and maintain limits about fair treatment of everyone in a class. Children have to learn what respectful treatment means; they learn this best from the words and actions of adults. It also means clearly stating the behaviors that we will **not** tolerate; e.g., degrading or hurting others.

Examples. "Hold the kitten gently, like this" (teacher demonstrates).
"Mitchell's name is on the list before your name. He goes first."
Mr. Claiborne to Vinnie: "Susan is crying, Vinnie, because you called her 'fatso.' One of our rules is that we treat each other with respect. It is disrespectful to call someone names."

Good limits, e.g., "Be quiet around the gerbils," teach children about respectful treatment of other people and animals. (The Web site *http://aphe.vview.org/packrat* lists articles that help teachers state limits about treatment of animals.)

As you can see, this includes rules about humane treatment of animals. **Humane** means kind, caring, and compassionate treatment of animals, something that children must learn. (Consider using the Web sites at the end of this chapter to learn how to teach caring, compassionate treatment of animals to children).

STATE LIMITS EFFECTIVELY

Authoritative caregivers have a clear, direct, and validating communication style. If a goal in guiding children is to help children, we can best help them understand necessary limits by stating these limits effectively.

Speak naturally, but speak slowly enough that the child hears everything you say; use concrete words and short sentences when stating limits

"Put your puzzle in this first slot of the puzzle rack." This limit tells a child exactly where the finished puzzle goes. It is a more effective than saying, "Put it over there." Avoid using abstract words or phrases such as "in a little while," "be a good boy," or "knock it off."

Tell a child exactly what to do rather than what not to do, and be as positive as possible

It is more helpful to say, "Use this tissue to clean your nose" rather than "Don't pick your nose!" We do need to be clear about what children may not do, but it is most helpful to focus on what we want children **to** do.

Use suggestions whenever possible

Suggestions are persuasive statements. Suggestions describe an acceptable behavior to a child in an appealing way; they do not order a child to do anything. Children cooperate more frequently and willingly when adults use suggestions (Baumrind, 1993, 1996).

Example. Sarah's mom (in the chapter-opening case study) said, "I have an idea, Sarah. Let's write what we want to buy at the store on this piece of paper and take it with us today."

Use direct, self-responsible statements when you think it is necessary to make a reasonable request

Authoritative adults do occasionally have to state a very direct request, but their style is highly responsive.

Example. Mrs. Vargas had given an appropriate warning about cleanup on the playground but Jackie was still zipping around on his trike. "Whoa, there!" said the teacher as she signaled Jackie to stop. "I gave the signal for cleanup and now I want you to park the trike." Then she put her hand on the handlebars, pointed to the row of trikes parked against the shed, turned Jackie in that direction, and said, "There's a spot for your trike right next to the yellow trike. Let's go and fit it in that space."

This type of direct request is firm but still responsive because it relies on persuasion. Self-responsible adult communication elicits much greater cooperation than do power-centered orders, such as "Jackie, put that trike away right now!" Ordering others around is a type of communication based on power and stirs up anger and resistance, not cooperation (Baumrind, 1996).

Give choices whenever possible

Making wise choices is a skill and must be learned and practiced; it does not happen automatically. Authoritative caregivers skillfully offer manageable choices to children.

Example. Mrs. Vargas first used a **when-then** statement to communicate clearly that the limit was that children had to wear paint aprons when painting. She said, "When you put on your paint apron, then you may paint at the easel."

Then she gave Ralph a choice: "Do you want to wear the green or yellow paint apron?" Alternatively, she could have given a different choice: "Would you like to snap the Velcro pieces together yourself or do you want me to help you?"

Avoid giving a choice when the child really has no choice

For example, avoid saying things such as "Do you want to wear a paint apron?" or "Do you want to go home now?" A logical response from a child to these questions is a **yes or no** answer because this is a closed type of question. It is unfair and confusing to give a child a choice when she really does not have one. You also set yourself up for an argument with a child who says "No" to such questions, because you then must backtrack and tell her why she really has no choice.

Issue only a few suggestions at a time; avoid giving a chain of limits

It is difficult for children to keep a string of limits or suggestions in their minds. If a child cannot remember a part of your string of limits, chances are good that she will not comply with all of the limits. Children comply more easily with limits when we state them in small chunks, small enough for children to remember. For example, "Use the clothespins to hang your painting." "Good, it will dry nicely. Now, wash the part of the table where you worked with this sponge." "OK, nice and clean. Now, wash your hands and hang up your apron."

Allow enough time for the child to process information and complete a task before issuing another suggestion (Schaffer & Crook, 1980); repeat a limit if necessary, but do it effectively

Suppose that a child ignores your request. Frustrating? Yes, but do not take the child's behavior personally. Avoid getting angry and remember that your job is to help this child accept a simple limit. You will be most effective if you

- Manage your emotions well and repeat the limit calmly and with good will.
- Call the child's name again.
- Pick up the item, and matter-of-factly hand the item to the child.
- Repeat the request.
- Avoid simply restating the limit in a snappish, peeved way because your irritation will show and will likely bring out anger and stubbornness from the child; then you will have a full-blown argument on your hands. (See Figure 4.3.)

HELP CHILDREN ACCEPT LIMITS

Authoritative caregivers and teachers help children willingly accept good limits. They do several things to set the stage so that children will accept legitimate boundaries on behavior. Here are some practical ways to get you started on helping children to willingly accept limits.

Set the Stage So That Children Can Accept a Limit

Researchers demonstrated many years ago how important it is to set the stage so that children can accept a limit (Schaffer & Crook, 1980; Stayton, Hogan, & Ainsworth, 1971). Adults who effectively help children accept limits believe that children are naturally compliant (Haswell, Hock, & Wenar, 1981). Authoritative adults tune in to a situation, help children focus on the task at hand, and give good cues.

Observe what the child is doing before stating a limit

Be responsive and take into account what a child is doing because her activity is important to her. If Moua is putting together her favorite puzzle when the cleanup signal is first given, she will very likely try to finish her work before putting things away.

Limit Setting

Things to Remember About Stating Limits

- Involve children in developing some limits in a classroom or other setting.
- Tune in, help children focus on the task, and give good cues.
- Speak naturally but slowly enough that a child hears the limit clearly.
- Use concrete words and short sentences.
- Use natural, normal sentences; e.g., "It's time to put the teacups away."
- Tell a child exactly what **to** do; e.g., "Take small bites of your bread."
- Be as positive as possible.
- Give choices when appropriate.
- Give short, clear, fair reasons for limits.
- Issue only one or two suggestions at a time.
- Give a child enough time to carry out the limit or to complete something else before she carries out the limit.
- Restate limits appropriately. Restate limits when it is necessary to do so.

Avoid These Behaviors When Stating Limits

- Avoid giving choices when children really do not have a choice; e.g., "Do you want to go to the library?" when the whole class goes to the library.
- Avoid giving a chain of limits.
- Avoid using "cute" reasons; e.g., avoid saying things such as, "I think that the teacups want to be put away now." This makes a teacher sound silly.
- Avoid telling children only what *not* to do; e.g., "Don't take such big bites of your bread!"
- Avoid vague limits; e.g., "I'm not sure that you should be doing that."
- Avoid stating arbitrary or trivial limits.
- Avoid arguing or playing the "why game" about limits.
- Avoid complex or excessive reasoning about limits.

Figure 4.3.

Give children a reasonable amount of time to complete their work

Consider cleanup in a classroom. Before officially beginning to clean up, announce cleanup quietly to the whole group, to small groups, or to individuals, and then allow the children a bit of time to finish up their work.

Decrease distance between you and a child

Avoid calling out limits from across the room. Decrease horizontal distance by walking toward a child. Decrease vertical distance by bending or stooping so that you can talk directly to a child.

Get a child's attention, politely

Touch a child on the arm or say her name quietly. Using nonthreatening verbal or nonverbal cues and appropriate physical contact[14] is essential with toddlers and is highly recommended with preschoolers, especially those who have not learned to live with reasonable boundaries and limits at home.

Direct a child's visual attention to a specific object or task

"Here's one of the puzzles that you worked on, Moua," you say as you show her the puzzle you are holding and then point to the puzzle table. This is **orientation compliance;** its purpose is to orient the child properly (direct her attention toward something) before stating a limit or making a request.

Have the child make contact with a specific object

For example, place a puzzle with which a child has worked in her hands and say, "Please hold the puzzle while we walk over to the puzzle table." This is **contact compliance;** its purpose is to help the child tune in to the task at hand before she is asked to do anything specific.

Make your specific request (ask for task compliance)

A child is much more likely to comply with your request when you have properly oriented her. It is much easier for a child to accept the cleanup limit when she is at the puzzle table holding the puzzle rather than when she is sitting in another area listening to a story when you announce cleanup.

Give Reasons for Rules and Limits

Children accept limits much more readily when they understand the rationale behind them (Baumrind, 1996). Three practical suggestions will help you use reasons well: give short, simple, concrete reasons, decide when to state the limit, and decide whether you need to restate the limit.

Give short, simple, concrete reasons along with a limit

   Example. "Put the lid on the paint cups" (the limit). "It will keep the paint fresh" (the reason).

Decide when to state the reason

State reasons for limits either before or after stating the limit, or after a child complies with the limit.

---

[14]A note on appropriate physical contact: this is a source of comfort to a young child and is a part of the style of sensitive, supportive, encouraging adults. Appropriate physical contact reassures a child, is never imposed on a child, and is given in response to the *child's* needs. With recent concern about child abuse in preschools, it is prudent for center personnel to be clear about the center's policy of appropriate physical contact between staff and children. This policy must also be clearly communicated to and discussed with parents (Phyffe-Perkins & Birtwell, 1989).

Examples. State the rationale **before** you give the limit: "We need tables cleared of toys before we can have snack" (the reason). "Put each puzzle back in the rack" (the limit). Some children tend to argue less about a rule if they hear the reason first and the limit second.

State the rationale **after** you state the limit: "I want you to put the puzzles away" (the limit). "Then the table is clear for snack" (the reason).

State the rationale after the child accepts the limit: "The puzzle table is clear! Now we can eat snack at that table."

Decide whether you need to repeat the rationale if you restate the limit

Repeating the rationale is a good idea when you want to emphasize the reason for the limit, perhaps when children are first learning a limit.

Example. Mrs. Vargas said before going out to the playground on the second day of school, "Tell me our safety rule about how many children are allowed on the sliding board at one time." "That's right, only one at a time so that nobody gets hurt." She also showed a picture of one child on the slide and a cue.

Be aware, however, that some children might try to distract you from carrying through with a limit by playing the "why game"; i.e., repeatedly asking, "Why?" Ignoring their "Why?" is one of the most helpful things you can do for them. You can also say, "I think you're having fun asking me why and I'll tell you why one more time and then the game is over" (Seefeldt, 1993).

COMMUNICATE LIMITS TO OTHERS; REVIEW LIMITS PERIODICALLY

Communicate Classroom Limits to Every Person Who Works in Your Classroom

It is important that everyone who works in your classroom, however short the time, understands and uses the same limits. This includes, but is not limited to, parents, other volunteers, specialists, the principal or director, children from upper grades, college students in a practicum, and persons invited to do a presentation. Some children are confused when adults in the same classroom use different limits. Other children quickly figure out that the adults are inconsistent and use the inconsistency to their advantage.

Example. Mrs. Vargas forgot to tell a new volunteer about some of the classroom rules. The volunteer told two boys that they could just leave the blocks out and that she would put them away. The classroom rule is that children put away things that they have used.

Figure 4.2, the checklist for hand washing by adults, showed that volunteers in Mrs. Vargas's class did not know proper hand-washing technique. The lead and assistant teacher learned that they had to communicate clearly information on proper hand washing to every person working in the room.

Communicate classroom limits by posting the list on a large poster board in a conspicuous place. Point out the list when the person first comes to the classroom.

Alternatively, have a number of copies of a handout titled "Classroom Limits" ready to give to anyone who works in the room. Talk with all classroom workers and visitors about how important it is for all adults to use the same limits. Demonstrate limits when necessary, as with proper hand washing.

Communicate Information on Limits to Parents

Bring parents into the guidance circle. You can make classroom limits even more effective by telling parents about the limits. First of all, this highlights limits for parents and reassures them. Second, communicating effectively with parents tells them that you think they are worthy of your time. This will help you develop a good working partnership with parents. Third, talking with parents about limits might help some parents ask questions about limit setting at home.

Parents tend to like the topic of how to set and maintain reasonable limits when it is offered as a parent education topic. Communicate information to parents about setting limits in a variety of ways: with handouts, newsletter write-ups, appropriate articles, formal parent meetings, and videos either used in meetings or borrowed by parents. See the "Working with Parents" box and the list of Web sites at the end of this chapter. You will find many handouts and other free or inexpensive material about guidance and discipline to use with parents.

Working with Parents. Bring Parents into the Guidance Circle

Teachers must clearly communicate a school or center's policies, including discipline policies and strategies, to parents. You will have to think through this issue and be able to articulate the center's policy without insulting parents who, according to Socolar (1995), believe in using physical punishment such as hitting (spanking). Your goal is to establish rapport and then maintain a good relationship with parents so that you can work effectively with each family and child. There are a number of steps you can take to explain school policies about positive discipline strategies to parents.

✓ **Write it down!** Let parents know about the child guidance policies of the school. Use the NAEYC Code of Ethical Conduct (National Association for the Education of Young Children, 1998) as a base and write your own center or school policies from that. Incorporate your guidance policies in a policy manual written just for parents. Then it will be clear to parents that the school has a guidance policy, that it is based on a professional group's guidelines, and that it is positive in nature.

✓ **Focus on teaching.** Are you going to do home visits? As a small part of your visit, plan to talk with each parent about a few of the specific positive strategies that you use. Does your school have a newsletter? Write a brief article explaining a specific discipline strategy. Does your school have a parent's bulletin board? Use this space to display information about a specific strategy. Are you having a group parent meeting? Explain the guidance policy along with all the other policies and highlight one or two positive discipline strategies.

For example, explain how you set limits and how you restate them if a child does not seem to listen the first time. Many parents react almost reflexively with spanking when their children do not obey immediately. Explain how you use redirection.

✓ **Do a needs assessment.** Effective teachers work as partners with parents. Make a list of the many positive discipline strategies that your school uses and ask parents to check off the ones about which they would like to know more. Work with parents by giving them information on the strategies that they have identified as areas of need. Do this through an early childhood family education program that includes one-on-one interaction with parents as well as more formal methods such as group meetings.

✓ **Listen with respect, avoid being judgmental, and don't argue.** Some parents will ask questions that simply call for clarification of a specific policy. A few parents will challenge a policy. Some might even want to engage you in a protracted debate about controversial discipline strategies such as spanking that they see as acceptable. In all cases, you will best help parents by remaining calm and professional; do not argue with a parent.

Suppose a father says, "I was spanked when I was a kid and it never hurt me!" You can neutralize such a statement and avoid arguing by **not** taking his statement as an attack and by saying respectfully, "Yes, lots of people were spanked and believe in spanking. Our school does not want to force ideas on anybody. But we do want parents to know that we guide children with positive discipline strategies."

TEACH HELPFUL OR APPROPRIATE BEHAVIOR

Help children construct knowledge about self-control by teaching them about helpful behaviors. The goal is to facilitate their understanding of knowledge and skills that will help them the most. Children must learn so many behaviors that they do not know automatically. Here are just a few examples:

- How to ask for something.
- How to listen when others talk, not interrupting them.
- How to join a play or work group.
- How to put things away when they complete a project.
- Skills for participating in a group, such as where and how to sit, how to listen, how to offer an idea, and how to get the teacher's attention.
- Mealtime manners, such as passing things and waiting their turn.
- How to wash their hands properly (Niffenneger, 1997) and that they should wash their hands at certain times.

Plan lessons on teaching the skills. Choose from your large collection of teaching strategies and incorporate them into your regular teaching plan. Teach individuals, small groups, or large groups. Use songs, stories, finger plays, flannelboards, demonstrations, films, videos, guest speakers, or other methods.

Example. At the beginning of the school year, Mrs. Vargas observed that several of the children did not understand the concept of passing things. For instance, the children seemed confused about how to pass baskets with snacks, and did not know how to pass pitchers with juice or milk. Here are two examples of the lessons through which she taught the children how to pass things.

Lesson #1: Large group. Mrs. Vargas held a basket filled with colored squares of paper. She said, "I'm going to take one of these squares from the basket. Then I'm going to **pass the basket** to Nellie" (who sat next to the teacher). Nellie takes the basket. "Now, Nellie will take one square out of the basket and pass the basket to Ralph. Ralph takes a square and passes it to Justine." After all the children had a chance to pass the basket, Mrs. Vargas showed them a basket used at snack time. She said, "We will **pass** baskets like this one when we eat snack."

Lesson #2: Snacktime. "Here's the basket that we will **pass**! I'll start today." Mrs. Vargas softly chanted as she took a cracker and then passed the basket,

> *"Mrs. Vargas takes a cracker and passes them to Jordan.*
> *Jordan takes a cracker and passes them to Chelsea.*
> *Chelsea takes a cracker and passes them to Ralph."*

They continued singing until every child had passed the basket.

Observe a child or a group to ascertain the skill that you need to teach. Consider using checklists, anecdotal records, or rating scales to assess the needs and abilities of your students (Marion, 2004). Use observation to assess a child's understanding after you have taught a skill. Mrs. Vargas observed during large group when she introduced the concept that every child except Calvin seemed to understand the meaning of "passing a basket." By the end of snack time, however, Calvin, too, seemed to understand the concept because he passed the basket quickly when it was his turn.

SET UP PRACTICE SESSIONS AND GIVE "ON-THE-SPOT" GUIDANCE

Give children a chance to practice what you show or tell them, as Mrs. Vargas did when they practiced passing baskets. Mr. Nellis had observed that Willis did not wait his turn for the computer stations in the K–2 classroom. Consequently, he had taught Willis the steps in getting a turn (putting his name on the list if necessary, checking the list and waiting, and working somewhere else until his name was next). He knew how important it is for children to practice what they have learned and so planned a simple practice session for Willis about waiting for a turn.

Mr. Nellis started the practice session (Mr. Nellis worked with Willis individually) by saying, "Let's practice waiting for a turn at the computer, Willis. You already know the main things that you have to do. Please tell me the first thing."

Willis:	I have to put my name on the list.
Mr. Nellis:	That's right. Write your name now on this list. (Willis prints his name at the bottom of the list.) Good. Now, check to see how many children are ahead of you.
Willis:	Sandi and Michael. That's two.
Mr. Nellis:	Right again! You won't have to wait very long at all. What would you like to do while you wait?
Willis:	. . . work on my math.

The next day, Mr. Nellis introduced a new math game to use at the computer and Willis was eager to get a turn. Mr. Nellis gave "on-the-spot" guidance to Willis. He quietly reminded him about how to get a turn and used this real-life situation as another practice session. Willis did very well. He had learned the steps, had practiced them with the teacher individually, and finally had practiced them in the classroom.

GIVE SIGNALS OR CUES FOR APPROPRIATE BEHAVIOR

Children might not remember to do things, in spite of learning how. **Cues** are hints or suggestions that remind children about a limit in a low-key way. The signals or cues can be verbal, nonverbal, pictorial, or written (for older children). Good cues are developmentally appropriate; they are age- and individually appropriate for a variety of children—typically developing children, children with disabilities, and a child for whom English is a second language.

Example. At the end of group time Mrs. Vargas verbally reminded the children to wash their hands for snack time. The group sang the action song and then she sent them to the bathroom (the song was the **cue** or reminder).

Example. Shortly after that, she showed one of the pictures of a child washing her hands to the group. "Where can we hang this picture so that it reminds us to always wash our hands after going into the bathroom?" (The picture is the **cue.**)

Example. The teachers at Oaklawn School (Thompson, Vargas, Claiborne, Nellis, Lee, and others) have many children in their classes for whom English is a second language. The teachers have found that picture cues help these children understand limits and deal with transitions. At transition from work and play time to large group, for instance, Mr. Claiborne showed each child two picture cues, one of a child playing and the other of the child in a circle with other children. At the same time, the teacher described moving from play to large group. (The pictures are **cues.**)

ENCOURAGE CHILDREN'S EFFORTS TO ACCEPT LIMITS AND TO BE COOPERATIVE OR HELPFUL

Children need more than limits—they also need encouragement for their efforts to accept limits and to behave in prosocial way, cooperatively or helpfully. There are many ways to encourage children's efforts.

Some new behavior is "self-encouraging"

Think of ways to set things up so that a child will find a new behavior so attractive that she will eagerly comply.

Example. Larry did not wipe his paint smock when he painted. Mrs. Vargas made a new job for the job chart and assigned that job to Larry for two days. The new job entailed being the person who ran the paint smock wash. This person wore a special hat and smock, was in charge of checking all the smocks to make sure they were clean, and was responsible for the new sponge and bucket.

Example. Mr. Nellis wanted his children to place leftover art paper in a neat pile when they finished a project. He glued a cutout of a hippopotamus head onto a basket and showed the basket plus hippo to the class. His class immediately named the hippo "Harvey," and Mr. Nellis asked the children to feed their leftover papers to Harvey. The class enthusiastically fed their papers to their new friend.

Checklist: Proper Use of Tissues						
	Susan	Tom	Ryan	Reese	Moua	Pae
Knows technique	X	X	X		X	
Uses proper technique willingly	X		X	X	X	
Throws tissue away when done		X	X	X	X	X
Washes hands after using tissue	X	X	X	X	X	X

Figure 4.4.

Observe children to determine whether they have learned what they need to learn and whether they have accepted a limit

Mr. Claiborne wanted all children to use a tissue when sneezing and wiping their noses. He taught them how to use the tissue with a demonstration and a song about using tissues. Then he developed a checklist (Figure 4.4) to help him determine who had learned the techniques. He observed children use a tissue and checked off names when they demonstrated proper technique. He also observed to determine whether children used a tissue at appropriate times.

Recognize and encourage a child's efforts

Children need our support. Recognizing and acknowledging their efforts demonstrates our support and appreciation. Some adults recognize an individual child's efforts; they also acknowledge the effort of the entire group.

Examples. Two days after introducing Harvey the hippo, Mr. Nellis said to his class at opening group time, "Harvey is a happy and well-fed hippo, you know! He very much appreciates getting your leftover art paper and he thanks you." The class made hippo mouth movements.

Mrs. Vargas said to her children at the lunch table (after they had washed their hands), "Hold up your hands. Just look at all these clean hands. You have really learned how to scrub away dirt and germs."

The principal visited Mr. Claiborne's room to read a story for the class. The children had just cleaned up after their morning work period and they sat on the floor for the story time. Mr. Claiborne introduced the principal. He showed a large photo of the entire class with the label "We are good helpers!" He said to the principal, "We have lots of children in this class and we are all good helpers." He then noted how every child had helped during cleanup.

CHANGE SOMETHING ABOUT A CONTEXT OR SETTING

Behavior communicates. Behavior does not occur in a vacuum—it happens in a context or setting. The context of a behavior has an effect on that behavior. With these statements in mind, consider reframing or rethinking the concept of a discipline encounter by asking a question. "What can I do about this context, this situation that will help this child be safe or help her choose a different behavior more helpful to the child?" For example, "Do I want to keep telling these two children to stop arguing over the blocks, or can I change something to help them accept the idea of cooperating?"

There are three major ways to change a situation to be helpful and to prevent or stop potentially dangerous or inappropriate behavior:

- change the physical environment and time schedule,
- increase options, or
- decrease options.

Change the Physical Environment and Time Schedule If Necessary

Guide children effectively by managing the environment well.[15] You can easily change something about a situation by evaluating how you have structured the physical environment. You can then decide that a slight change might be very helpful to children.

Example. When Mrs. Vargas was a first-year teacher she was surprised to find that the children ran, not walked, from the dramatic play area to the block area. Her principal observed one morning and said that the classroom had a **zoom area** in it—a tunnel-like space that just invited running. The teacher changed something about the situation by rearranging the room to eliminate the zoom area. The running stopped.

Example. Mr. Nellis's student teacher found that his opening large group time was almost unpleasant because of all the talking and squirming. Mr. Nellis, during the evaluation of group time, asked the student teacher to reflect on how long the lesson had been. The student teacher discovered that the group time was too long and made a simple adjustment. The adjusted schedule resulted in a much shorter, much more productive and peaceful group activity.

Increase Options Available to a Child

Authoritative adults closely supervise and monitor activities. They recognize when children need more options from which to choose. They realize that children might be stuck on a nonproductive course of action and require additional information or choices. Here are three practical ways to increase options for children.

Prevent predictable problems

Prevent problems whenever possible. Authoritative, responsive caregivers understand that young children have a difficult time controlling themselves. They know that it is their responsibility to observe the group for signs that adult intervention is necessary. One way to do this is to identify the times in a group's schedule when things could go wrong and prevent these problems.

---

[15]Chapter 5 describes and explains how to manage an early childhood classroom.

Mrs. Vargas knew that transitions are often stressful for children. Consequently, she made sure that there were as few transitions as possible in the schedule. In spite of this, she had observed and identified two times when transitions were difficult for several of the children. One problem transition was from nap to waking activities. The other troublesome transition was from large group to outside play. She reflected on the transitions and tried to make them as appropriate as possible.

Examples. Transition from nap to waking activities: Some children awoke from their naps before the others but still had to be quiet. Instead of just asking them to sit quietly, she prevented the potential problem by gathering a special group of toys and books for quiet play and then brought these materials out only after the nap. The children chose one of these activities.

Transition from large group to outside play: The teacher cut out and laminated simple squares of different-colored construction paper, and kept them in a basket in the large-group area. At the end of the activity, each child took one square from the basket. She then sent the five children with blue squares to put on coats, and then continued with the other colors. This simple method helped children focus on the transition and seemed to decrease anxiety about it.

Introduce new ideas to children engaged in an activity

Our goal is let play sessions unfold and not to dominate play. Occasionally, however, children benefit from getting ideas from adults. Offer a new idea when it would extend the play or help children get beyond an argument. Sometimes, children will use the idea, and sometimes they will not.

Example. Mrs. Vargas noticed that some of the children had worked cooperatively on building a train from large blocks for about ten minutes. When she heard an argument about who would be the driver of the train, she said, "Here is that book about trains. Look here (points to passengers). We do need a conductor but we need passengers, too. The conductor helps passengers find a seat on the train." Ralph immediately shouted, "I want to be the passenger!"

Introduce new materials into an activity

First, assess the situation and decide whether new materials would be helpful. Second, decide how to present the new materials to the children. One way is to add the new item, simply and quietly, without comment. Another way is to introduce the new materials to work sessions as needed.

Examples. Mrs. Vargas gave red or blue tickets and small suitcases to the train "passengers." She also gave the conductor a hat and a hole puncher with which to punch one hole in each passenger's ticket. Another time, she brought out plastic farm animals and placed them near the children working on building a farm. A final example took place at the playdough table. After children had worked with dough for one day, she brought out new rolling pins, taught them the term *rolling pin*, and asked them how they might use the new item with playdough.

Decrease Options Available to the Child

Occasionally, the problem is not that children need new ideas or materials but that they need *fewer* options. Too many choices can easily overwhelm children, especially impulsive children. Guide children effectively by limiting choices or changing activities.

Limit choices

Making wise choices is a skill that develops over time. Helpful adults teach young children how to make choices from only a few alternatives.

Example. Mr. Claiborne knew that Pae (pronounced "pay") had great difficulty zeroing in on one activity. He helped Pae focus attention and he limited his choices by asking, "You said yesterday that you wanted to write a story about your kitten and you wanted to make labels for your leaf collection. Which of those two things would you like to do first today?"

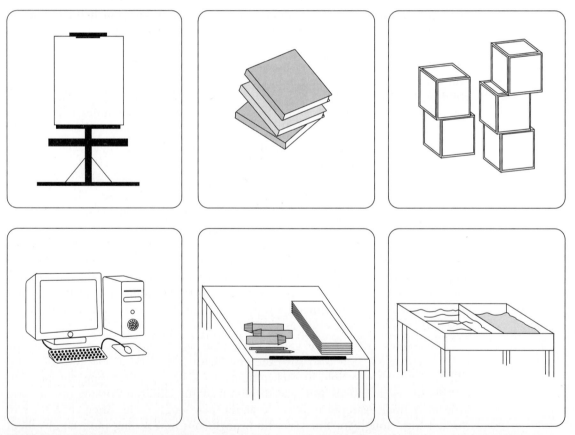

Figure 4.5. Children who have difficulty making choices might benefit from having their choices limited. A child chose three reminder cards out of the six cards to help her stay on track during the morning work session.

Example. A few of Mrs. Vargas's preschool children had trouble making choices during work periods. She helped them by narrowing the number of choices for them. She made a simple card for each center that was available. Each card had a picture on it signaling that center's purpose (Figure 4.5). When Justine arrived at school, Mrs. Vargas showed her the cards and said, "Start with three cards, Justine. Then you will know what you want to do this morning." Justine carried the three cards and worked in those centers.

Change activities

Authoritative caregivers understand that a variety of things might affect children's attention or behavior. They are skillful enough and have enough confidence in their ability to modify plans or to abandon a plan if necessary.

Examples. Mr. Claiborne had just gathered the entire group for story time when the roaring noise started. The earthmovers had come onto the school grounds to start digging the swimming pool. There goes group time, he thought, but remained calm. To the children he said, "Let's walk outside and stand out of the way so that we can watch for a little while. Then I'm going to tell you the story of an earthmover called 'Mike Mulligan!'"

IGNORE BEHAVIOR (ONLY WHEN IT IS APPROPRIATE TO DO SO)

Ignoring behavior: no longer paying attention to a specific action. The **ignore** strategy is appropriate for some behaviors but completely inappropriate for others. Ignoring certain things, when it is appropriate to do so, decreases the number of times that a teacher will see or hear the actions. This occurs because the adult stops giving attention for a behavior to which the adult has mistakenly paid too much attention. The main idea here is for the adult to change what she herself does, reminding herself to stop paying attention to the child's behavior (Figure 4.6).

Do Not Ignore These Behaviors

I usually like to state things as positively as possible. However, in this section I will use the phrase "Do not ignore . . ." several times for emphasis. Some behaviors are clearly dangerous, destructive, or hurtful. Do not ignore them because doing so might well place someone in danger. I will also describe a better way to approach the situation.

Do not ignore children when they treat someone rudely, embarrass someone, are intrusive, are disrespectful, or cause an undue disturbance

Young children do some of these things because they might not yet know a better way of behaving, and some older children may act this way because they have not learned to treat others with respect. With younger children, state guidelines and teach the better way. Avoid ignoring inappropriate behavior. Older children must learn from adults to value politeness, to respect boundaries, and to adhere to limits that convey these values.

Example. Nellie charged right up to the computer station and sat down just as Ralph was about to take his turn. Mrs. Vargas said quietly to her, "You are really anx-

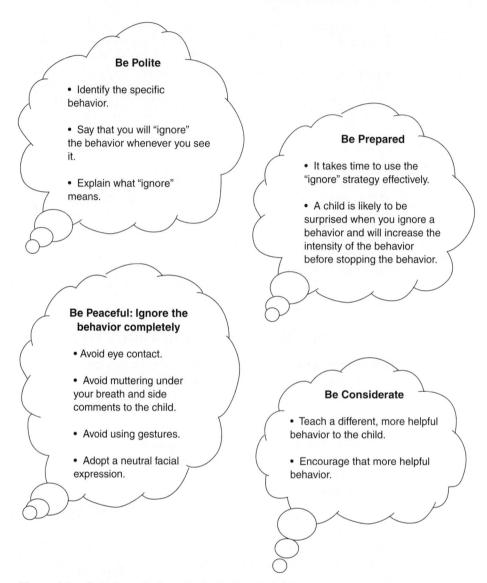

Be Polite

• Identify the specific behavior.

• Say that you will "ignore" the behavior whenever you see it.

• Explain what "ignore" means.

Be Prepared

• It takes time to use the "ignore" strategy effectively.

• A child is likely to be surprised when you ignore a behavior and will increase the intensity of the behavior before stopping the behavior.

Be Peaceful: Ignore the behavior completely

• Avoid eye contact.

• Avoid muttering under your breath and side comments to the child.

• Avoid using gestures.

• Adopt a neutral facial expression.

Be Considerate

• Teach a different, more helpful behavior to the child.

• Encourage that more helpful behavior.

Figure 4.6. Guidelines for ignoring behavior when it is appropriate to do so.

ious to work at the computer, but it's Ralph's turn right now. Let's put your name on the list. You'll get your turn soon!"

Example. Jordan said to a volunteer who told him that it was time to get ready for lunch, "You can't tell me what to do. You're not the teacher." Mrs. Vargas took Jordan aside and said, "Jordan, you were disrespectful to our visitor. It was his job to remind everybody about washing hands before lunch."

Do not ignore a child who endangers anyone, including himself

Authoritative adults do not hesitate to forbid certain classes of behavior, including dangerous, aggressive behaviors or behaviors that degrade others. Adults who ignore dangerous, destructive behavior lead children to believe that the environment is unresponsive to them (Baumrind, 1996). Ignoring aggressive, destructive, or ego-damaging behavior (toward animals as well people) gives it unspoken approval. In this case, the aggression will usually increase, which can also lead other children to think that adults will not protect them from aggressive outbursts.

Do not ignore a child who damages or destroys property

Again, ignoring such destructive or potentially destructive behavior conveys adult approval. Instead, give children a clear, direct, nonblaming message of disapproval for destructive behavior.

Example. Mrs. Vargas kindly, firmly, and simply says to Jordan, "Keep the trike on the path, Jordan. Stop hitting the tree. You'll damage the tree and the trike if you keep banging into it."

Guidelines for Using the Ignore Strategy

It is safe to ignore some behaviors, usually behaviors that are not hurtful, not destructive, not disrespectful, and not dangerous. In fact, it is a good idea to ignore behaviors such as

- whining or arguing about limits.
- any other effort to distract you from following through on a limit.
- efforts to pull you into an argument.
- a child's efforts to try to make you angry.

Adults who use the ignore strategy successfully follow these guidelines:

Tell the child that you will ignore a specific, targeted behavior whenever it occurs

Mrs. Vargas decided to use the **ignore** strategy when Nellie argued about limits. The teacher knows that telling Nellie about the strategy will make things easier. So, she politely but clearly told Nellie that she would stop paying attention to her when Nellie argued about a limit, "Nellie, I've made a mistake and paid attention to you when you argue about some things. I'm not going to pay attention to you when you argue with me. I won't look at you, and I won't talk to you when you argue."

Realize that it takes time to effectively use the ignore strategy

The difficulty is that adults usually give a lot of attention to the very behaviors for which their attention has caused problems for the child. When an adult decides to use the ignore strategy, a child who has received so much attention for unhelpful behavior (such as arguing or whining) will be surprised and is likely to increase the intensity of the arguing or whining. Essentially, her behavior says, "Look here, you've always argued back when I argue. Now you're ignoring me. Looks to me like I have to argue more loudly. Maybe that will get your attention!"

Example. Later that afternoon, Nellie, in her high-pitched voice, argued with Mrs. Vargas about cleaning up the paints. Mrs. Vargas followed through with her plan to stop giving attention to the arguing. Nellie was surprised, although the teacher had explained the procedure. The teacher had paid attention to Nellie's arguing in the past, giving her what she wanted.

Nellie did not stop after the teacher ignored her arguing only one time. Like most children whose irritating behavior is being ignored for the first time, she tried even harder to recapture the teacher's attention by arguing even more insistently. Her teacher was prepared for the "bigger and better" arguments. She knew that she would have to carry out the procedure at least one or two more times before Nellie finally realized that her teacher really had resolved to stop paying attention to her arguing.

Decide to ignore the behavior completely, to give no attention

This is difficult because the adult has decided to change her own customary behavior. In order to help herself stop paying attention to and encouraging the arguing, the teacher wrote the following list of reminders:
"Resist the urge to mutter to myself under my breath."
"Resist the urge to make eye contact."
"Resist the urge to communicate with this child, either with words or gestures."

Teach and encourage more acceptable behavior

Go beyond **ignoring** a behavior to teaching children some other, more appropriate behavior. Mr. Claiborne ignored Vinnie's whining but also remembered to teach Vinnie how to ask for things in a normal voice. Mr. Claiborne modeled the "normal" voice.

REDIRECT CHILDREN'S BEHAVIOR—DIVERT AND DISTRACT THE YOUNGEST CHILDREN

Diverting and distracting: a form of redirection in which an adult immediately does something to distract a child from the forbidden or dangerous activity. The adult then immediately gets the very young child involved in a **different** activity.

Authoritative, responsible caregivers perform most of an infant's or young toddler's ego functions. For example, they remember things for the child and keep the very young child safe, because an infant's or young toddler's concept of danger is just emerging. Authoritative adults accept responsibility for stopping very young children from doing something by setting limits that discourage certain behaviors, but they do so in a helpful way.

Diverting and distracting the youngest children accomplishes both of these tasks. An adult can be most helpful by **immediately** doing something to distract the child from the forbidden activity and steering her toward a different activity.

Example. Mary, 16 months old, walked over to the bowl of cat food, picked up a piece, and started to place it in her mouth. Her father said, "Put the cat food back

Tony's dad used diversion and distraction when he scooped Tony up to get him away from the kitchen where pots were bubbling on the stove. "Oh Tony, look at the puppet!"

in the bowl, Mary" (a short, clear, specific limit). Then he picked Mary up and said, "You know, I think it's time for us to take a walk!"

REDIRECT CHILDREN'S BEHAVIOR—MAKE SUBSTITUTIONS WHEN DEALING WITH OLDER CHILDREN

Substitution: a form of redirection; an adult shows a child how to perform an activity or type of activity in a more acceptable and perhaps safer way. Substitution is an excellent strategy to use with children who are at least older toddlers or young preschoolers. Substitution is a good strategy to use with older children because it acknowledges the child's desire to plan and engage in a specific activity.

The adult must first accept the responsibility of developing the substitutions to demonstrate the first step in the process of problem solving.

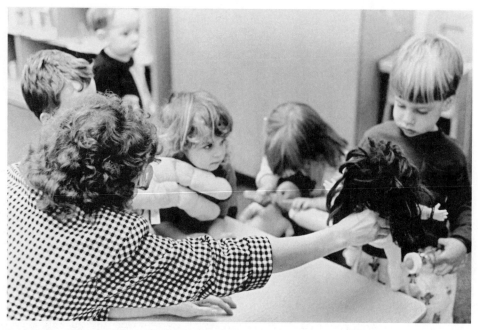

Redirect by using substitution: "You use this doll, Mike, but you may not take Jessica's doll."

Example. Mrs. Vargas saw Justine aim her brush at Calvin's picture. The teacher stepped in and said, "Paint on one of these pieces of paper, Justine, not on Calvin's. Which size do you want to use?" She then led Justine to the other side of the easel.

Children may test adult commitment to substitution by trying the inappropriate activity again—later in the day, the next day, or with a different person.

Example. Justine swung around from her side of the easel to try to paint on Calvin's paper. The teacher stayed calm and simply said, "Paint on your paper, Justine." Justine eventually accepted the substitution because the teacher resisted the power struggle that would have occurred had she become angry about Justine's challenge. She continued to make the substitution quietly and with good will.

Case Study Analysis: Redirection

Redirect by Diverting and Distracting

The teacher in the infant toddler room redirected by diverting and distracting (Chapter opening case study). Answer the following questions about his strategy.

- Focus on the child's actions. Which behavior did he need to stop for Pete, for Julianne, and for Georgio, the toddler?

- He used diversion and distraction three times. From your perspective, was he effective all three times? If yes, explain your reasoning for your decision. If no to any of the three times, state why.
- Suppose that Mr. Thompson used diversion and distraction effectively. Explain what you would do to make the strategy even more effective in one or more examples.
- Explain how **redirecting with diversion and distraction** is developmentally appropriate for infants and toddlers.

Redirect with Substitution

- Explain how Jordan's teacher redirected Jordan successfully. Consider noting when the teacher showed Jordan how to perform the same activity in a more acceptable way. How did Jordan test this substitution? Explain how the teacher effectively dealt with Jordan's testing of the substitution.
- Think about the differences between diversion and distraction and substitution. Why do you think that substitution is especially appropriate for preschoolers and older children?

LISTEN ACTIVELY[16]

Active listening: positive strategy useful when a child "owns" a problem. Adult focuses on what the child says, not interrupting, not offering solutions, listening for the feelings in the words, suspending judgment, avoiding preaching, and then feeding back perception of the feelings.

Example. Mrs. Vargas watched Ralph try to mix colors to get orange paint. She watched as he forcefully jammed one brush in the cup, clenching his jaw at the same time (comment: seemed frustrated), twisted his face in a frown, and blew out a deep breath.

Mrs. Vargas: "Looks like you might be tired of dealing with that paintbrush!"
Ralph: "Yeah, I want to make orange."
Mrs. Vargas: "You want orange but could not get orange?"
Ralph: "I got pink!"

Mrs. Vargas said, "I see that you mixed red and white and got pink." Ralph turned back to the easel and looked at the two paint cups. Teacher continued, "So . . . those two colors together don't make orange."

Ralph replied, "Can I get another cup of paint?" He pointed to different colors.

Mrs. Vargas said, "Sure. Here's an idea. Keep your red paint and put the white away. Get one different color to mix with red." Ralph got blue paint. When that did not work, he tried yellow with the red.

Ralph had a problem and the teacher used active listening to help him work through it. An authori**tarian** caregiver would have dealt with Ralph's rough use of a paintbrush very differently, very likely by punishing Ralph. Authoritarian teachers do not take the time to find out what a child is feeling and thinking, or what is

---

[16]Active listening is described more fully in Chapter 11.

bothering the child. They miss the chance to "hear" what a child's behavior says. Children very often communicate their deepest fears or try to tell adults through their behavior that something is wrong. We will discover what is wrong only if we take the time to listen actively.

Active listening, then, is the skill that responsible adults use when a child **owns a problem,** when something is troubling a child—the child is afraid, is angry, is jealous, cannot do something, or is frustrated. The adult can best help a child by listening actively and responsively to the feelings implied in the child's words.

DELIVER I-MESSAGES

I-message: positive, self-responsible strategy useful when an adult "owns" the problem in a relationship with a child. An adult owns the problem when a child has done something that interferes in some way with that adult's needs. Here are a few examples:

- Child does not clean up after an activity.
- Child interrupts group time quite frequently.
- Child curses at teacher.
- Child takes scissors and cuts into the glue bottle.
- Child tosses library books on the floor.

Adults who see behaviors such as these usually feel afraid, irritated, or annoyed—all normal, natural feelings because the behavior usually tangibly affects the adult in some way. For example, a teacher would have to spend her time cleaning brushes and aprons left by a child; the teacher would have to use her own money to replace the ruined glue bottle.

I-messages are easy to learn to use. It is difficult, however, to use an I-message if an adult has not experienced hearing them. The key to using I-messages well is to acknowledge the feelings of irritation, annoyance, sadness, anger, or fear. Adults who use I-messages well fully realize that a child has done something annoying which has cost them time, energy, or money, but they know that they are the ones experiencing the feelings. They avoid accusing the child of causing these feelings. They simply take responsibility for communicating the feelings to the child in a firm but respectful and nonaccusatory way.

Example. Mrs. Vargas had a discipline encounter with Tahisha, who immediately left a center when the signal for cleanup was given, leaving whatever she had been working on to somebody else (usually the teacher) to put away. Mrs. Vargas knew that she owned the problem, that she was annoyed, and that she should tell Tahisha in a nonaccusatory way. She used an I-message.

Four Parts of Effective I-Messages

Give data

I-messages give data about the child's behavior but avoid accusing a child, i.e., what did you see, hear, smell, touch, taste?

"Tahisha, when I gave the signal for cleanup, I saw you leave the block area and go to another center." (Data: Teacher saw something; child left area without cleaning up. Mrs. Vargas told Tahisha what she saw; but did not accuse.)

Describe the tangible effect

I-messages tell the child how his behavior tangibly affects the adult. Say how the child's behavior has cost you time, effort, and money.

"That means that I would have to pick up the blocks." (Tahisha's behavior tangibly affected the teacher because the teacher would have to do the extra work of straightening the block area.)

Communicate feelings

I-messages tell the child how the adult feels. "I get frustrated when I have to pick up things that somebody else has worked with." (Teacher states the feeling but clearly says that she has the feeling. Mrs. Vargas did not accuse Tahisha of causing that feeling.)

Tell how to change things

If you, an adult, heard an I-message, you would very likely know what to do to change things. A child, however, most often does not know how to do this. In the example above, a child would hear that her teacher was irritated and that the teacher had to do some extra work. The child would not necessarily know what to do to correct the situation. The teacher can follow up an I-message with a simple statement telling a child how to change things: "I want you to come with me to the block area and put away the blocks." (See Figure 4.7.)

Practice Delivering an I-Message

Discipline Encounter: Mr. Claiborne observed Reese walk away from the writing center, having left markers, paper, pencils, and rulers strewn over the table. Moua wanted to use Reese's spot at the table but would have to straighten up first. Mr. Claiborne decided to use an I-message with Reese. Practice writing an I-message by filling in each part.

Give data: (what did you see, hear, touch, taste, smell?)

Tangible effect: (avoid telling about your feelings here)

State feelings:

Tell how to change things:

Reflection: Adults are important models for children. What has Mr. Claiborne modeled for Moua by delivering an I-message to Reese?

Figure 4.7.

TEACH CONFLICT RESOLUTION (PROBLEM SOLVING)

Conflict in Mrs. Vargas's Classroom

Tahisha and Ralph had been working in the block corner, building a road and a yard with a large building. Then Mrs. Vargas heard the shouting.

> Tahisha: "It's a barn!"
> Ralph: "No! It's my garage."
> Tahisha: "It's a barn! It's for the tractor."
> Ralph: "It's for the cars!"

Tahisha stuck the tractor into the building and Ralph thrust it aside, putting his cars into the building. Tahisha, face red (comment: seemed angry), grabbed one of the cars. Ralph grabbed it back and shouted loudly, "Put it **back,** Tahisha!"

Think About Conflict as an Opportunity to Teach a Skill to Children

This teacher knows that conflict is inevitable and not at all necessarily bad. She believes that relationships can become even stronger when people resolve conflicts peacefully and with good will. She believes in supporting children in learning how to recognize and manage conflict. She takes the stand that everybody in the conflict can "win," that there really do not have to be any "losers."

Some teachers might simply punish Tahisha and Ralph by taking away all the blocks or by placing each child in time-out. Both strategies are forms of punishment and do not teach anything positive. The bickering might irritate the teacher but she realizes that her job is to support children in learning a brand new skill—conflict resolution (Clark, 1999; King & Kirschenbaum, 1992; Kohn, 1996; Marion, 1993, 1994; 1997).

You will find that you use other guidance strategies along with the steps described for conflict resolution. For example, you will very likely use **calming techniques, active listening,** or **I-messages** when you teach children how to resolve conflict.

Adults who teach conflict resolution acknowledge that children's needs are important and communicate trust in their ability to construct and carry out decisions. Using this method, therefore, requires that adults truly accept the child's feelings and needs as valid and important. This is not a strategy that an adult can "fake."

Teaching Conflict Resolution

Mrs. Vargas heard the argument and walked quickly to the block corner. "We need to talk, but first, let me just move the car and tractor over here for a minute." She unobtrusively took the car and the tractor and set them aside, then turned to both children. "It sounds as though you have a problem. Two children, one building."

> Tahisha: "It's a barn!"
> Ralph: "No, a garage!"

Mrs. Vargas says, "First, let's take a slow breath." She does deep breathing with them (a calming technique).

She then continued, after checking to see that both children were calm enough to talk, "OK. Listen carefully. You have one building. Tahisha, you want it to be a barn. Ralph, you want it to be a garage. Is that right?" The children nod.

Mrs. Vargas responded, "I see. We do have a problem then. Two children and one building." She then looked at both children. "Let's think for a minute about how to fix the problem. Do you have an idea?"

Tahisha: "Make another building?"
Ralph: "Make this building bigger!"
Mrs. Vargas: "Two ideas! Do you have any other ideas?"
Ralph: "Make a wall right here (points to middle of building). Then we can have a garage and a barn together." (The children had generated these three ideas).
Mrs. Vargas: "Good ideas. Do you have enough blocks for another whole building?" Children decide that they do not have enough blocks.
Tahisha: "We can't make another building, huh?"
Mrs. Vargas: "Probably not. Do you think that there are enough blocks to make the building bigger?"
Ralph looked at the block supply and said, "Yes."

Mrs. Vargas: "How about enough blocks to make a wall to divide the building?" Both children vigorously nodded.
Mrs. Vargas: "Which idea do you want to try—making the building bigger or dividing it to make two parts?"
Ralph: "Let's make it bigger!"
Mrs. Vargas: "Is that OK with you, Tahisha?"
Tahisha: "Uh-huh. If we make it bigger, then we can have a wall, too."

Mrs. Vargas said, "What do you think about that, Ralph? We could use two of your ideas together." Ralph shrugged and nodded, indicating that he agreed.

Mrs. Vargas said, "Tell me the first thing that you can do to get started on making your building bigger." (They discuss this a bit more.) The teacher then says, "OK. Start making the building bigger. Then make the wall and we'll look at how things work out when you are done. Call me if you need help." (See Figure 4.8.)

RECOGNIZE SIGNS OF STRESS, ANXIETY, OR STRONG EMOTION; PREVENT OVERSTIMULATION AND TEACH CALMING TECHNIQUES

Many times, the best thing that we can do for children is to look beyond or under the behavior that we see. You read about the need to observe children's behavior in Chapter 3. Children often have difficulty controlling themselves when they are under stress or when they are anxious (Figure 3.3, Chapter 3). Children often lose control because they are under so much stress (Goleman, 1995). At these times,

---

It's a Barn! It's a Garage!: Steps in Teaching Conflict Resolution to Children*

✓ **Identify the problem and define it as a shared problem.**

Young children do not take the perspective of others very well. Adults have to help them understand that they can share a problem with someone else. Children will likely see the problem mainly in terms of what they want (Ralph wanted a garage, Tahisha a barn). How has the teacher carried out this step?

✓ **Invite children to participate in fixing the problem.**

Children think about what they want, not about solutions. Teachers or parents must get and keep them focused on moving toward solving the problem together. A good, constructivist approach is to invite their participation. How did Mrs. Vargas do this?

✓ **Generate possible solutions as a group.**

This is brainstorming. Encourage a variety of solutions. Do not evaluate solutions at this stage. You might have to teach children not to evaluate now. When did Mrs. Vargas do this?

✓ **Examine each idea for its merits or drawbacks. Decide which idea to try.**

Encourage children to think through each idea. Facilitate an evaluation of each idea and let the children decide which idea to try. Acknowledge the children's participation and thank them for working together. How did Mrs. Vargas do this?

✓ **Work out ways of putting the plan into action.**

Children need help in taking action after coming up with ideas. They do not automatically move from the problem to working on a solution. How did Mrs. Vargas help Tahisha and Ralph start to put their plan into action?

✓ **Follow up. Evaluate how well the plan worked.**

Children need to learn that some plans work nicely and some do not work at all. Teachers have to help them through this process. Children who are just learning how to resolve conflicts might get frustrated when a new idea does not work for some reason. Teachers can then step in and help them figure out why the plan did not work and anything else that they might do to create a better plan. The children learn about "fine-tuning" a plan. When did the teacher do this?"

"We figured out how to make it a barn and a garage!"

*Source: Carlsson-Paige and Levin (1998).

Figure 4.8.

children have difficulty thinking clearly and adults need to help them. We help them best, not by punishing, but by

- recognizing signs of anxiety and stress,
- preventing overstimulation, and
- teaching calming techniques.

Example. Mr. Nellis noticed right away that first-grader Gene was acting differently as they talked about the visit from the firefighter. Gene bit his lip and was very agitated. Mr. Nellis recognized the signs of anxiety and stopped talking about the visit right then.

Instead, Mr. Nellis and the children did their favorite "rubber band" exercise. They stretched out both arms and stretched one as far as they could. Then they slowly brought the arm back to its original position. After this they did slow, deep breathing with their eyes closed. Only then did the teacher proceed with talking about the firefighter's visit. Later, Mr. Nellis discovered that Gene's family home had burned the year before and that several fire engines had responded to the fire. (See Figure 7.3, Chapter 7 for suggestions on teaching calming techniques.)

Example. Mrs. Vargas knew about the effects of a holiday season on preschool children and tried to prevent overstimulation. She realized that many of her students would become overstimulated if she stressed the holiday too much, and the effect would last for several hours or days. She approached holiday seasons carefully. She did nothing to whip the children up into a holiday frenzy. They proceeded with the curriculum, bringing the holiday in only when it seemed relevant to a project at hand, and then in a low-key way.

For Valentine's day, one of the few things that the children did for the holiday was to bake a heart-shaped cake with red frosting. This was a part of an ongoing project about creating colors and color mixing and was really done to focus on helping the children to remember the list of ingredients and the steps in preparing the cake.

See the following Web site for a list of articles on children and stress: *www.extension.umn.edu/distribution/Familydevelopment/components/7269-1.html.*

HELP CHILDREN SAVE FACE AND PRESERVE THEIR DIGNITY

Our most important role is to protect children. Therefore, our ultimate responsibility is to help children save face and preserve their sense of dignity no matter what positive guidance or discipline strategy we use. Authoritarian adults degrade children by using negative discipline strategies. Some continue to humiliate a child; they might tell others about what the child did in front of her, or they might humiliate her by saying "I told you so," or something such as, "Now, let this be a lesson to you," to the child.

Use your perspective-taking skills. Put yourself in a child's place and think about how it would feel to have an adult urging you to calm down. You would want the other person to treat you in a dignified way. Children also deserve dignified treatment.

This means that once you have completed the guidance strategy you let the episode go, let it become history, and allow the child to get on with things. You never bring the episode up again (continuing to refer to an episode from the past is inappropriate). No speech or reasoning is necessary. This is especially important when a child has become enraged and lost control, and you have helped him regain control.

YOUR BELIEFS ABOUT DISCIPLINE INFLUENCE YOU WHEN YOU CHOOSE DISCIPLINE STRATEGIES

> "Memory believes before knowing remembers."
> *(William Faulkner)*

Beliefs Versus Practices

Early childhood professionals study developmentally appropriate practices. They must examine their own practices and their beliefs about those practices. For example, a teacher attends a workshop on appropriate room arrangement and curriculum. The teacher thinks through her curriculum and discovers that she has arranged her room inappropriately. She reflects on this and eventually changes her practice by rearranging her room. The next time she thinks about her room arrangement, she immediately remembers the workshop and the ideas she learned there. She "remembers" her "knowing" (new knowledge) from the workshop.

Another teacher attends a series of workshops on appropriate guidance and discipline. She learns the strategies. She, however, does not use the new strategies in her classroom. In this case, the teacher's past experiences and beliefs about discipline more strongly affect her practices than anything that she learned in formal classes. She strongly believes, for example, that time-out is acceptable and uses it even after learning that it is a form of punishment.

This teacher's "memory" of past experiences, then, "believes" some things about inappropriate discipline; these inappropriate beliefs will be difficult to modify. To make any real changes, this teacher will have to examine her beliefs about discipline before she thinks about specific strategies (Haupt, Larsen, Robinson, & Hart, 1995).

An Opportunity for You to Examine Your Beliefs About Discipline

Take the time to examine what you really believe about discipline. What did you experience as a child? What, if you are already a parent, have you tried with your own children? If you are a teacher or have worked with young children, what strategies have you used? It is important to examine some of this because your experiences so strongly affect what you believe about discipline.

This chapter described many positive discipline strategies. When a person is confronted with such a large number of possibilities there is a tendency to feel overwhelmed. Avoid this feeling by looking at things differently. Adopt an optimistic perspective by keeping three things in mind.

- **Knowledge base.** First, you should be able, at this point in the book, to describe each strategy and state why it would be effective in some cases. That is a knowledge base, the beginning of expertise.
- **Skill building.** Second, you will have a chance at the end of this chapter to build your professional self-esteem by doing some skill development in the **Apply Your Knowledge** section. You will have an opportunity to use several

positive guidance strategies. Then, as you work with children in classrooms, you will practice using these strategies: you will become more skillful over time.

- **Decision-making approach.** Third, this book teaches the Decision-Making Model of Child Guidance (Chapters 1 and 12). It teaches how to make decisions about which strategy to use in specific discipline encounters. You will be able to do this because you have learned and practiced the strategies. Chapter 12 takes you through the Decision-Making Model of Child Guidance and shows you in a systematic fashion how to make wise decisions about which strategy to use.

Case Study Analysis: Positive Solutions for Sarah's Mother

Sarah's mother (in the chapter-opening case study) was embarrassed and angry and used a negative discipline strategy. Boost her confidence as a parent by teaching her more positive ways to deal with the same discipline encounter. Teach the skills that will enable her to use the positive strategies.

Help Sarah's Mom Learn to Set Limits

- Show Sarah's mom how to set a limit, before going to the store, on what they would buy. (Be specific and follow the guidelines for limit setting.)
- People forget things! Suppose that Sarah's mom simply forgot to state a limit. Then, in the store, Sarah started whining. Tell Mom how she could state the limit in a direct, nonaggressive way by saying: _____.

Help Sarah's Mom Teach and Cue More Appropriate Behavior

- Show Sarah's mother how to teach Sarah a new behavior that is different from whining, such as asking for things in a normal, conversational tone of voice. Consider showing her how to model and give direct instruction.
- Show Mom how to use cueing when they are in the store if reminding Sarah is necessary. Explain why it is best to cue her daughter in a matter-of-fact, low-key way in a public place. Be prepared to role-play what this would look like.

Help Sarah's Mom Ignore Behavior

- This time, help Sarah's mom ignore certain behaviors. Suppose that Mom *had* set limits before going into the store and that she had restated the limit when Sarah said she wanted a lunchbox.
- Explain why it would be appropriate to ignore Sarah's whining and arguments once Mom has clearly stated appropriate limits. Tell Sarah's mom specifically how to effectively use the *ignore* strategy in this case. List the essential things that you would tell her to do—or not to do.
- How do you think Mom might feel when Sarah reacts with a bigger and better whine? Give her some hints on how to cope with the feeling and with other adults in the store who say that she "should do something to that kid to stop her squealing!"

Help Sarah's Mom Use an I-Message

- Mom needs to know that even the most positive strategies do not always work. She needs to know what to do when this happens so that she does not start using negative strategies out of frustration again. Suppose that they missed their clinic appointment because Sarah whined, and Mom has to reschedule. Show Sarah's mother how to use an I-message by writing exactly what you think she should say in each section. This skill is easy to learn but difficult to carry out because a person is usually feeling some sort of unpleasant emotion such as irritation, anger, or frustration.
- Name the exact behavior that caused her a problem:
- Say how the behavior tangibly affected her (not how she felt, but the actual effect on her time, energy, and plans):
- Then Sarah's mom has to say how she feels, because Sarah's whining has tangibly affected her. (Remember, the goal is not to induce guilt but simply to say how she feels. Sarah did not cause the feeling.) Mom owns that feeling and says: "I feel _____ because now I _____ ."
- Tell Sarah how to change things:

Help Sarah's Mom Recognize Signs of Anxiety *and Help Her* Preserve Sarah's Dignity

- Children whose goals are blocked experience a great deal of frustration and even anger. They might even lose control. Explain to Mom why it might be best just to withdraw with Sarah to a spot (such as the store's bathroom) and help Sarah regain control. Show Mom how to do this by holding Sarah's hands, encouraging her to breathe deeply, washing her face with a cool cloth, and saying little besides "It'll be OK."
- Help Mom take Sarah's perspective again when they are ready to leave the bathroom. Explain that the other customers will be curious. Tell her how to prevent any further embarrassment for Sarah. I believe that Mom would be most effective if she said the following to Sarah before leaving the bathroom (remember: no speeches, no preaching, and no reminding of limits now. Remind her later. This is the time to let Sarah know that this episode is **over**):
- I believe that, under the circumstances, Sarah should have a choice about whether to continue shopping this day, even if they think they should buy the backpack. I would ask her what she wanted to do by saying: _____.

REFLECTING ON KEY CONCEPTS

1. What do you see as the main focus of a positive, as opposed to a negative, discipline strategy? What is the major difference between the two?
2. Authoritative adults are skillful in using a cluster of positive discipline strategies. Explain to someone who has not read this chapter why it is so important for teachers and parents to understand and know how to use a large number of positive discipline strategies.
3. Some parents will have questions about a school's policies on positive discipline strategies, and some parents will challenge the policies. Describe at least three practical and time-efficient ways in which teachers can help parents understand the child guidance policies of the school, including the use of positive discipline strategies.

APPLY YOUR KNOWLEDGE

Discipline Encounters and Appropriate Solutions: Each adult in the following vignettes faces a discipline encounter. Help the adult deal effectively by offering advice on how to use the specific strategy mentioned. Refer to information in this chapter when writing your solution.

- Discipline Encounter: Cami walked over to the piano and started to bang on the keys. Her teacher called out, "Stop banging on the piano!"

Appropriate Strategy: I think that this teacher would be helpful and effective by telling Cami **what to do instead of what not to do.** The teacher can be positive, polite, and firm as she says, "_____."

- Discipline Encounter: Ed and Jim rode their trikes at breakneck speed and their teacher said, "Stop driving so fast!"

Appropriate Strategy: This teacher would be more helpful and effective by telling the boys **what to do rather than what not to do.** I would advise that she say, "_____."

- Discipline Encounter: Tim's parents had been sitting in the booth at a fast-food restaurant for 15 minutes. They had finished eating and were talking to each other. Three-year-old Tim wiggled off the bench, ran around, and then crawled under the table. His dad scooped him up and told him, "Now, you sit here and be quiet." Five minutes passed, and Tim, who had missed his morning nap, started screaming in frustration. His dad grabbed Tim's arm to try to quiet him, but Tim continued screaming.

Appropriate Strategy: I would **change this situation** by . . . (Note: Tim must be supervised constantly, so sending him to the restaurant's playground is not an option unless the parent goes with him). Start your solution by stating whether you would **increase options, decrease options, or change the physical environment or time schedule** and then state exactly how you would proceed.

- Discipline Encounter: Dad was frustrated when 10-month-old Richard kept crawling right to the uncovered electrical outlets. He said "No-no," every time his son approached the outlet.

Appropriate Strategy: I suggest that Dad **change this situation** by . . .

- Discipline Encounter: John, 4 years old, has been working for 20 minutes in the sand pile constructing a "canal" for water (he has no water yet) when you glance over and notice that he is tossing sand into the air.

Appropriate Strategy: In addition to stating a safety rule, I would **change this situation** by . . .

- Discipline Encounter: Sylvia finger-painted on the window because, she says, she likes how the sun shines on the colors.

Appropriate Strategy: I would **use the following substitution** (Note: The substitution must be appropriate and safe for the child and acceptable to you): _____.

- Discipline Encounter: Jake pulled a chair over to the shelf holding the record player and twisted all the knobs, trying to see how they worked.

Appropriate Strategy: I would **use this substitution:** _____.

- Discipline Encounter: Pat wiped his nose on his sleeve.

Appropriate Strategy: I would **use this substitution:** _____.

1. **Should I Ignore This Behavior?**

   Look over this list and decide which of the behaviors you should not ignore. Which could you safely ignore? Give a rationale for your choices.

- One child tells another child, "You're stupid!" Ignore?

   Yes   No   Reason: _____.

- A 3-year-old girl smashes her playdough creation. Ignore?

   Yes   No   Reason: _____.

- The same child smashes another child's playdough structure. Ignore?

   Yes   No   Reason: _____.

- One of the children in your group forcefully splashes water from the water table onto the floor. Ignore?

   Yes   No   Reason: _____.

- Jan pulled Rachael's hair. Ignore?

   Yes   No   Reason: _____.

- "You clean up! I don't want to clean up. Why do I have to clean up?" a 7-year-old said argumentatively to her teacher. Ignore?

   Yes   No   Reason: _____.

REFERENCES

Baumrind, D. (1993). The average expectable environment is not good enough: A response to Scarr. *Child Development, 64,* 1299–1317.

Baumrind, D. (1996). Parenting: The discipline controversy revisited. *Family Relations, 45,* 405–414.

Bukatko, D., & Daehler, M. (1992). *Child development.* Boston: Houghton Mifflin.

Carlsson-Paige, N., & Levin, D. (1998). *Before push comes to shove: Building conflict resolution skills with children.* St. Paul, MN: Redleaf Press.

Clark, J. I. (1999). *Time-in: When time-out doesn't work.* Seattle, WA: Parenting Press.

Eaton, M. (1997). Positive discipline. *Young Children, 52*(6), 43–46.

Goleman, D. (1995). *Emotional intelligence.* New York: Bantam Books.

Haswell, K., Hock, E., & Wenar, C. (1981). Oppositional behavior of preschool children: Theory and intervention. *Family Relations, 30,* 440–446.

Haupt, J., Larsen, J., Robinson, C., & Hart, C. (1995). The impact of DAP inservice training on the beliefs and practices of kindergarten teachers. *Journal of Early Childhood Teacher Education, 16*(2), 12–18.

King, C. A., & Kirschenbaum, D. S. (1992). *Helping young children develop social skills.* Pacific Grove, CA: Brooks/Cole Publishing Company.

Kohn, A. (1996). *Beyond discipline.* Alexandria, Virginia: Association for Supervision and Curriculum Development.

Marion, M. (1993). Responsible anger management: The long bumpy road. *Day Care and Early Education.* April 4–9.

Marion, M. (1994). Encouraging the development of responsible anger management in young children. *Early Child Development and Care, 97,* 155–163.

Marion, M. (1997). Research in review: Guiding children's understanding and management of anger. *Young Children, 52*(7), 62–68.

Marion, M. (1999). *Guidance of young children* (5th ed.) Uper Saddle River, N.J.: Merrill/Prentice-Hall.

Marion, M., Swim, T., & Jenner, L. (2000). Preconference session, National Association for the Education of Young Children, Atlanta, November.

Marion, M. (2004). *Using observation in early childhood education.* Upper Saddle River, NJ: Merrill/Prentice Hall.

National Association for the Education of Young Children (1998). Code of ethical conduct and statement of commitment—revised 1997 (brochure). Washington, DC: NAEYC.

Niffenegger, J. P. (1997). Proper hand washing promotes wellness in child care. *Journal of Pediatric Health Care, 11*(1), 26–31.

Phyffe-Perkins, E., & Birtwell, N. (1989). Comprehensive child abuse prevention: Working with staff, parents, and children. Presentation at the Annual Conference of the NAEYC, Atlanta, November.

Schaffer, H. R., & Crook, C. K. (1980). Child compliance and maternal control techniques. *Developmental Psychology, 16,* 54–61.

Seefeldt, C. (1993). Parenting. Article in St. Paul Pioneer Press. Sunday, May 23.

Socolar, R. (1995). Spanking children is in even though it's out. *The New York Times,* Jan 15, *144,* Sec. 1, p. 26(L, col 1).

Stayton, D. J., Hogan, R., & Ainsworth, M. D. S. (1971). Infant obedience and maternal behavior: The origins of socialization reconsidered. *Child Development, 42,* 1057–1069.

✓ CHECK OUT THE WEB SITES RELATED TO THIS CHAPTER

✓ **American Psychological Association.** One section of this Web site deals with public communication and news releases. Here are two examples of articles from scholarly publications on discipline:

www.apa.org/releases/behave.html. An article about strengthening parenting skills.

www.apa.org/releases/familystress.html. An article on the relationship between family stress and beliefs possibly leading to harsh discipline.

✓ **Association of Professional Humane Educators**

http://aphe.vview.org. Main Web site for the organization.

http://aphe.vview.org/packrat/index.htm. Index of APHE's quarterly newsletter. A good list of articles that will help children learn about humane treatment of animals. Helps teachers state limits about treatment of animals to children.

✓ **Council for Exceptional Children (CEC).** Here is one of the many resources available from CEC:

http://www.ideapractices.org. Except of a booklet by S. Walsh, B. Smith, & R. Taylor (2000): *IDEA requirements for preschoolers with disabilities: challenging behavior.* Q & A format; designed to help EC general educators understand what the IDEA (Individuals with Disabilities Education Act, amended 1997) requires for children birth through age five and their families. Focuses on discipline requirements in the IDEA: prevention of discipline problems, interference with class activities.

✓ **Cornell University Extension**

www.cce.cornell.edu/publications/children.cfm. An extensive list of publications. Here are two on discipline: "Discipline is Not a Dirty Word (revised 1995), 24 pages, 321HDFS51, $6.25; "Discipline: What Is It?"(1994), Fact Sheet, 321HDFS538, $2.00. Order on-line, by telephone, or by mail.

✓ **Nevada Humane Society**

www.nevadahumanesociety.org/children.htm. Tells how to **set limits** for a young child about how to hold, pet, give attention, and give treats to animals. Specific about the need to supervise closely children's play with a new pet.

✓ **University of Illinois Extension**

http://www.urbanext.uiuc.edu Many links. Go to "Parenting & Seniors,"

www.urbanext.uiuc.edu/family/index.html. Then go to the links "Dealing with Toddlers" and "Nibblers" for information on guidance and discipline.

✓ **University of Minnesota Extension.** An excellent site for information on discipline.

www.extension.umn.edu/. This is the general site for the Extension. It contains many different links, some of them to sources on family life, parenting, and discipline.

www.extension.umn.edu/family. This is the link to family life information. Here is one example of what you can find:

www.parenting.umn.edu. A list of parenting education resources. See the link on the left side of the screen INFO-U for a series of fact sheets. See the facts sheets on discipline.

www.parenting.umn.edu/#pp. An index of parenting education resources, including information on guidance and discipline.

✓ **University of Nebraska Extension**

www.ianr.unl.edu/pubs/family/. This is a list of publications about children and families. Go to the link "childhood" for very good and inexpensive publications on discipline.

✓ **Your state's extension.** Find the Web site for Extension in your state or any state in the union.

Search for information on guidance and discipline.

✓ **NAEYC,** The National Association for the Education of Young Children. This is the Web site of this national professional association for early childhood researchers and practitioners.

www.naeyc.org. Go to the catalogue or resources link. Look for publications or posters on guidance and discipline. Find the Code of Ethics.

Early Childhood Classroom Management: Indirect Guidance

"Accomplished teachers use their knowledge of child development . . .
to design and adjust the physical space . . . the schedule, materials . . . ."
(NBPTS Standards for EC certification, page 71)
"Candidates use their understanding of young children's characteristics
and needs, . . . to create environments that are healthy, respectful,
supportive, and challenging for all children."
(NAEYC, 2001, Guidelines Revision: NAEYC Standards for Early Childhood
Professional Preparation: Initial Level)

CHAPTER 5

After reading and studying this chapter, you will be able to

❑ **Identify** principles of designing DAP early childhood classrooms.

❑ **Summarize** effects of developmentally appropriate and **in**appropriate classrooms.

❑ **List and describe** well-designed and managed activity areas for early childhood classrooms for children aged 3 to 8 years.

❑ **Briefly describe** curriculum, activities, and materials in a DAP early childhood classroom.

❑ **Summarize** research findings on the impact of the physical environment on cognitive development of infants and toddlers.

❑ **Explain** how these findings can help early childhood teachers make decisions about designing the physical environment.

❑ **Explain** several ways to adapt the early childhood curriculum for early childhood–inclusive classrooms.

Case Studies: A Preschool and a Third-Grade Teacher Manage Their Classrooms

Mrs. Vargas's Preschool Classroom

Mrs. Vargas, the preschool teacher, and her assistant teacher use the Project Approach (Helm & Katz, 2001) to curriculum development, working closely with the children, observing, and consulting with them, to determine children's interests. The current project started with a trip to the hardware store to get a gallon of paint mixed for the trike storage shed (the trip was a shared experience for every child in the class). Mrs. Vargas had visited the store ahead of time and talked with the person who would mix the paint, giving her suggestions on what she might say to the children.

The "paint lady," as the children called her, opened the can and showed the light base color, almost white. She showed the paint chip with the color the school needed. Then she used the rotating device holding concentrated colors and carefully added the three different colors they needed to the base color, showing and naming each new concentrated color. "I need a teeny-tiny bit of black," she said, using her thumb and forefinger to illustrate such a tiny amount, "but we need a lot more blue (space measured by finger and thumb widened). Here's the gray—only four drops. Count with me!"

She showed them the base color, now with the dark spots of coloring agents. When she put the paint can on the shaker, she asked, "What do you think is happening to the little spots of paint now? Why do we need to shake the can?" In addition, finally she said, "What do you think that the paint will look like after it has been shaken?" When she opened the can, the children confirmed their hypothesis about a new color and she made a color chip for each child. The teachers decided that a project centering on color and color mixing was appropriate and practical, as well as interesting to the children.

Mrs. Vargas and her 19 4-year-olds investigate things from their classroom base, a busy but calm place. She has organized the classroom into activity areas. The activities in small-group learning centers, for example, reflect the principles of developmentally appropriate practice (hereinafter called DAP) and current projects under investigation. On arrival each day, children find areas ready for work/play, and Mrs. Vargas encourages each child to choose an area. On Monday, the children worked in different areas on the following activities.

Art area

"Squish-squash, closely watch," said Mrs. Vargas as four children joined her around a small table. She had placed one lump of smooth, white playdough that the children had made on Friday in front of each child. Today's focus was to add one drop of blue food coloring to a little depression in each lump of white dough and to encourage squishing, squashing, predicting, observing, and describing color changes. Investigating color changes continued at the finger-painting table, where blue and yellow paint was available, while red and white paints waited at the easel. (The playdough, finger painting, and easel are all art and science activities in this integrated curriculum.)

Library area

This is a serene, quiet, enticing area, with good lighting and high-quality books displayed on the rack. One of the books was about mixing colors, the current topic for the investigators of color in her class. She put out the flannel board with figures for retelling the story of Little Blue and Little Yellow and put out the tape recorder and headset along with a set of pictures illustrating a story on the table.

Writing area

This is also a high-interest area. Mrs. Vargas set out transparencies of the color of the paints mixed for the shed. Children placed the transparencies on top of each other to approximate the new color of the shed. Two children dictated a summary of that process just as the entire group had dictated a thank-you note to the paint store. Now, some of the children wrote notes to parents about the trip, attached their notes to the paint chip, and took the notes home. Two other children wrote in their trays of damp sand with a stick.

Science/math area

Math and science are "hot topics" with these young investigators! Today, they made a graph showing the proportion of each color in the paint for the shed. Mrs. Vargas also placed three ice cube trays with clear water in each compartment on a separate table. Next to each tray were two eyedroppers, one with blue dye and one with yellow, for a color-mixing experiment. The parents have helped the teachers develop many homemade math materials (these items are packaged, labeled, and stored for easy retrieval). Two boys used some of the materials to work on the concept of larger/smaller "sets" on the table. Three other math-related games rested on shelves in the math area.

Dramatic play area

Dramatic play center activities usually stay up for several days, depending on the children's needs. This week, girls and boys working in the "fix-it shop" wore special "inspector" shirts. They checked books and puzzles for needed repairs, inspected trikes for squeaks needing oiling, examined dolls for necessary bathing and washing of clothing, determined whether blocks had splinters and needed light sanding, and inspected animal housing for required cleaning and repair. They dictated needed repairs to a teacher, who wrote them in a notebook. Then, over several days, with a student teacher's supervision, they completed one or two tasks per day from the notebook, checking off completed jobs.

Block area

To follow up their one-half block walk to watch the traffic signal change colors, Mrs. Vargas set out a model traffic signal the children could operate to change its colors. Several of the children worked on building a replica of the street outside the school, with their traffic light at the intersection.

Puzzle and "manipulative" toy area

The school invests a little each year in small, manipulative toys and a good storage system, so Mrs. Vargas has access to a multitude of these items. On Monday she placed three old, frequently used but well cared for puzzles on the table and set two tubs of small, interlocking blocks on the floor. The children could also choose from among seven or eight other manipulative toys stored neatly in clear plastic containers on low, open shelves.

Mr. Pelander's Third-Grade Classroom

Jim Pelander teaches third grade in the Charles Wright Academy in Tacoma, Washington. He has written about his transition from a conventional to a more developmentally appropriate practices (DAP) primary classroom. One of his biggest challenges was to be brave enough to encourage children to make choices and be in control of their learning. For example, he used to list work to be done on the board and each child completed the work in sequential order (Pelander, 1997).

Now he provides a menu of activities that children can complete in any order that they wish. Assignments from the menus are due in seven or eight periods rather than in one period. Children may choose where they sit when working—at their table, on the floor, at a study carrel, or in the library. Here is a sample menu for morning work for a week (Pelander, 1998):

English:

Journal/letter editing
Job cards
Daily oral language
Word search
Spelling
Compose sentences

Reading:

Comprehension cards (2)
Reading skill cards
Critical thinking cards

Handwriting

Five of each lowercase letter (get the coach's signature: _____)

Math:

Diffusion paper (choose either ½ page or full page)
Holey cards: Multiplication
Fraction cards: Write them here: _____, _____, _____, _____, _____
Math safari: Multiplication

Social Studies:

Geo Safari
States puzzles
Choose a "differently abled" book. Read at least four pages and explain what you learned from the book. Explain why what you learned is important. Use complete sentences. Consider doing this with a partner.

Science:

Hypothesis/stop watches (done in pairs; please check boards)

Computer

Math
Oregon trail
    (Check Post-it Notes on management chart)

Writing

Copy your first writing of the year with your opposite hand. With your regular hand, tell about your experience.

This chapter will help you understand what a DAP classroom is like, what it looks like, how it was designed, the type of activities in it, and how a DAP classroom tends to affect children. Most important, the chapter will describe and explain a set of principles that you can apply when designing an early childhood classroom for children in preschools, kindergartens, or the primary grades.

PRINCIPLES OF DESIGNING DAP CLASSROOMS AND EFFECTS OF DAP/DIP CLASSROOMS

At first glance, classrooms for infants, toddlers, preschool, kindergarten, and primary children might seem to have very little in common. A classroom/caregiving space and curriculum for infants would certainly be different from a classroom and curriculum for second-grade children. Preschool classrooms would differ from a classroom for all other age groups in the early childhood years.

Our goal as early childhood educators is to create a developmentally appropriate learning environment for children regardless of their age. All DAP early childhood classrooms share certain characteristics. There is a common thread that ties all DAP classrooms together—that thread is a set of principles, the base for designing space and planning curriculum and activities.

Principles of Designing DAP Early Childhood Classrooms

DAP early childhood classrooms are based on the following principles, which emphasize developmental needs of children; provide options; encourage choice, movement, and interaction; and emphasize positive guidance and concrete experiences.

- **Developmental needs.** Base the design of the physical environment on the developmental needs of the children using the space.
- **Developmentally appropriate curriculum.** Plan a developmentally appropriate curriculum based on the needs, interests, and abilities of the children. Integrate curriculum across traditional domains (math, science, social studies, language arts, music, art) through meaningful and relevant activities in which children are actively involved (Hart, Burts, & Charlesworth, 1997; Krogh, 1995).
- **Learning environment.** Plan and develop a learning environment so that it is full of concrete experiences (Hart, 1993; Hart et al., 1997; Helm & Katz, 2001; Kostelnik, 1992). There are, for example, more stories, music, and center activities in DAP classrooms and more worksheets, waiting, and transitions in developmentally **in**appropriate (DIP) classrooms (Burts, Hart, Charlesworth, Fleege, Mosley, & Thomasson, 1992).
- **Options.** Provide options for children. Do not expect all children to be doing the same thing at the same time (Hart, Burts, & Charlesworth, 1997).
- **Choice.** Encourage children to make choices from among the options.
- **Active involvement.** Encourage children to be actively involved with materials, peers, and adults.

- **Movement.** Arrange space to make it easy for children to move among equipment and materials. Allow and encourage children to move about the room (Caples, 1996; Marion, 1999; Pelander, 1997).
- **Child guidance.** Use developmentally appropriate child guidance and positive discipline strategies (Marion, 1999).
- **Adaptations.** Acknowledge and accommodate individual differences and needs among children (See Figure 5.12, near the end of the chapter. It lists several ways for adapting the curriculum in inclusive early childhood classrooms.)

Effects of DAP Classrooms

Both researchers and practitioners have been interested for quite some time in the effect of a DAP classroom on children's development and behavior (Charlesworth, Hart, Burts, & DeWolf, 1993; David & Weinstein, 1987; Kritchevsky & Prescott, 1977). A classroom based on DAP principles helps children become independent, learn to make sound choices and decisions, and to take initiative (Howes, 1991; Jones & Prescott, NAEYC film #806; King, Oberlin, & Swank, 1990). Several studies suggest that children who attend developmentally appropriate programs have better academic achievement (Marcon, 1993) and fewer behavioral problems (Marcon, 1994) than those in DIP classrooms.

The physical design of the environment and equipment influences children's play and social interaction. Gandini (1993) described the schools in Reggio Emilia, Italy, and said that the layout of physical space in these schools encourages positive encounters, communication, and relationships, all of which are elements of a DAP classroom. The physical arrangement of specific activity areas influences children's play. For example, children engage in more sophisticated dramatic play when play spaces are well designed (Petrakos & Howe, 1996).

Effects of DIP Classrooms

On the other hand, a developmentally **in**appropriate practice (DIP) classroom or program can contribute to poor academic achievement and behavioral problems (Marcon, 1994). A group of researchers has studied and continues to study the effects of inappropriate and more appropriate classrooms on stress in young children. They have found that there are higher levels of stress behavior in DIP versus DAP preschool and kindergarten classrooms. The stress in DIP classrooms contributes to some of the discipline problems (Burts, et al., 1992; Hart, Burts, Durland, Charlesworth, DeWolf, & Fleege, 1998).

SETTING UP THE PHYSICAL ENVIRONMENT: DAP CLASSROOMS FOR PRESCHOOL, KINDERGARTEN, AND THE PRIMARY GRADES

Research done more than 25 years ago demonstrated that children more easily develop self-control, independence, competence, and prosocial behavior in well-organized classrooms (Stallings, 1975). Figure 5.1a is a floor plan of Mrs. Vargas's preschool classroom, and Figure 5.1b is the floor plan of Mr. Pelander's third-grade

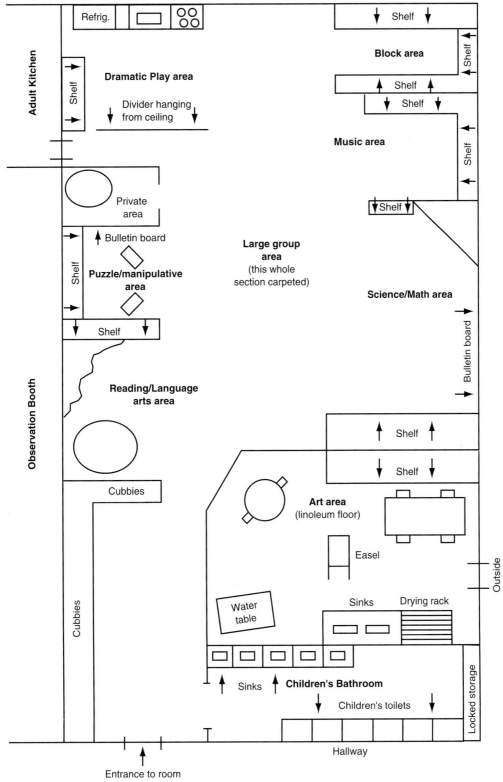

Figure 5.1a. Floor plan of Mrs. Vargas's preschool classroom.

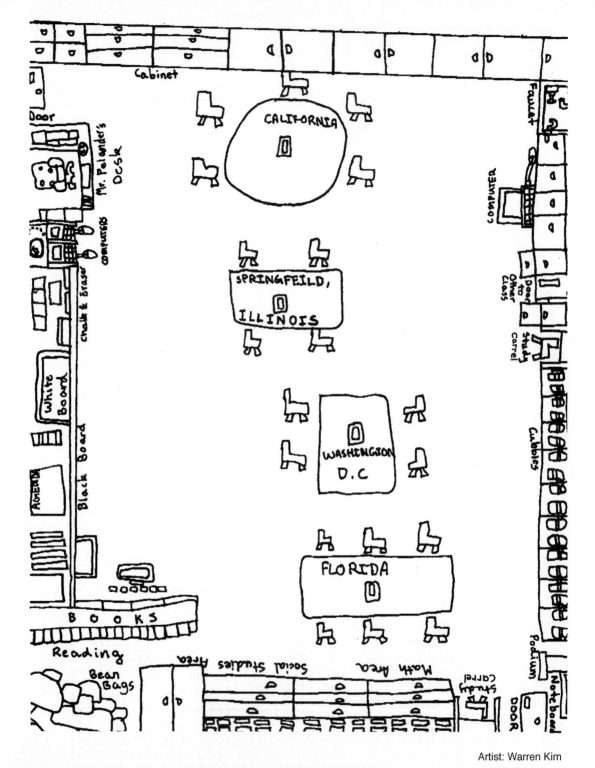

Artist: Warren Kim

Figure 5.1b. Floor plan of Mr. Pelander's third-grade classroom.

classroom (the teachers in the chapter-opening case study). One of Mr. Pelander's third-graders drew the floor plan. These are obviously classrooms for children at different points in the early childhood period, but there are striking similarities.

A big part of early childhood classroom management is managing the physical environment of the classroom as well as the curriculum, activities, and materials. There are several practical things to consider when setting up or designing the physical environment in early childhood classrooms. Teachers must organize the classroom into activity areas and develop enough of them. They have to arrange activity areas logically, create attractive and sensory-rich areas, and use a variety of indirect ways to make it easier for children to work and play in the classroom.

Organize the Classroom into Activity Areas

DAP classrooms are organized into areas or zones of activity. A good classr arrangement of areas embodies the principles of DAP that you just read. In sp this common thread, teachers in DAP classrooms develop and arrange activity that support the overall curriculum goals that have evolved for the children classroom.

There are several different types of classroom activity areas. Some of are small, some large; some have seating, others do not. Specific ma stored in some areas, but other areas have no materials stored there rooms usually contain individual or small-group learning centers, a area, and some sort of a private area.

Learning center: small group

Small-group learning center: permanent or semipermanent space] n for five or six children. Well-designed small-group learning center /ecific function reflecting the age of the children in that class as well as /'s cur- riculum goals. Examples of well-defined small-group areas inc /lowing: math and science, computer center, a "manipulative" area (pu /er small- muscle equipment), library and writing, dramatic play, block /a creative arts area (see Figure 5.2 for two examples).

Teachers in DAP classrooms create the types of centers /ne needs of the children in that class. Therefore, not all classrooms w /same small- group learning centers. One teacher might emphasize wr /ath with per- manent, well-stocked centers for each. Another teacher mig. provide those centers but with far less emphasis, stressing instead art, blocks, and music.

Seating arrangement. The seating arrangement varies with the purpose of each center, making this type of center quite flexible. Some centers call for a table and chairs, as in the preschool's manipulative toy area (Figure 5.2b). Some small-group learning centers do not require a table and chairs, such the preschool's block area or the third grade's reading area. You may also decide to arrange a center so that children can work either at a table or on the floor, as in the preschool's manip-ulative center (Figure 5.2b). Small-group learning centers in DAP classrooms are well separated from other areas, which clearly communicates each area's function.

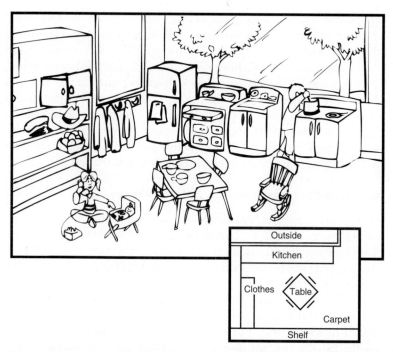

Figure 5.2a.   Dramatic play area set up as a home kitchen. For Figures 5.2a and 5.2b, each center accommodates five to six children. Materials for activities related to centers are stored in the centers. Children have access to some materials but not to others, and know where to return materials when they finish working. Mrs. Vargas uses good boundaries and limits traffic through areas.
(Source: Adapted from Alward, K. R. [1973]. *Arranging the Classroom for Children.* San Francisco: Far West Laboratory for Educational Research and Development. Reprinted with permission.)

Some primary teachers who have taught in traditional classrooms are gradually moving toward a more developmentally appropriate approach. This entails allowing children to choose the order of the activities that they will complete in a work period and then giving children more choices about where they work. Pelander (1997) said that during work periods children in his third-grade classroom have the choice of sitting at one of the tables, on the floor, or at a study carrel (Figure 5.1b).

Materials for the center. Store materials related to the activity in the area. Avoid storing materials **not** related to the function of the area in that location. Guide children indirectly by storing materials to which you want children to have access within their reach; store materials, however, to which you do not want children to have access out of their reach. Store items not currently in use, for example, in closed cabinets or on higher shelves (Figures 5.2a and 5.2b).

Learning centers for small groups change over time. Small-group learning centers in DAP classrooms change as the needs, interests, and abilities of the children change and as they engage in different projects. Teachers in DAP classrooms,

Figure 5.2b. Puzzle and manipulative area (small-group learning center).
(Source: Adapted from Alward, K. R. [1973]. *Arranging the Classroom for Children*. San Francisco: Far West Laboratory for Educational Research and Development. Reprinted with permission.)

in their long-range and daily planning, evaluate the learning centers for modifications that might be needed. They regularly add materials for new activities, rearrange the seating of a center as needed, reorganize materials as necessary, and remove materials no longer required.

Example. At the beginning of the school year Mrs. Vargas set up the dramatic play area as you see it in Figure 5.2a. The children enthusiastically used the center for a while but then she noticed less and less play in that area in spite of placing different items of interest in the kitchen area.

Mrs. Vargas concentrated on changing the area to rekindle interest in dramatic play. She recruited parent volunteers to develop prop boxes (Myhre, 1993) and collected some great dress-up clothes. The "office," the "backyard," the "gardening center," and the "fix-it shop" (see the case study opening this chapter) were all hits. In the "backyard," children used a small picnic table, umbrella, toy lawn mower set on a green carpet, and hand gardening tools along with a planting tray for starting plants from seed for the outside garden.

Figure 5.3. Individual learning centers. There are many easy and inexpensive ways to create individual centers.
(Source: Adapted from Alward, K. R. [1973]. *Arranging the Classroom for Children*. San Francisco: Far West Laboratory for Educational Research and Development. Reprinted by permission.)

Learning center: individual

Some early childhood teachers include learning/work centers for individuals when designing their classroom. Mr. Pelander, the third-grade teacher, put in individual study areas and computer desks for individuals (Figure 5.1b). Figure 5.3 shows several examples for creating individual learning or work centers. This is a flexible area because the same comments about seating arrangements and materials for the small-group learning area also apply to individual learning centers. These centers block some stimulation, allowing a child to concentrate on a specific activity. They also give children a chance to work alone in a busy classroom.

Example. Mr. Nellis, the teacher in the mixed-age K–2 classroom, developed three individual learning spaces in one corner of his room. When children chose their activity, he often asked them where they would like to work. "Where would you like to write your story, Philip? You can sit at the big table with the other boys or you can pick one of the one-person work stations. There is still a space open in the one-person work stations. Which would you prefer today?"

Large-group area

Large-group area: a space large enough to accommodate most or all of the children for large-group activities (Alward, 1973) or several children during a work period. This space should be large, open, and flexible to accommodate group activities such as music, language arts, creative dramatics, stories, nutrition education, dance, and other activities that a teacher thinks would be appropriate to do as a group.

Seating arrangement. This depends entirely on the activity that takes place in the area. Some preschool teachers have a permanent large-group area in their rooms (Figure 5.4). Some teachers move a table or two to make room for a large-group activity. The third-grade classroom teacher does a large-group activity in several ways. Mr. Pelander's children sometimes sit at their group tables, and at other times the class pushes aside a few tables and they sit in chairs or on the floor for a group activity.

Materials for the center. The large-group area serves many purposes. Therefore, specific materials are not stored in the large-group area but are brought there by the teacher. Mrs. Vargas, the preschool teacher (see Figure 5.4), has brought items for an obstacle course to the large-group area.

Many teachers do store items there that help them manage the large-group area well, such as individual pieces of carpeting that can be arranged in seating patterns and indicate to children where they are to sit before group begins. Some teachers keep items there used in transitions out of large group (picture cue cards or printed names, for example, or the puppet that introduces the activity for the day).

Private space

Private space: a small, partially enclosed space with room for only one or two children, visually isolated from other children but easily supervised by adults (Bowers, 1990; Marion, 1999). There are no chairs, tables, or special materials in the private

Figure 5.4.   Large-group area in a preschool classroom. The teacher has set up an obstacle course in the large-group area. It provides exercise as well as focus on the abstract words "in, out, through" and the verbs "tumble, crawl, jump, wait."
(Source: Adapted from Alward, K. R. [1973]. *Arranging the Classroom for Children.* San Francisco: Far West Laboratory for Educational Research and Development. Reprinted by permission.)

area. Figure 5.5 shows the private space for Mrs. Vargas's classroom. A teacher would follow the same principles for developing a private space for a kindergarten or primary classroom.

Reason for having a private space

Healthy systems acknowledge the right to privacy and the right to choose or limit contact with others. Teachers in DAP classrooms pay attention to the needs of both the entire class and of individuals. Like adults, children need breaks from large groups. Well-designed private spaces can help us make a special effort to teach children how to take these breaks and to pace their interactions (Bredekamp, 1987). Children encouraged to pace their interactions and control the degree of contact they have with others tend to be more independent and cooperative than children who are not permitted such control (Stallings, 1975).

Classroom management of the private space

Manage this part of your classroom well by clearly defining how everyone—teachers and children—may use the private space. Make sure that every adult who works in your room knows that the private space is a place of refuge and relaxation. Never

Figure 5.5a. Private area in the preschool classroom. No special materials are stored here. There is room for one child. The private area is a place for quiet relaxation.

use the private area as a time-out/punishment area, *never.*[17] Make sure each child knows that she can retreat to this spot to be alone and will not be disturbed. Teach each child the strategies for politely telling another person that he does not wish to be disturbed when in the private area. Set and state limits about the number of children who may use the private space.

Develop Enough Activity Areas

The principles of designing DAP early childhood classrooms call for children to have choices, to move about the classroom, and to be actively involved with materials, other children, and adults. Teachers who put this principle into action design a classroom with enough activity areas so that children do indeed have choices, are actively involved, and can easily move from one activity to another.

Consider the number and age of the children in the classroom when deciding how many of each type of area to include in the room. Provide one third more spaces than there are children so children can change activities without having to wait. The general formula is $x = n + (n \div 3)$ where x = number of spaces needed and n = number of children in a classroom.

---

[17]Time-out is punishment and is an **in**appropriate practice. Teachers in DAP classrooms do **not** use time-out.

Example. A kindergarten classroom for 21 5-year-olds would need 27 work spaces—$x = 21 + (21 \div 3) = 27$ spaces, or one third more spaces than children. This means that any child who completes a project in one area can move on to another activity because there are always more work spaces in the classroom than there are children. These 27 spaces might consist of one small, private space, five small-group areas, and a large-group area.

Example. Mr. Pelander's third-grade class has 18 children. This classroom (Figure 5.1b) has six learning centers based on the needs of his children—reading, social studies, math, art, science, and writing centers. In addition, there are three computers, an individual study carrel, and room for large-group activities. Applying the formula here, $x = 18 + (18 \div 3) = 24$ spaces.

Figure 5.5b shows how many of each type of space would be useful, depending on the number and age of the children. It is possible to create a classroom that is too "busy," so it is wise to avoid filling your classroom with so many activity areas that children are overstimulated, frustrated, and unable to move around easily.

Arrange Activity Areas Logically

Another important step in designing a DAP physical environment is to logically arrange activity areas. Do this by thinking about the type of work or play in each center, by separating centers from each other, and by regulating the flow of traffic in the classroom.

Type of play in each center

Design centers that are both stimulating and peaceful. DAP classrooms contain quiet, purposeful, enthusiastic, and even vigorous interaction. DAP classrooms,

Number of Activity Areas Needed Based on Ages and Numbers of Children in Class				
Area	Ages of Children	Number of Children in Class		
		up to 9	10–14	15–24
Private area	3–4	1	1	1
	5–6	1	1	1 or 2
	7–9	1	1	1 or 1
Small-group area	3–4	1	3	4 or 5
	5–6	2	3	4 or 5
	7–9	2	3	5
Large-group area	3–4	1	1	1
	5–6	1	1	1
	7–9	1	1	1

Source: Adapted from Alward (1973).

Figure 5.5b.

however, **are not** excessively noisy. Recent research shows that a DAP classroom is a far less stressful place than is an inappropriate classroom with excessive noise and seemingly unconnected or purposeless activity (Burts et al., 1992; Hart et al., 1998).

"Quiet" learning centers. Some learning/play centers lend themselves to relatively quiet, less vigorous work or play. Children tend to sit or stand and work quietly on projects or activities in these centers even if they work with several other children. This does not mean that children are silent in these centers. On the contrary, children in DAP classrooms talk quite a bit as they work together on math, at the computer, or on puzzles. The overall tone of these quiet centers is simply more subdued. The quiet centers typically include:

- private space
- library/writing centers (reading, writing, listening)
- science
- math
- puzzles and other small-table toys
- computer center

"Less quiet" learning centers. Other learning/play centers lend themselves to somewhat noisier, more vigorous work or play. Children seem to move around more in certain centers because the nature of the work or play encourages a lot of movement. As they move around, children engaged in these centers tend to talk to each other. Activity in these centers is less subdued than in the quieter centers, but still not excessively noisy. This movement and talk is what makes certain centers into less quiet learning centers, which typically include:

- dramatic play
- blocks
- physical education
- music
- arts
- water or sand table
- large-group area

Logically arrange areas so that quieter areas are placed near other quiet areas and so that they are well separated from areas encouraging more active play.

Example. Figure 5.1a shows how Mrs. Vargas appropriately placed the dramatic play area near the block area because both are high-activity areas and dramatic play flows so easily from one to the other. She wisely placed the language arts center close to the puzzles/manipulative toy center, with both of these centers well separated from the noisier areas. She also developed and clearly stated limits on noise level. Children in her class work and play together without disrupting other people, and she emphasizes everyone's right to a quiet place in which to work. The children are learning that one of their basic classroom values is respect for the rights of others, including the classroom animals.

Create physical boundaries for areas

You learned about setting appropriate limits in Chapter 4. Here, you will learn why it is necessary and how to create good **physical boundaries, or physical limits** for activity areas.

Creating proper boundaries for activity areas is not trivial. It is both age and individually appropriate. Creating good boundaries among areas is age appropriate because all children need to know how to function in the physical environment, and good boundaries give them good cues. Creating good boundaries is individually appropriate because some children especially need help understanding limits and boundaries.

Creating good boundaries may well be one of the most appropriate things you do for children from chaotic, disorganized homes. People in **un**healthy systems tend to violate the psychological and physical boundaries of others. One of the clearest marks of a healthy system, however, including a developmentally appropriate classroom, is the idea of clear and distinct boundaries. These boundaries include psychological boundaries (e.g., no hitting, no name-calling) and the physical boundaries within the classroom itself.

On a practical level, this information tells us to very clearly define and properly separate classroom areas from each other. Children tend to be more cooperative and far less disruptive when they understand where one area ends and the next begins (Olds, 1977). Clear physical boundaries, along with well-organized materials, also help children know where each piece of equipment belongs and encourage them to put things in their proper areas.

There are "inset pictures" in Figures 5.2a and 5.2b showing how each area looks from an overhead view. You can see in these insets how teachers have separated each area from the rest of the classroom. Figures 5.3 and 5.6 show close-ups of ideas for practical and efficient boundaries.

Define good "traffic patterns" in a classroom

Classrooms that have well-arranged activity areas and good physical boundaries give children cues about the traffic pattern in the room (Kritchevsky & Prescott, 1977). The **traffic pattern** refers to the flow of movement in an early childhood classroom. DAP early childhood classrooms encourage children to move about the room through logical traffic patterns. Good traffic patterns are created with **open pathways** that clearly lead to areas and that make it easy for children to move among areas (Colbert, 1997). (Try this: in Figures 5.1a and 5.1b, use your finger to trace a path from the entrance of the room and then around the room to the bathroom and each area. Read the next paragraph and judge how effective the traffic plan is in each room.)

Make pathways wide enough for wheelchairs, long enough to make moving among areas easy, and short enough to discourage running. Regulate traffic by making only one entrance to a center, and develop a closed circuit around the room with the pathway so that children may stop off at each center if they wish (Bowers, 1990).

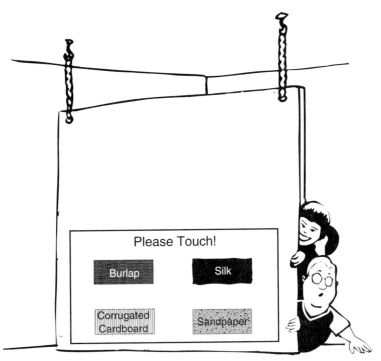

Figure 5.6. One example of how to create boundaries between activity areas. Other figures of the preschool classroom show that the teacher has used shelves and other dividers as boundaries. The teacher has also used one side of the boundary marker to create a "touch wall."
(Source: Adapted from Alward, K. R. [1973]. *Arranging the Classroom for Children*. San Francisco: Far West Laboratory for Educational Research and Development. Reprinted by permission.)

Create Attractive, Sensory-Rich Activity Areas

Children who spend a large part of their day in a classroom have a right to a clean, attractive, and sensory-rich space. The design of the room does not have to be extravagant, and furnishings need not be expensive. However, a children's classroom should be aesthetically pleasing and serene. One good way to create such an environment is to pay attention to such seemingly commonsense matters as lighting and the sensory environment. Following are several specific and practical suggestions.

Strive for a sensory-rich but clean and uncluttered classroom

Many early childhood teachers do a good job of adding interesting items to the classroom, but it is also important to weed out items that have served their purpose. A cluttered, disorderly, or dirty room is unpleasant and distracting. Eliminating clutter helps children focus on new material because the number of stimuli to which they must attend is decreased (Alexander, 1996; Marion, 1999).

Example. Mrs. Vargas realized that lots of the children in her class were fascinated by all the butterflies in the area, so she encouraged the study of butterflies. After adding a beautiful book on butterflies, two large color photographs, and several real butterfly models to the science area, she was puzzled at the children's lack of interest. A close look at the science corner showed that the butterfly book was on the table with old cups of seeds, the rock collection, a magnet, and a magnifying glass. The pictures had been pinned to a somewhat cluttered bulletin board, the butterflies dwarfed by a large, green plant.

Mrs. Vargas cleared the table and the bulletin board, and then set out only "butterfly" things—the collection of butterflies, books, and the magnifying glass. She arranged the pictures of butterflies attractively on the bulletin board so that they were the central focus. She also placed a picture of butterflies on the door of the classroom with a note to parents to "join us in learning about butterflies."

Modify the lighting

Skillful use of lighting is an indirect method of guidance. Many schools are equipped with bright lights, and although it is desirable to have adequate lighting, it is boring, stressful, and overly stimulating to be in a harshly lighted room for an extended period of time. Classrooms are often equipped with only one or two light switches, giving adults only two options: all the harsh lights on or all of them off. Installing dimmer switches is quite inexpensive and enables teachers to control the intensity of lighting in different sections of the room.

Modify ceiling height or floor level

Create safe, cocoonlike spaces that define the areas in a classroom. Many schools, for example, build a safe, inexpensive platform (see Figure 5.7) to give some dimension to the flatness of a room. Children use platforms for a variety of activities. My university lab school also made good use of the space **under** a platform to house the manipulative/writing areas. Figure 5.7 shows the platform right next to the block area with block storage and play under the platform.

Further, consider defining an activity area by draping strips of cloth across and between dowels hung from the ceiling. This strategy softens an area and room and actually makes the ceiling appear to be lower, especially useful when children need a private, quiet, partially enclosed activity area. This idea can be applied to almost any area in the room.

Example. Mrs. Vargas, in her first year at her school, was disappointed that the children did not seem to enjoy the reading area. She followed Colbert's advice (1997) and assessed the area. She drew a floor plan of the reading area and decided that she needed to make some changes:

- Use bookshelves to better separate the reading area from other areas.
- Add a fluffy carpet.
- Place large pillows against a wall.
- Suspend cloth across two rods hanging from the ceiling.

Figure 5.7. A platform set in a corner against the wall in a kindergarten classroom. The platform is next to the block area and the space under the platform is a storage/play area for blocks.
(Source: Adapted from Alward, K. R. [1973]. *Arranging the Classroom for Children*. San Francisco: Far West Laboratory for Educational Research and Development. Reprinted by permission.)

- Occasionally, but not always, play soft classical music in the area (one dad suggested this because his family likes this type of music and plays it while they read).

The children loved their new area and reading activity soared. They even make special requests for specific music while they read.

Modify the sensory environment

DAP classrooms are pleasant and attractive because the teacher has created visual, auditory, olfactory, and textural interest.

Create visual interest. Enhance the aesthetic appeal of your early childhood classroom by keeping it clean and tidy. Make a real effort to keep clutter to a minimum. Judiciously add well-chosen, inexpensive items such as paintings, posters, safe green plants, photographs of the children, cloth hangings, and artwork. Do not feel compelled to fill every square inch of wall space with these things, though. Leave some blank space where children get relief from stimulation.

Create auditory interest. We have already discussed the importance of a calm and peaceful environment where children are free to move and to talk but not to make excessively loud noise. It is much easier to use sound to create a pleasant environment in such a calm environment. How pleasant and relaxing it is for children to be able to hear their favorite composer's music when they arrive at school! Other sounds help create this kind of atmosphere if the children are tuned in to the sounds and are not distracted by unnecessary noise. Some ideas:

- New musical instruments
- The gerbil gnawing a box, scratching around in his bedding, running in his wheel
- A tinkling mobile
- The quiet hum of the computer
- Other ideas?

Create olfactory interest. Exquisite fragrances (lilac shrubs in bloom as we brushed by, the garden after a rainfall, homemade bread, fresh oranges shared with a friend) often call forth joyful memories. Other odors trigger unpleasant memories (the disinfectant odor of a hospital, the skunk odor reminding us that one of the critters sprayed the dog).

Here are some easy ways to make a classroom pleasant through fragrance. Start by eliminating unpleasant odors by maintaining cleanliness. Add pleasant aromas from safe sources:

- Bake bread, muffins, or cookies.
- Vary ingredients in baking, urging children to identify scents.
- Add food-grade extracts such as peppermint, orange, or almond to playdough.
- Place inexpensive scented soap in the bathroom on occasion. Introduce this at group time with reminders about hand-washing procedures.
- Occasionally place safe (real) flowers at the snack table or in the library (in a plastic vase).
- Place safe fragrance-filled plants in the room or yard.
- Other ideas?

Create textural interest. DAP means attending to needs of individual children, and children with impaired sight benefit perhaps to a greater degree from a room rich in textures. All children benefit from such a room, however. Some ideas:

- If appropriate, install carpet on selected sections of the floor. Carpet on certain sections of the wall is also a nice touch.
- Cover bulletin boards with cork or burlap.
- Hang a children-created large collage of cloth scraps.
- Create a **touch wall** with an expanse of corrugated paper and other materials (see Figure 5.6 for an example).
- Clear one wall of all signs and pictures and put up a fabric wall hanging.
- Make it a custom in your classroom to hang a differently textured fabric in a place where children are likely to see and want to touch it; for example, near lockers or cubbies. You will have created a way to start conversations with children who touch the fabric; you can ask, "How did the new fabric feel when you touched it? Did it feel the same as the strip of burlap we had up last week? How did it feel compared to the silk?"
- Other ideas?

Specific Indirect Guidance Ideas for the Physical Environment[18]

Our goal in managing an early childhood classroom is to be helpful to children. We can manage the classroom, for example, so children have an easier time cleaning up the block corner. We can manage group time so that it is easier activity in which to participate. We can manage things so that all children can more effortlessly choose their next activity. We can help children by using indirect guidance in the physical environment in many ways. Here are a few ideas. What is the possible benefit to the child when the teacher uses any of these indirect guidance methods?

- Unit block shapes painted on front of the shelf on which the blocks go. (Benefit to the child?)
- Musical instrument shapes painted on pegboard for hanging instruments. (Benefit to the child?)
- Transparent storage tubs for art or writing materials. If not transparent, attach a sample item from the box to the end of the tub facing the room. (Benefit to the child?)
- Paint apron on the back of each chair for a messy activity. Aprons right next to a water table. (Benefit to the child?)
- Picture choice cards for available activities. Used by teacher in transitions or by children throughout work time. (Benefit to the child?)
- Day planner—an index card on which a young child draws or writes a daily plan for activities. (Benefit to the child?)
- Carpet squares arranged in a specific pattern before group activities, such as semicircle, cluster, lines, circle. (Benefit to the child?)
- Symbol (animal, flower, etc.) for each child placed in the child's cubby or on locker door. (Benefit to the child?)
- Pictures or drawings of children properly washing hands placed over sink. (Benefit to the child?)
- Song about playground limits. (Benefit to the child?)

CURRICULUM, ACTIVITIES, AND MATERIALS IN A DAP EARLY CHILDHOOD CLASSROOM

Curriculum

A DAP curriculum for young children is based on how young children think and learn (Berk & Winer, 1995; Bredekamp & Rosegrant, 1992; Charlesworth, Hart, Burts, & DeWolf, 1993). Hart, Burts, & Charlesworth (1997), in a chapter on integrated developmentally appropriate curriculum, express concern about the

---

[18]I thank one of the reviewers for the suggestion to include ideas such as these in this chapter. I have gathered these ideas from many classrooms in which I have observed.

emphasis on instruction for young children that is merely a copy of the type of formal instruction used in upper elementary grades. Several years ago, Charlesworth (1985) warned that this type of skill-based instruction fails to meet the developmental needs of young children.

Children, then, are the source of a DAP curriculum and teachers who are good at observing children's development in all areas can develop activities that nurture children's growth in those areas (Helm & Katz, 2001; Marion, 2004; Williams, 1994). Teachers who maintain DAP classrooms believe that young children learn in an active, not a passive, way. They believe that young children **construct** or build knowledge as they interact with people and things (Berk & Winsler, 1995; Piaget, 1952; Vygotsky, 1978). Therefore, teachers in DAP classrooms tailor the curriculum to **meet the needs of every** child.

Teachers in DAP classrooms offer options to children and allow children to participate in ways that best suit each child's learning style. The DAP curriculum is integrated rather than being compartmentalized into separate areas. Teachers provide concrete experiences that actively involve children. Play is an integral part of the DAP curriculum and is valued by teachers inside as well as outside the classroom (Hart, 1993; Hart et al., 1997; NAEYC, 2001).

Example. Mrs. Vargas (from the case study) focuses on literacy in her integrated curriculum. She wants her children to know how reading and writing, as well as listening and speaking, are useful before she carries out any type of formal instruction. Her encouragement of literacy pervades the curriculum and is evident throughout the room. Here are just a few examples:

- Large sheets of paper and pencils for writing/dictating stories about play in block and dramatic play areas.
- Several types of paper, markers, pencils always available for drawing, writing, copying, inventing, spelling.
- Charts displayed and changed when appropriate, such as the arrival chart with the printed name of each child. Next to the printed name is a space for a child to copy his or her name with a dry-erase marker. Parents sometimes help.
- Menus for each day's food (snack and lunch) displayed near cubbies. Parents and children read the menus.
- Large recipe cards for one or two items occasionally displayed during snack or lunch. Children and teachers read the recipes, recalling steps in preparing the food as they eat.
- Chart with pictures of all the new vegetables and fruits that the class has tried. Words describing each item next to the picture; e.g., for the raw carrot—crunchy, orange, sweet, hard. Words describing the cooked carrot—soft/not crunchy, orange, sweet.
- "Emotions" chart, with a drawing of a happy face on one side of the chart. Children and teacher generate several synonyms for "happy" and list them on the other side of the chart.
- Tickets issued to watch a video. Tickets contain the name of the video.

Activities

Activities in a DAP classroom come from a careful analysis of what might help children answer their questions about a topic. DAP activities help children investigate topics that interest them. Teachers assist children in identifying topics of interest and then develop activities that will help children investigate their topic. Teachers and children go through two phases in deciding on activities that will be a part of the investigation (Helm & Katz, 2001).

Phase one

The first step in developing a project is usually a shared experience. The event that all the children experience triggers interest in a topic and then becomes a project. Teachers lead children in asking questions about the event, i.e., children generate questions about "What we want to know." The teacher creates a web of the questions (Helm & Katz, 2001).

Examples. A kindergarten class generated questions about a recycling truck that they had seen when they were on the playground. Their teacher created a web of questions about the truck (Figure 5.8a).

Mrs. Vargas's preschool class generated questions about colors after the shared experience of the trip to the paint store (in the chapter-opening case study). Mrs. Vargas created a web of their questions (Figure 5.8b).

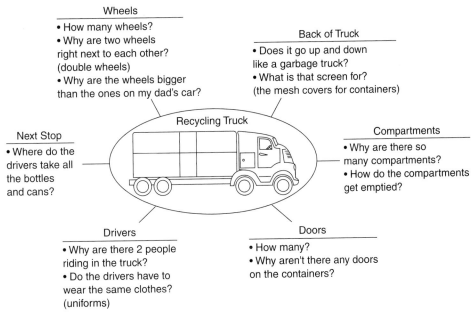

Figure 5.8a. This is the web of questions about the recycling truck that the kindergartners created and the teacher recorded.

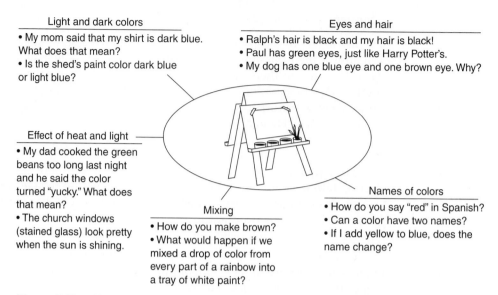

Light and dark colors
• My mom said that my shirt is dark blue. What does that mean?
• Is the shed's paint color dark blue or light blue?

Eyes and hair
• Ralph's hair is black and my hair is black!
• Paul has green eyes, just like Harry Potter's.
• My dog has one blue eye and one brown eye. Why?

Effect of heat and light
• My dad cooked the green beans too long last night and he said the color turned "yucky." What does that mean?
• The church windows (stained glass) look pretty when the sun is shining.

Mixing
• How do you make brown?
• What would happen if we mixed a drop of color from every part of a rainbow into a tray of white paint?

Names of colors
• How do you say "red" in Spanish?
• Can a color have two names?
• If I add yellow to blue, does the name change?

Figure 5.8b. Mrs. Vargas used the children's questions to create this web of questions about colors.

Phase two

This step involves deciding on activities that help children begin to answer their questions. The investigation of the topic with different activities spans several days (Helm & Katz, 2001).

Example. The kindergarten teacher arranged the following activities to help her students answer some of their questions about the recycling truck:

- Day 1. Visit from recycling truck and driver. Children observed, and asked questions of the driver. Back in the classroom, they dictated their observations to the teacher, who listed the observations on a chart.
- Day 2. Children began constructing their own recycling truck from cardboard and other safe recycled items. They put together a driver's uniform from clothing in the dramatic play area. They printed a sign for their truck. The teacher showed a film about recycling trucks.
- Day 3. Construction of the recycling truck continued. One of the fathers brought his heavy-duty pickup truck to school to show the double wheels. Children asked questions about double wheels. They doubled the wheels on the back of their mock-up of the recycling truck.
- Day 4. Children collected classroom items for recycling, placing them in the recycling bins of their truck. They made up a recycling song to the tune of "Bingo."
- Day 5. The children dictated a letter to parents about their project in progress. The teacher documented the project with photos, which she placed on a photo board in the classroom. The teacher also duplicated the letter and sent it home with each child.

- Day 6. The children invited the principal to see their truck and the photo display. They talked to him about their project, teaching him the recycling song.

Case Study Analysis: Rating Scale
Preschoolers Investigate Colors and Color Changes

Review Figure 5.8b, which lists questions generated by Mrs. Vargas's preschoolers about colors. Then review the case study for Mrs. Vargas's class and pick out the activities that help the young investigators answer questions about colors or color changes.

1. From your perspective, how well will the activities help children answer some of the questions? Circle the number on this numerical rating scale that best indicates your judgment.

    1 is a waste of time

    2 will not be very helpful

    3 will make no difference

    4 will help but not extremely so

    5 will be extremely helpful

2. State the reasons for your analysis: _____

Criteria for DAP activities

Early childhood activities, whatever the project and whatever the questions investigated, are developmentally appropriate when:

- there is a wide, but not overwhelming, variety of age-appropriate activities that occur throughout the day.
- children know that some activities will occur at the same time each day.
- children are actively involved and engage in concrete experiences.
- children choose their own activities from among the large number of activities set up by the teacher.
- children have options about when and how to complete activities.

See the case study analysis about DAP activities.

Case Study Analysis: Discovering DAP in Classroom Activities

Both Mrs. Vargas and Mr. Pelander (from the chapter-opening case studies) have developed activities based on principles of DAP. Please find examples of how both Mrs. Vargas's preschool and Mr. Pelander's third-grade classrooms meet the criteria for developmentally appropriate activities.

Both classrooms have a wide, but not overwhelming, variety of age-appropriate activities that occur throughout the day.

    Examples for the preschool classroom:

    Examples for the third-grade classroom:

Both classrooms schedule activities so that they occur at the same time each day.

> Examples (preschool):
> Examples (third grade):

Both teachers emphasize concrete activities that actively involve the children.

> Examples (preschool):
> Examples (third grade):

Both teachers encourage children to choose their own activities.

> Examples (preschool):
> Examples (third grade):

The children have options about when and how to complete activities.

> Examples (preschool):
> Examples (third grade):

_____

Materials

Choosing materials

Teachers in DAP classrooms provide appropriate materials with which children work and play. **Appropriate materials,** as we know from some older research, refers to a moderately rich assortment of exploratory and safe items which encourage competent, independent behavior in children (Stallings, 1975; Wachs & Gruen, 1982; White & Watts, 1973). These materials reflect the needs, interests, and abilities of the children.

Managing materials well

Bowers (1990) notes that teachers have to be able to manage materials well in addition to choosing appropriate materials. **Management of classroom materials** refers to how well materials are gathered, whether they work well, how well organized and displayed they are, and whether they are available to the children. See Figure 5.9 for a rating scale on managing materials.

DAP CLASSROOMS FOR INFANTS AND TODDLERS

Brief Summary of Infant/Toddler Development (Fogel, 1984)

Developmentally appropriate physical environments are based on the developmental level of the children using them. This section briefly summarizes child development during the first 3 years of life. Adults support infant/toddler development first by understanding infant/toddler development and then by designing the physical environment to be safe, cozy, and appropriate for the care and education of each child in the group (Fu, 1984).

Rating Scale: Classroom Management of Materials

Use this rating scale to evaluate classroom management of materials and equipment in this early childhood classroom. Rate each item using the scale. "1" indicates the lowest rating you can give. "5" is the highest rating you can give. A space is provided for comments.

The teacher has taken leadership in *gathering materials*.	1	2	3	4	5
All materials needed for an activity are there.	1	2	3	4	5
Materials appear to have been gathered well in advance of the activity.	1	2	3	4	5
Equipment is correctly sized for children using it.	1	2	3	4	5
Equipment works well.	1	2	3	4	5
Children will be able to use the materials without a lot of adult help.	1	2	3	4	5
Equipment is clean.	1	2	3	4	5
Materials are organized logically.	1	2	3	4	5
Items within centers are stored so that they are easy for children to get to and then to put away.	1	2	3	4	5
If children are expected to clean up after any activity, this teacher appears to have thought it through and has provided necessary items.	1	2	3	4	5
If children are expected to set up an activity, necessary materials are available.	1	2	3	4	5
Materials not intended for children's use are stored out of their reach.	1	2	3	4	5

Comments and suggestions:

Figure 5.9.

Very young infants, up to 3 or 4 months of age, spend most of their time getting bodily and physiological systems in order. Parents and teachers spend a lot of their time with new infants holding and rocking them, giving them tactile stimulation, and helping them establish a schedule of eating, sleeping, playing, and exercising.

A caregiver's touch seems to help moderate the production of a hormone that affects an infant's reaction to stress. Institutionalized Romanian orphans without such attention show wide fluctuations of that hormone level. Abnormal levels of the hormone have been linked to changes in a part of the brain involved with learning and memory (Rubin, 1997).

As time goes by, infants are gradually able to cope with slightly more complex stimulation because they continue to develop in all of the domains—physical, motor, cognitive, social, and emotional. An example is the rapid perceptual and motor development in infancy, which allows the infant to engage in one-on-one interactions, to play with any of hundreds of "things" in her physical environment, and to experience the pleasure of these new abilities.

Infants are partners in social interaction from the moment they are born. But there are important changes in their interaction with others as their cognitive development evolves during the first year or so of life. Older infants and toddlers realize or seem to "sense" their status as partners in social interaction and become aware that they "cause" things to happen.

Changes in cognitive development in the first 3 years are dramatic. By her first birthday, an infant has a better sense of the permanence of objects; i.e., that Mom and Dad still exist even if she cannot see them. She now understands the value of words and has become a real "communicator." Perception and memory change and affect her understanding of such things as emotions. Emotional development is tied to cognitive development over the next few years, meaning that toddlers will develop fears and some anxiety. Infants and toddlers can begin to deal with these uneasy feelings if they have understanding caregivers to help them.

Ever-changing cognitive and emotional development allow very young children to begin to see themselves as separate individuals and to be conscious of the "self," a phenomenon that increases as infants and toddlers interact with others. Motor skills advance, enabling toddlers to act in an increasingly autonomous way. Development during this period and in the next few years allows toddlers to experience the joy of living, to begin to understand the world around them, and to develop feelings of competence and confidence.

Supportive Physical Environments for Infants/Toddlers

Fogel (1984) believes that it is not possible to think about infants without also considering the child's environment. He identified two types of environments—the **physical environment** and the **caregiving environment**—for children from birth to age 3. The **caregiving environment** includes caregiver behavior as to how the caregiver interacts with the baby. For example, does a caregiver talk to a baby when changing baby's diaper? How does the caregiver respond to crying? How warmly does a caregiver respond to an infant? The **physical environment** includes all objects and situations, such as:

- the cleanliness and safety of a home or center
- the types and availability of toys
- the size and nature of the home or center
- the adequacy of nutrition, health care, and sanitary practices

Perception and memory, problem solving, spatial relations, perspective taking, planning strategies—all of these are a part of cognitive development, and an infant's physical and caregiving environments affect cognitive development. Teachers in DAP infant/toddler classrooms understand that they are professional teachers. They believe that how they structure the physical and caregiving environments affects infants or toddlers. They know that even the youngest infants are active information processers who need the right type of stimulation for optimal development. They know that infant and toddler cognition and learning is enhanced in a DAP classroom.

Problem solving in infants and toddlers

Children's cognitive development is enhanced when they actively explore their surroundings. We want infants and toddlers to begin to be able to solve problems based on their safe explorations. Therefore, an infant or toddler's cognitive development is affected by how well teachers design and then manage the physical environment. For example, children in their second and third years have better problem-solving skills and engage in more exploratory behavior when teachers and parents provide safe objects for them to explore; e.g., mini-hollow blocks, playdough.

Spatial relations and perspective taking

These skills have their roots in infancy and continue to develop over a period of years. Our goal is to create the type of environment in which the youngest children have a good chance of developing excellent spatial relations. We also want to help them begin to understand that they are separate from other people and that they can have an effect on their environment. Young children develop better spatial relations and perspective taking in well-organized and peaceful environments rather than in chaotic, stressful environments.

Learning to plan strategies

Play materials affect a very young child's ability to devise new ways of doing things and to plan effective strategies. Children are better able to figure out how to do things and to plan effective strategies when teachers provide play materials appropriate to their developmental needs, interests, and abilities.

Implications for teachers

The principles of DAP classrooms apply here. Draw implications from the information just given and you will see that it is wise to plan the physical environment so that it enhances cognitive development during infancy and toddlerhood.

- Provide objects that are responsive to an infant's actions, such as busy boards, nesting blocks, and shape sorters.
- Avoid noise, confusion, and overcrowding in environments for infants and toddlers.
- Organize the physical environment well. Develop activity areas to meet the specific developmental needs of infants and toddlers.
- Provide age-appropriate play materials for infants and toddlers.
- Introduce certain forms of environmental stimulation at specific ages (Figure 5.10).

Designing Physical Environments for Infants and Toddlers

Infants and toddlers are usually in Piaget's first stage of cognitive development, the sensorimotor stage. They take in information and act on their world through sensory and motor schemes. Very young children learn through experimentation and repetition, and teachers encourage learning by providing a safe and stimulating physical environment and an emotionally supportive caregiving environment. "Routines are the curriculum" (Bredekamp, 1987), and sensitive teachers take

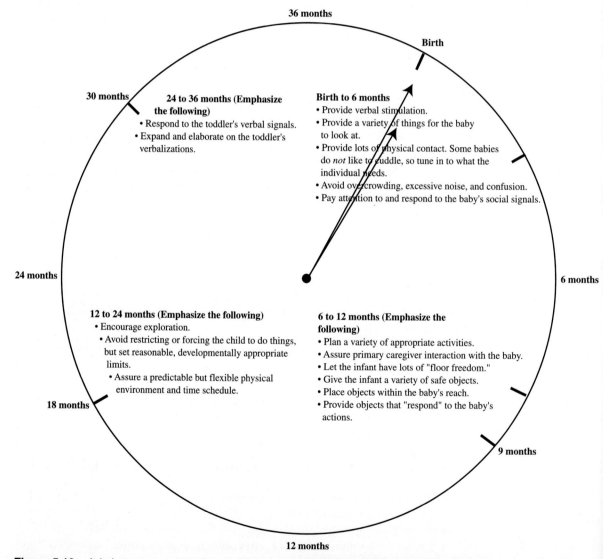

Figure 5.10. It is important to "time" environmental stimulation for infants and toddlers well.
(Sources: Laliberte [1997]; White House Conference, reported in the *New York Times* [April 1997].)

advantage of routine situations such as eating, bathing, diapering, and dressing to help very young children feel safe and learn at the same time.

Well-organized infant and toddler rooms contain activity areas but are not just scaled-down versions of classrooms for children 3 to 8 years old. Infants and toddlers should be able to practice sensorimotor activities in a well-designed space. A DAP infant and toddler room is clean and has spacious bathing and dressing areas. It encourages crawling, scooting, and walking in safe, open areas; pushing, pulling, rolling, emptying, and filling safe, clean toys; and climbing on safe structures. A DAP infant or toddler room encourages children to gaze at objects at their level and to do messy, active things such as finger painting or creating the swish-swish of a water table. Figure 5.11 suggests appropriate activity areas based on the infant's or toddler's level of development.

Supportive Caregiving Environments for Infants and Toddlers

The caregiving environment includes a caregiver's behavior as she interacts with an infant or toddler. A DAP caregiving environment is intertwined with the physical environment; together, they enhance an infant's or toddler's development. Chapter 2 described different styles of caregiving and explained that the authori**tative** style is the one most likely to enhance an infant's or toddler's development in different domains. An infant or toddler teacher with an authori**tative** caregiving style has expectations for a young child and is highly responsive to an infant's or toddler's needs.

Figure 5.11. Divide infant and toddler rooms into activity areas to meet the needs of our youngest children.
(Sources: King, Oberlin, & Swank [1990]; Wilson [1990]. These plus Herr and Swim (2002) and Bredekamp (1987) give excellent suggestions on specific DAP activities for infant/toddler centers.)

Activity Areas for Infants

- Well-designed and maintained diapering, dressing areas
- Comfort corner (soft spot)
- Pleasant eating area
- Manipulative area
- Exercise mat
- Sensory table
- Reading

Activity Areas for Toddlers

- Well-designed and maintained eating, toileting, dressing, and sleeping areas
- Music
- Private space
- Block
- Dramatic play
- Creative arts
- Large muscle
- Sensory table (e.g., water, sand)
- Playdough table
- Reading
- Comfort corner (soft spot)
- Small muscle

Supportive teachers of infants and toddlers take a lot of responsibility for infants because our youngest children cannot function on their own. Authori**tative** caregivers understand, for example, that babies and toddlers cannot control themselves, have limited memory, and are restricted in how they tell us what they need. Responsive teachers anticipate what babies and toddlers need and know when and how to adjust support gradually. They also know how to transfer control to children little by little.

Examples. Mr. Zimmer, head teacher in the toddler room, understands that his children have not yet achieved self-control. He believes that his job is to model self-control and to gradually transfer control to the toddlers. He does this when setting limits by giving positively worded statements such as "Hit this ball," rather than just restricting a toddler and saying what *not* to do.

Mr. Thompson, head teacher in the infant room, realizes that babies cannot stop crying just because somebody tells them to do so. Additionally, he knows that babies cry for lots of different reasons and that he can do some specific things to help a baby who is crying. He also gives this information to the parents of the infants.

Working with Parents. Babies Cry for Many Reasons[19]

Here at the center, we have found that the babies cry for a variety of reasons. Have you noticed the same thing? One of the things that we always keep in mind (we have a sign in our office with this saying) is: "Babies do not cry to annoy adults! They cry because something is wrong." Crying is a baby's way of telling us what she needs. It's a good idea to try to figure out what might be causing her to cry. We've also discovered that a baby cannot stop crying just because you tell her to do so.

Here are the main reasons that your baby cries and some practical things you can do to help the baby. "Babies cry when they are . . ."

✓ **hungry.** Babies often cry when they're hungry. If it has been at least 2 hours since she ate, see if she is hungry.

✓ **lonely.** If a baby calms and stays calm as soon as you pick her up, she missed you! A baby's need for closeness is real. You can't spoil a baby by cuddling her when she needs it.

✓ **cold or hot.** Feel the baby's back or tummy to see if she is too cold or too hot. Adjust her clothing to make her comfortable. Dress a baby as warmly as you or one layer warmer.

✓ **overly stimulated.** Give her calm and quiet. Rocking her in a dimly lit room may help.

✓ **undressed.** Put a cloth on her tummy until you redress her.

✓ **startled.** A baby may move suddenly, startle, and cry. Wrapping a blanket securely around her and holding her securely may calm her.

✓ **in need of a diaper change.**

✓ **in pain.** A baby might be ill or uncomfortable because something is hurting her. Always, always check this out.

✓ **sleepy.** Some babies need to fuss a bit before sleeping.

[19]Source: Parenting the first year. Wisconsin Children's Trust Fund, Madison, WI. (From the newsletter for the first month of a baby's life.)

Ways to Adapt Curriculum and Instruction for Early Childhood Inclusive Classrooms[20]

✓ **Environment:** Adapt materials for individual needs. Adapt the setup of the room or seating.
Example: Siri has trouble grasping and then releasing things. You provide a variety of items in the small manipulatives area to allow for this difference.

✓ **Presenting Information:** Adapt the way that you present information and materials, including your language. Demonstrate instructions or simplify language.
Example: You have observed that several children, and not just those with special needs, have difficulty making transitions. You decide to use picture cues during transitions. When moving from large group to snack, you hold up a picture cue card, an actual photograph of snack time in your class while you **say** the words about going to snack.

✓ **Difficulty:** Adapt how a child might approach an activity.
Example: Laurie has difficulty cutting, so you encourage her to tear paper for her collage. You write the adaptation into the lesson plan.

✓ **Level of Support:** Observe to assess how much help a child needs and then vary the amount of help given.
Example: Luke does not need hand-over-hand assistance for playing outside but does seem to need it for brushing his teeth.

✓ **Alternative Goals:** Adapt goals and outcomes for children within the same lesson plan or learning activity.
Example: Suppose that your goal for a story is for children to see how to use words to express angry feelings. You have adapted goals for Jafar. He needs to understand the content of the story but you have adapted your guidance plan for him during the lesson so that he also learns how to listen without interrupting others when they are talking.

✓ **Participation:** Adapt activities for different levels of participation by children.
Example: Most of your children sit upright and respond to questions during a story or group lesson. You have noticed, however, that Aaron seems less distracted if he just leans against the wall and listens. You have adapted your guidance plan for Jafar, too. He also seems much more relaxed and attentive if he lies down and listens to a story. Yesterday, you noticed that he lay on his side, his head on one hand. For the first time ever, he just listened without interrupting others when they talked.

✓ **Time:** Adapt the amount of time for children to complete an activity or task. You can determine who might need more time for a variety of activities through careful observation.
Example: You have observed that Joshua needs a little more time, but not much more, to put away blocks. He uses the extra time to find the outline of the blocks on the shelves and then does a great job of putting away the blocks.

✓ **Child's Response:** This is really for the teacher. Adapt how much you expect children to accomplish. Be flexible in terms of how you expect a child to respond.
Example: You have noticed that Siri seems to like art and seems to need two sessions to complete most art activities; e.g., today she did a part of a collage and you told her that you would put the collage materials out for her again in the afternoon. You have also noticed that Aaron will sometimes answer you by looking at something if you ask him to make a choice. Today you asked if he wanted grape or orange juice and he looked at the grape juice.

Figure 5.12.

[20]Source: Adapted with permission from Cross & Dixon (1997). *Adapting curriculum & instruction in inclusive early childhood classrooms.* Bloomington, Indiana: Center for Innovative Practices for Young Children.

REFLECTING ON KEY CONCEPTS

1. Suppose that you are giving a tour of your preschool classroom for a parent who is thinking about enrolling his child in the school. You point out each small-group learning center, the individual learning centers, the large-group area, and the private space. Explain why you have organized the classroom into activity areas and tell the parent about what goes on in each area. The parent asks you why the block area is adjacent to the dramatic play area and why the books are next to the puzzle and writing areas. What would you say?

2. The teachable moment: You meet a person who teaches eighth grade and you start talking about curriculum. "So," says your friend, "just what do you early childhood teachers teach? Do you just drill them on numbers, colors, and shapes?" You realize that this person does not understand young children or how they learn. You decide to treat this as a **teachable moment.** Briefly explain to this friend the meaning of a DAP approach to curriculum for early childhood.

3. Name four of the most important things to remember about managing materials in an early childhood classroom. Why do these four seem most important to you?

4. Name the two main ways, in your view, that a classroom for infants and toddlers differs from a classroom for older early childhood children.

APPLY YOUR KNOWLEDGE

Observation: Finding Dap In An Early Childhood Classroom

Request permission to visit an early childhood classroom for preschool, kindergarten, or primary children. As a guest in the classroom, your goal is **not** to criticize; it is to look at how the teacher has designed activity areas, how the areas are bounded, the traffic patterns in the classroom, and the management of materials in the classroom.

Practice professionalism by making suggestions for change **after** you leave the classroom. Keep information on the classroom confidential. If you share information in one of your courses, remove information that could identify the teacher or class or school from your work. Present any suggestions in a positive way so that you are merely suggesting ideas that would make a good classroom even better.

Activity Areas

Draw a simple floor plan of the classroom that you have observed. Include the toilet area for children, doors to the outside and to hallways, small-group learning centers, large-group area, private areas, and boundaries among areas. Label each area clearly. Use the floor plan in the chapter as a guide. Then analyze the activity areas in this room:

- Private area. Explain whether and how the private space in this classroom meets the criteria for private spaces. Suggest any changes needed.
- Large-group area. Explain whether and how the large-group area in this classroom meets the criteria for large-group areas. Suggest any changes needed.
- Small-group learning centers. Number of centers: _____. Explain whether and how the small-group learning centers in this classroom meet criteria for this type of activity area. Suggest any changes needed.
- Individual learning center(s). This classroom (does or does not) have individual learning centers. Explain how these centers meet the criteria for this type of activity area.

Boundaries

Describe the boundaries used to separate activity areas from one another in this classroom. Which areas were especially well bounded? Why? Which areas would benefit from having more effective boundaries?

Traffic Pattern

Use a contrasting color and draw arrows from the entrance to the classroom and around the room to each center. Describe the traffic pattern in this room using information on "good traffic patterns" from the chapter. Suggest how to make the traffic pattern of this room even better.

Management of Materials In The Classroom

Use the rating scale (Figure 5.9) to evaluate classroom management of materials and equipment in this early childhood classroom. After you are done with the rating scale, name three ways in which this classroom's management of materials would most benefit from a change in how materials are managed.

Suggestions for Change

Draw a second floor plan for this classroom. Clearly show your suggestions for change in your drawing. If, for example, you note that the classroom does not have quite enough small-group learning centers, decide where you would put them and draw them on your "after" floor plan. Indicate changes with a colored pencil or pen.

REFERENCES

Alexander, N. (1996). How to organize your classroom. *Early Childhood News, 8*(4), 28–30.

Alward, K. R. (1973). *Arranging the classroom for children.* San Francisco: Far West Laboratory for Educational Research and Development.

Berk, L., & Winsler, A. (1995). *Scaffolding children's learning: Vygotsky and early childhood education.* Washington, DC: NAEYC.

Bowers, C. (1990). Organizing space for children. *Texas Child Care Quarterly,* Spring, 3–10, 22.

Bredekamp, S. (Ed.) (1987). *Developmentally appropriate practice in programs serving children from birth through age 8.* Washington, DC: National Association for the Education of Young Children (NAEYC).

Bredekamp, S., & Rosegrant, T. (Eds.). (1992). *Reaching potentials: Appropriate curriculum and assessment for young children* (Vol. 1). Washington, DC: National Association for the Education of Young Children.

Burts, D., Hart, C., Charlesworth, R., Fleege, P., Mosley, J., & Thomasson, R. (1992). Observed activities and stress behaviors of children in developmentally appropriate and inappropriate kindergarten classrooms. *Early Childhood Research Quarterly, 7,* 297–318.

Caples, S. (1996). Some guidelines for preschool design. *Young Children, 51*(4), 14–21.

Charlesworth, R. (1985). Readiness: Should we make them ready or let them bloom? *Daycare and Early Education, 12*(3), 25–27.

Charlesworth, R., Hart, C., Burts, D., & DeWolf, M. (1993). The LSU studies: Building a research base for developmentally appropriate practice. In S. Reifel (Ed.), *Advances in Early Education and Day Care: Perspectives on Developmentally Appropriate Practice, 5,* 3–28.

Colbert, J. (1997). Classroom design and how it influences behavior. *Early Childhood News, 9*(3), 22–30.

Cross, A. F., & Dixon, S. D. (1997). *Adapting curriculum and instruction in inclusive early childhood classrooms.* Bloomington, IN: Institute for the Study of Developmental Disabilities.

David, T., & Weinstein, D. (1987). The built environment and children's development. In C. Weinstein & T. David (Eds.), *Spaces for children: The built environment and child development.* New York: Plenum Press,

Fogel, A. (1984). *Infancy: Infant, family, and society.* St. Paul, MN: West Publishing.

Fu, V. (1984). Infant/toddler care in centers. In L. Dittmann (Ed.), *The infants we care for.* Washington, DC: NAEYC.

Gandini, L. (1993). Fundamentals of the Reggio Emilia approach to early childhood education. *Young Children, 49*(1), 4–8.

Hart, C. (1993). *Children on playgrounds: Research perspectives and applications.* Albany: State University of New York Press.

Hart, C., Burts, D., & Charlesworth, R. (1997). Integrated developmentally appropriate curriculum. In C. Hart, D. Burts, & R. Charlesworth (Eds.), *Integrated curriculum and developmentally appropriate practice: Birth to age 8.* Albany: State University of New York Press.

Hart, C., Burts, D., Durland, M. A., Charlesworth, R., DeWolf, M., & Fleege, P. (1998). Stress behaviors and activity type participation of preschoolers in more and less developmentally appropriate classrooms: SES and sex differences. *Journal of Research in Childhood Education,* 176–196.

Helm, J. H., & Katz, L. G. (2001). *Young investigators: The project approach in the early years.* Published simultaneously by New York: Teachers College Press; and Washington, DC: NAEYC.

Herr, J. & Swim, T. (2002). *Creative resources for infants and toddlers.* Albany, NY: Delmar.

Howes, C. (1991). Caregiving environments and their consequences for children: The experience in the United States. In E. Melhuish & P. Moss (Eds.), *Day care for young children.* New York: Routledge.

Jones, E., & Prescott, E. *Environments for young children.* Washington, DC: NAEYC, Film #806.

King, M., Oberlin, A., & Swank, T. (1990). Supporting the activity choices of 2-year-olds. *Day Care and Early Education, 17*(2), 9–13, 67–70.

Krogh, S. (1995). *The integrated early childhood curriculum* (2nd ed.). New York: McGraw-Hill.

Kostelnik, M. (1992). Myths associated with developmentally appropriate programs. *Young Children, 47* (4), 17–23.

Kritchevsky, S., & Prescott, E. (1977). *Environments for young children: Physical space.* Washington, DC: NAEYC.

Laliberte, R. (1997). Inside your baby's brain. *Parents, 72*(9), 48–53.

Marcon, R. (1993). Socioemotional versus academic emphasis: Impact on kindergartners' development and achievement. *Early Child Development and Care, 96*, 81–89.

Marcon, R. (1994). Doing the right thing for children: Linking research and policy reform in the District of Columbia public schools. *Young Children, 50*(1), 8.

Marion, M. (1999). *Guidance of young children* (5th ed.). Upper Saddle River, NJ: Merrill/Prentice Hall.

Marion, M. (2004). *Using observation in early childhood.* Upper Saddle River, NJ: Merrill/Prentice Hall.

Myhre, S. (1993). Enhancing your dramatic play area through the use of prop boxes. *Young Children, 48* (5), 6–19.

National Association for the Education of Young Children (2001). *NAEYC guidelines revision. NAEYC standards for early childhood professional preparation: Initial level.* Washington, DC: author.

New York Times (1997, April 28). Nurturing development of the brain. *New York Times, 146* (50776), A14.

Olds, A. R. (1977). Why is environmental design important to young children? *Children in Contemporary Society, 11*(1), 58.

Pelander, J. (1997). My transition from conventional to more developmentally appropriate practices in the primary grades. *Young Children, 52*(7), 19–25.

Pelander, J. (1998, February 3). Personal communication.

Petrakos, H., & Howe, N. (1996). The influence of the physical design of the dramatic play center on children's play. *Early Childhood Research Quarterly, 11*, 63–77.

Piaget, J. (1952). *The origins of intelligence in children.* New York: International Universities Press.

Rubin, R. (1997). The biochemistry of touch. *U.S. News & World Report, 123* (18), 62.

Stallings, J. (1975). Implementation and child effects of teaching practices in follow-through classrooms. *Monographs of the Society for Research in Child Development, 40*(78).

Vygotsky, L. (1978). *Mind in society: The development of higher psychological processes.* Eds. and Trans. M. Cole, V. John-Steiner, S. Scribner, & E. Souberman. Cambridge, MA: Harvard University Press.

Wachs, T. D., & Gruen, G. E. (1982). *Early experience and human development.* New York: Plenum.

White, B. L., & Watts. J. C. (1973). *Experience and environment: Major influences on the development of the young child* (Vol. 1). Englewood Cliffs, NJ: Prentice-Hall.

Williams, L. (1994). Developmentally appropriate practice and cultural values: A case in point. In B. L. Mallory & R. S. New (Eds.), *Diversity and developmentally appropriate practices* (pp. 155–65). New York: Teachers College Press.

Wilson, L. C. (1990). *Infants and toddlers* (2nd ed.). New York: Delmar.

CHECK OUT THE WEB SITES RELATED TO THIS CHAPTER

✓ **Cornell University Extension, Ithaca, New York**

www.cce.cornell.edu. This is the main page for the Web site. Go to *www.cce.cornell.edu/publications/catalog. html.* This is the link "Children & Family Relations," which is filled with good items on different topics. See "Designing Child Care Settings," 327DCCS, $15.75.

✓ **Institute for the Study of Developmental Disabilities (ISDD), Indiana University—Bloomington.**

www.isdd.indiana.edu. Go to the link for the center serving young children. The institute promotes inclusionary services for individuals with disabilities across the life span. Find materials here for managing inclusive early childhood classrooms.

✓ **NAEYC, National Association for the Education of Young Children.**

www.naeyc.org. Go the link for the catalogue. It describes videos, books, booklets, and other materials related to developmentally appropriate early childhood classroom management. For example, are you interested in how to manage a block area well? Look for the books or other materials on "blocks" in the catalogue.

✓ **Project Approach Listserv.** Offered by the ERIC Clearinghouse on Elementary and Early Childhood Education. This is not a Web site but an e-mail address. Contact this group if you want to know more about the project approach with children: *Projects-l@postoffice.cso.uiuc.edu.*

Special Topics in Child Guidance

There are five chapters in this part of the book, each designed to help you apply your knowledge of DAP child guidance to a specific special topic in guiding children.

Chapter 6. Authentic Self-Esteem and Moral Identity. DAP child guidance helps children develop a healthy and balanced sense of self and self-esteem that is firmly rooted in a strong set of personal values. The chapter does not give you a set of "cute activities" but it does give you several practical suggestions on how to use DAP child guidance to guide children toward healthy self-esteem.

Chapter 7. Resilience and Stress in Childhood. This chapter concentrates on the positive when describing children and stress. You will read about the nature of stress and how it affects children. Its main focus is to help you develop knowledge and skills for assisting children in coping with specific stressful events.

Chapter 8. Emotional Intelligence and Anger Management. Young children feel and express anger but they do not understand it—this is an extremely important concept to keep in mind as you work with children. This chapter will guide you in applying DAP child guidance so that you can help angry children begin to understand and to manage this strong emotion.

Chapter 9. Preventing Violent Behavior and Understanding Aggression in Children. Children today are growing up in a world awash with violence and aggression. They face a tidal wave of trash and violence on television, in videos, and in the news. Many children are abused or neglected. Anger and aggression blossom in a violent culture.

Anger and aggression are related but different issues. This chapter will help you understand how some children become excessively aggressive. You will learn how to help aggressive children develop more positive ways of dealing with others.

Chapter 10. Guiding the Development of Prosocial Behavior. Nurturing the roots of compassion, generosity, helpfulness, and cooperation in children gives them an alternative to aggression. This chapter will help you understand how a child's development affects prosocial behavior. You will also learn specific and practical strategies for helping children grow in compassion and other aspects of prosocial behavior.

Authentic Self-Esteem and Moral Identity

"Children with uncaring parents or caregivers will learn to view themselves as unworthy, unlovable, and incompetent in school-related and cognitive tasks."

(Lowenthal, 1999)

After reading and studying this chapter, you will be able to

❏ **Explain** how negative self-esteem might have long-term negative effects on a person.

❏ **Tell in your own words** how a person with a positive view of himself could also be arrogant and narcissistic.

❏ **Define** self-esteem and **explain** it as one part of the "self."

❏ **List, explain in your own words, and give an example** of the three building blocks of self-esteem.

❏ **Explain** how social interaction affects the development of a child's self-esteem.

❏ **List, explain, and give examples** of specific adult practices that affect a child's self-esteem.

❏ **Acknowledge** the importance of helping children develop a strong moral identity as well as healthy and balanced self-esteem.

Case Study: Self-Esteem

Teachers and administrators at the Oakwood School identified self-esteem as the topic for professional development and hired Mrs. Chen, an early childhood consultant, to work with them on understanding the issue of self-esteem. She interviewed each teacher to find out what they currently believe about self-esteem and then observed in their classrooms before making recommendations. Here are some samples from her interviews and visits.

Preschool classroom: Mrs. Vargas, teacher

"I want my children," the teacher said, "to feel good about themselves but I **don't** believe in doing a lot of cute activities focusing on self-esteem. I also think it's **in**appropriate to give them a lot of empty praise and flattery." Mrs. Chen watched this teacher treat her class with great respect, use positive guidance strategies, and give them positive meaningful feedback instead of empty flattery. For example, the teacher expressed appreciation for a child's effort: "Ralph, you were so careful when you put all the puzzles in the rack." To another child, she expressed appreciation by saying, "Jordan, you remembered to wait for a turn on the swing!"

K–2 classroom: Mr. Nellis, teacher

"I want to help my children," said Mr. Nellis, "to realize that a big part of themselves (and self-esteem) is tied to helping and working cooperatively with others." He and the children had placed a large display on one wall entitled, "We are a class filled with helpers." Under the sign was a group picture of the class. Then the teacher had taken pictures of small groups of children working together or helping each other. He made sure that each child was included in a picture. Mr. Nellis displayed each group picture with a brief description of how the children had worked or cooperated with each other.

Second-grade classroom: Mr. Janis (substitute teacher for 2 months)

"My main goal," said the teacher, "is to boost the self-esteem of the children." During the classroom observation, Mrs. Chen heard lots of praise, but for trivial things. Every child who came down the slide heard the teacher say, "Good job!" Whenever any child hung her coat on a hook the teacher said, "Way to go!" Each child in the class made a book titled "This is Me!" The books consisted of duplicated pages asking a child to provide facts such as "My favorite thing to eat is _____." Others were "I want to buy _____ when I go to the store," and "I want a birthday cake that looks like this _____." This teacher also made an "I Am Special Because . . ." book for each child. The children completed the sentences on each page; e.g., "I am special because my favorite color is _____," or ". . . because I have _____ hair."

This teacher also said, "I think that the children will do well in school when they feel good about themselves. Eliza and Gordy are having trouble with the new math concept. But math really isn't as important as how these children feel about themselves, so I'm not going to focus on their trouble with math."

The principal, when asked about this teacher's approach, was astounded. He pulled the children's records and showed the consultant the substitute teacher's note to the parents that these two children were doing excellent work in math.

First-grade classroom: Mr. Claiborne, teacher

"You asked for my opinion. I think," said Mr. Claiborne in response to the consultant's question, "that **real** self-esteem grows from a child's own real effort and persistence. I cannot "give" self-esteem to my students. They'll earn it through their effort and persistence."

This teacher's approach to working with a child having trouble with math, for example, was to individualize his instruction so that the child could learn the concepts at her own pace. He talked with the parents about the issue: "Janet understands most of the math concepts but is having difficulty with two specific concepts. I'm certain that she can master these and we are working on it. Here's a sample of how she is improving. One of Janet's best qualities is her persistence, which will work well for her."

The consultant asked him if the children did the "This is Me!" book. He did not criticize the other teacher, but instead said, "I have done that in the past but now take a different approach." He pointed to a chart. "We did this chart: 'All About Us—Here Is the Information!' I was trying out this idea to get the children away from focusing so much on themselves as individuals. It's Katz's idea, really.[21] We gathered information about each child: number of teeth, eye color, number of lost teeth, shoe size, current weight, weight at birth. Then, we pooled all the information on each item and made graphs. What you see on the wall chart is information, for example, on how many children in the class have brown, blue, or green eyes or the average weight of first-graders in our room. This way, we did not single out any one child."

Mrs. Chen looked around the room and commented, "Your classroom has real framed artwork, pictures of real animals, and photos of real fire engines, dump trucks, and the like. You even have that quilt hanging on the wall in the reading area and have Native American baskets and pottery in different areas of the room. You don't have the usual cute posters with talking animals. I also noticed that your chart has photographs of the children weighing each other, counting their teeth, checking each other's eye color. The graphs are well done. But you haven't decorated the chart with talking animals, bright colors, smiley faces, or similar charming items. Why?"

Mr. Claiborne replied, "Well, the children learned a lot from this project. They also seemed to enjoy the process. They seem to be bombarded with bright colors and talking animals almost everywhere they turn. I didn't think that they needed all that in this project. I wanted them to be involved and challenged. The work was absorbing and really did not need cutesy drawings to 'sweeten the deal.' The room? These children see enough cartoon animals outside of school. I just want to surround my children with real things, not cartoon creatures, not fluff, but the real thing."

SELF-ESTEEM: A LIFELONG PROGRESS

Building self-esteem is an active process that continues throughout a lifetime. The wonderful thing about working with children is that we are present as children start to evaluate themselves (Bakley, 1997) and we can help children formulate a healthy and balanced view of themselves. Children's initial self-esteem develops slowly in early childhood and tends to be stable (Verschueren, Marcoen, & Buyck, 1998).

[21]Source: Katz, L. (1993)

Authentic self-esteem—positive, healthy, confidant, and balanced—provides a secure foundation for further growth and development.

Negative, unhealthy, unbalanced self-esteem, on the other hand, provides a shaky foundation for a child's development. Children with damaged self-esteem make a negative evaluation of their competence, control, or worth. This negative evaluation stays with a person for many years or even decades and affects many aspects of a person's life. Such a negative evaluation might well result in a lifelong struggle to meet these needs or to avoid situations where deficits would stand out. Here are two examples.

Example. Cassandra is 16 years old. She is 5′6″ and weighs 93 lbs. At age 14, she went on a diet, and then began to diet excessively. Cassandra has anorexia nervosa, an eating disorder that threatens her life. She was clinically overweight until she was 14. Her mother has always told her that she was fat because she "stuffed her face." Her mother always implied that the weight problem was Cassandra's responsibility. Her mother also implied that other children did not like fat people. Both of these attitudes very often lead overweight children to have negative self-esteem (Pierce & Wardle, 1997).

Consequently, Cassandra has had negative self-esteem for several years. Specifically, she does not think that she has much control over things in her life. Her therapist realizes that Cassandra has placed herself in grave danger in her effort to control her eating, one of the few things over which she thinks she has control.

Example. Ted is 38 years old and was physically and psychologically abused (rejected) throughout childhood and adolescence. He was and felt **un**loved as a child and has developed a very negative view of his worth. He has never felt that he had much control over anything. His negative self-esteem has caused problems for him at work, with friends, and in his marriage; e.g., he tries to make all decisions, both major and minor, for his wife. At a department store, for instance, she put a set of mixing bowls in the cart. Ted said, "Whoa, look at that price! Put 'em back." His wife said, "Ted, these are only $3.98 and we get three bowls." Ted snarled and replied, "I said to put them back, so PUT THEM BACK."

It is also possible for a child to have a positive view of his abilities and be conceited, arrogant, narcissistic, and egotistical at the same time (Katz, 1993; Baumeister, 1996).

Example. Hector, age 16, a high school junior, is a good mathematician and takes math courses at a university. However, Hector is also arrogant about this ability and laughs quietly but openly at others who are less gifted. One of his high school classmates, struggling with calculus, finally asked Hector for help. Hector grimaced in disgust and responded, "Look, I'll give you a few hints but this is your problem." The other students dislike him because of his excessive pride and because he degrades them, not because he outstrips them in math. Hector seems not to have respect for others.

MORAL IDENTITY: CHILDREN NEED A STRONG MORAL COMPASS AND NOT JUST POSITIVE SELF-ESTEEM

Moral Identity

Moral identity: a person's use of moral principles to define the self (Damon, 1999). A child gives clues about his moral identity by the words that he uses to describe the self. Hector, for example, uses words such as "smart and honest" to describe his self. Yes, he is smart. He is honest about his opinion. He is also unkind and inconsiderate at times. Other students use words such as smart, mean, overbearing, and selfish to describe Hector. Hector needs a stronger moral compass to guide his behavior.

A compass can be a lifesaving instrument because it indicates direction. Likewise, a strong moral compass or direction finder gives direction and guides behavior. Helping children develop healthy and balanced self-esteem takes so much more than a collection of activities, although appropriate activities can enhance self-esteem. Consequently, this chapter is **not** a collection of activities to boost self-esteem. Too strong an emphasis on the development of self-esteem in young children can lead to self-centeredness.

Egotistic, arrogant behavior, such as Hectors's in the example above, often results in mean-spirited treatment of others. Children need to feel good about themselves but they also need a strong, objective **moral compass** that guides their behavior (Baumeister, 1996; Damon, 1991; Lerner, 1996). Without such a guide, even children who have positive self-esteem, as Hector does about his ability in math, cannot acquire a stable sense of right and wrong.

A child's **moral identity** takes shape in later childhood and governs two things. First, moral identity governs what a child thinks is the right thing to do. Second, moral identity determines why a child should take a specific course of action (Damon, 1999).

Example. Hector knows that the right thing to do is to help someone who needs help and he does, indeed, agree to assist his classmate, but only minimally. However, his reasoning gives a clue about his moral identity. He seems to resent having to help. Hector needs not only to know that it is good to help another person, but also to want to help that person because it is the right thing to do.

Example. Sam is also in Hector's class. Sam is a talented ice skater. Not only is Sam truly modest about his athletic skill, but he also holds an unofficial skating clinic for other students one Saturday each month. A teacher asked him why he took the time for the clinic and Sam shrugged and replied, "I don't know. It's not a big deal. My mom and dad paid for so many lessons for me and I want to spread around all those lessons. I like to teach and the other kids really like to skate once they learn some good basic techniques. We have a good time."

We cannot wait until late childhood to think about children's moral identity. Early childhood is a good time for guiding children so that they eventually know the right thing to do and so that they are willing to act to do the right thing. Some of the best ways to help children develop a strong moral identity include (Buzzelli, 1992):

- Using positive discipline.
- Setting and maintaining appropriate limits.
- Requiring children to be self-responsible.
- Teaching them that some things are wrong.
- Emphasizing the right of others (people and animals) to respectful treatment.

PARTS OF THE "SELF"

Self: mental structure or construction consisting of four different parts. Humans gradually construct or build a set of ideas about these four components of self (Curry & Johnson, 1990; Harter, 1983). Children begin to construct their sense of self during infancy and continue to develop this concept throughout their lives. The four parts or components making up a child's "self" are:

- self-awareness
- self-concept
- self-control
- self-esteem

See Figure 6.1.

Self-Awareness

Self-awareness refers to two things:

First, **self-awareness:** the idea that a child views himself as separate from others; e.g., Mom is a person; I am separate from Mom. Infants gradually learn that they are separate from other people as the infant's perceptual system develops during the first year of life. Self-awareness emerges during infancy and toddlerhood and continues to develop during early childhood.

Second, **self-awareness:** also means that a child realizes that he can make things happen. For example, an infant learns that he can make things happen when someone hears his cry and picks him up. A preschool child knows that he can get the teacher's attention by asking for help.

A child must be aware of her **self** as separate from others and as capable of causing things to happen before she can ever develop self-esteem.

Self-Concept

Self-concept: the knowledge that a child acquires about her **self**. Children go through a long process of learning about the self. Children gradually gather information about themselves; e.g., about things such as physical appearance, physical abilities, gender, intellectual abilities, and interpersonal skills. Gathering such knowledge occurs at about the same time as more general changes in cognitive development.

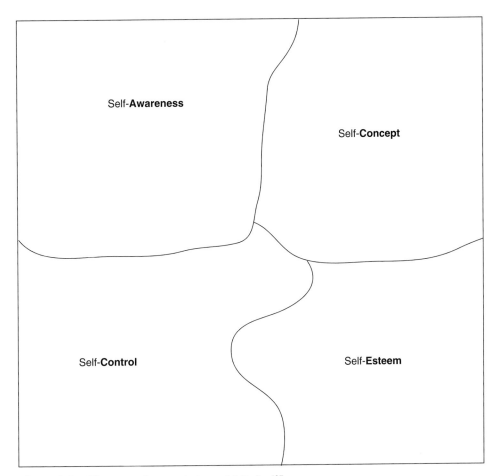

Figure 6.1. There are four parts to a child's "self."

Example. Six-year-old Vinnie carried out one of the classic Piagetian conservation experiments with Mr. Claiborne and said, "You have the same amount of water in that short glass as you have in that tall glass . . . because the short glass is so fat that it holds just as much as the tall glass." (Conservation is one of the general changes in cognitive development.)

During that same week the teacher heard Vinnie say to his friend Reese, "Yeah! We're boys and we'll always be boys. They're girls (pointing to a group of girls) and they're always going to be girls." (This is called **gender constancy** and children understand that gender remains the same when they understand the concept that some things remain the same despite apparent changes.)

A child's set of ideas about himself affects how he behaves (Harter, 1983). For example, a 6-year-old boy who believes that washing dishes is "girl's work" is very likely to refuse to comply or at least protest when his father tells him to wash dishes.

And a 7-year-old girl who thinks she can run fast would more likely enter a race than her friend who believes that she cannot run fast.

Self-Control

Self-control: behaviors that make it possible for children to regulate their impulses, tolerate frustration, and delay immediate gratification. Expect to see the begin-

---

Observe to Discover What Children Are Constructing About the Parts of the Self

Children gradually build ideas about the self and their current knowledge reveals itself in simple everyday statements that they make to other children or teachers. They also reveal their current knowledge about their self through behavior. Here are a few examples.

Self-awareness (child knows he is an individual and can influence events)
"Mommy! (toddler points to his mother). "Jose!" (toddler points to himself).
"When I curse, everybody looks at me and then they giggle or laugh" (preschool child's behavior indicates this).
"We have five people in my family: Mommy, Dad, John, Sarah, and me" (kindergarten child says this when he and Mr. Nellis looked at pictures of families).
"When I call my dog, she trots over to me and then I pet her or give her a treat" (primary child).
"I swing at the mobile and it moves" (infant's behavior).

Self-concept (child learns things about herself)
"My Grandma told me that I look like my Aunt Gail."
"Sam and Ralph like me" (child learns that others like him).
"I am a girl" (child learns that her gender is female).
"I can run fast. I'm still learning how to swim" (child learns about athletic ability).
"I can speak Spanish and English!" (child learns about ability to speak languages).

Self-control (children use these behaviors to regulate impulses, tolerate frustration, and delay immediate gratification)
"I used WORDS to tell Pete that I wanted my book back."
"I wanted to tell the teacher something, but he was talking with Susan, so I waited."
"I'd better look at the list to see who is next at the computer."

Self-esteem (child evaluates the "self" she has come to know)
"My Dad called me a dummy this morning. I feel bad."
"My uncle helped me with my math last night and said that I'm a 'natural-born' mathematician."
"My brother and I finally figured out how to attach the wheels to the car. Mom said that we are persistent and that is a good way to be."
"My teacher told the class that we work well together. We are a class full of helpers."

Figure 6.2.

nings of self-regulation or self-control in children who are about 24 months old. Children become better able to use certain strategies to regulate their own behavior as they get older. Self-control (or regulation) enables children to stop themselves from hurting somebody, to think before acting, and to use words instead of hitting. Parents and teachers can choose guidance strategies that help children learn to regulate their own behavior.

Example. Mrs. Vargas has been working on helping 4-year-old Jordan use words to say that he is upset. The teacher wanted to help Jordan to refrain from striking out at others when he was upset. So Mrs. Vargas said, "Jordan, just as soon as you know that you are angry, put up your STOP sign and say to yourself, 'Stop! Use words.' "

Self-Esteem

Self-esteem: a child evaluates the self about whom she has learned (Coopersmith, 1967; Harter, 1983; Tafarodi & Swarm, 1995). A child pays attention to all the information that she has gathered about herself and makes some sort of judgment about the self. A child who evaluates her self as competent, in control, and worthy will likely develop healthy, balanced judgment; she is likely to have predominately positive self-esteem. A child who evaluates her self as unworthy, unloved, and not competent will likely develop a negative view of the self; she will very likely have predominately negative self-esteem.

COMPETENCE, CONTROL, AND WORTH: THE BUILDING BLOCKS OF SELF-ESTEEM

What is it in the self that a child examines and evaluates so that she can develop her self-esteem? Self-esteem is not just one overall global concept; it can be broken down into distinct parts (Coopersmith, 1967; Curry & Johnson, 1990; Harter, 1983). The parts or dimensions of self-esteem are:

- competence
- control
- worth (Figure 6.3)

Competence

Competence: the ability to meet demands for achievement (Harter, 1982; Tafarodi & Swarm, 1995). Authentic, healthy self-esteem is earned. People with healthy self-esteem have learned that they cannot just wish for competence but that they must work for it. They understand that they have to make things happen through their own effort rather than trying to force or manipulate others into doing things for them. People with healthy self-esteem have earned a positive self-evaluation through hard work that results in increased competence (Lerner, 1996).

Lerner (1996) believes that children congratulated for mediocre work do not develop healthy self-esteem. Giving good feedback means that teachers give positive feedback, as well as suggestions for change when appropriate. Failing to give

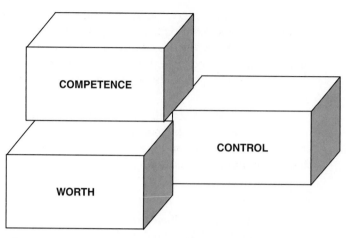

Figure 6.3. Competence, control, and a feeling of worthiness are the building blocks of a child's self-esteem.

suggestions for change or implying that everything a child does is excellent is highly inappropriate.

It is important to help children develop self-esteem that is realistic, positive, and healthy. It is highly **in**appropriate to artificially boost children's view of themselves (Lerner, 1996). Artificially boosting self-esteem gives children inflated self-esteem and an unrealistically positive view about the self (Curry & Johnson, 1990). Children who have an honest and balanced sense of self can look at themselves in several dimensions and make realistic judgments about how they are doing in a particular area. It is possible to feel extremely competent in one area and only moderately competent in another, and still have positive self-esteem.

Example. Sandi, in Mr. Claiborne's first grade, is 6 years old and is very competent socially; she gets along well with adults and other children. She makes friends easily and knows how to get her parent's or teacher's attention without whining. She deals with angry feelings in a positive way. She is only moderately competent in physical skills but seems to enjoy them anyway because her mother and father have never made fun of her physical skills.

Other children have a far less balanced view of themselves. They might not recognize their competence in an area and might even dwell on poor performance in some other area. Children with a negative view of their competence might have had their lack of ability pointed out by adults. Some children have even been humiliated for being competent.

Example. Veronica is 5 years old and loves and is very good at physical activities. Her mother, however, teases Veronica about "turning into a boy" when she gets physically active. Mom has begun to put her daughter in dresses so that is impossible for Veronica to climb or jump. Veronica has begun to think about her physical abilities in a negative way even though she is skillful.

A child's motivation affects how she achieves. Some children are primarily interested in understanding something new or in acquiring some new skill. They are oriented toward learning (Elliott & Dweck, 1988). They will fail at some tasks or make mistakes but will not just give up but will try to overcome the problem.

Example. Pete, a third-grader in Mr. Lee's class, realized that he did not understand the new science concept. He seemed puzzled but not upset about his confusion and said to his teacher, "I don't understand this. Can you help me?"

Other children are motivated differently. Some children go to great lengths to avoid having anybody make unfavorable judgments about their competence. They dread mistakes and often react to them by giving up a project instead of trying again, practicing, and overcoming the difficulty.

Example. Eight-year-old Ramon went to a day camp during the summer and one of the projects was to collect, preserve, and identify a variety of leaves. Ramon forgot to press the leaves as instructed and ended up with crinkled, dry leaves that cracked when put in his book. When the camp counselor offered to help Ramon gather new leaves, Ramon started crying. The next day, Ramon refused to go back to the camp.

Some children have confidence that they can achieve their goals, while others expect that they will not be able to achieve their goals even when they have the capacity to do so. Children who expect to perform well on challenging tasks are able to analyze the skills needed for effective performance. Children who expect to be able to perform well realistically analyze tasks. They are not overly optimistic, but they do not overestimate the difficulty of a task and don't say "I can't do it" (Elliott & Dweck, 1988; Dweck & Leggett, 1988). They also tend to deal well with failure or minor setbacks.

Control

Control: the degree to which a child thinks that he is responsible for how things turn out. Control is a lifelong issue (Wong, 1992). A child's sense of control is a critical aspect of self-esteem. Some children believe that they do have a measure of control, that they can "get things done," and that their actions influence whether they achieve a goal. They also believe that they can decide how much effort to expend in achieving goals—that they have control over their effort. They have a positive and healthy view of control.

Example. Mrs. Chen observed an interaction between 4-year-old Nellie and Mrs. Vargas, the preschool teacher, that will very likely help Nellie develop a positive view of her control. Nellie was doing a science experiment—adding food coloring to white playdough to change the color of the dough. She tried to match a light color of blue on a chart but added far too much coloring.

The teacher said, "You have a problem. What do you think would happen if you took this big glob of white dough and mixed it with your small glob of dark blue dough? It will take a lot of squishing and squashing!" Nellie pummeled and pushed the dough until she got the light color that she wanted. She smiled and called out,

"Look! I made the color of the sky!" The teacher then said, "You really worked hard at mixing that dough, Nellie."

Nellie had had a minor setback. Something had not gone well for her and she essentially failed at what she had set out to do. It is important for children to learn to deal with such minor setbacks if they are to develop authentic self-esteem (Katz, 1993). It is hundreds of such interactions with adults who help them deal with setbacks which show children that they can, indeed, control many of the outcomes in their lives.

Many children have been discouraged from viewing themselves as "in control." Authori**tarian** teachers or parents, for example, exert a great deal of arbitrary control over children, discouraging them from making decisions and from engaging in appropriate verbal give-and-take with adults. Abusive parents go even further and model an extremely rigid, external type of control. It is difficult for children from these types of families to evaluate themselves as controlling, to any degree, what happens to them. These children tend not to think that their own actions influence whether they achieve goals.

Worth

Worth: a child's general sense of his own social value, of his significance to others (Tafarodi & Swarm, 1995). He evaluates how much he likes himself and whether he thinks that others also like or love him. Whether a child judges himself worthy also grows from feeling accepted by and deserving of attention from others. Children who feel accepted, well liked, and deserving the attention of others are likely to evaluate themselves as worthy. Others see themselves as unloved and unworthy of attention and are likely to evaluate themselves as unworthy.

HOW SELF-ESTEEM DEVELOPS

Self-Esteem Develops in a Social Context

Any child's view of herself develops in a social context or setting. Infants are born with a basic temperamental style and certain physical, psychological, and emotional characteristics. These characteristics influence that baby's behavior as well as adults' reactions to the infant. An infant's "self" depends on both things—the child's characteristics and interaction behavior with other people (Brazelton, 1997; Kernis, Brown, & Brody, 2000; Tafarodi & Vu, 1997).

This implies that both the child and the adult have an active role in a child's developing sense of self; a child's sense of self is not just a mirror image of the adult's attitude toward that child. However, adults always have a greater share of responsibility in any interaction with a child.

Example. Mr. Thompson, infant teacher, noticed that Amelia, 5 months old, cried a lot in spite of loving and appropriate caregiving. The teacher thought that something was bothering Amelia, that Amelia needed something. The caregiver thought, "Hmm, how can I help Amelia?" To this caregiver's credit, he recognized his responsibility to figure out how to mesh his responses with the baby's style.

The "self" that an infant comes to know depends on the infant's characteristics *and* the behavior of other people.

Example. Mrs. Vargas, the preschool teacher, knew that Ken, a child new to her class, had been physically abused by his biological parents and was now in foster care. Ken demonstrated his negative view of his worth and control by striking out angrily at other children. Understanding that Ken's sense of self was at stake, Mrs. Vargas spent considerable effort helping him acquire a more accurate and positive view of his self.

Adults Influence a Child's Self-Esteem: Garbage In, Garbage Out (GIGO)

Teachers, parents, grandparents, brothers, sisters, and others make up a child's social environment; a child's opinion about her competence, control, and worth develops out of close involvement with them. Adults observe children, have attitudes

You know the old saying, "garbage in, garbage out."

Figure 6.4.   Poor computer programs result from careless programming. Similarly, negative self-esteem in children results from degrading, demeaning adult behavior.
(Source: Stone, M. *Data Processing: An Introduction.* Reprinted from INFOSYSTEMS, copyright © 1978 by Hitchcock Publishing Company.)

about them, interact with them, and interpret a child's behavior and characteristics. Adults reflect their attitudes about children to children. Children evaluate the self and develop **self-esteem,** to some extent, because of the attitudes of others important to them. Parents and teachers affect children's self-esteem because young children believe that adults possess a superior wisdom and children tend to rely on adult judgments (Harter, 1983).

The process that adults use to influence children's self-esteem is similar to the process that a computer programmer employs to develop information "output." Computer programmers feed data into the computer.

Significant adults feed data to the child through words, facial expressions, and actions, which essentially outline the adult's attitude toward the child. The adult data say things such as:

"You sure have lots of friends!"
"You're so gentle with Sam [the puppy]. I'll bet he feels safe with you."
"I like being with you."
"It's OK to feel angry when somebody takes something that belongs to you and you remembered to use words to tell him that you were upset."
"It was thoughtful of you to whisper when you walked past the baby's crib when she was sleeping."
"That computer game was fun. Let's play it again sometime."
"This class really works well together on projects."
"You tell funny jokes. Let's call Grandma so that you can tell her!"

Unfortunately, adult data can also bruise self-esteem with hurtful statements such as these:

"No wonder nobody plays with you!"
"You're really a lazy person."
"Yuck! What muddy colors you used for painting."

"Don't bother me. Play by yourself."

"Grow up! Stop whining because she took your puzzle."

"Why don't you stop cramming food into your face? You're fat enough already."

"You know something? I wish you'd never been born!"

Computer scientists emphasize, as the cartoon implies, that if input is garbage (meaningless data), then we can expect output to be garbage as well. Similarly, adults who feed a child garbage messages that convey demeaning, degrading adult attitudes can fully expect that child's self-esteem will be garbage, too. **Garbage in, garbage out.**

PRACTICES THAT HELP CHILDREN DEVELOP AUTHENTIC SELF-ESTEEM

Adults use specific practices that affect a child's self-esteem. Authori**tative,** support-ive adults use strategies that enhance children's self-esteem. Enhancing practices help children to develop authentic—healthy, positive, and realistic—self-esteem. Other, more nonsupportive adults use strategies that degrade or humiliate chil-dren, thus contributing to the development of negative self-esteem (Pawlak & Klein, 1997). Other adults focus on activities that ultimately foster narcissism or excessively self-centered views of the self.

Believe In and Adopt an Authoritative Caregiving Style.[22]

Authoritative caregivers are demanding in an appropriate way. They are also highly responsive to what children need. The authoritative style helps children to comply with (obey) reasonable limits and assists them to be more helpful and cooperative and less aggressive.

Authoritative adults also help children to develop positive self-esteem (Pawlak & Klein, 1997; Kernis et al., 2000). Parents and teachers are most likely to help chil-dren develop healthy self-esteem by combining acceptance, affection, high but rea-sonable expectations, and limits on children's behavior and effort (Lamborn, Mounts, Steinberg & Dornbusch, 1991). Children also have a better chance of developing healthy self-esteem when parents have little conflict in their marriages (Pawlak & Klein, 1997).

Plan Appropriate Activities That Are Deserving of Children's Time

You really do not need to plan "cute activities" intended to boost self-esteem. In fact, "cute activities" are frequently developmentally **in**appropriate, as were the activities in the classroom in the chapter-opening case study. The "This is Me!" book focused the children's attention on themselves as consumers and the "I Am Special Because . . ." book focused on trivial facts about each child.

---

[22]Review the authoritative style of caregiving in Chapter 1 of this text.

Katz (1993) believes that children are most likely to develop authentic self-esteem when they participate in activities for which they can make real decisions and contributions. Katz and Chard's (1989) work on the project approach helps children focus on real topics, environments, events, and objects that are deserving of a young child's time and effort. Developmentally appropriate activities help a child see herself as connected to others, as a hard worker, as kind and helpful, and as a problem solver. These are enduring traits that will help children develop a healthy sense of self and self-esteem.

Express Genuine Interest in Children and Their Activities

Engage in joint activities willingly. Adults who show an interest in children believe that a child's activities—whether playing with measuring cups, finger painting, playing computer games, building a campsite, or playing in sand—are valid and interesting. An adult communicates belief that the child is a person worthy of the adult's attention by demonstrating concern about a child's welfare, activities, and friends. Children tend to be competent, both academically and interpersonally, when significant adults communicate genuine interest in them (Heyman, Dweck, & Cain, 1992).

Several decades ago, Coopersmith (1967) found that parents of children with both high and low self-esteem spent the same amount of time with their children. He explained this puzzling finding by stating that the mothers of children with high self-esteem spent time willingly with their children and seemed to enjoy the interaction. Mothers of children with low self-esteem, on the other hand, appeared to spend time with their children grudgingly.

Give Meaningful Feedback to Children

Giving feedback is one of the basic ways through which adults influence children. Information from adults about how a child has performed a task is an important source of information about the child's competence (Bandura, 1981). The Kernis research group found that children with unstable self-esteem had fathers who were critical; i.e., gave unhelpful feedback (Kernis et al., 2000).

We can help children learn to acknowledge what they do well without bragging about what they do well; i.e., to **take credit gracefully.** Adults who encourage humble credit taking focus on what a child has done well, thereby helping her recognize her competence, one of the dimensions of self-esteem.

Example. Mrs. Vargas knew that Justine recognized and could name a square and a circle. From her checklist she also realized that Justine did not know the name for a triangle. Consequently, she placed a large square, circle, and triangle on a bulletin board and had the same shapes in a box. "You know the names of some shapes, Justine. Please reach into this box, take out one shape, and put it on top of the same shape on the board." When Justine correctly matched squares, the teacher said, "You're right! This is called a 'square.'" When Justine matched the triangular shapes Mrs. Vargas simply said, "You've matched the triangles!"

Avoid empty praise and flattery

Some people use empty praise (constantly saying "Good job!")[23] and flattery, thinking that such information will boost self-esteem. We are most likely to help children develop a healthy sense of self and self-esteem when we use what Katz (1993) calls **appreciation;** i.e., meaningful positive feedback directly related to a child's effort or interest. Expressing appreciation is an appropriate practice that will help a child build a healthy view of her competence.

Example. Mrs. Chen, the consultant, observed Mr. Lee, the third-grade teacher, use appreciation as feedback. Bennie was working on a project about mammals and had a specific question. Mr. Lee had a book at home with some information in it that Bennie needed. The teacher brought the book to school the next day so that Bennie would have a good reference. This teacher was helping Bennie develop healthy self-esteem based on increased understanding of a specific concept. It is also possible that Bennie would view himself as worthy of the teacher's time because Mr. Lee took the trouble to search for the book.

Example. Third-grader Carl's grandmother said to him, "You really concentrate well, Carl. You had homework to do and did it in spite of all the noise outside."

"I see you talking gently to Bunny." The teacher has expressed *appreciation* for the children's efforts to be gentle with the animal.

---

[23]See Kohn (2001).

Acknowledge Both Pleasant and Unpleasant Feelings

A child is jealous of a new baby brother. Another child feels guilty about having hit someone. Another feels great anger when an older child takes his lunch money. A primary child envies the children who belong to the country club. A preschooler is sad about his puppy who had to have surgery. Still another child is angry with a grandfather who makes fun of him. These children are all experiencing unpleasant emotions or feelings.

The real test of support for children comes when they are sick, hurt, unhappy, angry, jealous, fearful, or anxious—when they have unpleasant feelings. It is difficult at times for adults to acknowledge unpleasant feelings. Some adults tend to focus on a young child's behavior that often results from these feelings. They become so upset themselves with the child's behavior that they forget how to or refuse to deal with whatever brought on the guilt, anger, or sadness.

Demonstrate Respect for All Family Groups and Cultures; Avoid Sexism and Judging Physical Attributes

Convey, with words and actions, your abiding belief that all children are valuable, *all* children. It is important that children observe adults demonstrating authentic respect for both genders, for children with different abilities, and for various family groups and different cultures (Bakley, 1997; Pierce & Wardle, 1997).

Example. Mrs. Chen observed that Mr. Claiborne, one of the first-grade teachers, needed help in carrying a bale of hay. He asked for two strong **children** and then chose a girl and a boy. Thus, he avoided treating boys and girls differently.

Example. This teacher knows his class well. Several children live in single-parent families and one child lives with her grandmother. When discussing the topic of families, he showed digital photographs on a large screen of each child's family taken at the school picnic. He acknowledged that each group was indeed a family. He said, "We all live in families. Some families have lots of people in them and some families are small."

Example. Moua's mother and aunt do intricate embroidery on cloth, producing beautiful and complex geometric designs. The children, other faculty, and administrators have admired the wall hanging that they produced and that Mr. Claiborne hung in the classroom.

Teach Specific Social Skills

Some children have poor social skills; for example, they might interrupt others, hit when angry, tattle, refuse to help others, call others names, or not know how to join others in play. Children with serious deficits on social skills are likely to view themselves as incompetent with others and in many social situations. They are also likely to evaluate themselves as having little control over things. Consequently, they are likely to develop negative self-esteem.

Rather than artificially boosting self-esteem, consider teaching such children real skills as a way of giving them positive social experiences with others; for example, they might need to learn how to take turns, how to ask for something, how to enter a group, or how to respond to someone's anger.

Example. Mr. Nellis was supervising on the playground when he observed one of the second-grade children trying to push his way into the line at the slide, only to hear other children shout, "Hey, wait your turn!" The teacher walked over and asked the child in private, "Would you like to take a turn on the slide?" When the child replied in the affirmative, the teacher then said, "I guess that you've noticed that others don't like it much when somebody crashes into the line. If you want a turn just get in the back of the line and wait until it's time for you to go up the ladder."

To summarize, there are many appropriate practices that you can use to guide children toward a healthy and balanced sense of themselves and self-esteem. Many children, however, come from families that use inappropriate and even hurtful practices. Such practices do **not** help children gain accurate self-knowledge or self-control. Hurtful, inappropriate practices batter and bruise children's self-esteem by degrading and demeaning them.

The next brief section describes these degrading practices so that you will know just how some of the children in your care have been treated. Children incorporate negative adult opinions into their sense of self; you will likely see a child's negative view of herself reflected in her behavior. Your job with these children will be to keep this in mind as you strive to reflect a more positive view.

PRACTICES LIKELY TO CONTRIBUTE TO UNHEALTHY SELF-ESTEEM

Child Abuse or Harsh Discipline

There are several forms of child abuse. Child abuse can be mild, moderate, or severe. It can be a one-time event or the abuse can be chronic, a continuous assault on the child. When abuse is severe and ongoing, a child's self-esteem is likely to be damaged (Bolger, Patterson, & Kupersmidt, 1998). Harsh discipline, even when it is not physical—sarcasm, threats, severe punishment, and humiliation—hurts and degrades children. Harsh discipline has a negative effect on self-esteem. It leaves children lacking in self-confidence, feeling inadequate and incompetent, and belittling themselves (Anderson & Hughes, 1989).

Failure to Emphasize Self-Responsibility

Some parents do not take the time necessary to help children assume responsibility. Chores are not specified, or if they are, there is no penalty for not doing them. Nonsupportive adults also often fail to require children to take responsibility when they have hurt someone or damaged property.

Unhelpful, Overly Critical, Negative Style of Communication

Constant negative feedback is degrading because it communicates the adult's belief that the child is incompetent and unworthy of better feedback. Younger children, who rely heavily on adult opinion, feel incompetent when they are constantly criticized. Children who are criticized by adults and who live in a negative verbal environment tend to judge themselves negatively, including judgments of their goodness (Heyman et al., 1992; Kernis, Brown, & Brody, 2000).

Denying Unpleasant Feelings

Denying feelings is akin to denying a child's self because even unpleasant feelings are real and are a part of the child. The implication is that "if my feelings are bad, then maybe I'm bad, too."

Example. "Janna! You're not angry. You really like the new shirt, don't you?" Janna obviously did not like the shirt and was angry, but this adult is denying her the right to her feelings.

Ignoring Children or Spending Time with Them Grudgingly

Ignoring children is one of the classic forms of psychological child abuse. Ignoring children sends them the message that they are essentially unlovable and unloved, that they are not worthy of an adult's time. Some adults, however, do not ignore children, but they are irritable when they interact with their children. They give their time grudgingly.

Example. Marty asked his mother to show him how to make cupcakes. Feeling obligated, Mom did teach him. However, she clearly communicated resentment, annoyance, and irritability by talking quickly and answering Marty's questions abruptly. It is quite possible that Marty will conclude that he cannot be very likable because his own mother does not like to do things with him.

Acting in a Judgmental or Sexist Way, or Showing Contempt for Some Families or Cultural Groups

Examples. A kindergarten teacher allows only boys to use woodworking tools and allows only girls to bathe dolls.

Example. Several children in Mrs. Olsen's class live in single-parent families. Vernon lives with his grandmother, and another child lives in a foster home. Mrs. Olsen demonstrated her insensitivity when she had children bring in pictures of families. Looking at Vernon's picture of him and his grandmother at the park, the teacher said, "This is not a family, Vernon. Why did you even bother to bring in this picture?" (This teacher has been insensitive and ill-mannered. She has been unkind as well as ignorant about different families.)

Case Study Analysis: Self-Esteem

Now that you have read the chapter, analyze the case studies from the beginning of the chapter by answering the following questions. Refer to information from the chapter to support your responses.

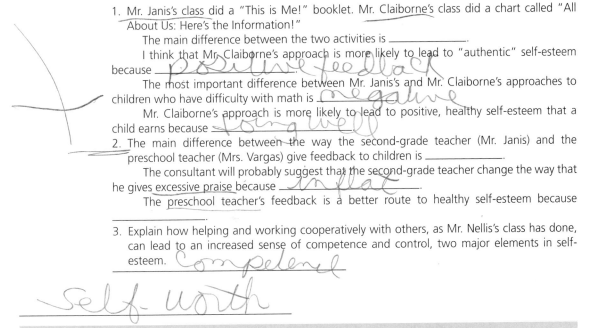

1. Mr. Janis's class did a "This is Me!" booklet. Mr. Claiborne's class did a chart called "All About Us: Here's the Information!"

   The main difference between the two activities is _____.

   I think that Mr. Claiborne's approach is more likely to lead to "authentic" self-esteem because ___*positive feedback*___

   The most important difference between Mr. Janis's and Mr. Claiborne's approaches to children who have difficulty with math is ___*negative*___

   Mr. Claiborne's approach is more likely to lead to positive, healthy self-esteem that a child earns because ___*doing well*___

2. The main difference between the way the second-grade teacher (Mr. Janis) and the preschool teacher (Mrs. Vargas) give feedback to children is _____.

   The consultant will probably suggest that the second-grade teacher change the way that he gives excessive praise because ___*in flat*___.

   The preschool teacher's feedback is a better route to healthy self-esteem because _____.

3. Explain how helping and working cooperatively with others, as Mr. Nellis's class has done, can lead to an increased sense of competence and control, two major elements in self-esteem. ___*Competence*___

___*self-worth*___

Working with Parents. The Road to Self-Esteem Starts in Infancy

Infancy is an important time for an infant's developing sense of self. Infants begin to construct ideas about their "self" as they interact with responsive parents. There some practical things that parents can do to help infants build the "self," thus giving their infant a good start on the road to authentic self-esteem (Curry & Johnson, 1990).

Early infancy. Make the environment predictable, secure, and gentle. Be flexible, not rigid, about feeding schedules. Make routines predictable and regular. Talk to the baby about what you are doing during diapering and feeding. Pay attention to the baby's cues and respond appropriately; e.g., respond to cries quickly.

4 to 9 months. Play games. Traditional games such as, "Where are baby's toes?" or "Peek-a-boo" help infants distinguish themselves from others. Use routine times to play word games.

Encourage play with appropriate toys. Offer safe and clean toys. Do not overwhelm the baby with too many toys at one time. Try offering a toy just within and outside the baby's grasp to encourage an infant to reach. Talk with pleasure about individual toys:

"Oh! Look at this pretty blue cube." Encourage babies to grasp toys and offer toys that make a sound and then focus on that sound. Remember that adult interaction with a baby is more important than any toy.

9 to 15 months. Create an environment that infants can manage—small groups with a moderate, not overwhelming, amount of stimulation. Provide simple props for pretend play—dress-up clothes, pots, pans, and dolls. Play games that help young children develop self-awareness; e.g., "Simon says touch *your* nose. Simon says hold *Daddy's* hand."

15 to 24 months. An adult's response to a toddler's struggle for autonomy influences a child's view of herself. Structure the environment and activities to give children as much control as is safe and possible. Short songs, finger plays, or walks around the block are all appropriate. Toys should encourage active manipulation, problem solving, and talking: blocks, playdough, telephones, books with short stories.

Decide how to look at the child's struggle for autonomy. You are most likely to foster all dimensions of self-esteem if you approach this period as a healthy and normal time rather than as a contest of wills and a power struggle. For example, do state limits but state them as positively as possible: "Walk in the house," rather than "Don't run!" Be prepared for a child's testing of the new limits.

24 to 36 months. Continue to provide safe and appropriate toys and to encourage children to play. Communicate genuine respect through words and actions. Give fair and honest feedback about a toddler's feelings and actions; e.g., "It really is hard to wait for the basket of crackers," or "I can see that you are upset about Mike taking your block. Let's think of some words to use to tell him that you're angry."

REFLECTING ON KEY CONCEPTS

1. Suppose that a child develops negative self-esteem in childhood. How might his negative view of himself affect him for many years into the future?
2. Many people confuse the terms **self-concept** and **self-esteem.** They treat these two terms as if they were the same thing. Explain how the two terms are different.
3. True or false? Explain each of your answers.
   a. Positive self-esteem means that a child will also be kind and thoughtful.
   b. Authentic self-esteem is earned.
4. Suppose that you are talking to a parent who thinks that her child has to be good at everything to have positive self-esteem. How can you help this parent with her misunderstanding?
5. "Garbage in, garbage out." Explain this statement to parents as a way to help them understand how they influence, but do not determine, their child's self-esteem.
6. Choose the strategy from the list in the text that you consider the single most important way to help a child to develop positive self-esteem. Why does that item strike you as most important?
7. From your perspective, why is it just as important to help children develop a strong moral identity and base of values as it is to help children develop positive self-esteem?

APPLY YOUR KNOWLEDGE

1. **Observation.** Observe an adult (parent or teacher) and a young child interacting with each other for a couple of hours. Focus on the practices that the adult uses that will likely help the child develop healthy and balanced self-esteem. State specific examples of the appropriate practices and be prepared to present your analysis to your classmates.
2. **Conversation with an expert.** Invite a professional who works with abused children to speak to your class. Ask this professional questions that will help you understand why abused children are likely to be **highly anxious, compulsive, withdrawn, or overly hostile.** Explain how abuse helps to

create negative (unhealthy and unbalanced) self-esteem in children; i.e., how abuse affects a child's evaluation of her competence, control, and worth.

3. **Problem for you to solve: Identify a more appropriate practice.**

For each situation, state specifically how someone has been demeaned. Describe how the adult could just as easily have used a more appropriate practice to enhance, rather than bruise, the child's self-esteem.

Situation: The baseball coach stared out at his team of 7- and 8-year-old boys and said, "You guys swing the bat like girls! Let me show you one more time how it's done."

How has the coach demeaned the boys?

How has the coach also degraded girls?

What more helpful statement could the coach have directed to the boys when he noticed that they used improper batting technique?

Situation: Five-year-old Matt, pointing to a tree, excitedly said to his grandfather, "Grandpa! Look! An oak tree! I'm learning the names of trees by looking at their leaves." Grandpa pointed to a willow tree and said, "What's the name of that tree?" Matt did not know. Grandpa continued, "Well, you have a lot of learning to do, don't you, young man?"

How has Matt been demeaned?

In your view, what would have been a more appropriate response from Grandpa?

Situation: Sam, the class's pet hamster, died during the night, and the aide found Peter crying after he heard the news. "Come on, Peter. Stop crying. You know that big boys don't cry."

How has Peter been demeaned?

In what way has this adult been sexist?

How has the adult demeaned girls as well as boys?

What would have been a better thing to say to Peter?

Situation: Dad and Jenna were in a restaurant and Dad asked if Jenna wanted spaghetti or pizza. "Pizza," said Jenna. Dad turned to the waiter and said, "Well . . . I think she'll have spaghetti."

How has Jenna been demeaned?

What do you think would have been a more appropriate response from Dad? State your reason.

REFERENCES

Anderson, M., & Hughes, H. (1989). Parenting attitudes and the self-esteem of young children. *Journal of Genetic Psychology, 160*(4), 463–465.

Bakley, S. (1997). Love a little more, accept a little more. *Young Children, 52*(1), 21.

Bandura, A. (1981). Self-referent thought: The development of self-efficacy. In J. H. Flavell & L. D. Ross (Eds.), *Development of social cognition*. New York: Cambridge University Press.

Baumeister, R. (1996). Should schools try to boost self-esteem? Beware the dark side. *American Educator, 20*(2), 14–19, 43.

Bolger, K., Patterson, C., & Kupersmidt, J. (1998). Peer relationships and self-esteem among children who have been maltreated. *Child Development, 69* (4), 1171–1197.

Brazelton, T. B. (1997). Building a better self-image. *Newsweek,* special edition, Spring/Summer, 76–77.

Buzzelli, C. (1992). Research in review: Young children's moral understanding: Learning about right and wrong. *Young Children, 47*(5), 47–53.

Coopersmith, S. (1967). *The antecedents of self-esteem.* San Francisco: W. H. Freeman.

Curry, N., & Johnson, C. (1990). Beyond self-esteem: Developing a genuine sense of human value. *Research Monograph* (Vol. 4). Washington, DC: NAEYC.

Damon, W. (1991). Putting substance into self-esteem: A focus on academic and moral values. *Educational Horizons, 70*(1), 12–18.

Damon, W. (1999). The moral development of children. *Scientific American,* August, 72–78.

Dweck, C., & Leggett, E. (1988). A social-cognitive approach to motivation and personality. *Psychological Review, 95*(2), 256–273.

Elliott, E., & Dweck, C. (1988). Goals: An approach to motivation and achievement. *Journal of Personality and Social Psychology, 54*(1), 5–12.

Harter, S. (1982). The perceived competence scale for children. *Child Development, 53,* 87–97.

Harter, S. (1983). Developmental perspectives on the self system. In P. Mussen (Ed.), *Handbook of Child Psychology* (Vol. 4). New York: Wiley.

Heyman, G., Dweck, C., & Cain, K. (1992). Young children's vulnerability to self-blame and helplessness: Relationship to beliefs about goodness. *Child Development, 63*(2), 401–415.

Katz, L. (1993). Self-esteem and narcissism: Implications for practice. ERIC Digest. ED358973.

Katz, L., & Chard, S. (1989). *Engaging children's minds: The project approach.* Norwood, NJ: Ablex.

Kernis, M., Brown, A., & Brody, Gene. (2000). Fragile self-esteem in children and its associations with perceived patterns of parent-child communication. *Journal of Personality, 68*(2), 225–252.

Kohn, A. (2001). Five reasons to stop saying "good job." *Young Children, 56*(5), 24–28.

Lamborn, S., Mounts, N., Steinberg, L., & Dornbusch, S. (1991). Patterns of competence and adjustment among adolescents from authoritative, authoritarian, indulgent, and neglectful families. *Child Development, 62*(5), 1049–1065.

Lerner, B. (1996). Self-esteem and excellence: The choice and the paradox. *American Educator, 20*(2), 9–13, 41–42.

Lowenthal, B. (1999). Effects of maltreatment and ways to promote resiliency. *Childhood Education, 76* (Summer), 204–209.

Pawlak, J., & Klein, H. (1997). Parental conflict and self-esteem: The rest of the story. *Journal of Genetic Psychology, 15*(3), 303–313.

Pierce, J., & Wardle, J. (1997). Cause-and-effect beliefs and self-esteem of overweight children. *Journal of Child Psychology and Psychiatry and Allied Disciplines, 38*(6), 645–650.

Tafarodi, R., & Swarm, W. (1995). Self-liking and self-competence as dimensions of global self-esteem: Initial validation of a measure. *Journal of Personality Assessment, 65,* 322–342.

Tafarodi, R., & Vu, C. (1997). Two-dimensional self-esteem and reactions to success and failure. *Personality and Social Psychology Bulletin, 23*(6), 626–636.

Verschueren, K., Marcoen, A., & Buyck, P. (1998). Five-year-olds' behaviorally presented self-esteem: Relations to self-perceptions and stability across a 3-year period. *Journal of Genetic Psychology, 159* (9), 273–279.

Wong, P. T. (1992). Control is a double-edged sword. *Canadian Journal of Behavioural Science, 24*(2), 143–146.

✔ CHECK OUT THE WEB SITES RELATED TO THIS CHAPTER

✓ Childswork/Childsplay

www.childswork.com. Go to the "products" link and then to the "self-esteem" link for books, posters, and games focusing on self-esteem. This company also has a catalogue: "The Building Blocks of Self-Esteem." It includes games and other materials for building healthy and balanced self-esteem. Phone: 800.962.1141.

✓ National Black Child Development Institute
www.nbcdi.org. Click on "PEP." This is the "Parent
  Empowerment Program." NBCDI believes that
  informed, effective parents can help their children
  to thrive.

✓ Parents Magazine
www.parents.com. Many links. Go to the articles section
  or type "self-esteem" in the search box.

Resilience and Stress in Childhood

"Growing up means meeting a variety of challenges, many of which can cause stress."

(McCracken, 1986)

After reading and studying this chapter, you will be able to

❑ **Define** resiliency and **explain in your own words** how children become resilient.

❑ **Define** stress for young children and **explain** it as a child/environment relationship.

❑ **Identify** two major sources of stress for children and **give examples** of each.

❑ **List** the stages of the stress response and **summarize** the elements of each stage.

❑ **Explain** how a young child's developmental level makes it difficult for him to cope with stress on his own.

❑ **List** and **give examples of** general guidelines for helping children cope with stress.

❑ **Analyze** a case study in which a teacher attempts to buffer the effect of stress for a child.

Case Study: Josiah's New School

Tuesday, 5:30 P.M.

Mr. Nellis waited for Josiah, a new child in his kindergarten class, and Josiah's father to arrive. "Hello Josiah. I'm pleased to meet you," said Mr. Nellis. To the father he said, "Please come in and we'll all look around Josiah's new classroom." "This is where you hang your coat. I've printed your name on your locker already, Josiah." He showed the pictures of the children in the class and took Josiah's picture to place with the others. He pointed out areas in the classroom and asked Josiah about the classroom at his other school. Mr. Nellis showed Josiah the children's bathroom where the 5-year-old demonstrated that he knew how to turn on faucets, use the soap dispenser, and reach the paper towels. Josiah looked at the toileting area, which was in a room right next to the classroom. "You can go to the bathroom whenever you want to," said Mr. Nellis. "Your other teacher told me that you usually had a carton of milk for snack. Here you can still have milk if you want it but you can also choose juice."

Mr. Nellis asked Josiah about his favorite activities (building with blocks, puzzles, and singing). Mr. Nellis told Josiah that he could play with blocks and puzzles every day and that everyone would be learning a new song tomorrow. Then they looked in the nap room, and Josiah smiled when he discovered that he already had a cot with his name on it. The teacher gave Josiah's father a copy of his class schedule so that Dad would have a clear idea of how the day was structured. "Why don't you look this over and just talk casually with Josiah about the flow of the day? It might help him make the transition."

"Thanks," said Dad, "for meeting with us so late in the day. Can you think of anything else that *I* can do to help Josiah make this move to a new school?" "Yes, there is something," Mr. Nellis replied. "I have a children's book on moving. You can borrow it if you like. Josiah might like to read it with you. And here's a short handout on how you can prevent stress from this move for Josiah. A group of parents and teachers put it together and it has helped other parents and children who are new to our school."

Thursday morning

Josiah stood next to his locker while all the new faces swirled around him. Mr. Nellis decided to let him watch the other children for a while, but brought him one of the unit blocks to hold while he looked. Soon he brought Louie over to him and said, "Louie, would you please show Josiah the rest of the blocks and explain how we put them away?" Mr. Nellis discussed the playground rules with Josiah when they went outside, and at naptime, Josiah knew that he had a cot with his name on it.

Children are not immune to stress. They face stress-inducing situations every day, like the one that Josiah and his family faced with the move to a new home and school. In this chapter, you will learn about **resilience** in children and about how **stress** affects children. You will also learn about stages of responding to stress, what it takes to cope effectively, and why young children have a difficult time coping with stress on their own. On a practical level, you will learn some **general guidelines** for helping children with stress and then discover how to help children who are facing a specific **potentially stressful event**—moving. In this way, you will learn how to help children become resilient.

RESILIENCE IN YOUNG CHILDREN

Many children face adversity in their homes and communities (Weinreb, 1997). These are the **high-risk** children about whom we worry so much. What we know, though, is that many, but certainly not all, children who face multiple and severe risks show great **resilience** as they overcome the odds. **Resilience is a set of qualities enabling a child to adapt successfully in spite of risk and adversity.** A person who is resilient is socially competent, can solve problems, can reflect critically on issues, is autonomous, and has a sense of purpose (Benard, 1995).

Children develop resilience in their families, schools, and/or communities

Resilient children have been able to connect with at least one caring and compassionate person, often a teacher, who serves as a good model of confidence and positive action. Children learn to understand and manage potentially stressful events in caring and compassionate adult/child relationships.

Protective Factors That Foster Resilience

What separates families who foster resilience from those who do not? A relisience-building family or school would make you feel like spending time there, that the adults really seem to care about the children. Adults in these systems have a philosophy or basic core values with protection of children at the center—the most important thing that they do—over and above their stated role.

Adults in resiliency-building families or schools tend to be authori**tative**, a style fostering resilience. Authoritative adults give children three things, **protective factors** that enable children to navigate the bumpy road of frustration or adversity. These three protective factors are

- a caring relationship,
- high expectations, and
- opportunities for participation.

Caring relationships

An authori**tative** teacher, for example, is high in responsiveness and one of the most important aspects of high responsiveness is a warm and caring attitude toward children. This teacher tries to develop a good and caring relationship with all children in a class. The teacher acknowledges each child's existence, what that child does and creates, and how she feels. The teacher knows that a good relationship is especially important for children who do not have a close relationship with parents.

High expectations

Authori**tative** caregivers, parents or teachers, are high in demandingness and have reasonable but high expectations for children. This helps children become resilient, partly because of how the expectations affect a child's self-esteem. Authoritative adults who have high but reasonable expectations help children develop

A caring relationship helps a child become resilient.

competence, control, and worth, the building blocks of positive self-esteem. Competence, control, and a belief that one is worthy of affection also form the foundation of a resilient spirit.

Opportunities for participation

All humans have a great need to be valued and validated. There is a strong urge for humans to be members of a group. Children have these needs, just as we all do. They require chances to operate as a member of a group, and adults in protective systems make sure that their children get those chances. This can be something as simple as participating in making the limits or rules for a classroom in which caring adults have high expectations. It can also mean participating in family events, activities in one's religious group, Cub or Brownie Scouts, 4-H, library reading groups, care and feeding of animals, theater or other arts group, or athletic teams.

The list of ways for children to participate is long. Children do not need to participate in a large number of activities, only those that give them pleasure and a sense of real belonging. Adults who want to help children become resilient can do two practical things. One is to help a child identify or find those activities that he likes and wants to do. For parents, this might mean spending "registration fees" for activities and letting a child try out the activity. For teachers, this means observing children carefully to discover what they really like to do. And once a child has found an activity that he likes, make sure that he has opportunities for participating and for feeling like a valued member of the group.

THE BIOLOGY OF STRESS

Specific parts of the brain and nervous system, as well as parts of the endocrine system affect one's reaction to potentially stressful events. Figure 7.1 defines biological terms. Understanding these definitions will help you understand the biology of stress in childhood.

Biological Definitions and Terms for Understanding the Concept of Stress[24]

Homeostasis A state of equilibrium or balance in which the internal environment of the body remains relatively constant. Survival depends on maintaining homeostasis.

Stressor A factor capable of stimulating a stress response.

Stress Condition produced by factors causing changes in the body's internal environment. Some of the changes are potentially life threatening. Disrupts body's homeostasis (state of equilibrium or balance).

General stress syndrome A set of reactions, controlled in large part by the hypothalamus when it detects a loss of homeostasis, and directed toward reinstating homeostasis.

Hypothalamus A portion of the brain located below the thalamus. Connected to other parts of the brain. Can receive impulses from other parts. Can send impulses to other parts. Plays a key role in general stress syndrome; i.e., in maintaining homeostasis, by regulating heart rate, blood pressure, and body temperature, among other things. Impulses originating here are sent via the sympathetic nerve fibers to the adrenal medulla. The impulses tell the adrenal medulla to release its hormones.

Autonomic nervous system The portion of the nervous system which functions independently without conscious effort on a person's part.

Sympathetic nervous system Portion of the autonomic nervous system. Arises from two specific regions of the spinal cord, the thoracic and lumbar regions. Receives impulses from the hypothalamus. Relays impulses to the adrenal medulla. Function: primarily preparing the body for stressful or emergency situations in which energy has to be expended; for example, during stressful situations, sympathetic division increases breathing rates and heart rate. Prepares body for "flight or fight."

Adrenal glands Endocrine glands located on top of the kidneys.

Adrenal medulla The inner part of the adrenal gland connected with sympathetic division of the autonomic nervous system. Receives impulses from sympathetic nerve fibers, and thus is stimulated to release its hormones. Secretes hormones; e.g., "stress" hormones, cortisol.

Figure 7.1.

---

[24]Source: From Hole, J. (1981). *Human anatomy and physiology.* Dubuque, IA: Wm. C. Brown.

TYPES OF STRESSORS

Stressors: factors producing stress, some form of excessive stimulation. Some of these factors are psychological; others are physical. At times, physical and psychological stressors are combined and they interact (Hole, 1981).

Physical Stressors

Physical stressors: forms of excessive stimulation that injure or can potentially injure the tissue of some part of a child's body. There are a variety of such physical stressors—excessively loud noises, extremely harsh lighting, decreased oxygen or lack of oxygen, extreme heat, extreme cold, injuries, infections, drugs. Children who experience these stressors usually perceive them as painful or unpleasant.

Example. Ronnie, 4 months old, sat in the car seat of his 19-year-old mother's car, with the windows opened about 1 inch. The outside temperature was 80 degrees, but the temperature inside the car, despite the slightly opened windows, had risen to an even greater, dangerously high temperature. Ronnie had been there for almost an hour when a passerby noticed him and called the police. Ronnie was unconscious; he later died at the hospital. Stressor: extreme heat. Tissue of the body affected: Ronnie's brain.

Example. Sarah's family was spending a month on vacation at the beach. Sarah's baby-sitter failed to put sunscreen on 4-year-old Sarah when the child played outside. Sarah was sunburned and her skin blistered. Stressor: unprotected and excessive exposure to sunlight. Tissue of body affected: skin.

Psychological Stressors

Psychological stressors: forms of excessive stimulation with the potential to threaten a child's sense of well-being or to keep a child from developing a sense of well-being. Children might perceive several things as psychologically stressful and children have varying views about what a psychological stressor is. One child might see the death of a beloved grandparent, for example, as extremely stressful. Another child might not view a grandparent's death as stressful at all. Psychological stress, then, is a relationship between a child and his environment. Stress is not an *event*, such as the death of a grandparent, but is instead a relationship between a child and his perception of that event.

This relationship involves whether a child understands and can evaluate an event as well as a child's ability to cope with the event. A child is most likely to feel psychological stress when he cannot understand, evaluate, or cope effectively with some internal or external event. He then feels overwhelmed by the inability to cope, thus resulting in stress (Holroyd & Lazarus, 1982). Children often feel stress when conditions keep them from fulfilling any of several fundamental needs—for security, bonding, acceptance, status, meaning, and mastery (Zimbardo, 1982).

Example. Juan goes to a school in which close to a third of the children were not born in the United States and who have been here for fewer than four years. The school district was not prepared to meet the needs of this influx of children with special requirements, and is now struggling to do so. Juan is having a great deal of trouble adjusting to life in a new country, as are his parents. Juan, 6 years old, does not understand and therefore cannot cope with several aspects of his new school. He is very likely to experience psychological stress because he feels overwhelmed in this new environment.

Some people automatically view specific **life events** as stressful, such as a move, a new school, a parent's death, or parents divorcing. In reality, these are merely life events (Zegans, 1982), which makes them only **potentially stressful.** They create stress only if a child does not understand the event, cannot evaluate the event, or does not have the skills for effectively coping with the event.

For example, many people believe that moving is automatically a stressful life event (Jalongo, 1986b). It would probably be more accurate to call moving a **potentially stressful event;** it has the potential to create psychological stress, but whether it does depends on a child's understanding of and ability to cope with the move. Juan, in the example just given, did view moving as stressful.

Combination of Physical and Psychological Stressors

Physical and psychological stressors frequently interact in a child's life. Thoughts about a physically stressful experience are tangled with psychological stress connected with the physical stress. Children physically injured in some way might then fear or display anxiety about similar situations.

Example. Daniel is a 2-year-old whose father deliberately burned him with a cigarette as punishment for an accident during toilet learning (often called potty training). Physical stressor: hot tip of the cigarette. Tissue of body affected: skin between two of Daniel's toes. Psychological stress: fear and anxiety in the relationship with a parent who uses sadistic punishment.

Example. Jordan, in Mrs. Vargas's class (and having much trouble with aggression) has a mother and father who argue loudly almost every day in front of their children. Jordan shows signs of fear during and after the arguments. Physical stressors: loud arguing and objects thrown against walls by parents. Tissue of body affected: arm (welt raised when Dad threw a bowl at the wall, but hit Jordan). Psychological stress: heightened emotional arousal from all of this background anger. Jordan seems to be in a constant state of high alert at school and often misreads other children's intentions.

ACUTE AND CHRONIC STRESS

Suppose that a child has perceived a potential stressor as stressful. He does not understand the stressor or might not have the skills for coping with it. The stress that he experiences can be either **acute** (profound, deep, extreme, intense, short-lived) or **chronic** (persistent, unceasing, continuous) stress.

Acute Stress

Acute stress: intense stress that occurs suddenly. Acute stress can be physical or psychological, or a combination of the two. It occurs quite unexpectedly but tends to subside as abruptly as it arose; for example, a visit to the emergency room to have a broken arm set (physical and psychological stress). How an event affects a child depends, in large part, on how others deal with the event and on how the child appraises it.

Example. Six-year-old Jessica stood alone on the front steps of her house, crying. Just minutes before, the fire truck had zoomed into her family's driveway, sirens blaring. The firefighters were at the back of the house in the garage, putting out a fire. Jessica's mother, along with two friends, watched them, looking as though they were at a party, with cigarettes dangling from one hand and drinks in the other. Not one of them explained anything or paid attention to Jessica, other than to tell her to get to and stay in the front of the house. Jessica's apparent upset escalated until she screamed with fear. Her mother strode around the side of the house and angrily regarded her daughter.

Chronic Stress

Chronic stress: persistent stress, which comes into a person's life and remains for a long period or even forever. Chronic stress is like a chronic disease, such as diabetes, in that it is a constant part of a person's life. The children in your classes come from a variety of backgrounds. Chances are very good that, in any one year, several of the children will be under chronic stress. They will have experienced grinding poverty, illness, child abuse, irresponsible or inept parenting, long-term bitterness after parents divorcing, seemingly never-ending daily hassles, and loneliness or not having friends. The effects of chronic stress seem to accumulate to cause problems (Bullock, 1997) even for children who are well adjusted (Honig, 1986).

SOURCES OF STRESS

There are two major sources of stress for young children—internal and external sources. **Internal** sources come from within the child (Honig, 1986). **External** sources originate outside the child.

Internal Sources of Stress

Internal sources of stress include things such as hunger pangs in a neglected infant or child, shyness (Zimbardo, 1982), or headaches (Sargent, 1982). Thoughts about real or imagined dangers can be a source of stress, too. Emotions are also potentially internal sources of stress. Anxiety, anger, jealousy, guilt, and even joy are potentially stressful for children if parents and teachers do not help them understand and deal with these emotions. Children do not automatically comprehend and know how to handle an emotion such as anger (Kuebli, 1994; Marion, 1997).

Example. Bill has experienced a lot of anxiety over usually being chosen last in pickup games of basketball in his neighborhood park. His dad has not helped Bill deal with this feeling and has not shown Bill how to practice basic basketball skills. Bill, now clearly stressed about this situation, has begun to avoid the park.

External Sources of Stress

Other potential sources of stress for children are **external;** that is, they come from the child's environment. Some of these external sources of stress exist within a child's family, while others are in a child's caregiving arrangement. Some external sources of stress exist in schools, others come from peers, and still others have their roots in the interaction of several systems. These stressors can be:

- child abuse or neglect, experiencing it directly (Terr, 1991)
- witnessing child abuse but not experiencing it firsthand
- inept or harsh child guidance practices (Baumrind, 1996)
- anger-arousing social interactions (Fabes & Eisenberg, 1992; Marion, 1997)
- background anger; i.e., anger that a child hears and observes, but is not directed at him
- loneliness or not having friends (Bullock, 1997)
- DIP (developmentally **in**appropriate practices) classrooms (Burts, Hart, Charlesworth, Fleege, Mosley, & Thomasson, 1992; Hart, Burts, Durland, Charlesworth, DeWolf, & Fleege, 1998; Hyson, Hirsh-Pasek, Rescorla, & Cone, 1991)
- standardized testing (Fleege, Charlesworth, Burts, & Hart, 1992)
- observing violence and aggression in newscasts, movies, videos, video games, real life, and cartoons (Surgeon General, 2000)
- going to a new school (Kerbow, 1996)
- death or injury of a friend or even another child, who is not a friend, but who goes to the same school; death of a pet; death of a family member
- poor-quality child care (Matlock & Green, 1990)
- divorce (Amato, 1997)
- joint-custody arrangements (McKinnon & Wallerstein, 1987)
- moving (Prestine, 1997)
- daily hassles for parents (Crnic & Greenberg, 1990)
- overcrowded living conditions
- illness and hospitalization (Bull & Drotar, 1991; Stuber, Nadar, Yasuda, & Pynoos, 1991)

HOW STRESS AFFECTS CHILDREN

Professionals who work with children can fully expect to experience firsthand a child's reactions to stress. You might wonder why one child suddenly has problems focusing on projects, why another behaves aggressively, or why still another is highly anxious. Stress affects children in a variety of ways, just as it affects adults. Stress takes its toll on children physically, behaviorally, or psychologically. If a child used words to express the stress that he feels, he might say, "There's something wrong in my life."

Physical Effects of Stress

A racing heart rate, dry mouth, a sick feeling in the stomach, a headache: most adults have experienced such physical reactions to some situation that they perceived as stressful—giving a speech, or seeing the flashing lights of a police car on the interstate. Children can and do experience the same physical effects of stress. Any or a combination of these physical effects usually shows up in cases of acute stress. Given enough stress (as in a chronically stressful situation such as child abuse or a developmentally inappropriate classroom), a child might have even greater physical effects from the stress.

Stress, white blood cells, and resistance to infections

Stress can eventually play a major role in disease (Hole, 1981; Stein, Keller, & Schleifer, 1981; Zegans, 1982). For example, stress often disrupts a child's immune system response and makes it difficult for the child's body to deal effectively with infections. Here is how this works: white blood cells (leukocytes) defend a child's body against invading microorganisms.

Example. A child gets a splinter in his foot; the splinter breaks the skin and introduces bacteria. The bacteria multiply (the infection) and white blood cells move through the blood to the site of the infection. White blood cells, which contain digestive enzymes, destroy the bacteria in a process called phagocytosis; literally, "cell eating."

The number of white blood cells changes when an abnormal situation arises. A child's white blood cell count may drop with mumps, chicken pox, flu, or polio. It also drops when a child is anemic or has been poisoned from a heavy metal such as lead, arsenic, or mercury. Additionally, a child's white blood cell count tends to drop when a child is overwhelmed by a stressful event. Thus, the child has less protection from infections. A child who is chronically stressed, say from child abuse, is likely to have a lowered resistance to infectious diseases.

Stress, brain size, and synapses

Lowenthal (1999) reviewed the literature on the effect of child abuse and neglect, a major stressor, on children's development. A startling, unfortunate, but preventable outcome of continued abuse and neglect is the effect on a child's developing brain. As you read in a previous section, a major stressor such as abuse signals the child's body to prepare for "fight or flight"; i.e., the body prepares to defend itself from danger.

A child under constant threat of abuse is nearly always in this state of readiness. The child's body may then produce an excessive amount of stress hormones and an excessively high level of stress hormones can kill brain cells and reduce the number of connections among brain cells (the synapses). Neuberger (1997) noted that adults subjected to long-term abuse as children have brains in which the parts responsible for tasks such as memory or regulating emotions are smaller. Abused children's brains can be up to as much as 30 percent smaller than the brains of children who do not experience the stress of child abuse (Perry, 1993).

Behavioral and Psychological Effects of Stress

Nail biting, bullying, fatigue, aggression, withdrawal, anxiety, fear: all these and others are behavioral or psychological indicators of childhood stress. The psychological distress that children feel, for example, when abused, when they move, or when rejected very often shows up in **behavior.** See Figure 7.2, Behavioral Indicators of Stress in Young Children. Some children react to stress with passive behavior while others display a more active approach. You might find that some children react to stress as they play or work with specific objects.

An issue to ponder about behavioral indicators of stress

Oppositional Defiant Disorder (ODD) is a psychiatric disorder in childhood. It is quite normal for children to test limits and be what some people call **oppositional** at specific junctures during development; i.e., during toddlerhood and early adolescence. The psychiatric community believes, however, that "openly uncooperative and hostile behavior becomes a serious concern when it is so frequent and consistent that it stands out when compared with other children of the same age and developmental level," and when it seriously impairs a child's functioning (American Academy of Child & Adolescent Psychiatry [AACAP], 1999).

Children diagnosed with ODD have frequent temper tantrums, are touchy, are easily annoyed by others, show a lot of resentment or anger, and argue frequently with adults. The AACAP (1999) advises that a child labeled as ODD also

---

Behavioral Indicators of Stress in Young Children

Children show us that they are experiencing stress in a number of ways:*
Reactions to stress might be passive.
    Excessive fatigue
    Withdrawing and putting head on table or desk
    Excessive fears
Reactions to stress might be more active with behaviors that involve only the child.
    Nail biting
    Manipulating one's hands or mouth
    Repetitive body movements
Reactions to stress might show up when children interact with others.
    Stuttering
    Bullying, threatening, or hurting others (See Seth in Chapter 9)
    Nervous, inappropriate laughter
Reactions to stress might show up as children work with objects.
    Excessive squeezing or tapping of pencils, markers, or crayons
    Clumsy or fumbling behavior

*Sources: Listed in Chapter 3, Figure 3.3.

Figure 7.2.

receive a thorough evaluation to screen for other disorders coexisting with ODD; these other disorders must also be treated.

It is quite possible that some children diagnosed with ODD are also under a great deal of stress. The AACAP even notes that symptoms of ODD tend to increase when a child is "under stress." One of the treatment methods for ODD is training parents. It is possible that parents of some children with ODD have had a major impact on their child's problem with inept or harsh parenting. Inept or harsh parenting is a major psychological stressor for children. Irresponsible parenting is also frequently a physical stressor for children if the parenting includes physical, including sadistically physical, punishment.

The thorough evaluation recommended by the AACAP should not be just an evaluation of the child. It might be more proper and accurate to diagnose a family system as having a problem when a child is given the label "ODD." We might need a new label for the family system problem. The child would then not be the "identified patient"; the family system is the patient.

STAGES IN RESPONDING TO STRESS

A child goes through a series of stages in responding to an event that he does not understand and cannot control. Each of the three stages—**alarm, appraisal, and searching for a coping strategy**—places different demands on a child's body (Zegans, 1982).

Alarm

A child stops what he is doing and orients toward or focuses on the potentially stressful event. A child is aware of the potentially stressful event for the first time. He might become aware of danger in this new situation or remember danger from similar situations in the past. He will be alarmed.

Example. Ben, 7 years old, heard his mother's words and closed his eyes (stage of alarm): "We're moving. You have to help me pack your toys and books tomorrow." He and his mother and brother were moving yet again, putting Ben in another new school, his third in two years.

Example. David, 6 years old, looked up from his game, startled (stage of alarm), when his mom said, "Your father will be here to pick you up soon." David's parents had joint custody of him after their divorce and David had come to dread visits with his dad, who had married a woman with an 8-year-old child. This older boy bullies David and Dad knows about it but has not done anything to protect David.

Appraisal

The **appraisal** stage is complex and involves reviewing what this event meant in the past. Ben, for example, thought, "I was scared when I went to the last new school but the teacher helped me find things." Children also try to figure out how to cope as Ben did: "Maybe the new teacher will help me find things."

Several things affect a child's appraisal of a potentially stressful event. One is his **developmental level in terms of memory and perception.** Infants and very young children will obviously not be able to perceive and remember or evaluate a stress-inducing event like a much older child or an adult would.

Another factor is a **child's experience with adults who have modeled how to look at and evaluate events.** A child whose parents model poor anger management skills, for example, will probably appraise an anger-arousing event differently from a child whose parents show responsible anger management.

Positive self-esteem is another factor that affects an older child's appraisal. Older children with high self-esteem have a much more positive view of stress-inducing events and their ability to cope with the stressor. Feeling competent is one of the building blocks of positive self-esteem, and in regard to stress, a feeling that "I can handle this."

Example. Ben is a resilient child who has a positive and realistic view of himself. He appraised the situation and said to himself, "The teacher in my last school told me that I know how to make friends and that other children like me."

Searching for a Coping Strategy

The third stage in responding to stress involves searching for a coping strategy. Children, like all of us, do not always cope effectively with stress-inducing events. We know from some older research that children have a better chance of coping successfully when they believe they can control or master an event (Levine, Weinberg, & Ursin, 1978). Controlling or mastering an event depends, first, on whether the child is familiar with and understands an event, and second, on whether he can generate successful coping strategies. The following possibilities were outlined by Zegans (1982).

First possibility: A child is familiar with an event, has actively dealt with it in the past, and used a good coping strategy

This is the best-case scenario because the child has already successfully dealt with a similar stress-inducing event. This enables him to think that he can master the current event.

Example. Tyrell was to get his first barbershop haircut. He had has been to the shop on several occasions with his father whenever Dad got haircuts, and Tyrell occasionally got to sit in the big chair on his own. The barber has demonstrated his haircutting tools, such as a comb, scissors, and towel. Tyrell was thoroughly familiar with the barbershop and, from Dad's observations, seemed not to fear it at all.

Second possibility: A child is familiar with an event, has actively dealt with it in the past, but used an ineffective coping strategy

In this case, the strategy did not work because it was applied incorrectly or was not a good strategy in the first place. This would make a child somewhat wary, or even downright frightened, of the same or a similar stressful event in the future, because he has not figured out how to cope.

Example. Luke, 7 years old, had been to the emergency room previously when he put his hand through a garage window. The hospital personnel were not mean to him, but they were efficient; their main goal was to stop the profuse bleeding from his hand and arm. They failed to explain procedures and Luke reacted, understandably, with great fear and upset. Now he was going to the emergency room again, but this time for a skin rash that erupted on a Saturday night. Luke's father also remembered the previous visit to the hospital and tried to reassure his son about the current visit. Despite his dad's calm explanation and reassurances, Luke still viewed the hospital as a frightening place because of his first experience there.

Third possibility: A child is familiar with a stressor but has not really dealt with it firsthand

The child only passively dealt with the stressor through secondhand experience and the secondhand source of information has an impact on his level of emotional or physiological arousal.

Example. Jake was Ben's friend in Ben's old neighborhood. Jake's family had never moved but Jake observed Ben's reactions to having to move to another new school. Jake is somewhat familiar with what happens when somebody moves because his teacher read a story about moving before Ben left. In spite of this, Jake has an incomplete understanding of the process.

Fourth possibility: A child is totally unfamiliar with a stressor

In this case, a child who has never dealt with such an event is now thinking about it for the first time and does not yet have a coping strategy. His degree of anxiety or confusion depends largely on whether adults help him understand the event and whether they assist him to figure out how to cope effectively with the stressor.

You can be most helpful to a child who is dealing with a stressful event for the first time in a couple of ways. Consider **changing the situation.** You can eliminate the stressful event altogether, as Diana's mother did by taking the new dog from next door back to his own yard after he ambled into Diana's yard.

When the stressor is inevitable and cannot be eliminated, assist a child in comprehending the meaning of an unfamiliar event. Help a child understand as much as he is capable of understanding. If you use this strategy, you will be acting as a "buffer" to a stressful event. Think of this as **"demystifying" the stressful event,** making it less mysterious for a child.

Example. When Tony's family moved (something they had never done before) they did not know anyone in their new neighborhood. Dad took Tony for a get-acquainted walk and met the new neighbors.

Example. Josiah's (chapter-opener case study child) first trip to the emergency room had all the earmarks of a stressful event when his parents ran to the car with him seconds after he fell off the swing and broke his arm. In the car, Mom kept her composure so that she could help Josiah because she realized how frightened he was. "Remember the hospital? We are going there now, to a special room called the emergency room. A doctor is waiting for you and she will take a special picture so she can see your arm bone. Then she'll fix the bone. Mom and Daddy will stay with you. Then we'll all come home. It'll be OK."

COPING EFFECTIVELY WITH STRESSORS

What Is Coping?

Suppose that you are working at your computer and your computer freezes; you cannot move the cursor and you cannot type. This has never happened to you before. You sit back and say, "OK, I have a couple of options. I can get out the manual and try to find out what has happened. I can just turn off the computer and try to reboot it." What you would have done in the process of thinking through your predicament is to have coped. You looked inside yourself and found the knowledge that you needed to get the computer going again and to keep yourself calm.

A person who **copes** looks for something inside or outside himself to come to terms with stressors (Haan, 1982). In the computer example, you coped by searching within yourself for the resources (knowledge) that enabled you to deal with the crisis. At other times, a person looks for something outside of himself to deal with a stressor.

Example. Another person has the same problem with his computer but calls an 800 number for help. He has coped by looking outside himself for the resources (the 800 number) that he needed.

Our goal in working with children is to help them to cope as effectively as possible with the stressors that they face. One thing that might help you is to remember that coping does not necessarily mean a child will have a happy or successful outcome. Some situations, such as child abuse, make it very difficult for a person to achieve a "successful" solution (Haan, 1982).

Different Ways of Coping with Stressors

There are many of ways of coping with potentially stressful events. There is no one-size-fits-all coping strategy. You will quickly learn to recognize different patterns in different children and in other adults. No one way is best for every person, and it is probably wise not to force any specific method of coping with stress on anybody.

Some people cope by getting information on the stressor

Somebody who copes with stress in this way searches his memory for information on how he has dealt with a similar stressor. A person might also look for information outside himself—from other people, self-help groups, a therapist, formal classes, books, pamphlets, movies, television, magazine articles, videos, or the Internet. Bookstores usually stock "self-help" books that people read for information on almost any stress-inducing event. Early childhood teachers give information on different stressors when they read well-written books to children about specific stressors such as death or moving (Jalongo, 1986a).

Others cope by taking direct action

Some people take direct action by leaving the scene. Withdrawal can be a healthy way to take direct action and to cope. The withdrawal can be temporary, as when a parent leaves a room to cool off rather than yell at or hurt a crying baby. Such a person chooses either to return to further deal with the stressor or to cope by permanently withdrawing. A person who withdraws as a way to cope might either announce his plan to leave or might just leave without notice.

Example. Rachel, 5 years old and in Mr. Nellis's kindergarten class, was tired of hearing Louie tell her and the other girls that they didn't know how to do certain things because they were girls. She was weary from irritation when Louie kept telling her that girls could not play with certain toys. She dealt with the stress of her irritation by announcing, "You can just play by yourself, Louie. I'm not going to play with you anymore!" She then left the science table.

Others take direct action by asserting their rights. This implies that the person sees an injustice, which is causing him some stress. For example, asserting one's rights by using words to express the emotion is a good way to deal with the stress of anger.

Example. Rachel was clearly upset when Louie sat at her place for lunch. She took direct action this time by asserting her rights and using words, as Mr. Nellis had suggested: "Hey, Louie. That's my chair! Your chair is over here."

Some people cope by restraining movements or actions

A person might control his actions because he understands that it would be the most sensible way to deal with a stressor. For example, a teacher instructed a child who did not have friends in class on how to make friends and taught him how to join a group. Specifically, the teacher showed the child how to control his movements and control his tendency to push his way into the group. The next day he practiced and controlled his actions by waiting and observing what the other children were doing before joining them.

It is also possible for children to control their actions out of fear or anxiety. Children who are abused often try to be as quiet as possible around the abuser, hoping to seem to disappear and not be noticed.

Still others cope with stress by denying or avoiding the problem

As you remember from your study of psychology, denial is a basic defense mechanism that protects people by allowing them not to face certain situations or to remember unpleasant events.

Example. Elena, 8 years old, is the fourth child in a family of seven children and her parents are seasonal farmworkers. Elena's parents love their children; nevertheless, they have to move frequently. All of the school-age children in Elena's family change schools frequently as the family moves from one farm to another. Elena, clearly upset by the turmoil of constant moving, has begun to deny that the family is about to move again as a way of coping with the stress.

Denial is also evident in abusive families, with abused children often denying that abuse is even occurring. Denial, in fact, is one of the hallmarks of an abusive family system. Denial does not solve problems, however, and people who are in denial often cope with their problem by engaging in some unhealthy or dangerous activity, such as excessive eating, drinking alcohol, taking illegal drugs, or gambling.

What Does It Take to Cope Effectively? Do Young Children "Have What It Takes" to Cope Effectively on Their Own With Stressors?

Children's cognitive, physical, social, and emotional development affects whether they have what it takes to cope with stressors on their own or whether they need adult guidance in order to cope. This section first focuses on the requirements for coping successfully (Haan, 1982). Then the focus shifts to explaining why young children cannot cope effectively with stressors on their own.

To cope well you have to be able to think about more than one thing at a time

A person who can sift through several options or solutions has one of the abilities that it takes to cope with stressors. Looking at option A as well as option B requires that the person have the basic cognitive ability to consider at least two things at a time. Essentially, what the person must be able to do is to look at a problem from different angles. He might have to take a perspective different from his own.

Can young children think about more than one thing at a time? Usually, they cannot. Young children are not as capable as older people of taking different perspectives (see Chapter 2 for a discussion of perspective taking). They tend to focus on only one thing at a time and cannot seem to pay attention to all helpful and relevant facts. A 4-year-old child who gets upset when he slips away from Dad at the grocery store and then cannot find his way back would most likely focus only on one thing, the fact that he was lost.

To cope well you must be able to invent alternative ways of solving a problem

First, a person must have the concept that "I can move from this problem to a solution to this problem." Second, he must also be able to generate creative solutions for the problem; e.g., "I'm locked out of my car. How can I solve this problem?" The person must also be able to look at an array of solutions and categorize or classify groups of options.

Can young children invent different ways to solve problems? Usually, they cannot do this on their own. When children are upset, their emotions often overshadow their ability to solve problems. The preschool child lost in the grocery store would **not** be likely to think about different ways to handle his problem. He would not say, "I can go to the manager and ask her to call my dad on the speaker; I can search each aisle; or I can call out to my dad." He would likely focus primarily on the fact that he was lost.

Young children have difficulty seeing how things can change because they tend to focus on the "before" and then the "after" but cannot seem to focus on how they could get from before to after. Consequently, young children have difficulty creating solutions because of their inability to deal with the process of change.

Young children also have limited classification skills. They are not able to look at a number of solutions and then to classify them into logical groups; for example, "I can wait here," or "I can search for Dad," or "I can find somebody to help me" (three different groups of things to do).

To cope well you must be able to manage unpleasant emotions

This implies that a person can pay attention to and that he understands emotions such as anxiety, fear, or anger, emotions often associated with stress. He can evaluate what those emotions mean for him: "I'm anxious about giving this speech because the sale depends on how well I present my ideas today." A person who can manage emotions effectively and appropriately has learned good strategies for managing emotions: "I am well prepared for the speech and I know how to do deep breathing prior to beginning to speak."

Can young children manage unpleasant emotions? Young children, even babies, **have** emotions and they certainly **express** them. However, young children tend not to understand their emotions or be able to deal with them (Kuebli, 1994). The research on anger tells us that children learn to understand or deal with anger when their development allows them to and then only if they have good models and instruction in managing anger (Marion, 1997).

To cope well you must understand how your reactions affect situations

Again, this implies that an individual can think about at least two things at the same time—his reaction and the stressful event. He could also think about the impact of his actions as well as how another person might feel about them. Again, this requires good perspective taking. It also implies that the person has a broad enough knowledge base and enough experiences from which to draw the understanding.

Can young children understand how their reactions affect situations? A young child usually is not able to understand how his reactions to a stressor will affect the situation. The child lost in the grocery store does not understand, for example, that his frantic crying (his reaction to stress) affects his ability to listen to or answer questions from the manager.

Young children in general have a limited knowledge base and some of the children that we teach have an even more restricted knowledge base than do others their age. Young children have less knowledge and experience from which to draw when they face a stressor such as getting lost.

To cope well you must be able to think purposefully

Such a person would be able to think about the obvious in a stressful event but also be able to acknowledge and think about less obvious or hidden factors. Thinking purposefully brings together a person's conscious and preconscious thoughts. Thinking purposefully demonstrates that you know that you have thoughts. You also show that you can think about those thoughts—you can "think about thinking."

Example. Starting college for the first time is perceived as stressful by many students. The ability to think about this stressor purposefully, however, enables an older person to cope successfully. He would be able to think about the obvious, such as where everything is and how to register for courses. He would also be able to think about what is less obvious, such as his anxiety about meeting new people and making friends, because he understands the concept of anxiety and can think about it.

Can young children think purposefully? Young children are not able to consciously reflect—think about thinking—on matters such as how they feel, why others do things, or how others feel. Young children tend to focus on the obvious—their own agitation—and cannot reflect on the less obvious psychological aspects of stressful situations.

GENERAL GUIDLINES FOR HELPING CHILDREN COPE WITH STRESS

Children gradually learn how to manage stress, but only if we actively teach and encourage them to practice stress management. Many young children's families model, teach, and reward poor coping skills. The parents themselves in these families often do not know how to manage stress, so it is nearly impossible for them to teach helpful strategies to their children. These children will come to your classroom having already learned poor coping skills. Other children, fortunately, learn better coping skills.

What follows are general guidelines for encouraging young children to develop good coping skills. After studying the general guidelines, you will have an opportunity to read about a specific experience that is very likely to cause great stress for young children.

Model Good Stress Management

The process of modeling is a powerful teaching tool. Children observe many models of stress management—parents, teachers, other adults, and people in videos, movies, video games, and cartoons. These models influence a child's style of stress management. Children need teachers to model calm, thoughtful approaches to dealing with daily hassles. This is particularly important for children who observe a frenzied, inappropriate approach to stress management in their families or on television (Honig, 1986; McBride, 1990).

Manage a Classroom So That It Is a Low-Stress Environment

It is impossible to create a classroom or any other environment that is totally free of stress. However, taking the time and effort to create a developmentally appropriate physical environment will result in a low-stress (not stress-free) classroom. Develop suitable activities and make sure all materials are appropriate. Use positive guidance strategies when dealing with discipline encounters. Chapter 5 in this text explains how to develop a DAP classroom.

Acknowledge and Learn About the Variety of Stressors in Children's Lives

This chapter lists several of these stressors and then describes one of them in detail. You will learn the general principles in dealing with stressors, study one or two specific stressors, and then make a commitment to continuing education in this area.

Act as a Buffer Between a Child and a Stressor

You can be helpful to children facing a stressor by acting as a **buffer** if you stand between them and the stressor as you help them. You will shield them even as you teach them. You cannot always make the stressor disappear; nor would you always want to do so. You can soften (buffer) the effect of the stressor by supporting the child in any of several ways as he deals with the stressor.

Example. The manager of the grocery store acted as a buffer between the 4-year-old and the stressor of getting lost. She squatted down so that she was at the child's level, used a calm and even tone, and assured him that they would find his dad. She did not order him to stop crying but instead continued her soothing talk. He eventually gulped, stopped crying, and stared at her. "I know you're a little scared," she said. "I'll bet that you can tell me your name. Then I can talk on our microphone and tell your dad where we are."

Teach Children the Skills of Calming Themselves and Relaxing

Calming oneself and relaxing are essential skills in managing stress. All children must learn these skills, so it is age appropriate to teach them. Children who live in indifferent, chaotic, abusive, or neglectful families need the lessons even more, making it individually appropriate for an adult to teach them.

Calming down or relaxing helps a person to get the autonomic nervous system under control. The autonomic nervous system, as you read in a previous section, is that part of the nervous system that operates automatically, without our control. The sympathetic nervous system is a part of the autonomic nervous system and puts us in the high-alert stage of alarm when we face a stressor. Learning how to interrupt the action of the sympathetic nervous system is useful in managing stress. You can learn such techniques, and you can teach them to children.

Without understanding the biology of the stress response, older preschool, kindergarten, and primary children can learn to control how their bodies react under stress by learning how to relax. Children who can actively control their bodies by deliberately relaxing one or more body parts or by breathing slowly have strategies that they can use when they are under stress. Adults will undoubtedly have to remind them to use the relaxation strategies because children tend to focus on one thing—their problem—and might well forget about relaxing when they face a stressor. Figure 7.3 gives a few suggestions on teaching children how to calm themselves and to relax.

Learn and Teach Good Coping Skills

This often involves direct instruction, and specific strategies will depend on the particular stressor that a child faces. For example, if a child does not have friends, you might consider teaching him how to approach other children. If a child is under

---

Teach Children to Stay Calm and to Relax

Use these ideas to teach older early childhood children to soothe themselves, to calm down, and to relax. Write lesson plans for teaching these relaxation strategies and teach only one at a time. Consider using one of the calming, relaxing techniques that the whole group can do together at open group times. Encourage children to choose the group-time opening relaxation technique. Make sure that you carefully observe your children and know whether they can perform the physical movements in any of the activities. Plan adaptations for children as necessary.

✓ **Rubber band.** Use a real rubber band to demonstrate stretching it s-l-o-w-l-y. Children then stretch one arm up or to the side just as slowly. Hold the stretch and return slowly to the starting point. Try stretching shoulders down slowly and returning to the starting point.

✓ **Gentle waves.** Create gentle waves in the water table or a sealed jar of water as the children watch. Then listen to the recorded sound of gentle waves. Children move their arms in a slow, wavelike way.

✓ **Swim, fish. Swim!** Children quickly learn that watching the fish swimming in the aquarium is relaxing. Give them permission to pull up a chair and watch. Older children might even enjoy sketching the fish.

✓ **Hum or sing softly.** Sing a favorite song with the children, not loudly but calmly and very quietly. Then ask them if they know how to hum. Teach them how to hum the tune softly. Then have them close their eyes and hum. Tell them that you hum softly to yourself when you get a little nervous or when you have to wait in line.

✓ **Melting ice cube.** Prepare for this by placing an ice cube in a dish on the science table. Children observe that it melts. At group time, the children become ice cubes, all hard and cold. Then they begin to melt (relax) slowly.

✓ **Yoga stretches.** Teach three or four simple yoga stretches. Place pictures of the poses in the room so children can do the poses whenever they feel the need to relax.

✓ **Paint, sand, and other sensory items.** Remember the power of finger painting (even for primary children) to calm and soothe. The same thing is true for sensory materials such as clean sand or water in a tub or sensory table.

Figure 7.3.

stress because of a lot of anger, you would do well to teach him how to deal with anger and how to do deep breathing. Use books to teach about specific stressors (Jalongo, 1986a; Marion, 1997).

SUGGESTIONS FOR HELPING CHILDREN WHO FACE THE SPECIFIC STRESSOR OF MOVING

We live in a mobile society. By the end of early childhood (end of the third grade), one in six of the nation's third-graders had changed schools at least three times since beginning public school (Department of Education, 1994). Some groups, such as migrant, urban low-income, or abused children move even more frequently than others do. For example, 58 percent of one sample of urban low-income students had changed schools at least once (Mehana & Reynolds, 1995).

Kerbow (1996) also described the high mobility in large urban settings, noting that in Chicago there were clusters of schools tied together by the students they exchange from year to year. Abused children move twice as frequently compared to other children (Lang, 1996). Migrant children, who can move several times in one year, are especially vulnerable to stress from moving (Prewitt Diaz, 1989).

Teachers today experience frequently and firsthand the effects of a mobile society just as they have for the last several decades. Teachers start the school year knowing that some of their students will move to a new school and that they are likely to get new students anytime during a year. Teachers witness the stress that moving often produces in children, families, and schools.

Why Moving Is Stressful for Many Young Children

Moving to a new area is among the most stress-inducing experiences a family faces. Moves are especially difficult for preschool and primary children (American Academy of Child & Adolescent Psychiatry [AACAP], 1998; Cornille, 1993). For children, moving is a type of loss just as are death or a parent's divorce. A child loses friends, a home, and a school; the losses often result in feelings of sadness and anxiety or even anger. Moving is stressful for many young children for the following reasons.

Moving interrupts friendships and children lose social support (AACAP, 1998; Lang, 1996)

Children who move to a new area or a new school often think that everybody at school or in the new neighborhood is in a group or has a best friend. Children who lose friendships are likely to go through a mourning process for those friendships. Having somebody dismiss or laugh at the loss intensifies the sadness over the loss. If a child is shy or aggressive or has poor social skills, the move and the need to make friends will be even more difficult and stressful. Many children lose the support of older people, too. Moving away from trusted teachers, a Scout leader, religion teacher, relatives, and neighbors means that a child will not have these adults to turn to for support.

Moving elicits unpleasant emotions (Prestine, 1997)

Children tend to feel anxious and sad when they move. Young children, however, do not understand their emotions and do not know how to manage them on their own. So added to the already stressful situation of moving is the stress that goes along with emotions that the child cannot manage.

Moving interrupts the separation process (AACAP, 1998)

Moving is especially troublesome for children during early childhood because they are in the process of separating from parents and adjusting to adults other than their parents in centers and schools, as well as adjusting to peers. Relocating often pushes young children to return to a more dependent relationship with parents than they might want, thereby interrupting the normal separation process.

Moving requires children to adjust to a new curriculum in school and different teacher expectations (AACAP, 1998; Lang, 1996)

Children often find that they are behind in some curriculum areas or ahead in others, resulting in boredom or anxiety. Children can withstand the stress if their parents and teachers give them the support that they need. However, the children who move most frequently are the least likely to get the help that they need for managing the stress of curriculum changes (Department of Education, 1994). Their families and schools are often not prepared to give them the support they require.

For example, Prewitt Diaz (1989) studied the culture of migrancy and noted that there is a survival-oriented way of thinking among migrants of different ethnic and cultural backgrounds. This survival orientation makes it very difficult for migrant children to do well in school. Migrant children are negatively affected by many things; among the most important are the fragmented education received between moves and low self-esteem related to the trauma of constant moving.

Abused children also move much more frequently than most children, and Lang (1996) reports that frequent moving accounted for many problems in English and reading. Moving frequently also accounts in part for abused children having to repeat grades.

Moving interrupts school and social services

Kerbow (1996) noted that some public school systems, such as those in Chicago, are undergoing reforms that center on promoting greater local school autonomy. Greater local autonomy is based on the assumption that children will attend one specific school consistently enough so that the school can make a difference in the child's achievement. Urban low-income children who frequently change schools lose the benefit of any school or social services that go along with such school reform.

Act as a "Buffer" Between a Child and the Stress of Moving

Schools, teachers, and policymakers can buffer the stress of moving and changing schools for children. Moving and changing schools does not necessarily have to affect children adversely. With proper support, moving can be a positive experience for children (AACAP, 1998). Teachers, directors/principals, schools, and policymakers must take the first step and make a conscious effort to help children who are about to move away from or who have just transferred to their center or school (Prestine, 1997).

Buffering the effects of moving and changing schools is important for all children but it is crucial for children who move frequently (Department of Education [DOE], 1994). The DOE's report underscored the urgency of the need to help children who change schools frequently. It said that these children will continue to be low achieving in math and reading and they may have to repeat grades unless a school makes a greater effort to help them when they change schools. For example, one of the major changes the DOE recommended is that states implement a more effective student record transfer system. Similarly, child-care centers could help children who change centers by transferring a child's records to the new center after parents give approval.

When a child moves *AWAY FROM* your school/classroom

Consider doing some of the following things to help a child deal with the stress of **moving away** from your classroom. Our goal is to acknowledge our regret at his leaving but also to help this child find the strength from within to enable him to deal with his feelings and uncertainties about the move. Another goal is to work with parents so that they can also help their child cope with a move.

- Talk with the child about moving away and help him understand something about his new school. It would help greatly if you would take the effort to find out where he is going, the name of his school, and his new teacher. Present this information in a positive way.
- Listen carefully and encourage him to talk about his feelings about moving away. Avoid being intrusive, however, and do not force a child to talk about feelings.
- Help him say "good-bye" to his school in a low-key and positive way.
- Give the child a picture of the entire class with him included.
- Make sure that his records are up to date and accurate and that the records are transferred quickly to the new school.
- Follow your center or school's policy about contacting the new school so that you can give positive information to the new teacher about the child. The goal here is to help the new teacher make the child's transition as smooth as possible.
- Work with the child's parents. Answer their questions and give them information that will enable them to help their child make the move with as little stress as possible (see the Working with Parents box).

When a child moves *TO* your school/classroom

Consider the following suggestions as you welcome a child who is **moving to** your classroom. Your goal is to draw your classroom circle to include this new child. Adding a new member to a family or a classroom involves adjusting the boundaries to include that person.

- Obtain the child's file and read it carefully. Follow your school's policy if you need to contact the previous teacher for clarification on any issues.
- Make a home visit if your school encourages teachers to do so. Home visits are a good way to get to know the child.
- Familiarize the child and family with the new school. Invite them to come to school for a tour so that the new school is not so new on the child's first day.

- Make sure that the child and his family know the schedule in your room. Give them a handout of your schedule and encourage parents to talk about their child's new schedule.
- Create a space for a new child by preparing a locker or cubby, cot for napping, and any other individualized area or material. Create his space before he arrives.
- Take a new group picture with the new child included. Do this on the first day that the new child enters your room.
- Walk through your classroom's and center or school's routines; e.g., bathroom, snack, or lunch, getting on the bus, waiting for parents. Take your class through the fire safety drill so that **everyone,** including the new child, knows the procedure. Get the child to tell you about how the new routines are different from or similar to those in his old school.
- Talk with the child and find out what he likes to do in school.
- Include the child in activities of his new room at his pace.
- Request that other children in the class act as guides for the new class member. Be specific in your requests: "Joe, please walk with Robert to the lunchroom. He will be sitting next to you and I thought that you could show him how lunch is served in our school," or "It's time to put the carpet squares down for group time, Cindy. Please help Jean choose her carpet square and then sit next to her during her first group time with us."
- Be sure that every child wears a name tag so that a new class member can get to know names.
- Read a book about moving with the child or with the class.
- Listen carefully for the feelings that the new class member has about moving. Acknowledge them and avoid commanding him to feel differently.
- Work with parents. See the Working With Parents box for information that you can use with parents to help them buffer the effect of moving on their children. Your school might have a formal policy or program in place through which you help children who are moving away. Even if there is no formal program, you can do some things to help parents decrease the stress of moving for their children.

Information in the Working With Parents box will help parents of the children who you teach learn some simple but powerful and practical strategies for helping their children adjust to a move. Offer these strategies to parents of children who are leaving or who are new to your classroom or school. A simple handout with this information might well be the most efficient way to reach parents in the midst of a move.

Working with Parents. Is Your Family Moving? Tips for Helping Your Child Cope with the Move[25]

Explain and listen. Explain clearly to your child why the move is necessary. Are you being transferred? Are you starting school in another section of the state? Is the home you've been building finally finished? Is his school closing? Your child will understand the reason for the move if you state it simply and clearly. Get comments from your child about what you've explained. Listen closely, clarify anything that your child did not seem to understand, and "listen for feelings" such as fear or anxiety.

Read. Read a book about moving with your child (Jalongo, 1986a). *Moving Is Hard* is a picture book that will help children understand the process of moving and deals with some of their feelings.

Familiarize and describe. Acquaint your child with the new area as much as possible. Visit the new area and take your child on a tour of the new house

and neighborhood. Consider visiting the public library or parks. Familiarize children with their new home by using maps (for older children) of the area or photos of a new house or apartment building. Consider taking the local newspaper early to acquaint your child with the comic section if he has a favorite cartoon.

Describe something about the new area that your child might like, such as a pool, a pond with ducks, or an amusement park. Give the information in a positive, "upbeat" way but do not force your child to be enthusiastic.

Get involved. After the move, get involved with your children in activities in the new community such as synagogue or church, parent's group at school, YMCA, a family education and support program, and volunteer groups such as the Humane Society.

Case Study Analysis: Buffering Josiah's Move to his New School

Analyze the chapter-opening case study to decide how well Mr. Nellis, the teacher, buffered the effect of Josiah's move to his new kindergarten class. Use the suggestions in the section of the chapter about when a child **moves to** your school/classroom as a guide for your analysis.

1. Identify, from your perspective, the three most helpful strategies that Mr. Nellis used.
2. If you had to choose the single most important thing that Mr. Nellis did to help Josiah, what would you choose? Why?
3. If you were the teacher, describe one additional thing that you would have done. Why? Which of the strategies used would you have eliminated, and why?
4. Now give your overall evaluation of how well Mr. Nellis has "cushioned" or "buffered" Josiah's move to his new school. Mr. Nellis did a/an _____ job.

(Excellent, Good, Adequate, Barely Adequate, Quite Bad)

---

[25]Sources: adapted from AACAP (1998); Prestine, J. (1997). Available from 299 Jefferson Road, PO Box 480, Parsippany, NJ 07054-0480. This book is a good resource for parents and accompanies a children's picture book called "Moving is Hard."

REFLECTING ON KEY CONCEPTS

1. Describe a **resilient** child. Describe the circumstances under which a child is most likely to experience stress from any life event.
2. **"Stress?"** asks a friend of yours unfamiliar with early childhood. "What do children have to be 'stressed' about?" Consider this a teachable moment. What would you say to this person?
3. **Alarm, appraisal, searching for a coping strategy.** All of these are stages of responding to stress. What sorts of behaviors would you look for in a child at each of the stages?
4. What does it mean when we say that a person has **coped** with a stressful event? In addition, what does it express to say that coping does not necessarily mean that a person has come to a happy or successful conclusion?
5. Which of the abilities required to cope well with stressors do you think is most important? Why? You hear a parent say to a child who is facing the stress of a new school, "Oh, just get over it!" Why is the parent's approach unhelpful?

APPLY YOUR KNOWLEDGE

Get a start on developing some expertise in one area that can cause stress for children. Do you want to know more about how death, divorce, hospitalization, child abuse, or neglect results in stress? Do you need to know more about how harsh parenting, not having friends, or loneliness causes stress for some children? Choose a specific stressor and then prepare yourself to help children deal effectively with it by completing the following application activities.

1. **Internet and other resources.** Here are some suggestions: the ERIC database on the Internet is an excellent resource for early childhood information. Also, use one of the other search engines to find information on your chosen stressor. Visit or call the extension office in your county and ask the family or child life specialist for written information on your topic. Collect magazine articles about your stressor. Make copies of the information and organize it in a file for later use.
2. **Children's books.** Develop an annotated bibliography of children's books about the stressor you have chosen. Find and read at least four children's books. Give a brief synopsis of each and then explain how you would use it to help children deal with that specific stressor.
3. **Your portfolio and interview.** Let others know that you have knowledge, skills, and materials for teaching children how to begin to cope with this specific stressor. Decide how to place information in your professional portfolio.
4. **Role-play.** Role-play being interviewed for a teaching position. The director/principal looks over your portfolio, pauses, and asks you, "I see that you've studied about how children deal with _____ (moving,

death, divorce, etc.). How would you see yourself using this information if you're hired to teach in this school?" Be prepared to explain how you would use the material on stress to help children and parents.

REFERENCES

American Academy of Child & Adolescent Psychiatry (1998). Children and family moves. *AACAP Facts for Families,* No. 14. www.aacap.org/publications/factsfam/14.

American Academy of Child & Adolescent Psychiatry (1999). Children with oppositional defiant disorder. *AACAP Facts for Families,* No. 72. www.aacap.org/publications/factsfam/72.

Amato, P. (1997). Life-span adjustment of children to their parents' divorce. In E. Junn & C. Boyatzis (Eds.), *Annual editions: Child growth & development.* (149–169). Sluice Dock, Guilford, Connecticut: Dushkin/McGraw-Hill.

Baumrind, D. (1996). Parenting: The discipline controversy revisited. *Family Relations, 45,* 405–414.

Benard, B. (1995). Fostering resilience in children. ERIC Digest, EDO-PS-95-9, (http://www.ericps.crc.uiuc.edu/eece/pubs/digests/1995/benard95.html). University of Illinois at Urbana-Champaign: ERIC Clearinghouse on Elementary and Early Childhood Education.

Bull, B., & Drotar, D. (1991). Coping with cancer in remission: Stressors and strategies reported by children and adolescents. *Journal of Pediatric Psychology, 16*(6), 767–782.

Bullock, J. R. (1997). Children without friends: Who are they and how can teachers help? In E. Junn & C. Boyatzis (Eds.), *Annual editions: Child growth & development.* (121–125). Sluice Dock, Guilford, Connecticut: Dushkin/McGraw-Hill.

Burts, D., Hart, C., Charlsworth, R., Fleege, P., Mosley, J., & Thomasson, R. (1992). Observed activities and stress behaviors of children in developmentally appropriate and inappropriate kindergarten classrooms. *Early Childhood Research Quarterly, 7,* 297–318.

Cornille, T. (1993). Support systems and the relocation process for children and families. *Marriage & Family Review, 19*(3–4), 281–298.

Crnic, K., & Greenberg, M. (1990). Minor parenting stresses with young children. *Child Development, 6*(5), 1628–1637.

Department of Education (Migrant Education Program). (1994). *Elementary school children: Many change schools frequently, harming their education.* Report to the Honorable March Kaptur, House of Representatives. Washington, DC: author. ERIC No. EC369526.

Fabes, R., & Eisenberg, N. (1992). Young children's coping with interpersonal anger. *Child Development, 63*(1), 116–128.

Fleege, P. O., Charlesworth, R., Burts, D. C., & Hart, C. H. (1992). Stress begins in kindergarten: A look at behavior during standardized testing. *Journal of Research in Childhood Education, 7*(1), 20–26.

Haan, N. (1982). The assessment of coping, defense, and stress. In L. Goldberger & S. Breznitz (Eds.), *Handbook of stress: Theoretical and clinical aspects.* New York: Free Press.

Hart, C., Burts, D. Durland, M. A., Charlesworth, R., DeWolf, M., & Fleege, P. (1998). Stress behaviors and activity type participation of preschoolers in more and less developmentally appropriate classrooms. *Journal of Research in Childhood Education, 12*(2), 176–196.

Hole, J. (1981). *Human anatomy and physiology.* Dubuque, IA: Wm. C. Brown.

Holroyd, K., & Lazarus, R. (1982). Stress, coping, and somatic adaptation. In L. Goldberger & S. Breznitz (Eds.), *Handbook of stress: Theoretical and clinical aspects.* New York: Free Press.

Honig, A. S. (1986). Research in review: Stress and coping in children. In J. B. McCracken (Ed.), *Reducing stress in young children's lives.* Washington, DC: NAEYC.

Hyson, M., Hirsh-Pasek, K., Rescorla, L., & Cone, J. (1991). Ingredients of parental pressure in early childhood. *Journal of Applied Developmental Psychology, 12*(3), 347–365.

Jalongo, M. R. (1986a). Using crisis-oriented books with young children. In J. B. McCracken (Ed.), *Reducing stress in young children's lives.* Washington, DC: NAEYC.

Jalongo, M. R. (1986b). When young children move. In J. B. McCracken (Ed.), *Reducing stress in young children's lives*. Washington, DC: NAEYC.

Kerbow, D. (1996). *Patterns of urban student mobility and local school reform*. ERIC No. ED402386.

Kuebli, J. (1994). Research in review: Young children's understanding of everyday emotions. *Young Children, 50* (3), 36–47.

Lang, S. (1996). Maltreated children move more often, do worse in school. *Human Ecology Forum, 24* (3), 24.

Levine, S., Weinberg, J., & Ursin, H. (1978). Definition of the coping process and statement of the problem. In H. Ursin (Ed.), *Psychobiology of stress*. New York: Academic.

Lowenthal, B. (1999, Summer). Effects of maltreatment and ways to promote children's resiliency. *Childhood Education*, 204–209.

Marion, M. (1997). Research in review: Guiding children's understanding and management of anger. *Young Children, 52* (7), 62–68.

Matlock, J., & Green, V. (1990). The effects of day care on the social and emotional development of infants, toddlers, and preschoolers. *Early Child Development and Care, 64*, 55–59.

McBride, A. (1990). The challenges of multiple roles: The interface between work and family when children are young. *Prevention in Human Services, 9* (1), 143–166.

McCracken, J. B. (1986). *Reducing stress in young children's lives*. Washington, DC: NAEYC.

McKinnon, R., & Wallerstein, J. (1987). Joint custody and the preschool. *Conciliation Courts Review, 25* (2), 39–47.

Mehana, J., & Reynolds, A. (1995). *The effects of school mobility on scholastic achievement*. Paper presented at the Biennial Meeting of the Society for Research in Child Development, Indianapolis, IN (March 30–April 2).

Neuberger, J. J. (1997). Brain development research: Wonderful window of opportunity to build public support for early childhood education. *Young Children, 52*, 4–9.

Prestine, J. (1997). *Helping children cope with moving: A practical resource guide for "Moving is hard."* Parsippany, NJ: Fearon Teacher Aids.

Prewitt Diaz, J. The effects of migration on children: An ethnographic study. ERIC No. ED327346.

Sargent, J. (1982). Stress and headaches. In L. Goldberger & S. Breznitz (Eds.), *Handbook of stress: Theoretical and clinical aspects*. New York: Free Press.

Stein, M., Keller, S., & Schleifer, S. (1981). The hypothalamus and the immune response. In H. Weiner, M. Hofer, & A. Stunkard (Eds.), *Brain, behavior and bodily disease*. New York: Raven.

Stuber, M., Nadar, K., Yasuda, P., & Pynoos, R. (1991). Stress responses after pediatric bone marrow transplantation: Preliminary results of a prospective longitudinal study. *Journal of the American Academy of Child & Adolescent Psychiatry, 30* (6), 952–957.

Surgeon General. (2000). *Youth violence: A report of the Surgeon General*. Retrieved from http://surgeon-general. gov/library/youthviolence/report.

Terr, L. C. (1991). Childhood traumas: An outline and overview. *American Journal of Psychiatry, 148*, 10–20.

Weinreb, M. (1997). Be a resiliency mentor: You may be a lifesaver for a high-risk child. *Young Children, 52* (2), 14–20.

Zegans, L. (1982). Stress and the development of somatic disorders. In L. Goldberger & S. Breznitz (Eds.), *Handbook of stress: Theoretical and clinical aspects*. New York: Free Press.

Zimbardo, P. (1982). Shyness and the stresses of the human condition. In L. Goldberger & S. Breznitz (Eds.), *Handbook of stress: Theoretical and clinical aspects*. New York: Free Press.

✓ CHECK OUT THE WEB SITES RELATED TO THIS CHAPTER

✓ **Center for Effective Parenting.** This is a collaborative project of the University of Arkansas for Medical Science, the Arkansas Children's Hospital, and the Jones Family Center. This site has numerous links for parent education information, including information about stress.

www.parenting-ed.org. The home page for the Center for Effective Parenting. The following is one of the many good links.

www.parenting-ed.org/handouts3. Handout on children's stress. Accurate, well written.

✓ **ERIC** Clearinghouse on Elementary and Early Childhood Education, University of Illinois at Urbana-Champaign. A valuable resource on many topics, including stress in childhood.

www.ericps.crc.uiuc.edu/eece. Main page.

www.ericps.crc.uiuc.edu/eece/pubs/digests. Page for a set of publications called ERIC DIGESTS.

www.ericps.crc.uiuc.edu/eece/pubs/digests/1995/benard95. html. An ERIC DIGEST on stress during childhood.

✓ **Extension divisions of land grant universities.** Each state has a university with an extension division, which is charged with providing information and education for people throughout that state. The extension produces written documents on many topics, including parenting. Here are examples of information on stress management for children from two different extension sources. Check the extension division in your own state, either on the Internet or at your county's extension office (Yellow Pages).

www.urbanext.uiuc.edu/champaign/connections/9812-family2.html. University of Illinois Extension. This is a handout on holiday stress in children.

www.extension.unr.edu/children&violence/child&stress. html. University of Nevada Reno. This link is a Fact Sheet on stress in children.

www.exnet.iastate.edu/publications/PM1660F.pdf. Iowa State University. This is a three-page article on stress.

✓ **University of Minnesota Extension**

www.extension.umn.edu/distribution/Familydevelopment/ components/7269cm.html. A list of articles on children and stress.

www.extension.umn.edu/distribution/Familydevelopment/ components/7269-1.html. An example of one of the articles in the aforementioned list; this one is entitled Rural Children Under Stress.

Emotional Intelligence and Anger Management

"Anger is more easily identified in the infant and young child than in the middle-school and adolescent child. This is why . . . communities are stunned by unexpected violent events. It is difficult to identify subtle anger so intense that the angry youth will plan precisely and secretly to kill others."

(Brown University Child and Adolescent Behavior Letter, 1999)

After reading and studying this chapter, you will be able to

❑ **List and describe** the three components of anger and explain how children can feel and express anger without understanding it.

❑ **Identify** types of interactions in early childhood settings that are likely to elicit anger and **describe** children's responses to each.

❑ **Identify and explain** how several factors affect how a child expresses anger.

❑ **List, explain, and give examples** of developmentally appropriate strategies adults can use to guide children's expressions of anger and help them develop emotional intelligence.

Case Study: Anger in an Early Childhood Classroom

Jordan

"Remember to use words, Jordan, to tell Ralph that you're angry," said Mrs. Vargas. Jordan, almost 5 years old, paused briefly and then replied, "Oh, yeah, that's my paint. Give it back! I'm **mad** because you took it." Mrs. Vargas sighed with relief. Saying, "Use words" seems so simple, but it wasn't with Jordan, who has learned from his family and from television to express anger aggressively.

This was March and she has been working with Jordan all year on expressing his anger in direct, positive, and nonaggressive ways. At times she has been extremely frustrated but lately Jordan has made some major changes and is beginning to understand his feelings and to express his anger more responsibly.

Here are some samples from the teacher's anecdotal records for Jordan, the observations recorded at least weekly throughout the year for each child. She recorded all of these observations early in the school year.

September 7.

Jordan and Ralph had both been building separate block structures. Ralph took one of many curved blocks from the shelf. Jordan had been watching Ralph and snapped up the block just as Ralph took it off the shelf, saying, "I want that block for my tower."

September 10.

Justine walked into the dramatic play area and started to put on a firefighter's hat when she heard Jordan say, "Hey, you get out of here. Girls are stupid and you're not allowed to be a fireman!"

September 21.

I (Mrs. Vargas) noticed that Jordan left the bathroom without washing his hands. I reminded him to "scrub away the germs." He continued to walk away and ignored the classroom rule. "Jordan, please come back and wash your hands." Jordan walked back to the bathroom, glaring at me as he turned on the water.

October 5.

Jordan seemed to be upset when Justine turned around suddenly and bumped into him. Shoving her with both arms, he hissed, "Get out of my way!"

Justine

Mrs. Vargas noticed almost immediately that Justine's style of expressing anger or irritation was very different from Jordan's. Justine has learned a different lesson about how to show angry feelings from her family and she now deals with the normal everyday anger-arousing situations in her classroom directly and nonaggressively. Here are the observations that Mrs. Vargas made early in the year.

September 9.

Justine was about to take the plate of carrots as it went around the snack table when Jenny grabbed it. "Hey," said Justine, a questioning look on her face, "it was **my** turn next. Give me the plate."

October 5.

> I reminded Justine to put her puzzle back in the rack as she was leaving the puzzle table. She pursed her lips and frowned at me but then brightened and said, "Okey dokey!" I've heard her dad say that to her!

October 6.

> Jordan put his face right up next to Justine's while they were standing by a wagon. He grabbed the handle of the wagon from Justine's hand and pushed her away, laughing as he pushed. She said nothing to him but came over to me and said, "It was my turn with the wagon and Jordan took it."

Emotional intelligence. Good anger management. These are both goals in guiding children well. Anger is a natural and a normal emotion but chronic, unresolved anger and hostility can be hazardous to a person's health. Chronic anger makes a person vulnerable to illness and weakens the immune system. Chronic unresolved anger makes pain worse and increases the risk of death from cardiovascular disease (Suinn, 2001).

Unfortunately, some individuals have developed an emotional life that seems dominated by anger (Cole & Zahn-Waxler, 1992; Jenkins, 2000). They are chronically and cynically hostile, displaying frequent anger and aggression. They also experience a great deal of stress from their anger. This high level of stress and hostility has consistently been the factor that best discriminates between adults with coronary heart disease and those without coronary heart disease (Baughman, 1992; Johnson, 1992).

Anger and hostility also make it difficult to function effectively in groups, whether at school or at work. Anger and hostility play roles in damaging relationships. Anger is the root of many murders and other violent crimes.

These are less than cheerful thoughts. However, early childhood professionals can take the positive approach, looking on working with children as an opportunity to help them learn responsible anger management. We can light the candle of responsible anger management rather than cursing the darkness of anger gone wrong. Teaching responsible anger management to young children might prevent future problems associated with poorly managed anger.

THREE COMPONENTS OF ANGER: STATE, EXPRESSION, AND UNDERSTANDING

Joy. Disgust. Anger. Envy. Pride. These are all examples of **emotions.** Every emotion has the same three components or parts—the emotional state, the expression of the emotion, and the understanding of the emotion. The three components of the emotion anger are:

- the emotional state of anger,
- the expression of anger, and
- the understanding of the anger.

Example. Mom told Ralph, 4 years old, to go out to the backyard to play. When he got there, he was surprised to see the brand-new wading pool and his dad filling it with water. The **emotional state** of joy washed over Ralph. He **expressed** the emotion by saying, "A pool!"

Anger: An Emotional State

Anger: an emotion, an affective state, or feeling. The first component of anger is the emotional state of anger. The emotion, anger, results when a person's goal is blocked. A person is also very likely to feel the emotion of anger when something prevents her from getting a basic need met (Campos & Barrett, 1984). Children are likely to experience the emotional state of anger when they encounter an obstacle to attaining any significant goal. Children also feel anger when they think that the obstacle will be difficult to remove.

Think about different levels of anger. All children get angry at times, some more than others, but they all experience anger; e.g., when someone swipes a toy. Even a child who has loving, responsible parents and a caring teacher gets angry occasionally. It is relatively easy to help children with this type of anger and several practical suggestions are listed in this chapter.

Other children come to us with damaged and bruised bodies and egos. Someone has aimed anger and aggression directly at these children. An adult has abused them physically, psychologically, emotionally, or sexually. An adult might have neglected them. Their most basic need for safety and security has been ignored. They have not developed trust; they feel insecure and unsafe. They have a deep reserve of confusion, fear, and anger. It is especially difficult for them to confront the normal, everyday, anger-arousing events in an early childhood classroom.

Still other children have seen a lot of background anger, anger between others but not directed at the child. They have seen high levels of anger-based conflict between their parents (Jenkins, 2000). These children have emotional lives dominated by and organized around anger. They develop an antagonist approach to relationships. These children are very angry and express anger readily during social interaction. They also show aggression in their relationships. Like their angry parents, they also act in ways intended to belittle, degrade, and provoke distress in others. They show contempt for the other person, mirroring the contempt modeled in their parents' marriages. For example, a child might laugh or smile while saying or doing something cruel to another person or animal.

Many people believe that anger is a negative emotion. On the contrary, the emotion anger, though unpleasant, has a potentially positive role to play. It might be more useful to look at anger as a signal, a red flag, that something is wrong. Even the youngest children (including infants and toddlers) get angry when something threatens their welfare. Infants, for example, clench their fists and scream during vaccinations. Infants react (scream or cry) with anger to a goal blockage even as newborns. This is long before they can consciously reflect on the feeling of anger.

This chapter emphasizes anger in early childhood settings. Children often feel angry when other children or teachers (or parents) block their goals.

Example. Nine-month-old Megan felt angry when her teacher put her in her high chair for lunch. The teacher's well-intentioned actions frustrated Megan by unintentionally blocking the baby's goal of continuing to play with a specific toy.

Example. Four-year-old Ralph felt angry when his goal of finishing a painting was blocked after another child took the paint he needed to complete his work.

Example. Seven-year-old Willis felt angry when his cousin said, "Stop calling me your cousin. You're adopted, so you're really not a part of this family." The cousin's rejecting statement threatened Willis's need for belonging.

See Figure 8.1.

Expression of Anger

The second component of anger is its expression; this unpleasant emotion is first expressed in infancy. Children who believe that an important goal has been blocked attempt to cope by expressing the anger that they feel. Infants encounter

---

Causes of Anger in Early Childhood Settings[26]

Young children face several types of stress-producing anger provocations in their daily interactions. Anger usually arises from problems involved in interacting with other children or adults; i.e., from social interaction.

- **Conflict over possessions:** One of the most common interactions in early childhood classrooms that provokes anger is a conflict over possessions, which involves someone taking or destroying the target child's property or invading her space. Most conflicts over possessions take place between a child and another child.
- **Physical assault** is the second most frequently observed cause of anger in early childhood settings and involves something done to a child's body; e.g., pushing or hitting. Children are assaulted by other children. They also can be and are physically assaulted by adults, as Jordan often is by his dad. Some forms of physical assault are classified as child abuse according to most state laws.
- **Verbal assault** involves taunting, teasing, insults, or degrading or demeaning statements and blocks a child's goal of psychological safety.
- **Rejection:** Other children either ignore or refuse to allow a child to play. Rejection by adults is one of the classic forms of emotional child abuse (Garbarino, Guttman, & Seeley, 1986). A teacher who belittles a child is engaging in emotional abuse.
- **Issues of compliance** involve asking or forcing a child to do something that he does not want to do. In this case, a child's goal for independence will seem to have been blocked by a teacher's request for compliance. Almost all anger over issues of compliance occurs between an adult and a child.

Figure 8.1.

---

[26]Source: Fabes, R., Eisenberg, N., Smith, M., & Murphy, B. (1996). Getting angry at peers: Association with liking of the provocateur, *Child Development, 67*(3), 943–958.

many events that elicit the feeling of anger, which they express with their faces and voices (Stenberg, 1982). Children express anger in many different ways. Early child-hood teachers are likely to observe that children express anger with one or more of the following behavioral coping strategies:

- venting
- active resistance
- revenge
- expressing dislike
- avoidance
- adult-seeking (Fabes & Eisenberg, 1992)

See Figure 8.2.

Early childhood teachers see the whole range of possible responses. Most young children express anger nonaggressively through active resistance, but some children express their anger aggressively. Children construct ideas about how to express emotions through social interaction, watching television or movies, playing video games, and reading books (Lewis, 1989; Michalson & Lewis, 1985; Russel, 1989). Teachers can use child guidance strategies to help all children express angry feelings in socially constructive, not destructive, ways.

Some children have learned to express anger by hurting others. They learned their aggressive approach to managing anger (Hennessy, Rabideau, Cummings, & Cicchetti, 1994) and then resort to using aggression when they face normal every-day conflicts at school, on the playground, or at home. Teachers face a challenge. On one hand, they want to encourage children to acknowledge angry feelings; on the other hand, they want to help children express anger in a positive and effec-tive way.

Factors Affecting How Children Express Anger

Age and gender

Younger children tend to express anger more readily than do older children because younger children have not yet absorbed their culture's rules for when and how to express anger. You will read in the section on understanding anger that younger children's developmental level keeps them from understanding their anger. They do not yet have the skills for managing how they express angry feelings.

There appear to be differences in how some boys and girls express anger. Girls are more likely to use active resistance, but boys tend to vent or to use mildly aggressive methods (Fabes & Eisenberg, 1992; Zeman & Garber, 1996; Zeman & Shipman, 1996). How we socialize boys and girls might account for these gender differences (Davis, 1995; Underwood, Coie, & Herbsman, 1992).

For example, Malatesta & Haviland (1982) found that mothers showed differ-ent reactions to anger in children as young as 3 to 6 months old. They responded to girls' anger with an angry expression, thus giving a message of disapproval for the feeling to the female infant. Mothers tended to respond to a baby boy's anger with sympathy, conveying the message that it was acceptable for a boy to express anger.

How Children Express Anger[27]

- **Venting.** Expressing anger through facial expressions, crying, sulking, or complaining. Little is done to try to solve a problem or confront the agitator. Some people think of venting as "blowing off steam." Considered an unhealthy way to express anger if this is all that the person does, i.e., if she does nothing to solve the problem that caused the anger.

   Example. Jake and Jim, 8 years old, were angry about the number of math problems that they had to do for homework and vented their anger by complaining all the way home from school.

- **Active resistance.** Expressing anger by physically or verbally defending one's position, self-esteem, or possessions in nonaggressive ways. Considered a healthy way to express anger.

   Example. Luis expressed his anger with active resistance when Linda tried to take the scoop from him as he worked at the sand table: "That's mine. You can't have it, Linda!"

- **Expressing dislike.** Expressing anger by telling the offender that he or she cannot play or is not liked because of an incident.

   Example. Justine was angry when Jordan pushed her (in the chapter-opener case study). Later, when Jordan wanted to sit at her table for snack she said, "You can't sit here, Jordan. We don't like you."

- **Aggressive revenge.** Expressing anger by physically or verbally retaliating against the provocateur with no other purpose evident—name calling, pinching, hitting, or threatening. Considered a negative way of expressing anger. Seen frequently in children who are physically assaulted or rejected.

   Example. After snack time the children went to the playground. Jordan, steaming from Justine's comment at snack time, was hanging from the climbing gym when Justine rode by on her trike. He sang out, "Justine is stupid. Justine is stupid."

- **Avoidance.** Expressing anger by trying to escape from or evade the person with whom the child is angry.

   Example. Justine, mildly irritated by the name calling, walked away and played on the other side of the playground.

- **Adult-seeking.** Expressing anger by telling an adult about an incident or by looking for comfort from the teacher.

Figure 8.2.

Does a child have any control over the situation?

Another factor that affects how children express angry feelings is whether they think that they have some degree of control in an anger-arousing conflict (Levine, 1995; Zeman & Shipman, 1996). Children tend to be on an equal footing with other children; both children have about the same amount of power. Therefore, a child's interactions with other children have a far greater give-and-take quality

---

[27]Source: Fabes, R., Eisenberg, N., Smith, M., & Murphy, B. (1996). Getting angry at peers: Associations with liking of the provocateur, *Child Development, 67*(3), 943–958.

Children see themselves and other children on an equal footing in terms of power. Therefore, children often express anger toward peers more directly than they do toward adults.

(Piaget, 1970) than do child/adult interactions. Children believe that they have some measure of control in interactions, including anger-arousing situations, with other children. Therefore, the angry child tends to use direct strategies such as active resistance with other children.

In a relationship with an adult, many children easily detect the difference in power between the adult and themselves. Young children tend to think that they have much less control when a teacher provokes their anger. With adults, children express anger more indirectly with strategies such as venting (Fabes & Eisenberg, 1992).

Curiously, some children express anger toward a popular child who provokes anger in much the same indirect way as they do toward an adult (Fabes, Eisenberg, Smith, & Murphy, 1996). Again, a child's view of his level of power or control is at work here. Children tend to see themselves as having far less control in angry interactions with popular children.

Understanding Anger

Understanding anger: the ability to interpret and evaluate the emotion. Understanding anger is the third component of the whole experience of anger. Suppose, for example, that a friend borrows one of your textbooks and returns it severely damaged by a coffee spill. You get quietly angry when you first see the damage. Your friend quickly tells you that she has already ordered a new copy of the book for you. Your anger subsides just as soon as you think about what your friend has just said. You have evaluated the situation. You understand the emotion that you felt.

What about children's understanding of anger? Dealing with angry and aggressive children is very difficult at times because:

- Children can feel anger.
- Children can certainly express anger.
- Young children can**not** understand their anger (Michalson & Lewis, 1985).

Children's feelings wash over them rapidly and it is startling to observe a young child who swings into the angry mode so quickly.

We want to help children eventually be able to regulate or control how they express anger. Our efforts will be hampered somewhat because children do not understand their feelings (Zeman & Shipman, 1996). Children have an extremely limited ability to reflect on their anger and therefore need our guidance to understand and then to manage their angry feelings; they cannot do so on their own.

There are reasonable explanations for why young children cannot understand—evaluate or interpret—how they feel (Marion, 1997). Four major developmental factors contribute to a young child's **in**ability to understand, and therefore to control, how he expresses anger:

- brain development
- memory
- language
- self-awareness and self-control

Brain development (Goleman, 1995)

The prefrontal cortex is the part of the brain that governs the regulation of emotion. The prefrontal cortex takes years to develop fully; i.e., the prefrontal cortex matures during adolescence. An adult, whose prefrontal cortex is fully developed, is equipped to understand and evaluate his emotions. A young child's prefrontal cortex is not fully developed, making it impossible for him or her to understand any emotion as an adult would.

The **amygdala** (amygdala: Greek word for almond) is also a part of the brain. The amygdala is an almond-shaped structure that sits on top of the brain stem. Humans have two amygdalas, one on each side of the brain stem. The amygdala is almost fully mature when a baby is born.

The function of the amygdala is to store the emotional quality of interactions. Then, the amygdala acts like a sentry, scanning each and every experience, checking to see if the person is in danger. Signals of danger often go directly to the amygdala, bypassing the more rational part of the brain. This causes children, as well as adults, to act on what they have seen; for example, to express their anger even before they have had a chance to rationally process what they have seen or heard.

Combine two bits of information about brain development here.

- One, the prefrontal cortex, that helps humans rationally process and then understand emotion, is immature in young children.
- Two, the amydgala, which often causes us to act before we can think, is almost fully mature at birth.

These two aspects of brain development account, in large part, for a young child's inability to understand or control anger. At the same time, the child feels and expresses a wide range of emotions (but does not understand them).

Memory

A child can understand any emotion only when he can pay attention to it (Kuebli, 1994) and can remember the emotion. Memory is a basic cognitive process. A child's memory is a part of the foundation that enables her to gradually understand the feelings of anger that wash over her. Memory improves substantially during early childhood (Perlmutter, 1986) and this enables young children to better remember aspects of anger-arousing interactions.[28]

This is a slow process. Mrs. Vargas, for example, knew that Jordan needed help managing anger. She started working with him just as soon as she had observed sufficiently. She used a number of strategies to give him better ways of dealing with his angry feelings and after a time, he seemed to understand what she meant.

Example. Mrs. Vargas showed Jordan how to use words to express his anger. She had him practice using words to express angry feelings. Could she expect Jordan to remember her suggestions or would he regress and use one of his old unhelpful ways of expressing his anger?

Young children such as Jordan remember an **in**correct perception (unhelpful way to express anger), even when it has been replaced by a more accurate perception of events (more helpful way to express anger) (Freeman, Lacohee, & Coulton, 1995). An incorrect idea seems to get held back or repressed for a short time so that a child can use a new idea.

Example. In Jordan's case, it seemed like he really understood Mrs. Vargas because he did use words a couple of times to express his anger. However, his previous memories of expressing anger were also very strong, and for the time being, stronger than Mrs. Vargas's help. He went right back to hitting when he was angry.

Jordan retrieved an earlier unhelpful strategy even after his teacher taught him a new, more helpful strategy (Miller & Sperry, 1987). This implies that teachers

---

[28]Chapter 2 in this text describes the development of memory during early childhood.

must be unrelentingly positive and remind certain children, often several times, about a less aggressive way of expressing anger. Overcoming old, unhelpful memories takes time. Children with deep reserves of anger need help in managing that anger, and getting angry with them when they revert to old methods does not help them; it only adds fear and confusion to their anger.

Language: Talk about emotions

Talking about emotions helps young children understand their feelings (Brown & Dunn, 1996). Talking about feelings helps them begin to evaluate them. Talking about feelings is a skill and, like most skills, must be learned and then practiced. Teach the skill of talking about emotions by:

- talking appropriately about your own adult emotions (modeling the skill). For example, "I watched a movie about a dog who was lost and felt sad that that the dog couldn't find his family. Then I felt so happy when his family looked for him and found him."
- teaching the skill directly to children in situations charged with emotion, when they are sad, happy, jealous, or angry.
- planning lessons on talking about emotions as a regular part of the social studies curriculum.

Example. Ralph got off his trike so that he could remove his jacket. Jordan seized the trike and zoomed away, making faces and laughing at Ralph. When Ralph realized what had happened, he narrowed his eyes and clenched his teeth together—he looked angry. Then, to the teacher's surprise, he started crying. She knelt down and quietly said, "You seem to be upset, Ralph. Tell me what has upset you."

Mrs. Vargas comforted Ralph as she also urged him to talk about how he felt. She acted appropriately and gave him an individual lesson quietly and quickly. She taught through active listening when Ralph was "hot with anger," when he most needed her support and help. Then she dealt with Jordan's aggression.

How well a child comes to understand emotions depends partly on his overall language skills (Denham, Zoller, & Couchoud, 1994). Children will have a much more difficult time learning to talk about emotions if they have poor language development. Ralph, for example, has very good language skills and has a large vocabulary, so Mrs. Vargas was confident that he could tell her what had upset him. She realizes, though, that two of the children in her class come from homes where adults do not talk to children, and the television is on constantly. These two children have small vocabularies and simply do not grasp the concept of talking about any matters, let alone emotion.

Language: Word labels

Make sure children have the vocabulary that they need for talking about how they feel. All children need to acquire an "emotion" vocabulary. All children must learn labels for emotions; they need to acquire words such as "angry, sad, happy." Knowing word labels for and naming the emotion of anger, then, is an important part of understanding and eventually managing anger.

The teacher is urging Carol to talk about how she feels. Talking about emotions helps children begin to understand their emotions.

A problem here is that preschool children produce very few labels for emotions before the age of 3. Even then, many children produce few labels, because nobody has taught them the words for feelings. We must help them learn and then use words for their feelings. This task should be easier when we realize that even preschool children make a connection between an expression on a face and the emotion word labels for that facial expression (Michalson & Lewis, 1985). What children beyond infancy need help with is actually using words to describe facial expressions or their own feelings.

Language: Different ways of discussing anger-arousing events

Some children discuss angry feelings easily after they know the words for the emotions. Other children have a great deal of difficulty talking about things that arouse their anger or resentment. A child's family has a major impact on her ability to label or discuss anger-arousing events. How a child's family discusses anger-arousing incidents affects the ease or difficulty that a young child has in labeling emotions or discussing feelings.

Some parents accuse, insult the perpetrator, or assert their own rights with threats. These parents forget or fail to label their feelings. They do not process their anger rationally. They model a very unhelpful way of talking about anger-arousing incidents. Their children tend to talk about angry conflicts in the same way.

Example. Jordan's father was angry about how long he had to wait in the drive-through at the bank. Slapping the steering wheel, he said, "Who do they think they are? I ought to go right in there and tell the manager what I think about this place." At school, Jordan was angry when Robert would not give him one of the puppets. Jordan slapped one of his fists into the other hand and said, "I'm gonna get my dad to beat you up! He'll make you give me a puppet."

Jordan fails to label his anger, but he does use language to threaten Robert and to accuse Robert of unfairness. Jordan has, like many children, adopted this style of talk by observing how his parents talk about anger-arousing events.

Other parents and teachers acknowledge their feelings, frequently putting a label on a feeling. They do get angry but avoid accusing the person with whom they are angry. They think through an incident even when they are angry. They are aware of their feelings even as an unpleasant feeling hits them like a wave.

Their awareness helps them to evaluate the situation (they **understand** their anger). They choose words carefully and are cautious about how they talk about angry feelings. These adults, through words and actions, model a more responsible way to manage anger. These parents are emotionally intelligent; their children observe this **emotion talk** and tend to imitate their parents. They use similar language and actions when talking about anger-arousing conflicts.

Example. Justine, the child from the chapter-opening case study, was sitting on the porch with Mom when her father came home from a fishing trip. Dad hadn't caught any fish. Mom said, "Oh, George! It's no big deal." Dad frowned and said, "I was looking forward to grilling some fish for all of us, and I'm a little disappointed that I didn't catch anything. Plus, I'm **irritated** that you would tell me 'It's no big deal.'" Mom said, "Sorry, honey. I know you're disappointed."

At school the next day, Justine and Nellie were in the dramatic play area. Nellie grabbed for the prop box first, inadvertently pushing Justine out of the way. Justine's face registered annoyance. She put her hands on her hips, looked directly at Nellie, and said, "I'm **irritated,** Nellie, that you pushed me. There's room for both of us to play, so please move over." Justine labeled her feeling and but did not accuse Nellie. Justine was confident in stating her rights. She had imitated how her parents manage anger.

Professionals working with young children should expect to see individual differences in children's ability to identify and label angry feelings because their families model a variety of approaches to talking about emotions.

Self-awareness and self-control

Self-awareness and self-control develop during early childhood. These two features of a child's self, along with memory and language development, set the stage for understanding and managing anger and other emotions (Kuebli, 1994).

A self-aware person sees himself as separate from others.

Example. Justine and Nellie, in the dramatic play area, surprised Mrs. Vargas when they kept changing dress-up clothes. The teacher observed and heard this. Justine, wearing men's clothing, said, "OK. This is my dad." She changed into a dress and said, "Now I'm Mom." Then she took off the dress-up clothing and, in her own things, said, "Now I'm me—Justine!"

Justine is fully aware that she is a person separate from other people. This allows her to look at situations in which she is angry with someone else and see that there are indeed at least two separate people involved.

A self-aware person also knows that he has a degree of influence over how some things turn out.

Example. Tahisha and Larry were both working on a color-mixing science experiment. Larry had begun to squeeze food coloring into a container of water when Tahisha said, "Hey, Larry. Put a little bit of blue in this cup, too, OK? But just a little bit." Larry carefully squeezed a tiny amount of blue coloring into the cup.

Children like Justine and Tahisha are aware of their selves, that they are people, but more important, they are people who can influence things. When they get involved in anger-arousing interactions, they will carry this knowledge with them. Justine will be able to see herself and the other person as separate people and she will think that she can influence how the interaction turns out. Self-awareness emerges during infancy and toddlerhood. Children continue to grow in self-awareness during early childhood, and this enables them to begin to think about themselves as angry and to think about the things that called forth their anger (Harter, 1983; Kuebli, 1994).

Self-control is another significant part of a child's self. A child who is self-controlled can control impulses, not perfectly, but in many cases. A self-controlled child can tolerate frustration that is not overwhelming. A child with self-control can also postpone immediate gratification. Self-control appears at around 24 months, and children become better able to use strategies to regulate or control their own behavior, including how they express anger, as they get older (Kopp, 1989). Parents and teachers can build on a child's budding ability to control the self. Adults can use strategies that help children use their self-control to begin to regulate how they express angry feelings.

IMPLICATIONS: GUIDING CHILDREN'S EXPRESSIONS OF ANGER

Teachers can give children the gift of a healthy approach to dealing with anger by guiding their understanding and management of anger. Some children in our classrooms have learned unhelpful and aggressive approaches to anger management, while others have learned a more direct, nonaggressive approach (Jenkins, 2000). The guidance practices described here will help children understand and manage angry feelings in a direct and nonaggressive way (Marion, 1994, 1997). Some suggestions focus first on adults and urge them to reflect on their own practices. Other suggestions focus on directly helping an angry child.

Create a Safe Emotional Climate

The leader in a parent education class on anger management asked the parents what happened in their families when they, as children, expressed anger.

"My dad used to get so mad at me when I was angry, even if my anger had nothing to do with my father," said Marv.

"How did you feel when he got mad?" asked the leader.

"It scared me to see him get so mad. After a while I just started hiding out when I was upset."

The leader asked, "Did you ever talk about what it was that you were angry about in the first place?"

"No, and, you know what? I ended up taking care of Dad by pretending nothing was wrong even if I was seething about something," said Marv. "I've never thought about this before!"

Others noted that their parent criticized or even punished them for being angry or expressing anger. The root of their anger was never dealt with and never resolved. They were punished or criticized for feeling angry. Their anger was shamed and the emotional climate was not safe.

A **safe emotional climate** permits children to acknowledge all feelings, both pleasant and unpleasant, and does not shame anger. They are not told to hide feelings, and they know that they will not be criticized for having the feeling, whatever it is. If Jamal has sad feelings when the gerbil dies, he knows that he can express them without fear. If James expresses tender feelings by gently stroking his puppy when it visits, nobody laughs or calls him a sissy. If Mary is irritated when somebody takes her puzzle, she will feel safe in knowing that her teacher will not also become angry just because Mary is mildly irritated.

All healthy systems, whether in a family or a classroom, have clear, consistent yet flexible boundaries. Adults who help children understand and manage anger responsibly convey a simple, firm, consistent message:

- You have the right to feel angry.
- I will help you learn to talk about and deal with your feelings.
- I will tell you clearly that you are not allowed to express anger destructively. You are not allowed to hurt or humiliate a person or animal because you are angry" (Baumrind, 1996).

Example. Mrs. Vargas watched Larry get ready to hurl a shovel at Ralph after Ralph ran over Larry's sand structure. From all indications, Ralph destroyed Larry's sand structure on purpose. The teacher was quick enough to grab the shovel, and said, "Larry! I'll take that shovel. Throwing the shovel is dangerous and I won't allow you to hurt children when you're mad." (The teacher then talked a bit more with Larry and dealt with Ralph's aggression.)

Model Responsible Anger Management

Adults influence children through modeling, and adults are powerful models of how to manage anger. Some adults model irresponsible anger management—they have "silent" arguments, argue or yell loudly, attack one another physically, and frequently belittle or humiliate others.

Children who witness such irresponsible anger management have a distorted view of emotions. They might be fearful of emotions because of the turmoil that adults create when they are upset. Children who observe such aggression tend to see anger-arousing situations as a signal that an attack is about to take place. This puts them on alert, ever ready for a fight or ready to hide. They do not view anger-arousing situations as mere problems that reasonable people can solve. They also experience great stress when adults are so aggressive and mean-spirited when angry (Cummings & Cummings, 1988; Denham et al., 1994; El-Sheikh & Reiter, 1996).

Other adults model a healthier, more responsible, and more effective way to deal with angry feelings. Children do not need to know about every little argument or disagreement to learn the social skills for avoiding some anger-arousing events with other adults. However, adults who work with children will feel irritated, annoyed, or even downright angry at times. They can model good anger management with the day-to-day anger-arousing events that occur when they are with children.

Example. Willis and Michael, second-graders, each scooped a handful of the applesauce from the cups on their lunch trays. Then, as their teacher, Mr. Nellis, watched in astonishment, the two boys both aimed the sugary mass directly at the window and threw. Mr. Nellis felt anger creep up and take hold, especially after Michael sang out, "Two points!" Mr. Nellis felt his face get hot and his heart started beating faster. He was angry.

How to Model Responsible Anger Management

Adults have varying approaches. They have different ways of saying things because of the region in which they live or because of their family backgrounds. This is merely a difference in style, and adults usually are more effective with children when they use their own style. Whatever one's style, though, there are some guidelines that will help all adults model responsible anger management.

Acknowledge the angry feeling

We cannot "not" have a feeling. Feelings come to us, many of them uninvited. Feelings are normal and natural, although some feelings are certainly unpleasant. Give yourself permission to feel angry when you are angry; you will model several important things. Children will observe that you feel the emotional energy of anger. They will observe that you do not think that you have to justify your feelings. They will observe that you think that anger simply is, and that there is nothing wrong with it or any other emotion. These are important lessons in emotional intelligence.

Example. The rest of the children watched the applesauce target practice. They looked from Willis and Michael to Mr. Nellis, who was clearly upset and surprised. They had never really seen their teacher in this type of situation. They watched as he closed his eyes and quietly blew out a stream of air. They watched him rub his hand over his face as he got out of his chair and walked calmly and directly over to the boys. "Willis and Michael, please come with me." He led them to a separate table and they all sat down.

This teacher was very upset and acknowledged his feeling. The children observed two important things: (1) an upset teacher who (2) consciously controlled how he showed his feeling.

Stay calm

An emotionally intelligent person is able to feel anger, not hide the fact that she is upset, but, at the same time, remain calm. Adults who work with children need this skill. Children benefit from observing a parent or teacher take the time to get that burst of angry energy under control, as Mr. Nellis does in the next example. He speaks directly to the boys and looks at them, but his tone and expression are neutral.

Example. After the teacher and two boys sat down, he said, "I am very upset about what you both did. I want both of you just to sit here with me until I can calm down. No talking while I take some deep breaths."

Choose how to express anger

Children clearly benefit by watching emotionally intelligent adults actively choose how to express anger. Mr. Nellis has refrained from simply venting his anger. He did not unleash his anger in front of the class; he did not "blow off steam." Some of his students see enough of that at home or on television and need a different example from their teacher.

Then he talked with the children. He had decided how to respond. Notice, in the next example, that he takes responsibility for how he felt. He does not blame the boys for causing his feeling but he did describe their part in the actual incident. His is direct, firm, and kind. He does not blame but he is clear that the boys will make restitution by cleaning the window.

Example. "I saw both of you throw applesauce at the window. Michael said 'two points.'" (Mr. Nellis simply gave the facts, the data. No blaming.) Willis giggled. Mr. Nellis ignored the giggling.

"There is applesauce all over that window and I know that the janitor works hard to keep this room clean for us." (He gave the tangible effects of the applesauce throwing.)

"I am upset that two children in my class have made their school so messy." (He states his feeling.)

"Please go and ask Mrs. Johnson (cafeteria worker) for paper towels. I want you to clean the window."

Willis responded, a smirk on his face, "She's paid to clean up after us. Why do I have to clean the window?"

Mr. Nellis resisted the urge to argue with Willis. His facial expression was neutral as he said to both boys, "Please go get the towels—now. I want you to clean the window before the applesauce dries."

Help Children Develop Self-Control

Infants and toddlers cannot control themselves; they do not have self-control. Therefore, it is unfair to expect an infant or toddler to show self-control. Teachers and parents who are empathic do most of the self-control work for very young children. For example, teachers put appropriate winter clothing on toddlers who otherwise would not remember to dress appropriately. As children get older, authoritative adults recognize when children are ready to assume more responsibility for controlling themselves. These adults gradually transfer control to children to help those children develop self-control.

Example. Mrs. Vargas knew that most of her 4-year-olds were ready to control themselves by listening quietly to a brief story. Consequently, she had requested that they be very quiet while she read one of their favorite stories. When Tahisha blurted out a statement, Mrs. Vargas helped Tahisha by saying softly, "Listen carefully, Tahisha," and turning back to the book.

This teacher's efforts are likely to help Tahisha and the other children achieve healthy self-control. Mrs. Vargas is an authoritative caregiver—highly responsive to children but also willing to make reasonable demands (that a 4-year-old listen quietly to a story). She demonstrates respect for her children in her day-to-day interactions with them. This should make it easier for the children to accept the teacher's efforts to give them, ever so gradually, responsibility for controlling themselves (Baumrind, 1996; Hart, DeWolf, Wozniak, & Burts, 1992).

Teach Children to Use Words to Describe Angry Feelings

"Use your words." Many teachers, thankfully, say this to angry or aggressive children. It is an appropriate statement and a good strategy. Use this strategy most effectively by coupling this phrase with these other suggestions.

- Help children understand that they are having a "feeling."
- Teach them that they can **use a word** to describe their feeling.
- Help them produce a label for that feeling of anger. Give examples of the words to use to children who do not have a good emotions vocabulary.

Example. Larry was clearly upset when Justine would not play with him. Mrs. Vargas stepped in and talked with Larry privately. "You really seem to be upset, Larry." She found out that Larry's feelings were hurt and then he acted upset. "You can use words to tell Justine that you are upset. How about this: 'I wanted to play with you. I'm upset because you said no.'" She had Larry say those words, for practice. Then she said, "Would you like to tell Justine now?"

Help Children Expand Their Feelings Vocabulary

Anger is a complex emotion with many levels of emotional energy, ranging from minor irritation to rage. Help children understand that at times one can feel "a little angry" but at other times feel "very very angry." After children have learned to use a word for angry feelings, encourage them to increase the number of labels or words they can use to describe the specific feeling they are having.

Many children will describe anger as feeling **mad.** Build their feelings vocabulary by adding synonyms to the list—words such as **angry, irritated, annoyed, furious, irate, enraged, upset**—that help them more accurately describe the level of emotion. Make a permanent record, such as a book or chart (see Figure 8.3) listing different words for angry feelings, and refer to it when discussing anger. (You can do the same thing with other feelings words, too.)

Example. "I think that the librarian was a little **annoyed** when we were late for our library period." "It seemed to **irritate** you when Nellie took the block again." "I noticed that you seemed **angry** when Jackie put a big blob of red paint on your paper." "Mr. Rogers seemed **upset** when he discovered that the puppy was lost." "That man was **furious** when his neighbor walked on the fresh cement."

Listen Actively When Children Are Having an Anger Conflict

Young children understand anger and other emotions best when adults explain emotions (Denham et al., 1994). Help children reflect on anger-arousing events by creating opportunities to discuss the events. Help children embroiled in a hot anger conflict by listening to them. Just listen, without judging, evaluating, or ordering them to feel differently. This is not the time to restate limits or to explain things. It is a time to listen, the first step in a true anger interaction.

Listening carefully and actively has an amazing effect on angry children. Anger arises when somebody has blocked a goal. Listening carefully tells a child

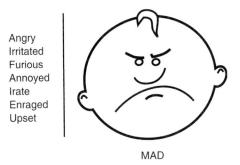

MAD

Figure 8.3.   Use a chart as a permanent record, listing different words for angry feelings. Refer to it when discussing anger.

that someone is finally interested in his problem. Listening carefully opens the door to problem solving. Discussing their angry feelings and interactions with an adult who listens actively helps children begin to understand the meaning of the interaction. Telling an adult about feelings prepares angry children for dealing more effectively with similar events in the future.

Example. Mr. Nellis said, "Looks like you might be a little irritated, Sandi. I saw you clench your fists when you looked at her and you're breathing very fast."

"Well, she said that my picture was ugly!"
"You got upset when she made fun of your drawing."
"Yeah. She shouldn't do that. It's mean."

By this time, Sandi was a bit calmer and was breathing normally. They then talked about how Sandi wanted to handle the situation.

Plan Discussions About Anger

Get creative. Be proactive. Avoid some, but certainly not all, angry interactions by creating opportunities to teach about anger management. Feed discussions about managing anger directly into your curriculum. There many times, calmer times, when children are not engaged in anger-arousing interactions. Treat this subject as you would any other important topic, as something you need to teach.

Many teachers plan activities involving discussions about anger. These discussions teach effective anger management skills. Carry out the instruction in small or large groups, or even with individuals. Here are a few ideas to get you started.

- Vignettes.

Make up scenarios or situations and then encourage children to generate a direct, nonaggressive response: "What could you do if you were washing your hands and somebody pushed you out of the way?" Or, "Here's a picture of a child who is upset because somebody just called her a stupid girl. What do you think that she should do?"

- Books and stories.
- "Thinking" puppets.

These puppets help children think about many things, including anger. Use them to demonstrate good anger management and then lead a discussion about how well they managed. Conversely, present a problem about anger through the puppets and help the children work to achieve a positive, responsible solution.

Example. Mrs. Vargas had done quite a bit of observing. Her assessment told her that most of her students needed to learn how to respond in a healthy way to incidents such as getting pushed or pinched. She planned a discussion about anger for large-group time, a discussion based on a formal lesson plan. She demonstrated a mild conflict in which one puppet pinched the other. "This thinking puppet is angry because this other puppet pinched him. Help him think about what he could do." A lively discussion took place.

This teacher has planned a "thinking puppets" session on appropriate ways to respond to anger-arousing events.

Use Appropriate Books and Stories About Anger Management

Books are helpful in anger management

Bibliotherapy refers to using literature to promote mental health. Use stories and books to help children understand themselves and other people, as well as to help them develop emotional intelligence (Rovenger, 2000). Books and stories in different forms help children to deal with the stress-producing emotion of anger. Books dealing with the emotion of anger can help a child cope more effectively with this strong emotion.

Reading crisis-oriented books, including those about anger, serves three purposes. Children:

- get information about anger from well-chosen books.
- make connections between what they hear about anger in and out of school.
- are more likely to view their own anger as natural and normal when a teacher plans, reads, and follows up on a story about anger (Jalongo, 1986).

Choose books wisely

The goal is "First of all, do no harm." Children's books advocating hurting somebody when angry do harm to children. Well-written books about anger teach one or more of the major concepts about anger management. Some of these concepts are that anger is a normal emotion, anger can be expressed with words, anger can range from mild irritation to rage, and a child should express anger without resorting to aggression. See Figure 8.4.

Checklist: Guidelines for Choosing Books on Anger

Follow selection guidelines for choosing any picture book (Jalongo, 1986). Check to be sure that the book meets additional, specific selection criteria for stories about anger (Marion, 1997, 1999). Evaluate a book on anger by completing this checklist.

1. **How does this book deal with words/vocabulary for angry feelings?**
   - ❑ Uses one word; e.g., "mad" or "angry" exclusively.
   - ❑ Uses two different words; e.g., "mad" and "angry," or some other combination.
   - ❑ Uses several different words; nicely illustrates how to describe anger with different words.

2. **Does this book identify the specific event that seemed to elicit the anger?**
   - ❑ Not at all. Anger trigger never mentioned.
   - ❑ Identified a trigger for the anger, but was inaccurate.
   - ❑ Identified the anger trigger, but in a blaming, accusatory way.
   - ❑ Correctly identified the specific thing that brought on the anger, without blaming.

3. **How well does this book convey the idea that feeling angry is a natural and normal experience?**
   - ❑ Not at all. It actually blames the child in the story for feeling angry.
   - ❑ Not very well. It acknowledges that the child is angry but in a guilt-inducing way.
   - ❑ Adequately. Acknowledges anger. Says nothing about it being OK.
   - ❑ Very well. Clearly conveys idea that anger is a normal emotion.

5. **How does this story urge children to manage their anger? (Goal: present nonaggressive, optimistic strategies.)**
   - ❑ With aggressive strategies exclusively; e.g., hitting others (an **in**appropriate strategy).
   - ❑ Sometimes aggressively (also an **in**appropriate strategy).
   - ❑ With positive strategies; e.g., using words (appropriate strategy).

My decision, based on my checklist analysis:
   - ❑ Reject outright (because it advocates aggression or it blames the child).
   - ❑ Read, but make adjustments to fix minor issues.*
   - ❑ Use with confidence that this book meets most of these guidelines.

*It is possible to use a book even if it is less than perfect (assuming it does not advocate aggressive strategies or blame children). Suppose that a book does not identify the event that angered a child. How might you use the book anyway? What might you do to help the children themselves come up with ideas about the anger trigger?

Figure 8.4.

Suggestions for using a book on anger

Sharply focus on anger throughout the discussion. Develop specific introductory remarks to motivate thinking and help children concentrate on the topic of anger. Prepare specific comments and questions to use when reading the book. Prepare a thoughtful follow-up. Avoid merely asking children to relate the chronological events of the story. Instead, clarify information presented on how to manage anger responsibly. Concentrate on reviewing concepts or vocabulary relating to anger. Most important, communicate your acceptance of anger as a natural and normal emotion and your approval of managing anger in a direct, nonaggressive way.

Teach Children How to Deal with the Stress of Anger

Anger is a useful but stressful emotion. Teach children how to recognize and deal with the stress that usually accompanies anger. When angry, for example, many people are jittery, feel their skin get hot, feel their heart beating faster, feel sweaty. Managing anger responsibly returns the body to a normal state. A person remains in a stressful state if she does not deal with anger appropriately.

Two of the most helpful stress-reduction strategies are relaxation training and deep breathing exercises. Both strategies allow children (and adults) to get the autonomic nervous system under control, gain control of breathing, get the heart rate back to normal, stop shaking, and calm down. A person can begin to evaluate his feeling most coherently when the stress subsides somewhat. This is the first step in dealing with anger responsibly and in avoiding doing anything irrational while in a highly stressed state.

Review the behavioral indicators of stress in Figure 7.2 in Chapter 7. Figure 7.3 describes several stress-reduction activities that you can use with children.

Work with Parents

Children exist in a family system. Teachers are more effective in helping children manage anger when they acknowledge and work with a child's family as well as with a child. Helping parents understand how to help their children manage anger also shows parents how to help their children develop emotional intelligence (Goleman, 1995).

Working With Parents. Parents Can Help Children Build Anger Management Skills and Emotional Intelligence

Offer information to parents about helping children understand and manage anger and build emotional intelligence. Use the same strategies that you employ when talking with parents about other areas of the curriculum or other concerns. For example:

- **Newsletter.** Write a newsletter article about learning to use words to label anger.
- **Group-based parent education.** Plan a group-based parent education session to explain some of the things you have done to help children manage anger nonaggressively.

- **Thinking puppets.** Introduce the **thinking puppets** to parents and explain how they are used in discussions about anger with the children.
- **Books.** Display books on anger management at the meeting, explain how you have used them with the children, and invite parents to read the books. Do the same thing with books on emotional intelligence.
- **Electronic communication.** Create a listserve for parents of children in your class or in a parent education group. This is a method for using the computer and e-mail for communicating with a whole group. Parents can also ask questions. You can post information via listserve.
- **Feelings chart.** Explain how you use the chart with the words for anger and give a handout of the same chart to parents so that they may have a reference.
- **Web sites.** Some parents like to get information electronically. Help them by suggesting good Web sites. See the suggested list at the end of the chapter.

Resources for Parents

Azerrad, J. (1997). *Anyone can have a happy child: How to nurture emotional intelligence.* New York: M. Evan.

Chapman, D. (1996). *Playwise: 365 fun-filled activities for building character, conscience, and emotional intelligence in children.* New York: G.P. Putnam's Sons.

Myers, D. E. (1996). *Heartful parenting: connected parenting & emotional intelligence.* Mesa, AZ: Blue Bird Publishing.

Shapiro, L. E. (1997). *How to raise a child with a high EQ: A parent's guide to emotional intelligence.* New York: Harper Collins Publishers.

Resources for Professionals

Goleman, D. (1995). *Emotional intelligence.* New York: Bantam Books.

Salovey, P., & Sluyter, D. J. (1997). *Emotional development and emotional intelligence: Educational implications.* New York: Basic Books.

(Video) Emotional intelligence—a new vision for educators. Daniel Goleman Presents, 1996.

Work with Other Professionals

Teachers are educated to teach but usually not trained as therapists. If a person is not a licensed therapist, he should not act as a therapist. Some children have problems diagnosable by a licensed mental health professional. Licensed mental health professionals know how to assess problems, make diagnoses, and then help extremely angry children whose anger springs from abuse or neglect or other major emotional problems.

Help these children by seeking the counsel of professionals trained to help angry children and their families. Consider getting the advice of such a professional when you suspect that a child needs help beyond normal classroom interventions and lessons. This mental health professional can also give you advice on how to talk to parents about a possible referral for the family or for the child.

Case Study Analysis: Anger in an Early Childhood Classroom

Both Jordan and Justine, in the case study at the beginning of this chapter, **felt** anger. Each child **expressed** anger. Now that you have read the chapter, analyze this case study by answering the following questions.

1. Each child felt angry because of a conflict over possessions. Identify one such interaction for
   a. Jordan
   b. Justine
2. Each child also felt anger over an issue of compliance with Mrs. Vargas. Identify one such interaction for
   a. Jordan
   b. Justine
3. From your perspective, which child, Jordan or Justine, has more stress related to angry conflicts? Explain your answer.
4. From information in the chapter, explain how Jordan's and Justine's families have influenced each child's ability to use words to express angry feelings.
5. Briefly describe how the families of these two children have modeled how to express anger and how it has affected Jordan's and Justine's behavior in their classroom.
6. How safe, in your view, is the **emotional climate** in Mrs. Vargas's classroom? (1 is not at all safe; 5, an extremely safe emotional climate.) Explain your choice.

1	2	3	4	5

REFLECTING ON KEY CONCEPTS

1. Why is it so difficult for young children to **understand** emotions, especially since they can feel emotions, and they certainly do express emotions?
2. Explain why arguing over possessions is the type of interaction most likely to call forth anger in preschool children.
3. A parent asks you this question: "OK, Tim is only 2 years old. He cannot manage anger on his own. I understand that. How will I know when he is ready to handle some of his feelings on his own?" What would you say to this parent?
4. Why is it so important to teach children how to use word labels for their feelings of anger? Why can you expect the children with whom you work to show individual differences in their ability to use word labels for emotions?
5. Choose two of the guidance strategies for helping children manage angry feelings described in this chapter that you would find the most helpful. Explain why.

APPLY YOUR KNOWLEDGE

1. **Help Jordan manage his anger.** Choose one of the observations that Mrs. Vargas made about Jordan in the chapter-opening case study. Using knowledge you have acquired from the chapter, state how she could have effectively dealt with how Jordan expressed his anger for that example. Be specific. Explain your solution thoroughly. Write out the words that you would have Mrs. Vargas use. Be prepared to role-play your solution.

2. **Analyze a book on anger.** Here are a few examples of children's books on anger. This is merely a list; decide for yourself whether each book meets the guidelines. Practice choosing wisely by evaluating one or more books from this list. Use the checklist from the chapter as a guide (Figure 8.4).

- Barshun, R. N., & Hutton, K. (1983). *Feeling angry.* Elgin, IL: Child's World.
- Carle, E. (1977). *The grouchy ladybug.* New York: Harper & Row.
- Duncan, R. (1989). *When Emily woke up angry.* Hauppauge, NY: Barrons.
- Mayer, M. (1983). *I was so mad.* Racine, WI: Western Publishing.
- Noll, S. (1991). *That bothered Kate.* New York: Puffin.
- Riley, S. (1978). *What does it mean? Angry.* Elgin, IL: Child's World.
- Simon, N. (1974). *I was so mad!* Chicago: A. Whitman.

3. **Portfolio development.** Analyze at least five children's books on anger by using Figure 8.4. Place the checklists in your portfolio with a note about your willingness and ability to choose appropriate books on anger.

4. **Read a story to children.** If you are currently working with children and find a book that meets the guidelines for choosing books on anger, arrange to read the story to a group of children. Write a brief lesson plan detailing how you will present the book to the children and get the plan approved by the children's teacher. Read the story to a single child if you are not working with children in a group setting.

REFERENCES

Baughman, D. (1992). Heal thyself: Reducing the risk of heart disease. *Optimal Health, 4*(2), 1, 4. (A publication of the University of Wisconsin-Stout, Menomonie, Wisconsin.)

Baumrind, D. (1996). Parenting: The discipline controversy revisited. *Family Relations, 45,* 405–414.

Brown, J. R., & Dunn, J. (1996). Continuities in emotion understanding from 3 to 6 years. *Child Development, 67*(3), 789–803.

Brown University Child & Adolescent Behavior Letter (1999). Commentary: The wellsprings of anger. *Brown University Child & Adolescent Behavior Letter, 15*(7), 8.

Campos, J., & Barrett, K. (1984). A new understanding of emotions and their development. In C. Izard, J. Kagan, & R. Zajonc (Eds.), *Emotions, cognition, and behavior.* New York: Cambridge University Press.

Cole, P. M., & Zahn-Waxler, C. (1992). Emotional dysregulation in Disruptive Behavior Disorders. In D. Cicchetti & S. L. Toth (Eds.), *Rochester symposium on developmental psychopathology.* Rochester, NY: University of Rochester Press.

Cummings, E., & Cummings, J. (1988). A process-oriented approach to children's coping with adults' angry behavior. *Developmental Review, 8,* 296–321.

Davis, T. L. (1995). Gender differences in masking negative emotions: Ability or motivation? *Developmental Psychology, 31*(4), 660–668.

Denham, S. A., Zoller, D., & Couchoud, E. Z. (1994). Socialization of preschoolers' emotion understanding. *Developmental Psychology, 30*(6), 928–937.

El-Sheikh, M., & Reiter, S. (1996). Children's responding to live interadult conflict: The role of form of anger expression. *Journal of Abnormal Child Psychology, 24*(4), 401–416.

Fabes, R., & Eisenberg, N. (1992). Young children's coping with interpersonal anger. *Child Development, 63,* 116–128.

Fabes, R., Eisenberg, N., Smith, M., & Murphy, B. (1996). Getting angry at peers: Associations with liking of the provocateur, *Child Development, 67*(3), 943–958.

Freeman, N., Lacohee, H., & Coulton, S. (1995). Cued-recall approach to 3-year-olds' memory for an honest mistake. *Journal of Experimental Child Psychology, 60* (1), 102–116.

Garbarino, J., Guttman, E., & Seeley, J. (1986). *The psychologically battered child.* San Francisco, CA: Jossey-Bass.

Goleman, D. (1995). *Emotional intelligence.* New York: Bantam Books.

Hart, C., DeWolf, M., Wozniak, P., & Burts, D. (1992). Maternal and paternal disciplinary styles: Relations with preschoolers' playground behavioral orientations and peer status. *Child Development, 63,* 879–892.

Harter, S. (1983). Developmental perspectives on the self-system. In E. M. Hetherington (Ed.), *Socialization, personality and social development, Vol 4. Handbook of child psychology* (pp. 275–385). New York: Wiley.

Hennessy, K., Rabideau, G., Cummings, E. M., & Cicchetti, D. (1994). Responses of physically abused and nonabused children to different forms of interadult anger. *Child Development, 65*(3), 815–829.

Jalongo, M. (1986). Using crisis-oriented books with young children. In J. B. McCracken (Ed.), *Reducing stress in young children's lives.* Washington, DC: NAEYC.

Jenkins, J. (2000). Marital conflict and children's emotions: The development of an anger organization. *Journal of Marriage and the Family, 62*(3), 723–736.

Johnson, E. H. (1992, February 25). The role of anger/hostility in hypertension and heart disease. Speech presented at the University of Wisconsin-Stout, Menomonie, WI.

Kopp, C. (1989). Regulation of distress and negative emotions: A developmental view. *Developmental Psychology, 25,* 343–354.

Kuebli, J. (1994). Young children's understanding of everyday emotions. *Young Children, 49,* 36–47.

Levine, L. (1995), Young children's understanding of the causes of anger and sadness. *Child Development, 66*(3), 697–710.

Lewis, M. (1989). Cultural differences in children's knowledge of emotional scripts. In C. Saarni & P. Harris (Eds.), *Children's understanding of emotion* (pp. 350–357). Cambridge, England: Cambridge University Press.

Malatesta, C., & Haviland, J. (1982). Learning display rules: The socialization of emotion expression in infancy. *Child Development, 53,* 991–1003.

Marion, M. (1994). Supporting the development of responsible anger management in children. *Early Child Development and Care, 97,* 155–163.

Marion, M. (1997). Research in review: Guiding young children's understanding and management of anger. *Young Children, 52*(7), 62–68.

Marion, M. (1999). *Guidance of young children* (5th ed.). Upper Saddle River, NJ: Merrill/Prentice Hall.

Michalson, L., & Lewis, M. (1985). What do children know about emotions and when do they know it? In M. Lewis & C. Saarni (Eds.), *The socialization of emotions* (pp. 117–139). New York: Plenum.

Miller, P., & Sperry, L. (1987). The socialization of anger and aggression. *Merrill-Palmer Quarterly, 33* (1), 1–31.

Perlmutter, M. (1986). A life-span view of memory. In P. B. Baltes, D. L. Featherman, & R. M. Lerner (Eds.), *Life-span development and behavior* (Vol. 7). Hillsdale, NJ: Erlbaum.

Piaget, J. (1970). Piaget's theory. In P. Mussen (Ed.), *Carmichael's manual of child psychology.* New York: Wiley.

Rovenger, J. (2000). Fostering emotional intelligence: A librarian looks at the role of literature in a child's development. *School Library Journal, 46* (12), 40–41.

Russel, J. A. (1989). Culture, scripts, and children's understanding of emotion. In C. Saarni & P. L. Harris (Eds.), *Children's understanding of emotion* (pp. 293–318). Cambridge, England: Cambridge University Press.

Stenberg, C. (1982). *The development of anger facial expressions in infancy.* Unpublished doctoral dissertation, University of Denver.

Suinn, R. (2001). The terrible twos—anger and anxiety: Hazardous to your health. *American Psychologist, 56*(1), 27–36.

Underwood, M., Coie, J., & Herbsman, C. (1992). Display rules for anger and aggression in school-age children. *Child Development, 63,* 366–380.

Zeman, J., & Garber, J. (1996). Display rules for anger, sadness, and pain: It depends on who is watching. *Child Development, 67*(3), 957–974.

Zeman, J., & Shipman, K. (1996). Children's expression of negative affect: Reasons and methods. *Developmental Psychology, 32*(5), 842–850.

✓ CHECK OUT THE WEB SITES RELATED TO THIS CHAPTER

✓ **American Psychological Association** (APA). A professional organization that also serves the public.

www.helping.apa.org/daily/anger.html. APA public information brochure; outlines various techniques to help those who experience anger learn how to better control it. This brochure is titled, "Controlling Anger Before It Controls You."

✓ **Parenting Toolbox.** This is a Web site devoted to giving information to parents.

www.parentingtoolbox.com. Go to "Family Anger." Several sites related to anger management.

✓ **University of Cincinnati, Psychological Services Center.** This is the part of the university charged with helping students deal with problems such as dealing with anger.

www.psc.uc.edu. Go to "Self-Help Information" and then to "Anger Management."

Preventing Violent Behavior and Understanding Aggression in Children

"You first learn violence within the family." Violence "is learned early and learned very well . . . violence is preventable"

(American Psychological Association, 1993)

"Viewing media violence can lead to increases in aggressive attitudes, values, and behavior, particularly in children."

(Anderson, Cook, Honaker, & Kestenbaum, 2000)

"Bullying . . . a vicious type of aggressive behavior, since it is directed, most repeatedly, towards a particular victim who is unable to defend himself or herself."

(Smith & Morita, 1999)

"Continuing abuse from bullying . . . results in feelings of humiliation, helplessness, hopelessness . . . victim feelings of anger have led victims to act out aggressively against their school peers."

(Hazler, 2000)

After reading and studying this chapter, you will be able to

❏ **Define** aggression and **list and describe** different forms of aggression.

❏ **Explain** age and gender differences in aggression.

❏ **Explain,** from a systems or ecological perspective, how children become aggressive or violent, and how they acquire scripts for aggression and violence.

❏ **Explain** the role of media violence in children's aggression.

❏ **List and describe** different forms of violence.

❏ **Summarize** the warning signs of violent behavior in young children.

❏ **List, discuss, and give examples** of specific guidance strategies that prevent or control aggression.

Case Studies: Oaklawn School's Effort to Prevent Violence and Aggression

Seth, Third Grade: Building on His Strengths

Mr. Santini, one of Oaklawn's guidance counselors, is also a clinical child psychologist licensed to provide psychological evaluation and treatment for emotional and behavioral problems and disorders (American Academy of Child & Adolescent Psychiatry [AACAP], 1999a). He has been working with several children, including Seth, 8 years old, recently labeled by classmates as a bully. Seth is not ADHD and has no learning disabilities or anxiety disorders. Seth's family is under great stress, and Seth has begun to show some symptoms of Oppositional Defiant Disorder (ODD) at school, especially when he is tired or stressed. Seth has lost the ability to manage his anger, and that presents problems for him in school. His behavior—occasional deliberate attempts to annoy other children, frequent anger and resentment, mean and hateful speech when upset, easily annoyed by others—has recently interfered with his relationships with his classmates (AACAP, 1999b). Some, but not all, of the children have begun to steer clear of Seth because of his bullying. Seth is still doing well academically.

Mr. Santini knows Seth's family well, having dealt with Seth's three older brothers, two of whom have been in trouble for about a year. He has observed changes in the family that have affected the parents and the time they have for their children. Seth's father is a partner in a law firm. Seth's mother has had breast cancer and is currently receiving chemotherapy, which has made her very sick and unable to care for or watch over her children. The housekeeper takes care of the house and the food but supervises Seth and his brothers only minimally. Seth's dad has taken a quarter-time family leave (he carries 75% of his normal client load) to take care of his sons and wife. He tries to spend some time with each of his sons. He takes Seth and the dog to dog training class and practices with Seth. In spite of all that this family faces, Seth shows good resilience, as you will see. Mr. Santini wants to help Seth and his parents.

Mr. Santini, who lives in Seth's neighborhood, has often seen Seth with his dog, Runner, and they talked about Runner at school in the counselor's office. Seth's sense of humor, still intact, was evident when he explained that "Runner is named Runner because we like to run together." Runner is Seth's friend, and Seth really loves the dog and treats him well. Seth has never hurt or bullied Runner.

When Mr. Santini told Seth, "Runner sure likes you, Seth," Seth shared a secret with his counselor. "We (Runner and I) watch a real old TV show called *Lassie*. I try to treat Runner the way that Timmy treats Lassie!" Seth wants desperately to have the same type of relationship with Runner that Timmy has with Lassie, and to his credit, he seems to be succeeding.

Recently, Seth cried in Mr. Santini's office and told him that the other boys would not let him play on the baseball team at lunch, although they know that he is a good shortstop. Mr. Santini has observed that baseball is Seth's favorite sport and knows how hurt Seth was by the boys' rejection. Mr. Santini and Seth's teacher, Mr. Lee, have also observed that Seth still shows flexibility and cooperation many times but that some of the other children, now afraid of him, do not notice. The guidance counselor and teacher have developed a specific plan for Seth, one that includes restoring Seth's view of himself as socially skilled with other children. They plan to model, coach him, set up practice sessions, and encourage his efforts at cooperative behavior. They intend to build on Seth's strengths.

To do this, they are giving him lessons in social skills that he appears to have forgotten. For example, he now frequently enters a group in progress by pushing his way in. He greets others, not politely but often by saying something rude, or by ignoring them. He does not read social cues very well (e.g., "Tommy is busy, not angry with me"). He has begun to see hostile intent, where there is none. The goal is to help him relearn good social skills.

They modeled and coached him on how to enter a group and how to ask politely for what he needs. They practiced with him until Seth seemed to remember the more helpful skill. Then they decided that Seth needed to practice the skills with the other children. He started just by sitting near another child quietly, working on a similar project. Talking with the other child was not the goal.

The plan: Seth was working on a "trees" project, as were all the other children. He decided to go to the writing center to do one of the writing options in the project. Randy, bullied in the past by Seth, was also there. When Seth got his paper and pencil and sat down at the round table, Randy looked up, flinched, and quickly put his head down. Seth knew that this might happen (Mr. Santini had role-played it with him). So, Seth just sat at the table and wrote his poem about pine trees.

Then Seth went beyond expectations for this lesson. Randy needed a green marker to illustrate his story, but Seth had most of the markers. Seth noticed and said, "Sorry, Randy. I took all the markers. I'll put the markers in the middle of the table and then we can share them, OK?" Randy, unsure about this new behavior from the former bully, merely nodded. Seth quietly said, "Whew. I did it!"

Tyler, Kindergarten: Warning Signs of Violence

Tyler is 5 years old. His family has adopted Bailey, a golden retriever, from a rescue group. Tyler's permissive parents do not monitor his play, and he is on his own a good bit of time each morning in the backyard where Bailey spends the day. Tyler, only when alone with Bailey, kicks and hits the dog (Tyler looks to see if anyone is around to see him). Another of Tyler's favorite things to do is to pull one of Bailey's back legs out sideways. Bailey learned early that barking in protest resulted in Tyler squeezing Bailey's mouth shut hard. One morning, Tyler's dad had to trim a tree branch and tied Bailey to a tie-out stake to keep him safe. Tyler, after making sure that Dad was way off in the back of the yard, got on his tricycle and zoomed to within about 10 inches of where Bailey was tethered. When Bailey jumped back, Tyler laughed, sped away, turned, and bore down on the dog again.

Mr. Nellis, Tyler's kindergarten teacher (from Oaklawn School), has called Tyler's parents three times with reports of Tyler's hitting other children. He was most alarmed when he saw Tyler reach into the gerbil house, pick up the gerbil by her tail, and let her dangle in midair. He and Mr. Santini have asked Tyler's parents to meet with them about Tyler's aggression.

Oaklawn's Parent Group: Taking Charge of Media

A high percentage of Oaklawn parents actively participate in their children's care and education. Some parents refuse to participate. Still others, like Seth's parents, are concerned about their children and have participated in the past but are now overwhelmed by other tasks and cannot participate. When actively involved parents watched reports of yet another high school student killing teachers and classmates, they contacted the principal and requested a meeting. Frustrated, they asked what they could do to keep their children safe in what one parent called a "world gone crazy." "I am so sick," one father said, "of what is on that TV—kids' shows, news, talk shows, and have you seen that wrestling? All they show is people hurting each other. Then there's the garbage on the Internet and all those video games where winning means killing somebody. I've had it! No wonder that teenagers are shooting other kids!"

The parents answered the principal's question: "What's the one thing that we can do together that will help you the most?" by agreeing that they most wanted help in dealing with all the violence in the media. The principal had never thought of this topic as the school's concern until the parents helped her realize that it would, indeed, take the entire community, including the school, to help parents deal with media violence.

So was born the "Helping Children Take Charge of Media in Their Lives" program.[29] To start, parents and teachers focused on three main ideas. (See the Working With Parents box.)

- They learned how to talk with children about media violence.
- They learned how to help children take charge of what they watch.
- They learned how to select toys that would foster creative play and learned about avoiding media-linked toys that foster aggression and violence.

AGGRESSION DEFINED

Aggression: a problem-solving behavior which is learned early in life, is learned well, and is resistant to change (Eron, 1986). Aggression is any behavior that injures or diminishes a person or animal in some way or damages or destroys property. Aggression takes several forms. Aggression can cause physical, verbal, psychological, or emotional damage. The attack can be direct or indirect, impulsive or well planned (Berkowitz, 1993; Potter, Vaughn, Warren, Howley, Land, & Hagemeyer, 1995).

Example. In Minnesota in 1997, three 18-year-old men broke into an animal shelter for cats and slaughtered all the cats living there. Two adolescents shot and killed 14 classmates and one teacher in Columbine High School in Colorado in April 1999 (premeditated, direct, physical aggression).

Example. Tyler, from the case study, kicks and hits Bailey, the family pet (intentional, direct, physical aggression). Tyler calls Bailey to him and then hits the dog (intentional and both psychologically and physically harmful aggression).

Example. Seth's brother (in the case study) has reacted to the family problems by getting mean. He calls Seth a "dummy" (verbal, psychologically harmful aggression).

Seth watched his oldest brother deliver a karate-like hit to another child's chest (direct, physical aggression). The brother had seen male adult entertainment wrestlers do the same thing (direct, physical aggression).

The same brother ripped Seth's list of spelling words to shreds (physical, direct aggression that damages property).

Aggression clearly takes several forms; it has many faces. Adults who work with children should have a common definition of aggression so that they can observe and then deal with aggressive behavior consistently and effectively. The common thread that ties together all acts of aggression is that the behavior, whatever it looks like, injures a person or animal or damages or destroys property.

---

[29]The program was based on Levin's ideas, explained in Levin, D. (1998).

Aggression is not the same thing as anger. Anger is an emotion, a feeling. Aggression is a behavior. Angry children might behave aggressively, but not always, and children can be aggressive without being angry. Therefore, this text treats anger (Chapter 8) and aggression separately.

FORMS OF AGGRESSION: INSTRUMENTAL, HOSTILE, ACCIDENTAL

Instrumental Aggression

Instrumental aggression is aggressive behavior that is aimed at obtaining or getting back some object, territory, or privilege (Hartup, 1974). This type of aggression usually springs from simple goal blocking; a child who uses instrumental aggression is usually not even angry with the person blocking his goal. He simply wants to remove whatever is blocking his goal and tends to do something offensive to achieve his end. He uses aggression as an instrument, a tool.

Example. Four-year-old Chelsea wanted to sit on the yellow carpet square at circle time. When she saw that Nellie was already sitting on the yellow square (Nellie was blocking Chelsea's goal) Chelsea sat down right next to Nellie and started to bump her. This surprised Mrs. Vargas, the teacher, since Chelsea was usually so withdrawn. Nellie shot a look of annoyance at Chelsea, who kept bumping Nellie, finally shoving her off the yellow square (instrumental aggression).

Observant teachers realize that they are going to have a certain amount of instrumental aggression in an early childhood classroom. As we know from many decades of research, this is the most common form of aggression during early childhood. Research from the 1930s, Dawe (1934), the 1970s, Hartup (1974), and the 1990s, Fabes & Eisenberg (1992), demonstrated that young children have most of their conflicts over space and resources (toys and other equipment). There tends to be little hostility involved. They push their way into line, grab things from others, yell "It's my turn!" and even bite (quite common in very young children). This type of aggression originates in a child's inability to take the other child's perspective and in his frustration about not having what he wants.

Helping children who use instrumental aggression

There are two main things that will most help children. One, view instrumental aggression as behavior that should not be ignored. Ignoring instrumental aggression rewards a child for being aggressive. Had the teacher allowed Chelsea to push people around, as Chelsea did with Nellie, and get what she wanted, the teacher would have rewarded Chelsea for aggression. There is a better way.

Two, acknowledge the child's frustration and help her construct another solution.

Example. In the carpet-square incident, Chelsea's teacher decided to acknowledge that Chelsea had a goal but also to refuse to let her use aggressive tactics to achieve it. The teacher also helped Chelsea construct another solution by saying, "Chelsea, Nellie was sitting on the yellow square. Nellie, use words to tell Chelsea to give it back." She did not allow Chelsea to victimize Nellie. (Chelsea

Miko wants part of Jake's lunch (her goal). She used *instrumental aggression* when she grabbed the cake.

handed over the piece of carpet.) "Thanks, Chelsea. Nellie has a right to sit on her carpet square. (She focused on the central issue of fairness to others.) "What other choice can you make?" "I can pick another square," Chelsea replied in a decidedly resigned tone of voice.

Hostile Aggression

Hostile aggression often strikes an observer as a nasty, distasteful sort of vengeful behavior; some forms of hostile aggression are tinged with evil. It is quite different from instrumental aggression because hostile aggression is rooted in the emotion of anger. Hostile aggression is behavior bound up with anger aimed directly at a person, animal, or even a country; it is anger-based aggression. Some anger-based aggression is truly vicious. The destruction of the World Trade Center in New York City on September 11, 2001, the bombing of the Federal Building in Oklahoma City in 1994, and the Columbine High School tragedy in 1999 are three of our nation's most glaring examples.

Hostile aggression is violence. The purpose of hostile aggression is clearly to hurt someone or to destroy something. Tyler's behavior (in the case study) is an obvious example of anger-based, deliberate, hostile aggression aimed at his dog. Cruelty toward animals is not a joke; it is outrageous behavior and a warning sign of potential deadly violence. Adults must take it seriously because a young child will not outgrow such cruelty. It is not just a phase (AACAP, 1997). Ignoring such behavior is akin to participating in the cruel behavior. Ignoring a child's cruelty toward an animal is like giving permission for the behavior. Children who are cruel to animals need help, and teachers must have the courage to observe, document, and then report such behavior to protect the animal and to help the child.

A person who is angrily aggressive usually is on guard, has his "antennae up," for any behavior that he perceives as a threat to his ego. He either disregards or is incapable of paying attention to relevant social cues, resulting in his belief that the other person has done something mean-spirited when the other person might well have had no such intention. Mistaken beliefs such as this are starting points for physically or psychologically **hostile** aggression. Mr. Santini, Oaklawn's psychologist, heard about the following incident from the teacher and from Seth when Seth was in his office.

Example. Seth (from the case study) and Theng (pronounced Teng), worked on their science project together. Seth's brothers have been calling Seth a "dummy" and so now, Seth is on guard at school. When Theng offered to help Seth solve a problem with Seth's part of the project, Seth perceived the offer as a sign that Theng thought him incompetent (perceived threat to self-esteem). Seth's face got red with embarrassment and anger, and he shouted at Theng, "I can do this, Theng! You think you're so smart" (hostile aggression).

Hostile aggression tends to show up most often in older children, adolescents, and adults (Szegal, 1985). Whether children are capable of expressing behavior such as hostile aggression parallels a more general change in their cognitive structure. Preschool children, usually in the preoperational or second of Piaget's stages of cognitive development, are somewhat **egocentric.** They are not yet able to understand or take another person's perspective; this explains why their aggression is most often instrumental.

A very young child who cannot take another person's perspective will also not be able to understand what that other person intended to do. An older child, in a different Piagetian stage, becomes less egocentric and better able to take another child's perspective. Understanding that other perspective also means that older children, such as Seth, can begin to guess at another person's intentions.

Some older children however, have deficits in several aspects of social problem solving. For example, in spite of a greater ability to detect others' intentions, some older aggressive children are inattentive to relevant social cues or signals. As a result, they frequently presume that another person had some sort of hostile plan in mind, even where no hostility was intended (Dodge & Frame, 1982). They repeatedly make mistakes about the intentions of other people, as did Seth with Theng's offer of help, but it is a person's perception of reality that matters, even if the perception is a faulty one. Seth acted on his perception, faulty as it was, and he reacted with hostile aggression.

Accidental Aggression

Accidental aggression is unintentional aggression (Feshbach, 1970). All teachers observe a certain amount of this sort of unintentional injury or damage. Whether this unintentional hurting of others is really aggression is a good question. What does happen, though, is that someone accidentally hurts another person or animal or accidentally damages something. The real problem with this type of aggression is that the child who is accidentally hurt often responds aggressively in turn.

Example. It was crowded in the coatroom of Mr. Nellis's classroom. Mr. Nellis had stored curriculum materials and had placed a small table there. When Mitchell stowed his backpack and turned to leave the room, he crashed into Louie (accidental aggression). Louie reacted by yelling at Mitchell.

Louie retaliated in a hurtful way. Like most young children, in addition to not being able to see things from Mitchell's perspective, he is also not very good at dealing with more than one idea at a time. For example, Louie would likely not be able to think on his own about these three things. "It's crowded here; Louie is rushing around; he bumped into me by accident." He does not understand yet the difference between an **accidental and an intentional** act.

Mitchell also had a part in this interaction. He does not pay attention to what he is doing at times. He is somewhat impulsive, but not excessively so. The crowded coatroom was perhaps just too much for him to handle.

Mr. Nellis observed Louie and Mitchell and decided to take some positive steps. He realized that the boys, as well as other children in the class, simply do not know some specific things. They lack some skills that he can teach them. See Figure 9.1 for examples of the lessons for which he wrote plans and then presented in large group. These lessons are appropriate for older preschool, kindergarten, and first-grade children.

The teacher also observed himself and the classroom. He realized that the physical setup of a space affects children's behavior. On inspection, he realized that the coatroom was cramped. Consequently, he decided to remove the table and boxes. Mr. Nellis noticed an immediate change in the children's behavior in this still small but less crowded space. He made one other change, this one in how he set limits. The teacher limited the number of children who went to the coatroom at any one time, a change which also supported the children's efforts (Figure 9.1).

DEADLY SCHOOL VIOLENCE

Pearl, Mississippi; Paducah, Kentucky; Columbine High School, Colorado (1999); Santana, California (2001). These and many others scenes of deadly school violence have shocked this nation into a new awareness about the real outcomes for a society awash in violence. In the past, some have dismissed school violence as just a major temper outburst, the result of a bad day. That view has given way to the idea that deadly school violence is now, in addition to being a juvenile criminal justice concern, a major public health concern (Heide, 1999; Surgeon General, 2000).

Students often do not feel safe either going to school or while they are at school. This unease or anxiety is often caused by peer abuse, with bullying the most common form (Center for Disease Control & Prevention, 1995). Deadly violence, a

---

Rush-Around Rabbit and Observant Owl[30] to the Rescue: Putting the Brakes on Accidental Aggression

Teacher uses puppets, Rush-Around Rabbit (impulsive, rushes around, does not stop and think) and Observant Owl (observant, more deliberate, slower), to help all children in the group understand the meaning of the phrases "by accident," "meant to," or "intended to." Teacher teaches children about paying attention or taking heed of their actions before acting. Teacher also demonstrates how important it is for children to practice new skills. This might well reduce the number of episodes of **accidental aggression** in an early childhood setting.

✓ **Rush-Around Rabbit does not pay attention.** Teacher demonstration: Rush-Around Rabbit, playing happily and not paying attention, bumps Observant Owl. Owl exclaims: "Hey, Rush-Around Rabbit! You bumped into me but I think it was an 'accident.' I think that you did not 'mean to' bump me. You just were 'not paying attention.'"

✓ **Observant Owl teaches Rush-Around Rabbit how to do "self-talk."** "Want some help, Rush-Around Rabbit? Watch me!" Observant Owl moves from the easel to the book corner—at a steady pace but deliberately and carefully. He uses "self-talk" to remind himself to pay attention: "OK, I'm done at the easel. I'll go now to the book corner. Whoa! Somebody is in my way. I'd better walk around her."

✓ **Rush-Around Rabbit practices.** Observant Owl to Rush-Around Rabbit: "Now, you try it with me, Rabbit. Go slowly, OK? Let's walk over to the dress-up corner. Watch out for other children." (They arrive at the dress-up corner.) "You did a good job, Rabbit! You were careful. Now, look to see who is playing here before we go in. Tell yourself to 'stop and look' carefully." Rabbit says, "OK, I have to stop and look. Now I count—one, two, three. Three other children." Owl observes and comments, "You talked to yourself and then looked and then counted the children. You are really paying attention, Rabbit!"

✓ **"Whoops! I'm sorry."** Rush-Around Rabbit slows down but then forgets and bumps into Owl. He wails, "Oh, no! I forgot, Owl." Owl replies, "I know, Rabbit. It was an 'accident' and you did not 'mean to' bump me. You just forgot. It's OK." Then Owl says, "My dad told me that when I forget to pay attention and bump into somebody that I might have hurt them. He says I should say, 'Whoops! I bumped into you. I'm sorry. I'll be more careful.'" Rabbit says, "Let me try, OK?" (Rabbit then practices this simple but straightforward apology.)

Figure 9.1.

complex issue, grows in part out of a progression of traumatizing events such as bullying, constant teasing, isolation, and rejection. Deadly school violence does have warning signs (Carney, 2000; Hazler, 2000) (Figure 9.2).

---

[30]Sources: Berk, L. E., & Winsler, A. (1995). *Scaffolding children's learning: Vygotsky and early childhood education.* Washington, DC: NAEYC; Frey, K. S., Hirschstein, M. K., & Guzzo, B. (2000). Second step: Preventing aggression by promoting social competence. *Journal of Educational and Behavioral Disorders* 8(2), 102–112; King, C. A. & Kirschenbaum, D. S. (1992). *Helping children develop social skills: The social growth program.* Pacific Grove, CA: Brooks/Cole Publishing Company.

Warning Signs for Violent Behavior in Children and Adolescent	
These warning signs should be like bright red flags. Warning signs of violence are a combination of any of several factors that increase the risk of violent behavior ("risk factor" column on left) and specific behaviors (right-hand column). Take the warning signs seriously.	
Factors Increasing the Risk of Violent Behavior	**Specific Behaviors**
• Past violent behavior (including uncontrollable angry outbursts) • Access to guns or other weapons • Bringing weapons to school • Recent experience with and a history of shame or humiliation • Pattern of threats • Witnessing abuse or violence • Being a victim of abuse or violence • Cruelty to animals • Fire setting • Inadequate monitoring by and inadequate supervision by parents	• Frequent intense anger • Frequent lost of temper or frequent blowups • Extreme irritability • Extreme impulsiveness • Extremely easily frustrated

Figure 9.2.

Source: AACAP (1997). Understanding violent behavior in children and adolescents. *Facts for Families,* No.55, Washington, DC: Author; AACAP (1998). Children's threats: When are they serious? *Facts for Families,* No. 65, Washington, DC: Author.

Different Forms of Violence

There is not just one type of school violence; there is a range of violent behavior (AACAP, 1998). Media response to the high school killings of the past several years has focused on homicide, and the danger is that the public might fail to recognize other forms of violence.

- Explosive temper tantrums
- Physical aggression
- Cruelty towards animals
- Threats or attempts to hurt others (including homicidal threats)
- Carrying out threats to hurt others (including murder)
- Use of weapons
- Fire setting
- Intentional destruction of property
- Vandalism

Warning Signs of Violence

You might be wondering why you are reading about youth violence in a text about early childhood. The surgeon general's report on youth violence (2000) views violence from a developmental perspective. This perspective has pointed to **two pathways of violence, one emerging before puberty,** and one emerging after puberty. The early-onset pathway provides the strongest evidence of a link between early childhood experiences and persistent involvement in violent behavior.

Some of the violence which we have witnessed, then, had its roots in early childhood. Deadly violence provides warning signs, some evident in early childhood.

GENDER DIFFERENCES IN AGGRESSION

There are clear differences in aggression between boys and girls, and these differences are evident during early childhood (Boyatzis, Matillo, & Nesbitt, 1995; Cummings, Iannotti, & Zahn-Waxler, 1989). The findings tell us that

- boys display more aggression than girls, both physically and verbally
- boys display more aggression after watching media violence
- boy's aggression stays stable during the early childhood years
- older boys are more likely than older girls to counterattack when physically attacked
- pairs of boys have more aggressive interactions than a boy/girl or girl/girl dyad (pair).

Researchers document gender differences, but explaining the differences is another thing. Gender differences most likely result from how we socialize boys and girls. Our culture has clearly defined attitudes about girls, boys, and aggression, and we can easily observe these attitudes by looking at differing child-rearing tactics used with boys and girls.

Some parents expect, permit, and then encourage aggression in boys. Parents tend to use more physical punishment with boys than with girls, and boys might adopt these aggressive methods in interaction with others (Block, 1978). Many parents also manage the environments of boys and girls differently. For example, they choose different toys for girls and boys, and toys often chosen for boys, such as guns or action figures, are **aggressive cues,** items that seem to elicit aggressive play.

CHILDREN GATHER "SCRIPTS" FOR AGGRESSIVE BEHAVIOR IN FAMILIES, FROM PEERS, AND FROM MEDIA VIOLENCE

Think Scripts

An actor knows exactly what to say and do onstage because he has a script. Children who behave aggressively also have **scripts,** files of information that tell them exactly how to hit, punch, kick, grab, insult, extort, threaten, or call names—how to behave aggressively. Other children might not have as many scripts about aggression. They have far less information on how to behave as aggressively as a child who has a large collection of scripts.

Think scripts whenever you observe aggressive behavior. Seth, the third-grader in the case study, has in the past year and a half activated one of his growing number of aggressive scripts when he wants something. Seth has also recently acquired scripts for bullying, an especially vicious type of aggression. The beginning of helping aggressive children lies in rooting out the sources of these scripts. Did Seth gather his stash of aggressive scripts from his family, especially the older brother who bullies Seth? Did he add to his collection of ideas about how to hurt people from his friends? How many scripts has he collected from the hours and hours of trashy talk shows and violent movies that now run constantly in his family's house when his father is not home? How much of his bullying springs from the violence-laden interactive video games that his oldest brother's friends bring to the house?

The most complete explanation of how children become aggressive is a **systems** or **ecological approach** (Bronfenbrenner, 1979). Professionals taking this approach acknowledge that a child is embedded in a variety of social systems and believe that these systems work together to shape a child's aggression (Huesmann, 1988). A child quite frequently first learns about aggression in his **family system.**

Almost equal in importance to a family's influence is the **media system;** i.e., television, videos, interactive video games, movies, and print media, in helping children learn aggression. The child's **peer group** is a system, which can teach and then reinforce aggression. Families and peer groups are themselves embedded in a larger setting, the **community and culture,** and it is the teachings about aggression from these settings that influence what some families learn and pass on to their children.

Scripts From Aggression-Teaching Families: Writing, Rehearsing with, and Activating the Scripts

Writing aggressive scripts

Aggression is a learned behavior, and some families teach aggression extremely effectively (Parke & Slaby, 1983). An observer would never see a lesson plan for aggression in aggression-teaching families but would definitely observe parents passing on their knowledge about how to hurt others. Aggression-teaching families teach hurtful or destructive behavior in a variety of ways, and teach it very effectively. Children in such families listen to and observe the family's ways of dealing aggressively with one another, with animals, or with people outside the family. This is the scriptwriting step.

Example. A stray cat wandered into Seth's yard and Seth watched his oldest brother yell at the cat, sending the animal running for cover (Seth was handed a new script called "Yell at Cats").

Rehearsing with scripts

In aggression-teaching families, children use newly acquired scripts to rehearse aggressive behavior. Such families give their children many rehearsal sessions with the aggressive scripts.

Example. Recently, Seth listened to a talk show on which a man used a racial slur and then laughed when the other person became embarrassed and angry (Seth

Children acquire *scripts* that tell them how to be aggressive by watching their parents argue.

learned a new script called "Use Racial Slurs"). Seth rehearsed the new script, calling forth laughter from two of his brothers. There was no adult around to stop them.

Children in aggression-teaching families have many chances to practice using their newly learned aggressive scripts. They practice over and over what they have learned about hurting others (Parke & Slaby, 1983). This is the rehearsal with script step. There is no guarantee, however, that the child will automatically use the script or act it out. Seth, for example, learned how to yell at cats but has never used that script. In spite of how one of his brothers now treats animals outside the family, Seth has never rehearsed the lessons.

Therefore, learning does not always mean putting the learning to use. In Seth's case, there is something in his personality that keeps him from acting out any script for hurting animals. He seems to have also gathered and stored scripts of his mother and father's kind treatment of animals. Seth has also such scripts from sources outside his family.

Example. Seth has two favorite television channels; their programming focuses on kindness, cooperation, and healthy relationships. Seth has his own television and automatically chooses these stations whenever he is alone (after school every day while Mom sleeps and the housekeeper fixes dinner, and at several other times during the week). He has been watching *Lassie* reruns and tunes in to whichever animal show he can find. His favorite is the emergency hospital for animals show. These shows add new, positive, scripts to his collection. They also trigger Seth's recall of scripts for healthier behavior that he had learned from his family in better days, and he has rehearsed the aggression-free scripts.

Activating the scripts

Children store the scripts for aggressive behavior in their memories and then activate icons for those aggressive scripts just as we activate specific files on our computer screens. A child then often retrieves and activates the scripts in settings both inside and outside his family.

Suppose that Seth, the case study child, is in your early childhood class. You observe Seth's behavior and realize quickly that he has a growing number of scripts for aggressive behavior in his memory. After observing Seth with the other children for a while longer, you begin to see a pattern. Seth's relatively new scripts for fighting and bullying seem to be stored so that he can retrieve and activate them in a flash. We store frequently used folders on our computers as shortcuts. Unfortunately, Seth's scripts for quick, aggressive responses are stored as shortcuts. He has only to select the shortcut icon that says, "shortcut to fighting."

Three things induce children to retrieve and activate aggression-packed scripts:

- rehearsal
- having cues for aggression
- continued exposure to aggression

Rehearsal. Some children call up scripts for hurting others if they have had many rehearsal sessions using an old standby script.

Example. Seth has activated his script for how to fight back or threaten several times with Randy, the other child in the case study. They have been in the same class since kindergarten and Seth had bullied Randy for several months before the guidance counselor started to work with him. Seth had rehearsed with his "threaten" script with Randy at least once each week.

Cues for aggression, including interactive videos. Some children retrieve scripts for aggression when they see war toys, guns, or aggressive videos. These are a class of items called **cues for aggression.** Putting an aggressive video on the VCR for a child, for instance, is like showing an actor a cue card. It says, "Be aggressive. Here is how to be aggressive." Children retrieve and activate aggressive scripts when they detect specific cues such as war toys or aggressive videos.

Children who play **violent video games** are exposed to and participate in these interactive games. They learn and then practice new aggression-related scripts. The scripts are then accessible for real-life conflict situations. The interactive nature of popular violent video games puts children right in the middle of the aggression in

These boys have all played the same interactive video game. They are imitating aggression from the video.

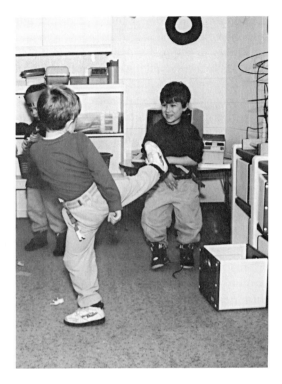

the video. The child becomes a part of the video. Active involvement with violence, even if it is in a video, is still practice. Such practice imprints that script indelibly in the child's memory, giving him a permanent, easily accessed reminder of how to hurt others.

Continued exposure to aggression. This provides even more scripts. Children who already have a large collection of aggressive scripts very likely will continue to observe aggression, increasing even further the number of aggressive scripts in their collection. The brand-new scripts for aggression, in turn, trigger the recall of existing aggression scripts. It is a vicious cycle.

Aggression-Teaching Family Systems Use a Coercive Process to Write Aggressive Scripts

Seth's family, like many aggression-teaching families, uses a specific process to teach aggression and then to maintain it. His family has also used the same process to increase aggression. Patterson (1982) observed patterns of family interaction, which he called a **coercive process.** Knowing that some of your students come from families using such a process for teaching aggression should help you explain, in part, the origin of the children's aggression. Coercion involves the use of psychological or physical force. These are the steps of the coercive process:

- **One system member does something aggressive.** For example, Seth's brother hit Seth.
- **A second system member is likely to respond in an equally hurtful way.** Seth hit his brother back.
- **The unfriendly interaction continues and escalates in intensity.** The boys start pushing each other around. Seth's brother slugged Seth hard and Seth cried.
- **Other system members are drawn into the process.** Dad heard the children fighting, raced to the backyard, and grabbed them. Clearly frustrated and puzzled about what to do, he yelled at them to stop the fighting.
- **One system member eventually withdraws the aversive or unpleasant stimulus and breaks the cycle of aggression for a short time.** Dad retreated to the house, thinking that he had stopped the fighting. The problem? Dad thought he succeeded in stopping the boys' aggressive behavior (actually, the children's aggressive behavior will probably increase). Dad, **negatively reinforced** for grabbing and yelling, is highly likely to shout at them again in future interactions.
- **System members reinforced for aggression victimize the same members of the system in future interactions.** Seth's brother will very likely use aggression with Seth again because Seth cried. Likewise, Dad will very likely use negative discipline strategies with both children again because he mistakenly believes these tactics to be effective.

Families inadvertently train each other to use aggression (Herrenkohl, Egolf, & Herrenkohl, 1997). They will play back the scripts again and again. Dad has a script that says, "Shout when the boys fight." He models aggression by yelling at Seth and his brothers. Seth and his brother reinforce Dad for using aggressive discipline strategies by **temporarily stopping their fighting.**

Seth has acquired, practiced, and used a script about how to fight. His brother is a model of how to be a bully. Seth has activated the bully script in the past when he bullied Randy, his main victim at school. Herrenkohl et al. (1997) noted that children whose parents used punitive discipline showed a lot of aggressive behavior when they were adolescents.

Children Gather Many Aggressive Scripts from Authoritarian Caregivers

Members of aggression-teaching family systems are not very responsive to each other. The parents are often, but not always, insensitive to and nonsupportive of their children, and their caregiving style sets the stage for heightened or increased aggression in children in a number of ways (Feshbach, 1970; Parke & Slaby, 1983). How can we explain how the authoritarian caregiving style fosters aggression?

Unmet needs

Unresponsive adults often ignore and fail to meet a child's basic psychological needs for protection, love, affection, nurturance, play, and self-esteem. Seth's father has never been an authoritarian parent. He has always been highly responsive, but for quite some time now, he has been overwhelmed with the changes in his family. Lately, Dad has even begun to yell at his boys (example of the coercive process above). He needs help so that he can again meet Seth's need for protection (from the brothers) and for affection and nurturance. Unmet needs result in frustration, and frustrated, angry children frequently act aggressively if other conditions are present.

Failure to teach social skills

On one hand, unresponsive adults do not seem have the concept that they should teach specific social skills to their children. They might also just not know how to teach what the child needs to know. Whatever the reason, their children miss out on learning important social skills such as how to deal with conflict nonaggressively, how to wait their turn, how to approach a group, or how to use words to express anger. Therefore, these adults omit something that their children need. Their children tend to be low in self-control or self-restraint, and children who are not self-controlled are likely to react with aggression under many circumstances.

Active teaching of ineffective social skills and rewarding aggression

On the other hand, unresponsive adults actively teach ineffective social skills. A parent might do this deliberately, as when he teaches his child how to hurt someone. A parent might also well carry out such teaching unknowingly, as when Seth's father modeled aggression by yelling at his sons. These adults also tend to reward aggressive behavior.

Use of negative or unhelpful discipline strategies

Using harsh physical discipline, failing to set appropriate limits, inconsistency in discipline, using humor as a weapon, using sarcasm or shame, nattering or nagging, and hurting children with punishment are all unhelpful methods of discipline. Adults in aggression-teaching systems tend to use not just one or two but a whole cluster of negative discipline tactics. Using several negative discipline strategies can increase aggression in children because the strategies demonstrate clearly how to be aggressive.

Providing cues for aggression

Adults in aggression-teaching systems indirectly influence aggression through their management style. This adult managerial role is probably just as important as the adult's direct role. Parents in aggressive systems provide many cues that elicit aggression—media violence in its many forms and toy guns (Boyatzis et al., 1995).

Example. The housekeeper listens to sleazy and aggression-laced talk shows in which people make fun of and denigrate others and allows the older boys to watch almost anything, even violent adult wrestling. Seth's brothers and their friends play violent interactive video games. Seth tends to shy away from much of this because the noise bothers him (he told the psychologist). Nevertheless, he cannot escape it all and does see and hear plenty of media violence. Other adults consciously avoid providing such cues.

Aggressive Peers Teach Aggression and Help Others Gather Aggressive Scripts

Aggression has its roots in a child's family, but aggression is also learned, maintained, and modified in a child's peer group. The children in your center or class will influence each other's aggression in several ways (Parke & Slaby, 1983).

Peers model aggression

Researchers first studied how children learn from peer models almost 40 years ago (Hicks, 1965). They discovered that young children learn just as effectively from models who are their own age (the models were peers) as they do from other types of models. The effect of the modeling lasted for at least six months after observing the peer model.

Example. Seth's three older brothers, 11, 13, and 14 years old, have started hanging out with some new, aggressive friends. Seth has learned aggression from these young models. For instance, he observed one of the friends extort lunch money from a girl at the bus stop. Seth has watched these children push their way in line at the bus for years but has only recently observed their aggression at closer range.

Peers reinforce aggression

Peers also reinforce other children's aggression. Aggressive children lack certain social skills, such as the ability to resolve conflict; they tend to solve conflicts with peers through aggressive means and do not seem to know how to resolve conflict in a positive way (Bullock, 1991). Fabes & Eisenberg (1992) found that almost 20 percent of children who were physically attacked by another child reacted with **aggressive revenge,** a hurtful way of responding to physical attack.

Example. Seth has observed that some children attacked by his brothers and their friends gave in to them, but others did not. He learned that his brothers picked their victims carefully. Seth quickly learned that the brothers picked a new victim when somebody stood up to them. In his own case, Seth found out that Randy would give in to his bullying.

Regarding recent incidents of deadly school violence, experts recognize that teasing, harassment, humiliation, or bullying have been factors in some of these homicides (Hazler, 2000). (I recommend reading Hazler's article if you want to learn about how victims of bullying and humiliation might themselves become, not only aggressive, but aggressive to the point of killing other humans.)

Peers regulate aggression by setting norms

Peer groups influence aggression of group members by **setting norms** about a number of things, including the expression of aggression. The norms tell children what the peer group will accept in terms of aggression. Some peer groups, like Seth's brothers' new friends, have norms that cheer on the use of aggression. Other groups, such as most of the children in Seth's class or those in some of the aggression-free television that he has been watching, forbid aggression through their norms.

Media Violence: An Effective Way to Gather Aggressive Scripts

There is an overwhelming consensus in the research, public health, and early childhood communities that watching and participating in media violence threatens the development and well-being of young children. Thirty years and well over 1,000 studies show that children watch an excessive amount of media violence (television, movies, videos, Internet sources, and interactive video games).

Children have a lot of screen time and watch a lot of violence (Gunter & McAleer, 1990; Huston, Rice, Kerkman, & St. Peters, 1990; Levin, 1998; National Television Violence Study Council [NTVS], 1997; Ridley-Johnson, Surdy, & O'Laughlin, 1991).

- 98% of American homes have one television.
- Over 50% of American homes have at least one extra television.
- Children are the main users of extra televisions.
- Over 50% of American homes have a VCR.
- Half of American homes with children aged 6–14 have video game systems. A majority of video games contain violent content.
- Approximately 33% of American homes receive cable programming.
- Children average 35 hours each week of screen time (television, videos, computer time, interactive video games).
- Infants, 6 months old, are exposed to an average of 1 hour of television per day.
- Many children spend more time watching television than doing anything else.
- Children watch 8,000 murders and 100,000 violent acts in the media by the time that they leave elementary school.
- By the end of kindergarten, children will have seen 4,000 hours of television.
- Children's cartoons contain a high number of violent incidents.

Heavy viewing of media violence has major behavioral effects. Media violence, family, and peer group are the principal socializers of children's aggression (Anderson et al., 2000; Boyatzis et al., 1995; Levin, 1998; National Association for the Education of Young Children [NAEYC], 1994; NTVS, 1997).

Major Risks of Watching Media Violence

Children who watch media violence develop aggressive attitudes, values, and behavior (Anderson et al., 2000). Media violence influences children in four ways: making them want to imitate what they see, reducing learned inhibitions against violent behavior, desensitizing them to violence through repetition, and increasing arousal (Black & Newman, 1995; Gunter & McAleer, 1990). Three major risks go along with watching media violence.

Risk #1: Media violence can and does increase subsequent aggression in children. This conclusion comes from basic research and reports of professional groups (Anderson et al., 2000; APA, 1993; Funk, 1992; Primavera, Herron, & Javier, 1996).

Risk #2: Media violence increases a child's passive acceptance of aggression by others. Not only do children themselves become more aggressive, but they also accept violence by others after watching media violence. Children are most likely to relax their standards if they view violence as effective, justified, reinforced, and commonplace (Anderson et al., 2000; NTVS, 1997).

Risk #3: Media violence often leads children to think that the world is a violent and scary place in which people hurt and degrade each other. It might create and then increase the fear of becoming a victim of violence. Children who are afraid of becoming a victim of violence develop behaviors through which they hope to protect themselves. It also increases mistrust of others (Anderson et al., 2000).

How is media violence portrayed?

Real violence is dirty—people bleed, jaws are broken, people are stabbed, dogs are mutilated, animals and people suffer and die. Real violence is not funny. Media violence does not show the results of real violence. A child who watches television wrestling, for example, does not see the demanding sport of wrestling from high schools or colleges where athletic prowess in important. Instead, he watches very large and strong males, who use loud and mean-spirited speech and who are trained not to wrestle, but to jump on opponents, kick, smash heads, and use headlocks. Some of this violence is simulated, but to a young child, simulated and real are the same thing. Therefore, this is entertainment violence, not wrestling.

Children see a distorted view of violence on television, in movies, and in video games (NTVS, 1997; Potter et al., 1995). Media violence portrays beatings, shootings, fighting, knifings, and murder as clean, justified, effective, rewarded, and humorous.

Children see media violence as an effective way to get things and to get things done. They see good guys get what they want by hurting others. Good guys such as Ranger Walker in *Walker, Texas Ranger*, for example, use violence as a way of punishing bad guys. Children also see that there are rewards for violence. Less than one aggressive act out of six is punished in any way on television; and twice that number are rewarded (Potter et al., 1995).

Producers of televised violence often show the violence as funny. Children's television is especially guilty of connecting violence and humor (Parke & Slaby, 1983). Laugh tracks frequently accompany violent cartoons, and linking violence and laughter tells children that violence is funny.

One research group investigated the effects of *The Mighty Morphin Power Rangers* on children's aggressive behavior. The National Coalition on Television Violence (NCTV, 1997) called this program the most violent children's program it had ever studied, averaging 211 violent acts per hour. Most of the aggression in the show is severe and hostile. The intent of most of the violence in the show is to harm or kill another character. The researchers were alarmed at the power of *The Mighty Morphin Power Rangers* to increase aggression. The children in the study who watched only a single episode were significantly more aggressive immediately after the show. This show had helped children write a script for social behavior that said, "Hit, punch, kick, hurt."

Diane Levin (1998) notes that "just saying 'no'" to shows such as this might not be the most effective thing for parents to do, although the goal is to decrease children's exposure to such media violence. She urges us to help children understand the violence in a show like this and to help children come up with alternatives to all the fighting and to search for ways to restrict imitations of the violence.

STRATEGIES FOR GUIDING AGGRESSIVE CHILDREN AND FOR PREVENTING VIOLENCE

The combination of aggressive children and media violence offers a challenge to early childhood teachers. While some aggression is normal as young children learn to live with others, e.g., grabbing toys, other aggression is much more deeply rooted in a child because the hurtful behavior has developed in an aggression-teaching family. The latter is more difficult to deal with.

There are several ways to help all children cope with aggression and with media violence. Some strategies are especially appropriate for children from aggression-teaching families. This section describes a number of strategies through which we can either decrease or prevent aggression. Some strategies focus on helping individual children. Other strategies are useful when we work with a child's family. We can also decrease or prevent aggression if we focus on events in a child's larger community.

Work with Individual Children

Set and clearly communicate limits prohibiting aggression

Create a **non**permissive atmosphere by establishing limits against hurting or disturbing other people and animals, or damaging toys or equipment. Lead a discussion with children about why it is important to treat other people and animals with respect. Firmly but kindly enforce limits. You will begin to help children construct the idea that other people and animals have a right to be safe and secure. You will help them develop values and internal controls about the rights of others.

Example. When Mr. Nellis restated a limit—"Lilly, I know that you want to sit in that chair, but I can't just let you push Roxanne off. Please pick one of these other chairs"—he clearly communicated his refusal to tolerate Lilly's aggression while he also presented other options to her.

Help children take charge of what they watch in the media

The main goal is to teach children to make conscious decisions about what they watch, and if they will watch at all. Another goal is to decrease the effect of the power and pull of the media—TV, videos, video games, and computers–on a child. This is a difficult task because of how well and attractively the media packages shows. The shows have a mesmerizing effect on a number of children, and many have developed habits of tuning in to the screen when they have a few minutes of downtime. They turn to screens (TV, videos, etc.), are entertained, and do not have to think or exert much energy at all.

Levin (1998) offers excellent ideas on how to help parents and teachers teach children about using media wisely and taking control of what they watch.

- Lead problem-solving discussions with children about the media; e.g., about the Power Rangers and all the fighting that they do. For example, why do they need to fight so much? Is there a way to limit where and when children play "Rangers" on the playground or in the classroom, so that children who do not like the "Rangers" play will not be bothered by it?
- Be clear about limits on imitating certain types of behaviors: Never allow children to imitate hurting animals, other people, or damaging property. Talk to them about the reasons, but be firm. This should be a nonnegotiable item.
- Teach children how to make good choices about their screen viewing (TV, videos, etc.).
- Teach children how to do advance planning for their screen time. Children need help understanding that screen time means a combination of TV, videos, video games, and computers. Give them specific skills for choosing screen time wisely.
- Help children observe themselves and think about the things that they most like doing. Encourage them to schedule time to do these activities in addition to choosing screen time wisely.

See Figure 9.3, a copy of a page in Jessie's log for play and screen time. Jessie is a third-grader whose parents, along with others at Oaklawn School (in the chapter-opening case study) have made a concerted effort to combat violence. One focus is to help children make wise choices about how to use time in general and another is to help them learn to choose screen time carefully.

The school makes no judgments about parents or their level of participation. The teachers realize that not all parents will help their children with this project and for this reason, the teachers decided to have all children fill out the charts at school. It was important to them that all the children, and not just those with actively involved parents, learn and think about how to take charge of the media. They also helped all children do the self-assessment of their interests (favorite things to play with, read, and do) other than screen time. This gave Seth, for example, the opportunity to have adult guidance when he would not have gotten it otherwise. Figure 9.4 is Seth's chart. Please note that his parents do not limit the amount of Seth's screen time.

Seth is indeed a resilient boy. In his chart, notice that his dad goes to dog training class with him. This is also the first time in almost a year that Seth has done anything with both parents (Friday's video). Seth is alone much of the rest of the time. Even when family members are all home, nobody pays attention to what Seth does, and the television is on almost constantly in the family room. Seth has figured out how to begin to avoid his brothers and their brand of television by going to his room to watch television or play video games on his own. He has been making different, better choices about what he watches. If he takes his log home, he hides it between his mattress and box spring so that his brothers will not find it and call him

Oaklawn School: My Plan for Play, TV, Videos, and Computer			

My name: *Jessie S.*
I am allowed to have <u>*60 minutes*</u> screen time on most days.
My favorite things to do (not screen time) are: *baseball, training my dog, reading, skating, building with Legos, playing with my friends.*
Family jobs that I have: *set or clear table, make my bed, feed dog, weed garden with Dad, and one job from "job jar" every week.*

	What I want to play with or read	TV show I plan to watch	Computer game I plan to play	Video I plan to watch
Monday:	*library book* *Skate with Tim* *(Tim stays for dinner)*	*After-school* *special (with Tim)*		
Tuesday:	*dog training* *class* *library book*			*Dog training* *(with Dad)*
Wednesday:	*Lego village (with Tim and Sandy after school)* *Family night (pizza and church)*			
Thursday:	*library book (new book)* *dog training*	*Footage of old time baseball teams (PBS special, with Dad and Uncle)*		
Friday:	*dog training* *read new magazine about baseball*		*Baseball*	

Figure 9.3.

a sissy. He takes the log with him to visits with the school counselor. He has shown the log to his dad, who thought that the log was a good idea.

He also decided to stay after school whenever he can to participate in the Boys and Girls Club after-school programs. The yoga class and the dog training allow him contact with other children. There is, however, little one-to-one contact in these activities, sparing Seth the stress often caused by his downwardly spiraling social skills.

Since he has been working with the school psychologist, Seth's social skills have gradually improved and he has again made a friend—Jeff, a new child in school who lives on Seth's block. They both like dogs. At school, some of the children who had begun to avoid Seth are now gradually changing how they see him. Mr. Santini, aware of the family's circumstances, got permission from Seth's father to work with Seth and Dad readily agreed, relieved and grateful for the help.

Oaklawn School: My Plan for Play, TV, Videos, and Computer				

My name: *Seth B.*
I am allowed to have _a lot_ of screen time on most days.
My favorite things to do (not screen time) are: *playing with Runner, reading about building things, baseball, Boys and Girls Club.*
Family jobs that I have: *I take care of Runner.*

	What I want to play with or read	TV show I plan to watch	Computer game I plan to play	Video I plan to watch
Monday:	*Yoga class after school (Boys Club)*	*Animal doctors*		
Tuesday:	*dog training class (with Dad!)*			
Wednesday:	*Book about skyscrapers* *Throw ball for Runner*	*Lassie*		
Thursday:	*Take Runner to Jeff's house to play with Jeff's dog*			
Friday:	*Play catch with Jeff* *Run with Runner in backyard* *Brush Runner*			*Dog training video (on loan from Jessie's Dad)* *Watch with Mom and Dad!*

Figure 9.4.

Watch television with children and comment on aggressive program content

A realistic approach acknowledges that children will have some screen time, some much more than others. Teachers and parents can still be proactive. They can gradually decrease the amount of television watched, monitor what children watch, watch with children, and teach them how to understand what they watch (Levin, 1998; Primavera et al., 1996).

Example. While John was watching television, his father said, "Why do you think that man kicked his neighbor's car, John? . . . Yes, I think he was mad at him for driving his car over the flowers. That still doesn't make it OK to kick his neighbor's car." Another example while watching a talk show: "That man sure seemed upset when his wife called him a bad name."

Children who watch media violence with adults and hear a negative evaluation of the violence, as John did, tend to be less aggressive than children who watch the same aggression alone (Singer, 1987).

Encourage children to be empathic

Teach aggressive children by telling them how the person they have victimized is feeling. Simply asking a young aggressive child how he thinks that the other might feel is an **in**effective approach because young children cannot take the other's perspective. Give them information by telling. The examples that follow are from a preschool classroom for 4-year-olds.

Example. "Oh, Susan! You really seem to have scared the gerbils when you banged on the glass. Look. They've run under cover and are hiding."

Example. Teacher to Tahisha, who grabbed the basket of bread at lunch: "Whoa, Tahisha! Let me take the basket back from you. Jordan had it first and looked startled when you grabbed it. Let's sing the basket-passing song while we wait our turns." Teacher then hands the basket back to Jordan.

The adult encouraged Susan and Tahisha to be **empathic.** Children encouraged to be empathic tend to be more sensitive to another's feelings and to be less aggressive (Feshbach & Feshbach, 1982).

Encourage consequential thinking

Help children develop a value system that encourages them to treat others with respect and to refrain from hurting others (APA, 1993). One way to help children develop a respectful attitude is to teach them **consequential thinking,** the understanding that a consequence of aggression is that somebody gets hurt or something is damaged. Consequential thinking is one key to changing or preventing aggressive behavior. A good way to encourage consequential thinking is to give gentle but direct instruction in thinking about consequences.

Example. In the dog training class, Seth has respect for the trainer, just as he respects his counselor at school, and wants to imitate her skill with dogs. Dad accompanies Seth and Runner to dog training class and then practices with Seth. Dad makes time to do this with Seth, partly because he wants to and partly because his wife asked him to do this. Seth treats Runner gently much of the time.

Seth, however, under great stress and having gathered quite a number of aggressive scripts, surprised everyone when one of the aggressive scripts crept into a training session. Seth yanked Runner's collar when Runner did not sit on command. The trainer said, "Hold it, Seth. You hurt Runner when you yank his collar like that. He looks real scared to me. Let's try the **sit** command again." Seth grimaced and said to Runner, "Sorry, Runner." He tried again, was successful, and rolled his eyes and grinned when he heard soft applause from his father, Jessie, Jessie's dad, his new friend Jeff, and the trainer.

This adult aroused empathy in Seth for Runner by feeding back the dog's fear; she is also teaching Seth the consequences of aggression—that someone gets hurt. He has also seen such kind behavior on television, especially on his secret favorite, *Lassie* reruns, and he has old scripts from his mom. The trainer reminded him that aggression is not a good thing. Then the admired adult went further to help him reactivate a different and more positive script. Jessie's father asked Seth and his dad if they would like to borrow a video on dog training that he and Jessie had watched. On the way home, Dad looked over at Seth in the car and said, "Say, what if we ask Mom if she feels up to watching that video with us, Seth?" There is hope for Seth.

Teach more positive behavior

Assertiveness, negotiation, cooperation, sharing, helping: all of these behaviors are incompatible with or contrary to aggression. We can essentially prevent or crowd out aggressive behaviors by teaching children how to cooperate or be assertive in place of acting aggressively. Aggressive children have a limited number of ways to deal with interactional problems. Help children gather scripts for nonaggressive responses to issues (Middleton & Cartledge, 1995).

Example. Mr. Nellis encouraged his students to help each other. He used Rush-Around Rabbit and Observant Owl (puppets from Figure 9.1) in a new skit about Rabbit needing help at the computer and Owl offering help. At group time, he encouraged the children to ask others for help when they needed it.

Recognize and encourage cooperative behavior and language

Noticing and then encouraging helpful, cooperative behavior (Brown & Elliott, 1965) is an effective way to decrease aggression. Seth's counselor has encouraged Seth's teacher to observe Seth carefully, to listen and look for instances of cooperation or helpfulness, and then to encourage the more positive cooperative behavior.

Example. Mr. Santini decided that Seth needed to practice requesting permission to work with a small group. The counselor went over the lesson with him and Seth then successfully approached a group of girls at the fish tank who were sketching fish. Mr. Lee, the teacher, later said to him, "You simply asked the group if you could join them, Seth. That was a good thing to do." The next day he observed as Seth approached Sue, who was working on a big puzzle. "Seth," he noted later, "I heard you ask Sue if you could work with her on the big puzzle. She seemed to like how you asked and it looked like you two had fun with the puzzle."

Encourage responsible anger management

Anxious or aggressive children are usually not skillful at managing strong emotions; e.g., jealousy, anger, or the fear of rejection that a child such as Seth has often felt in the past. Prevent some of the aggression that comes from this source by teaching children how to understand and manage their strong feelings. See Marion (1997) and Chapter 8 in this text for specific strategies for teaching children how to understand and manage anger.

Work with Parents and Get Involved in Preventing Violence at the Community Level

A teacher concentrates on working with children but is not a therapist and is not qualified or licensed to conduct therapy with aggressive families. However, teachers work with families by giving information and advice about any number of issues, including information on violence and aggression. See the Working With Parents box.

Early childhood professionals can also think about the "bigger picture" by keeping in mind the idea that families are embedded in communities, that families do not exist in a vacuum. A family's community and culture has an enormous influence over the family's value and belief system, including values and beliefs about aggression. There are several practical and realistic things that early childhood professionals can do to decrease aggression at the community level. An individual teacher would not be able to do all of the following activities alone, but might consider joining with others to do one or two to help decrease aggression within her community.

- Join and support the efforts of your professional organization to document and curb violence and aggression. The National Association for the Education of Young Children, for example, has had a national-level committee examining violence in the lives of children and provides information to its members on this topic (NAEYC, 1994).
- Understand television ratings systems and explain them to parents in your center or school, church, or synagogue. Make this an ongoing agenda item (see Levin, 1998).
- Give parents information about where to find a mental health professional who can help them and their aggressive child (AACAP, 1999a).
- Plan violence prevention activities for the Week of the Young Child. For example, prepare a display of books for parents to read to children that emphasize nonaggressive solutions to problems. Hold a conflict-resolution workshop open to all community parents. Invite pet trainers to give a workshop on kind treatment for animals.
- Use information from the Working With Parents box to help parents gain a sense of confidence about media (television, videos, video games, and computers). Share all or some of these ideas in ways that do not take much professional time: a group or individual parent meeting, a short newsletter article, or a separate handout. Get someone to interview you for an article in the local paper or get this information to parents during Week of the Young Child activities.

Working with Parents. Help Your Child Take Charge of Media and Screen Time

- **Slow the pace for and focus on your family.** Plan a "family night" every week. Do fun, non-screen things that everybody looks forward to and enjoys: board games, skating, taking a walk, reading, playing charades, playing music, learning about and looking for birds of **your** area. Other ideas?

- **Help your child take an inventory of favorite activities or new things** that she or he would like to try:
  Make a list.
  Refer to the list when planning things to do.
  Refer to the list when a child is bored.
  Revise the list when it seems appropriate.

- **Model wise, sensible use of your time, including screen time.** Let your child see you, not plunking down in front of a screen, but reading books and magazines, exercising, spending time with family, gardening, sailing, or whatever hobby you enjoy.

- **Help your child understand the concept of "screen time";** i.e., it includes television, videos, computer time, and video games.
- **Set a reasonable amount of "screen time"** your child may have each day.
- **Teach your child how to plan reading, play, or screen time.** Use Figure 9.3, the chart for planning how to use time wisely.
- **Write your family's rules for using television.** Let children help write the rules. Post, use, and evaluate the rules. Change them if necessary.
- **Make the television set a less prominent piece of equipment.** Turn on the TV only for specific, planned shows; avoid letting a TV run as background noise.

- **Have a motto that works for your family;** e.g., "homework first" or "chores first," or "play with and feed dog first" or "think first about what I really want to do," or "what are my choices here?"

- **Help your child understand "action figure" characters.** Talk with your child about why some of the action figures engage in so much fighting.
- **If your child wants to imitate the action figures,** consider trying to confine the imitation to specific times and places. Consider how "just saying no" might backfire. However, forbid certain things: hurting animals, hurting other people, and damaging property.

Case Study Analysis: Analyze Oaklawn's Violence Prevention Program

1. Think about Oaklawn's work with the parent group. The group has decided to focus on one specific aspect of violence prevention, helping children take charge of media in their lives. After reviewing the case study and the material in this chapter, answer the following question.

   - I think that Oaklawn's prevention effort for all children

___ 1 ___	___ 2 ___	___ 3 ___	___ 4 ___	___ 5 ___
will be quite effective	will be effective but not extremely effective	will make no difference	will not be very effective at all	is a waste of time

   - List and explain each of your reasons for your choice on this rating scale.
2. Now, consider the school's effort to help individual children such as Seth.

   - I think that Oaklawn's effort to build on Seth's strengths

___ 1 ___	___ 2 ___	___ 3 ___	___ 4 ___	___ 5 ___
will be quite effective	will be effective but not extremely effective	will make no difference	will not be very effective at all	is a waste of time

   - List all of the specific things that the school has done to help Seth. Of those, in your opinion, which will be the most effective? Why?

- One of our goals in guiding children is to build on their strengths. How has the school tried to build on Seth's strengths?

- Do you see signs that Seth is slowly making changes in how he behaves with other children? Explain.

Tyler

1. Using Figure 9.2, would you say that Tyler shows any warning signs of violent behavior? If you said yes, what are these signs?
2. How would you respond to a person who watched Tyler and his dog and then said, "Don't make such a big deal of it. He's just a kid and he'll outgrow it. It's just a phase!"

REFLECTING ON KEY CONCEPTS

1. Reflect on the concept of aggression by answering these "True/False" questions:

   - True or False? Anger and aggression are the same thing. Why, or why not?
   - True or False? Young children's aggression is usually instrumental in nature. Explain your answer.
   - True or False? Hostile aggression usually shows up in children as they get older. Explain your answer.
   - True or False? There are three forms of violent behavior. Explain your response.

2. Name two specific ways in which aggression-teaching families foster aggression in young children. Explain how a child's peers can teach her to be aggressive and summarize media violence's influence on aggression in young children.
3. Explain the effect of bullying, humiliation, and constant hostile teasing on the development of violent, aggressive behavior.
4. Choose at least three of the strategies for guiding aggressive children presented in this chapter and explain why they would be effective in either stopping or preventing children's aggression.

APPLY YOUR KNOWLEDGE

1. **Watch children's television.** Watch at least 1 hour of television designed specifically for young children. On a sheet of paper, break that hour into 10-minute segments. In each segment, keep a tally of the number of times that you see an act of aggression—any act of aggression—and give a total at the end of the hour. Write a brief description of each act of aggression.
2. **Visit a toy store.** Find several examples of and describe toys that you think would serve as **aggressive cues;** i.e., would likely bring out aggression in young children. Were these toys designated for a specific gender? If yes, state what led you to this conclusion.

3. **Teach a social skill.** Do one or two of the puppet plays from Figure 9.1 for older preschool, kindergarten, or first-grade children. Write a lesson plan for the chosen scripts. Seek permission from a teacher to present the play(s) to the class. Present the plays first to the teacher and have the teacher check your lesson plan. An alternative is to write a lesson plan for two of the puppet plays and present your lesson plan and the play to your class (if you cannot work with a group of children).

REFERENCES

American Academy of Child & Adolescent Psychiatry. (AACAP) (1997). Understanding violent behavior in children and adolescents. *Facts for families,* No. 55, Washington, DC: Author.

AACAP. (1998). Children's threats: When are they serious? *Facts for families,* No. 65, Washington, DC: Author.

AACAP. (1999a). Being prepared: Knowing where to find help for your child. *Facts for families,* No. 25, Washington, DC: Author.

AACAP. (1999b). Children with oppositional defiant disorder (ODD). *Facts for families,* No. 72, Washington, DC: Author.

American Psychological Association. (1993). *Violence and youth report.* Washington, DC: APA Commission on Violence and Youth.

Anderson, E., Cook, D., Honaker, L., & Kestenbaum, C. (2000, July 26). *Joint statement on the impact of media violence on children.* Presented at the Congressional Public Health Summit on Media Violence, Washington, DC.

Berk, L. E., & Winsler, A. (1995). *Scaffolding children's learning: Vygotsky and early childhood education.* Washington, DC: NAEYC.

Berkowitz, L. (1993). *Aggression: Its causes, consequences, and control.* Philadelphia: Temple University Press.

Black, D., & Newman, M. (1995). Television violence and children. *British Medical Journal, 310,* 273–274.

Block, H. (1978). Another look at sex differentiation in the socialization behaviors of mothers and fathers. In J. Sherman & F. L. Denmark (Eds.), *The future of women: Future directions of research.* New York: Psychological Dimensions.

Boyatzis, C., Matillo, G., & Nesbitt, K. (1995). Effects of "the mighty morphin power rangers" on children's aggression with peers. *Child Study Journal, 25*(1), 45–57.

Bronfenbrenner, U. (1979). *The ecology of human development.* Cambridge, MA: Harvard University Press.

Brown, P., & Elliot, R. (1965). Control of aggression in a nursery school class. *Journal of Experimental Child Psychology, 2,* 103–107.

Bullock, J. (1991). Supporting the development of socially rejected children. *Early Child Development and Care, 66,* 15–23.

Carney, J. V. (2000). Bullied to death: Perceptions of peer abuse and suicidal behavior during adolescence. *School Psychology International, 21*(2), 44–54.

Center for Disease Control & Prevention (1995, March). CDC surveillance summaries. *Morbidity Weekly Report, 44,* page ss–1.

Cummings, E. M., Iannotti, R. J., & Zahn-Waxler, C. (1989). Aggression between peers in early childhood: Individual continuity and developmental change. *Child Development, 60*(4), 887–895.

Dawe, H. C. (1934). An analysis of two hundred quarrels of preschool children. *Child Development, 5,* 139–157.

Dodge, K. A., & Frame, C. L. (1982). Social cognitive biases and deficits in aggressive boys. *Child Development, 53,* 629–635.

Eron, L. D. (1986). Interventions to mitigate the psychological effects of media violence on aggressive behavior. *Journal of Social Issues, 42*(3), 155–169.

Fabes, R., & Eisenberg, N. (1992). Young children's coping with interpersonal anger. *Child Development, 63,* 116–128.

Feshbach, S. (1970). Aggression. In P. Mussen (Ed.), *Carmichael's manual of child psychology* (Vol. 2). New York: Wiley.

Feshbach, N. D., & Feshbach, S. (1982). Empathy training and the regulation of aggression: Potentialities and limitations. *Academic Psychology Bulletin, 4,* 399–413.

Frey, K. S., Hirschstein, M. K., & Guzzo, B. (2000). Second step: Preventing aggression by promoting social competence. *Journal of Emotional & Behavioral Disorders, 8*(2), 102–112.

Funk, J. (1992). Video games: Benign or malignant? *Journal of Applied Developmental Psychology, 12*(1), 63–71.

Gunter, B., & McAleer, J. (1990). *Children and television—the one eyed monster?* London: Routledge.

Hartup, W. W. (1974). Aggression in childhood: Developmental perspectives. *American Psychologist, 29,* 336–341.

Hazler, R. J. (2000). When victims turn aggressors: Factors in the development of deadly school violence. *Professional School Counseling, 4*(2), 105–113.

Heide, K. M. (1999). *Young killers: The challenge of juvenile homicide.* Thousand Oaks, CA: Sage.

Herrenkohl, R. C., Egolf, B. P., & Herrenkohl, E. C. (1997). Preschool antecedents of adolescent assaultive behavior: A longitudinal study. *American Journal of Orthopsychiatry, 67*(3), 422–432.

Hicks, D. J. (1965). Imitation and retention of film-mediated aggressive peer and adult models. *Journal of Personality and Social Psychology, 2,* 97–100.

Huesmann, L. (1988). An information processing model for the development of aggression. *Aggressive Behavior, 14*(1), 13–24.

Huston, A. C., Rice, M. L., Kerkman, D., & St. Peters, M. (1990). Development of television viewing patterns in early childhood: A longitudinal investigation. *Developmental Psychology, 26,* 409–420.

King, C. A., & Kirschenbaum, D. S. (1992). *Helping children develop social skills: The social growth program.* Pacific Grove, CA: Brooks/Cole Publishing Company.

Levin, D. (1998). *Remote control childhood? Combating the hazards of media culture.* Washington, DC: NAEYC.

Marion, M. (1997). Research in review: Guiding young children's understanding and management of anger. *Young Children, 52*(7), 62–68.

Middleton, M. B., & Cartledge, G. (1995). Effects of social skills instruction and parental involvement on the aggressive behaviors of African American males. *Behavior Modification, 19*(2), 192–211.

National Association for the Education of Young Children. (reaffirmed 1994; original statement, 1990). NAEYC position statement on media violence in children's lives. Washington, DC: NAEYC.

National Television Violence Study Council (1997). National television violence study (NTVS), executive summary, Volume 2. J. Federman (Ed.), Santa Barbara, CA: Center for Communication and Social Policy, University of California, Santa Barbara.

Parke, R. D., & Slaby, R. G. (1983). The development of aggression. In P. Mussen (Ed.), *Handbook of child psychology* (Vol. 4). New York: Wiley.

Patterson, G. R. (1982). *Coercive family processes.* Eugene, OR: Castilia Press.

Potter, J., Vaughan, M., Warren, R., Howley, K., Land, A., & Hagemeyer, J. (1995). How real is the portrayal of aggression in television media programming? *Journal of Broadcasting and Electronic Media, 39*(4), 496–517.

Primavera, L., Herron, W., & Javier, R. (1996). The effect of viewing television violence on aggression. *International Journal of Instructional Media, 23*(2), 137–151.

Ridley-Johnson, R., Surdy, T., & O'Laughlin, E. (1991). Parent survey on television violence viewing. *Journal of Developmental and Behavioral Pediatrics, 13*(1), 53–54.

Singer, J. L. (1987). Is television bad for children? *Social Science, 71*(2–3), 178–182.

Smith, P. K., & Morita, Y. (1999). Introduction. In P. K. Smith, Y. Morita, J. Junger-Tas, D. Olweus, R. Catalano, & P. Slee (Eds.), *The nature of school bullying: A cross-national perspective* (pp. 1–4). New York: Routledge.

Surgeon General (2000). Youth violence: A report of the Surgeon General. http://www.surgeon-general.gov/library/youthviolence/report.

Szegal, B. (1985). Stages in the development of aggressive behavior in early childhood. *Aggressive Behavior, 11*(4), 315–321.

✓ CHECK OUT THE WEB SITES RELATED TO THIS CHAPTER

✓ **American Medical Association.** Lists many violence prevention resources and other Web sites.
www.ama-assn.org

✓ **American Academy of Child and Adolescent Psychiatry.** One of the best sites for information on violence and its prevention. Good links to other sites.
www.aacap.org
www.aacap.org/publications. Access to all of the publications of this organization.
www.aacap.org/press__releases. News releases of interest to professionals working with young children and their families.

✓ **National Association for the Education of Young Children (NAEYC).** Go to the link for position statements.
www.naeyc.org

✓ **Surgeon General's Office of the United States.** A governmental agency. The surgeon general is the nation's leader on health care issues.
www.surgeongeneral.gov. Main page.
www.surgeongeneral.gov/library. Link containing the surgeon general's full text reports.

Guiding the Development
of Prosocial Behavior

"Who raises altruistic children? Parents who themselves are highly concerned about the welfare of others."

(Shaffer, 1993, p. 547)

After reading and studying this chapter, you will be able to

❏ **State, in your own words,** what prosocial behavior is.

❏ **Identify, describe, and give an example** of types of prosocial behaviors.

❏ **List** developmental building blocks of prosocial behavior. **Explain** the role of each.

❏ **Explain** the benefits of encouraging prosocial behavior in children.

❏ **Identify, describe, and observe** developmentally appropriate strategies that foster prosocial behavior.

❏ **Apply** knowledge and **analyze** case studies.

Case Studies: Prosocial Behavior

Minda

Three-year-old Minda lives on a farm with her parents and three older brothers. When Dad takes care of his houseplants, Minda's regular job is to help by misting the plants needing moisture. After lunch her 12-year-old brother handed her plate to her and said, "Take your plate over to the dishwasher, Minda . . . Thanks!" She helped her mother feed the barn cats and watched as her mom picked up Puddles, a cat whose leg was cut. Mom said, "O-o-h, come here and let me take care of your cut. Please get that cloth for Mommy, Minda. I'll bet that Puddles's leg hurts, and I think she might be afraid, too. So, we have to tell her it's going to be OK."

Steve

Steve, almost 6 years old, lives with his mom and dad. Within a 1-month period, this is what he witnessed: Mom and Dad **really** shared the housework. He watched *Mr. Roger's Neighborhood* when Mr. Rogers talked about working together and showed what it meant. Steve and his dad and uncle made cookies for the preschool's bake sale, and Dad helped a neighbor fix the gate on his fence. "Glad to help," was Dad's reply to the neighbor's thanks. Mom took Steve with her when she showed Humane Society slides on taking good care of pets at the local elementary school. When she took vegetables from their garden to the food pantry, she quietly said, as they drove away, "There are a lot of people who don't have enough to eat, Steve. I like sharing the vegetables from our garden."

John

John is 8½ years old and lives with his dad in a single-parent family. "OK, partner. It's time to plan Project Winterizing," said Dad as they sat down at the table with hot chocolate and a pad of paper. "We have some garden chores to do before winter, and we should share the work. Let's list the jobs. I'll do some of the chores, and then I want you to do some, too." (They made the list and put John's name next to two jobs.) "Great! We'll get this done a lot more quickly if we work together. How about getting some pizza when we finish?"

"Let's start with covering the rosebushes. You've never done that, so I'd like to show you how to cover the rosebushes so that the cover stays put," said Dad. They shook hands as they headed off to the garage. John made a trumpeting sound and said, "Project Winterizing is under way!"

August 1996: An amazing thing happened at the Brookfield Zoo near Chicago. Binti Jua, a female lowland gorilla, rescued a 3-year-old human child who had fallen into the gorilla enclosure at the zoo. She cradled the boy in her arms and stayed with him near a door until the zookeepers arrived. She kept the child safe and away from the other gorillas. Binti Jua's actions touched off a storm of debate—does altruistic behavior exist in a nonhuman species? Her protective, compassionate behavior (rescuing the child) typifies the kind of behavior discussed in this chapter; it is **prosocial behavior.**

As an early childhood educator, you will rightly be concerned about encouraging children to act prosocially. You will encourage them to be helpful, cooperative, and generous in a world determined to shower children with quite another set of values—violence, hatred, mean-spiritedness, stinginess, and aggression. Some children, like Minda, Steve, and John, come from healthy family systems that foster moral development by showing concern for and responding to the needs of other people and animals. But many children come from less healthy family systems, in which interactions leave people feeling degraded or demeaned, where adults refuse to respond to the needs of others, and in which compassion is rarely, if ever, demonstrated.

This chapter focuses on the development of **prosocial behavior.** First, we will focus on what prosocial behavior is and what you are likely to see during early childhood. Then the focus shifts to figuring out what motivates people to share, help, and cooperate. This chapter emphasizes how development in a couple of important areas is the key to enabling children to act prosocially. Finally, you will learn some very practical and effective strategies for guiding children's sharing, helping, and cooperation.

UNDERSTANDING PROSOCIAL BEHAVIOR

What Is Prosocial Behavior?

Prosocial behavior: behavior that benefits another person or animal. Prosocial behavior includes sharing, helping, and cooperating.

Altruism: unselfish, benevolent behavior. To be true altruism, the person shares, helps, or cooperates with no thought about what is "in it" for him or her (Naparstek, 1990). See Figure 10.1.

Sharing, helping, and cooperating are intended to assist someone else. At certain times, each might be used to meet somebody's physical needs, as when a child willingly shares a blanket or a cracker with another child. We can also meet another person or animal's emotional needs by sharing, helping, or cooperating. We might also meet both physical and emotional needs with prosocial behavior.

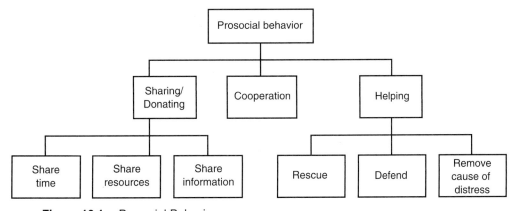

Figure 10.1. Prosocial Behavior

Example. Minda's mother in the (chapter-opener case study) took care of Puddles's (the cat) physical needs by cleaning a cut. She met the cat's emotional needs when she held Puddles and when she suggested that Minda "tell Puddles that it would be OK."

People communicate needs differently. Sometimes, it is clear that a person or animal needs help, as when a child asks for help finding a word on the word chart. At other times, it is more difficult to figure out what someone needs.

Example. Mr. Claiborne's class had been painting a large packing crate during playground time. On the second day that the crate was there, Pae (pronounced "pay") stood quietly by the packing crate, looking longingly at it. Mr. Claiborne, sensing that Pae, a shy child, might want to paint, asked, "Pae, do you need a paint-brush?" Pae seemed visibly relieved that his teacher had figured out what he wanted.

Forms of Prosocial Behavior: Sharing, Helping, and Cooperation

Sharing

Sharing: Dividing up, giving, bestowing. A person owns something, or at least currently has possession, and decides to let somebody use the item or even gives ownership of the item to the other person. People can share or donate materials, information, or time.

Examples. (all from Mr. Claiborne's first-grade class). Reese shared his markers with Vinnie (sharing materials).

Reese's father volunteers with Habitat for Humanity (donating time).

Pippin showed a new child in the class where things were in the cafeteria and library (sharing information).

Teachers and parents often see examples of young children sharing things simply because the child recognizes that someone needs something and the child wants to share. Teachers and parents see many examples of such generosity in young children.

Example. Mr. Claiborne observed as Moua went to his cubby to get his extra pair of mittens. Moua gave the mittens to Ryan, who had forgotten his mittens that day (sharing to meet Ryan's physical needs).

So young children do share altruistically, but sharing also seems to serve another important purpose for young children in social interaction. Offering things to others—often viewed as sharing—is one way that a young child can initiate social contact and then keep the interaction going once it has started. Children might occasionally share as a way of meeting their own need for contact with others. Young children's sharing often takes the form of simply offering objects to other children or adults during social interaction (Eisenberg, Wolchik, Goldberg, & Engel, 1992).

Example. Moua asked Vinnie to join him in play on the playground like this: "I have a hoop, Vinnie. You can roll it and jump through it. Come on over and play with the hoop" (offering something to initiate an interaction).

Judy is sharing her book with Janet. Judy has the cognitive and emotional competencies plus the skill for sharing.

Whatever a young child's reason, he is usually not highly self-sacrificing; i.e., he takes little risk (Eisenberg et al., 1992). There was little risk for Moua, for example, who shared his extra mittens with Ryan. Similarly, there was little risk for Pippin, who shared information with another child.

Helping

Helping: another major category of prosocial behavior evident in preschool children's behavior (Grusec, 1991). There are many ways to help someone:

- simple everyday acts of kindness
- rescue (Binti Jua, the gorilla, rescued the human child who fell into the gorilla enclosure; thousands of firefighters and others worked on the rescue operation when the World Trade Center was destroyed on September 11, 2001)
- defending others
- removing the cause of someone's distress

Examples. Steve's dad (in the chapter-opener case study) helped his neighbor fix his garden gate (simple act of kindness).

Later that afternoon Steve stopped the garden gate just as it was about to close on his sleeping cat's tail (rescue).

Steve was in his reading group and heard Ryan call Jack a "dummy" when Jack could not figure out a word. Steve said to Ryan, "Jack isn't a dummy. He's a good reader but just can't figure out that word" (defending another).

Steve's father had helped him once by taking a splinter out of Steve's foot (removing the cause of someone's distress).

All children are capable of sharing and helping, but a variety of factors influences their actual level of prosocial behavior. For example, children's willingness to help or share is heavily influenced by whether their teacher and parents value prosocial behavior (Eisenberg et al., 1992). A child might also share or help more easily if important adults have modeled prosocial behavior; e.g., helping someone or sharing something with somebody.

Example. Moua's father and uncle were fixing the uncle's car. Moua watched as his dad shared his tools with the uncle (Moua's father **helped** the uncle fix the car and **shared** tools).

Recent research with kindergarten children (Phillipsen, Bridges, McLemore, & Saponaro, 1999) and with middle-childhood children (Greener, 1998; Nelson, 1999) has documented gender differences in prosocial behavior, with girls seemingly more prosocial than boys. Earlier research found that the **differences might lie in how boys and girls express compassion** or generosity. In one study, girls who heard an infant crying expressed more verbal sympathy than did boys. However, girls were no more likely to assist than boys were when they were near a crying infant (Zahn-Waxler, Friedman, & Cummings, 1983).

Cooperation

Cooperation: working together willingly to accomplish a job or task. The motive for working together is altruistic.

Examples. Ryan and Moua cooperated by pulling a wagon with a heavy bucket of water to the outdoor painting area.

Pippin, Tom, and Janet cooperated to clean the gerbil's house. "There you go," Janet murmured to the gerbils. "Your house is nice and clean! Does it feel comfy?"

Lee's mother (volunteer firefighter) cooperated with the other firefighters to demonstrate the firefighting equipment to Lee's class.

Many children play cooperatively, as research demonstrated 70 years ago (Parten, 1932). In cooperative play children follow one another around and make mutual suggestions about what to do next. Such budding interest in others and in playing and working cooperatively is prosocial behavior when the **cooperation** benefits someone or a group, as Pippin, Tom, and Janet's cleaning the gerbil house did.

What Motivates People to Act Prosocially?

What you see when someone acts prosocially is a **behavior;** he helps, shares, or cooperates. What you do not always know is the motivation for behaving that way. People share, help, or cooperate for a variety of reasons, some of them altruistic (unselfish):

- genuine feelings of empathic concern

- the ability to imagine the inner experience of someone in need
- a sense of responsibility for relieving the other's distress

Others share, cooperate, or help for more personal and perhaps even somewhat selfish reasons:

- a need for social approval
- external pressure
- relieving one's own sadness, anger, or guilt
- a desire for social interaction

There is no judgment implied here. People have a right to their own reasons for doing things. My purpose is simply to explain different motivations for helping or coorperating. Consider a person such as Mother Teresa, who spent her entire adult life among the poorest people in India, ministering to their needs. Her life was an endless string of selflessness and prosocial behavior. Her motivation seems to have been an unusually high-level ability to take people's perspective, combined with the ability to imagine the inner experience of a leper or a starving person. She was empathic and had a sense of responsibility for relieving their distress. Most individuals would probably agree that someone like Mother Teresa was a good example of **selfless** altruism. Batson & Shaw (1991) believe that authentic prosocial behavior exists only when a person has altruistic (selfless) motives.

Another person volunteers many hours in a nursing home. Is this prosocial behavior? On the surface, yes, because he is helping people. When questioned about why he does this work, he smirks and says, "It'll look great on my resume." This person's helping benefits others but he is motivated by his own needs and not so much by the needs of those he helps. His motives are **not** altruistic and therefore Batson & Shaw (1991) would say his actions are **not** authentic prosocial behavior.

The same thing seems to hold for Robert, ordered by a judge to do 70 hours of community service as a part of his sentence. On the surface, his community service at the food bank looks like prosocial behavior (helping). Nevertheless, Robert grumbles about having to work at the food bank and works there only because he has been ordered to do so. His actions are not altruistic and therefore not true prosocial behavior.

What a Child Needs for Prosocial Behavior: Cognitive and Emotional Competencies and Specific Skills

Several of the children in Mr. Claiborne's class demonstrated prosocial behavior. Reese shared markers with Vinnie. Pippin helped a new child in school find the cafeteria. Moua shared his extra mittens with Ryan. All of these children are first-graders, between 6 and 7 years old. None of them could have acted prosocially (compassionately) when they were infants. When Moua was an infant, he could never have shared something as he did with Ryan.

Several things happened during his first 6 years of life through which infant Moua, who knew nothing about helping, sharing, or other prosocial behaviors, became a child capable of the beginnings of compassion and generosity. He developed very specific **cognitive competencies** that serve as the foundation for his ability to share. He has also developed the beginnings of specific **emotional competencies** that allow him to understand what Ryan needed. Finally, Moua learned some **specific skills** through which he could indeed share or help someone else (Zahn-Waxler, Radke-Yarrow, Wagner, & Chapman, 1992). When all three abilities come together or converge, prosocial development is only then possible. Having one or two of these competencies is not enough; a child needs all three (Figure 10.2).

Cognitive competencies

Moua developed the following cognitive abilities before he was able to share (Bohlmeyer, 1989):

- He realized that he was an individual and separate from other individuals (Bengtsson & Johnson, 1992; Hoffman, 1987). This occurred in infancy.
- He had to be able to take another's perspective; i.e., think about what that person would say that he needs (Rheingold & Emery, 1986; Selman, 1980). Moua and most 6-year-olds are in the beginning stages of learning to take another person's perspective. Moua had to be able to understand that Ryan did not have mittens and needed them to go outside to play in the snow.
- Moua also had to be able to see himself as a person who could make things happen (Kuebli, 1994); i.e., "I can help Ryan by sharing my mittens with him." This ability arises in infancy and continues to develop throughout childhood.
- He had to have good enough language skills to describe how others might be feeling and to describe how he himself feels; e.g., "Ryan didn't have mittens."
- His memory had to be sophisticated enough to allow him to keep Ryan's need in mind long enough to act on that need. Memory improves steadily from ages 3 to 12 and 6-year-old Moua could remember what Ryan needed.

All of these abilities have their roots in early childhood. Glimmers of these abilities appear in older infants and toddlers, allowing the youngest children to **begin** to act in ways that appear to be helpful or cooperative. These cognitive competencies, however, are not fully developed in very young children. For instance,

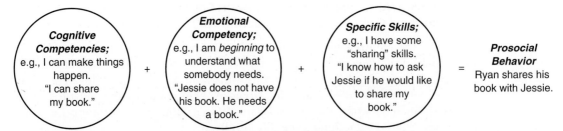

Figure 10.2. Children need to be competent in all three areas before they can help, cooperate, or be generous. If Ryan had had the cognitive and emotional competencies but did not have the skills for sharing, he would not have been able to share his book with Jessie.

young children can often tell that someone needs something but are not very good at reflecting on another person or animal's inner experience based on the need. They tend to focus on people's readily observable, external characteristics. As they get older, children tend to focus more and more on another person's **internal** psychological perspective (Bengtsson & Johnson, 1992).

Example. When Moua was 4, he and his 11-year-old brother, Bee, both saw a neighbor child fall off his bike and break his arm. Moua had said, "John was crying real loud, Mom!" (He focused on observable behavior, crying). Bee demonstrated an older child's ability to reflect on another's inner psychological perspective when he said, "Yeah, he cried. I think that he must have been afraid when the ambulance came."

Emotional competencies

Children also need to have specific **emotional competencies,** which seem to develop quite slowly (Kuebli, 1994). To act prosocially, Moua and other children must have the emotional capacity to respond to another's needs or distress.

- Decoding emotion in another person's face. High-prosocial children seem to be much more accurate than are low-prosocial children in decoding emotion in children's faces (Greener, 1998).

Decoding or figuring out the emotion in another person's face is an emotional ability that begins in infancy and continues to develop during childhood. Some children are better at decoding emotion than are other children. Teachers notice differences in children's abilities to "read the face" of another child. A child who decodes emotion very well has a far better chance of understanding how another child might be feeling.

Example. Mr. Claiborne discussed a playground incident with his class. The whole class had observed two older boys fighting, and the teacher wanted to get their reactions. Moua said, "Jason hit that other boy hard. Jason was mad!" "How do you know he was angry?" asked the teacher. Moua: "He had a real mad look on his face."

- Responding to the emotions of others. A very young baby responds to emotions in other people (Sagi & Hoffman, 1976) and seems to be able to discriminate among mother's different emotions; in some cases, the baby can imitate these emotions (Cohn, Campbell, Matias, & Hopkins, 1990; Termine & Izard, 1988). Babies can do this even when they do not have the concept that the other is an individual separate from them. They do this even without the ability to take the person's perspective.
- Develop and demonstrate empathy. **Empathy:** the ability to participate in another person's or animal's feelings; one person's emotional state is similar to the other person's emotional state.

Example. Renee, an adult, hears that a friend has had a biopsy for cancer. Renee understands that her friend is afraid and confused. Renee is empathic because she can take her friend's perspective and share the friend's emotions.

Example. Mr. Claiborne realized, on the first day of school for his first-graders, that they would probably be anxious. He has good perspective-taking skills and is able to feel what his children might be feeling.

Like most other aspects of development, empathy develops slowly. The road to high-level empathy starts in infancy. Researchers have thought for a long time that human children are biologically prepared for empathy (Hoffman, 1975) because they respond to another person's emotional state. However, the budding ability to recognize another person's emotional state is **not** real empathy.

The cognitive processes described above influence a child's level, quality, and intensity of empathy (Bengtsson & Johnson, 1992; Hoffman, 1987). For example, perspective taking affects a child's level of empathy (Hoffman, 1987). Children can demonstrate real empathy only when they develop good perspective-taking skills (Lupinetti, 1999).[31] Moua could see that Ryan did not have mittens. He also understood that Reese needed markers. Moua, at 6 years of age, however, does not have high-level perspective-taking skills. He does not understand Ryan's anxiety about losing brand-new mittens and about having cold hands.

High-prosocial children score significantly higher on self-reports of empathic response (Greener, 1998). In a study of prosocial behavior in 10- and 11-year-olds, Bengtsson & Johnson (1992) found that some children had a high level of empathy for a victim. They were able to take both the victim's **and** the victimizer's point of view, as shown in the next example.

Example. The children in the study were given an example. A young girl was turned away by force when entering a room where her older sister and a friend were playing. Some children showed **extended empathic reasoning** by showing empathy for the little girl as well as understanding of the victimizer, "I didn't like the way they pushed the little girl out of the room, but I can also understand that they wanted to be left alone while playing."

Children who reasoned like this about another person's situation showed the highest levels of prosocial behavior. These were 10- and 11-year-olds, not young children. We know that children in the early childhood stage are not capable of reasoning like this. It takes several years for children to develop high-level empathy and the ability to think about the perspective of both a victim and a victimizer. Some children never develop this high level of empathy. Growing older is an important element in developing empathy but, by itself, growing older is not enough.

Skill development

Children need to know **how to** help, share, or cooperate; they need specific skills. If Moua, for instance, wants to share something, Moua must have the social skill of approaching another child and must know what to say as he offers something. Zahn-Waxler et al. (1992) believe that young children have a better chance of

---

[31]Review the stages of perspective taking in Chapter 2.

developing such skills if they have had a firm attachment to their primary care-givers because their parents or caregivers shared, took turns, and cooperated with them.

Parents and teachers can teach the skills that children need for acting proso-cially.

Example. Susan was having trouble putting on her parka. Janet could put on her parka easily and watched Susan struggling. "Janet," Mr. Claiborne said quietly, "you could really **help** Susan by showing her how you lay your jacket on the floor and then flip it over your head."

Example. Mr. Claiborne decided to focus on teaching the skills needed for sharing to his entire class. He wrote lesson plans that incorporated puppets. The puppets demonstrated how to offer to **share** something with another person. They gave specific words to use.

Example. Mr. Claiborne showed Pippin, Tom, and Janet how to work together (**cooperate**) to clean the gerbil house. Figure 10.3 summarizes how very young chil-dren are likely to show prosocial behavior.

How Very Young Children Are Likely to Show Prosocial Behavior[32]

Up to approximately 12 months
- Pats or rubs. Almost all babies will pat or rub a person who appears to be upset or hurt.
- Gives an object. Some young infants will try to offer an object to someone who appears to be upset.

14 to 20 months
- Kisses or hugs
- Gives some object
- Might try to protect someone

20 months to 2½ Years
- All of the above, plus
- Gives physical assistance
- Tries to get help from a third person
- Asks questions indicating concern; e.g., "Does your finger hurt?"
- Gives advice to a person who is upset or hurt; e.g., "Tell your Mommy."
- Might offer reassurance to person or animal; e.g., "It's OK."

Figure 10.3.

---

[32]Source: Radke-Yarrow, M., & Zahn-Waxler, C. (1984). Roots, motives, and patterns of children's prosocial behavior. In E. Struab, D. Bar-Tel, J. Karylowski, & J. Reykowski (Eds.) *Development and maintance of prosocial behavior.* New York: Plenum Press.

GUIDE CHILDREN'S PROSOCIAL BEHAVIOR BY USING DEVELOPMENTALLY APPROPRIATE STRATEGIES

A child's relationships heavily influence his or her level of prosocial behavior. Adults can make it possible for kindness, compassion, and generosity to flower by understanding children's developmental level, by helping children understand how others feel, and by showing them how to share, help, or cooperate. Consider using the following practical and developmentally appropriate strategies to help children learn to act prosocially. See Figure 10.4.

Model Prosocial Behavior

In terms of generous, helpful behavior, the research shows that a child is highly likely to imitate models when it comes to prosocial behavior. Modeling is an extremely powerful way to encourage children to act prosocially (Oliner & Oliner, 1988). Children tend to imitate models who:

- are **powerful.** Power models control resources. Children usually perceive parents and teachers as powerful because caregivers do control resources.
- are **authoritative.** Children will imitate models who are highly responsive to their needs but who also make expectations known, the two major elements in authoritative caregiving (see Chapter 1).
- are **consistent.** Consistent models practice what they preach. Research done three decades ago showed that families who talk about generosity or volunteering (urge the family members to be generous) and then actually give or volunteer (practice what they preach) are likely to produce children who share or donate (Bryan & Walbek, 1970).
- **give without grumbling.** It is good for children to observe people who are quietly and effectively generous, cooperative, and helpful, who are genuinely pleased to be able to help someone else, and who don't seem to expect anything in return (Midlarsky & Bryan, 1972). Children are more likely to act prosocially if they vicariously experience the same good feeling as the model.

Provide models of prosocial behavior. Act as a model of prosocial behavior. Arrange regular viewing of prosocial media and video games because programs focusing on cooperation, helping, and sharing promote these behaviors in children (Honig & Wittmer, 1996; Stout & Mouritsen, 1988). Choose games and books focusing on helpfulness and cooperation.

Help Children Develop Helpful Emotional Scripts

Young children are able to identify another person's distressed state and the situation that produced the distress. Children seem to organize their understanding of the emotional state of others in the form of **emotional scripts** that they learn by the age of 5 to 6 years (Russell, 1989). These scripts include information about the appropriate emotion for the child and the emotion or affective state of another person or animal in specific situations (Lewis, 1989).

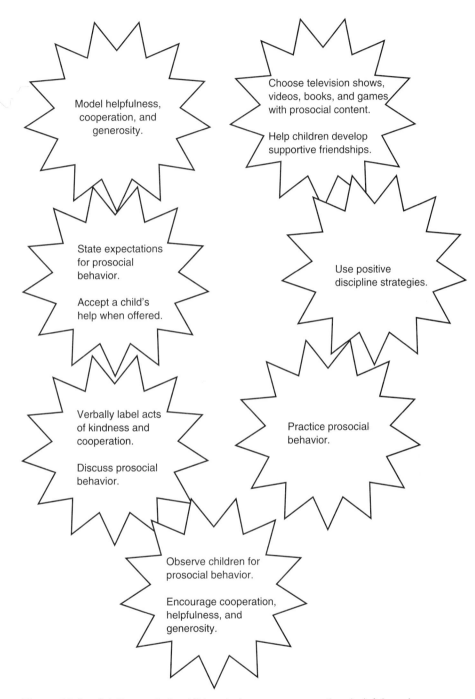

Model helpfulness, cooperation, and generosity.

Choose television shows, videos, books, and games with prosocial content.

Help children develop supportive friendships.

State expectations for prosocial behavior.

Accept a child's help when offered.

Use positive discipline strategies.

Verbally label acts of kindness and cooperation.

Discuss prosocial behavior.

Practice prosocial behavior.

Observe children for prosocial behavior.

Encourage cooperation, helpfulness, and generosity.

Figure 10.4. Adults can help children to become cooperative, helpful, and generous.

Acquiring emotional scripts through interaction

Children learn emotional scripts as they interact with parents, siblings, teachers, and others; as they watch television; and as books are read to them.

Example. Derek is an overweight 6-year-old. At snacktime, Ryan snickered when Derek took one of the snacks: "Hey, Derek. You're so fat! You don't even need to eat." Mr. Claiborne, the teacher, took Ryan aside and said, "Ryan, it hurts somebody's feelings when you make fun of him. I think that Derek probably feels bad because you called him fat. In this classroom, we treat everybody with respect."

Ryan's teacher is helping him develop an emotional script by helping him understand how Derek probably felt in this particular situation.

Children also develop emotional scripts as they play with friends. The quality of the friendship seems to affect a child's level of prosocial behavior. For example, children who have supportive friendships are more prosocial. Children who have conflicts with friends seem to be less cooperative and helpful and more aggressive (Sebanc, 1999).

Acquiring emotional scripts through reading

Reading stories about sharing is another excellent way to help children learn emotional scripts. In one study, this strategy increased children's willingness to share and their ability to take another person's perspective (Trepanier & Romatowski, 1981). Researchers read three books each week for three weeks, a total of nine books, focusing on sharing. They discussed with the children sharing, its relationship to the feelings of the characters, and the causes of the feelings.

Acquiring emotional scripts through screen time

Children develop emotional scripts as they play video games and watch television or movies. Children who prefer aggressive video games tend to be more aggressive and show less prosocial behavior than children who do not prefer aggressive video games (Wiegman & Van Schie, 1998).

One study explored the moral lessons of television situation comedies (sitcoms). The investigator wanted to know if sitcoms with a moral lesson helped children learn prosocial behavior. The first- and third-grade children in the study watched an episode of *The Cosby Show* and were then interviewed to determine if they comprehended the moral lesson.

An overwhelming majority of subjects understood the moral lesson from this show. Similarly, one third of the first-graders and one half of the third-graders were able to identify the moral lesson in an episode of *Full House*. Watching sitcoms with a moral lesson seemed to help these children to become more helpful and cooperative. This was especially so for the children who understood the moral lesson in the show (Rosenkoetter, 1999).

State Expectations for Prosocial Behavior and Accept Children's Help When Offered

State expectations for prosocial behavior

Children learn to be prosocial in families and classrooms when adults clearly communicate expectations for cooperation, helpfulness, sharing, and giving comfort. Adults in prosocial teaching families or classrooms help children learn **norms of social responsibility.** One of these norms deals with prosocial behavior. The norm or standard tells children that they are **expected** to help or cooperate with others (Bryan, 1975).

Example. Mr. Claiborne said to two children, "Jack and Pippin, I'm going to need some help taking the trikes and wagons out of the shed. I want both of you to come with me and help." (He stated his expectation that the two children should help.) Pippin uses a wheelchair but Mr. Claiborne includes her in every aspect of classroom life, including the work of the group, making appropriate adaptations as necessary.

Mr. Claiborne helped Jack and Pippin learn the norm of social responsibility when he told the children that he expected them to help someone else. It is very difficult for children to learn this norm of socially responsible behavior unless we teach it to them.

Accept children's offers of help and cooperation

Children are more likely to cooperate, help, share, or give comfort when adults accept a child's offer of help or cooperation (Child Development Project, 1991; Schenk & Grusec, 1987; Swanson, 1988).

Example. The next day Jack approached Mr. Claiborne, who was in the shed getting trikes out: "Can I help you again today, Mr. Claiborne?" The teacher replied, "That would be wonderful, Jack. Sure!" (The teacher accepted Jack's offer of help.)

Some adults hesitate to accept a child's effort to help, although the child offers to help often. It is important, at least some of the time, for adults to take the time to guide a child through a process after he offers to help, as Vinnie's dad does in the next example.

Example. Vinnie's dad was weeding his garden. Vinnie said, "Hey, Dad, need some help?" Dad wanted to get the weeding done quickly but was surprised and pleased that Vinnie wanted to help. So he said, "You've got a deal! I'll show you how to use the hoe so that you get the whole weed out, OK?"

Give children age-appropriate responsibilities

Communicate expectations that children are an important part of a family or classroom system by assigning age-appropriate responsibilities to them. Authori**tative** adults, high in demandingness, assign age-appropriate household chores and tasks. Baumrind (1971) found that children in authoritative families were the most cooperative when observed at school.

Base responsibilities on a child's developmental ability. A 3- to 4-year-old child can certainly mist plants, give pets food and water, clean out her own cubby at school, and place toys back in the spot where they belong. A preschool child can also help set and clean tables for meals, hang up her own clothes, and take good care of books, games, and other materials.

It is reasonable to expect older children to do their fair share of yard work and housework. They can carry out trash, rake leaves, shovel snow, make center-pieces for a dinner table (it is pleasant to be assigned a creative task occasionally), help plan menus, cook simple meals under supervision, wash dishes, write items on a shopping list, and wash the car. Children who grow up on farms and ranches have regular chores that make real contributions to the functioning of the unit.

Use Positive Discipline Strategies

Adults who use positive discipline strategies have an authori**tative** style of caregiving—they are highly demanding and responsive. For several reasons, this style of caregiving tends to foster prosocial behavior (Swanson, 1988). On the other hand, children whose parents are authori**tarian** tend to be less prosocial (Flory, 1999).

There are several reasons that authoritative adults foster prosocial behavior in children.

Adults who use positive discipline clearly communicate their expectations about helping, sharing, and cooperating

Because these parents or teachers make their expectations of the child's cooperation clear, they are more likely to get that cooperation.

Adults who use positive discipline encourage children to take someone else's perspective

Children are more likely to be cooperative, helpful or compassionate if they understand another's perspective (Lupinetti, 1999).

Examples. Mrs. Vargas observed as Nellie took a container of pegs from another child. "Jackie had the pegs first, Nellie. He wants to work with them just as you do."

Mr. Claiborne heard the commotion near the gerbil's house and said, "Whoa! You're making so much noise that the gerbils look afraid. Remember our rule: Play quietly when you're around the gerbils."

A word of caution: Emotionally vulnerable, depressed caregivers in one study overemphasized the child's responsibility for others' problems, leading children to believe that they had created problems for which they were not responsible at all (Zahn-Waxler, Kochanska, Krupnick, & McKnew, 1990). So while children need to learn that they are responsible for their own behavior, they should not be held responsible for matters beyond their control.

Adults who use positive discipline give suggestions on how to help, cooperate, or share

Stating expectations is an excellent strategy, but adults can be even more helpful if they also give specific suggestions on how to help or cooperate with someone. This means that adults have to teach some skill development by telling or showing children specifically how they can help or cooperate with someone.

Example. Mr. Claiborne said to Vinnie, "Here, Vinnie. I'm going to hold this wagon steady, and your job is to squirt just a little oil right here, on the spots where the wheels join the wagon body. We'll fix that squeak together."

Adults who use positive discipline tell children what TO do

Some adults dwell on telling children what **not** to do, such as "Don't yank on the dog's leash like that!" "Don't shut the door when someone is behind you." "Stop flipping crumbs all over the car." Authoritative adults try to avoid, as much as possible, telling children what **not** to do.

Authoritative adults prefer to tell children what **to** do, such as "Tell the dog to sit and give the signal like I showed you. You won't need to pull on the leash." "When somebody is behind you at a door, just hold the door for him." "Put your hamburger on the napkin and keep the crumbs in the napkin." We will be much more successful in helping children share, help, and cooperate if we tell them what **to** do rather than harping on what **not** to do.

Verbally Label Prosocial Behavior

Examples. Mr. Claiborne said to the children who made applesauce, "We all **worked together** to make the applesauce, and it's going to be a good snack for the rest of the group."

The aide said to two children after cleanup, "You **cooperated.** You put all the blocks on the shelf and cleared the space for group time."

In each, the teacher made an effort to **verbally label** prosocial behavior.

We acknowledge the need to help children learn to label many things, such as "You picked up the red square" or "This animal is called a timber wolf." Labeling is one aspect of direct instruction, a basic responsibility that teachers have, and one of the processes through which adults influence children. We should also label acts of kindness and compassion as a way to teach children about these traits.

Some verbal labels more effectively encourage sharing, helping, and cooperating. Statements that are mere preaching, such as "It is good to give," or "You should share with your friends," or "People should work together" are less effective in encouraging prosocial behavior. Statements focusing on how a child's sharing, helping, or cooperation affects others seem to be much more effective (Grusec, 1991). The examples from Mr. Claiborne's classroom showed adults noting how acts of kindness or cooperation affected others ("It's going to be a good snack for the rest of the group"; "You cleared the space for group time").

Discuss Prosocial Behavior

Discussing prosocial behavior goes beyond labeling. Discussing prosocial behavior is an excellent but often neglected technique for teaching about helping, sharing, and cooperating (Honig, 1998; Honig & Wittmer, 1991). Discussion helps children to focus on and to think about specific examples of sharing, helping, or cooperating. Teachers can easily plan discussions on prosocial behavior as a regular part of the curriculum.

Example. Mr. Claiborne showed a short segment of *Mr. Rogers's Neighborhood* and then led a discussion: "It was kind of Mr. Rogers's visitor to help him build the shelves. How could we tell that his friend wanted to help? How could you tell that his friend was happy about helping? What did Mr. Rogers say that made you think he was grateful for the help?"

Example. Mr. Claiborne took digital photographs of every child, either alone or with someone else, sharing, helping, or cooperating. Then he wrote a lesson plan incorporating the photos. His goal was to show that this group worked together, helped one another, and shared things.

He showed the photos on the computer at group time and led a discussion about each photo: "This is a picture of Vinnie and Tom reading Vinnie's book together. How are they **sharing?**" (Vinnie shared his book with Tom when Tom could not find his.) This is a picture of Reese, Jack, Janet, and Susan **cooperating.** Tell me how they worked together." (They made the applesauce for snack.) "This picture shows Pae, Ryan, and Jessie all working together, **cooperating.** How are they working together?" (They wheeled the cart filled with mulch to the garden.)

Mr. Claiborne had planned a discussion of the television episode on helping as a part of the lesson plan. He had also planned a discussion of the prosocial content of the photographs for group time. He set up the computer with the photos when the PTA met. Next to the computer, he placed a poster that said, "We are a class of helpers. We share. We work together. We cooperate!" Parents looked at every photo.

Practice Prosocial Behavior

Suppose that Ryan **learns** how to help and cooperate by observing models and by hearing the behaviors labeled. Does that mean that he will automatically **perform** the prosocial behavior? No, but chances that he will actually perform cooperative, helpful acts that he has seen modeled increase when his teachers set up opportunities for him to **practice the desired behavior** (Child Development Project, 1991; Rogow, 1991). Children taught to play cooperative games were later more cooperative in other settings. In addition, the cooperative game training resulted in increased sharing. Rogow's (1991) work suggested several ways to facilitate the practice of prosocial behavior of children with a variety of disabilities.

Give children the chance to practice by planning activities focusing on prosocial behavior. Teachers and parents can do a variety of things to ensure that children have an opportunity to practice prosocial behavior. Plan specific activities focusing on concepts of **sharing, helping, and cooperating.** Plan these activities just as you would math, science, language arts, and social studies activities. Write a lesson plan, for example, the objective of which is for children to practice cooperation.

Recognize and Encourage Prosocial Behavior

Children learn how to help or cooperate through modeling and labeling prosocial behavior. It is also important to observe a child so that you might recognize her efforts to share, help, or cooperate. Then it is important to encourage those efforts (Schenk & Grusec, 1987).

In the next examples, the adults encourage children's efforts at prosocial behavior. They use both verbal and nonverbal encouragement. Each teacher's verbal encouragement is specific to the task at hand. The verbal encouragement describes the child's actions; it is informative to the child. The verbal encouragement demonstrates appreciation for the child's efforts and does **not** evaluate a child's character. The adult gives verbal encouragement almost immediately after the child shares, cooperates, or helps. It is sincere, not phony. The adults are not trying to manipulate children with their encouragement. The adult also uses appropriate physical contact or nonverbal communication along with encouragement.

Examples. "You put your painting in your cubby, Reese, just as you agreed to do. Thanks!" said Mr. Claiborne as he also nodded his head approvingly.

"You both put the library books away. You followed my suggestions about where to place each book," noted the assistant teacher, a genuine smile on her face.

"Each of you had a second helping because Reese figured out how to break his second cookie into equal parts to share with Vinnie and Janet." The teacher clapped his hands softly. (Reese basked in the warm glow of success.)

Encourage groups of children

Consider showing appreciation to a group of children, rather than individuals, for prosocial behavior whenever possible. Group-administered recognition is more effective in fostering cooperation and friendliness and in decreasing competitive behavior than are rewards given to individuals (Bryan, 1975). Here are several examples of how adults can recognize the efforts of a group of children for prosocial behavior.

Examples. Mr. Claiborne played the class's favorite piece of classical music after all the children cooperated on the litter patrol on the playground. "Let's sit back and read our library books while we listen to the music. You all worked together so well, and the playground looks terrific!"

All the children in Mr. Claiborne's school held a carnival and then donated the money they made to the Humane Society to sponsor a cage for an entire year. The principal gathered the whole school together in the cafeteria and read a letter of thanks from the director of the Humane Society. It said, "Your **generous donation** will pay for food and care for cats in this cage for one year. Thank you for **helping** the animals."

A student teacher sang a short song with the children at group time about how each child had acted prosocially during the morning's activities (to the tune of "Mary Had a Little Lamb"):

Pippin, Tom, and Janet cleaned the gerbil house,
the gerbil house, the gerbil house
Pippin, Tom, and Janet cleaned the gerbil house
when they came to school.
Ryan and Lee fed the fish today,
Fed the fish, fed the fish,
Ryan and Lee fed the fish today
when they came to school.

Then the student teacher said, "I saw Jessie and Pae helping each other with writing. In addition, I saw Moua help Reese open his milk carton at lunchtime. Let's sing about that."

This student teacher did not just pull this activity "out of the air" or "do it off the top of her head." She **planned** it. She had written a lesson plan for it, and to carry it off well she had to observe carefully how each child showed prosocial behavior during the self-selected activity period.

Encourage cooperation, not competition

Make sure that you are actually recognizing and encouraging cooperation and not competition. Avoid forming groups, for example, and pitting one group against the others (e.g., at cleanup, for reading the largest number of picture books, for bringing in the most for a food drive). Although group members do have to work together, their goal in these examples is to trounce another group. They might well lose sight of their real goal—to gather food for a food drive, to read, or to work together to clean up.

BENEFITS OF ENCOURAGING PROSOCIAL BEHAVIOR

Chances are that you, like most adults, would probably agree that it is a good thing to encourage young children to help and cooperate with others. If you value and then take the time and effort to teach and encourage prosocial behavior, you will likely see the following outcomes.

Increased competence

A child who helps somebody tends to view himself as more competent, believing "**I am capable of helping**" after having cooperated with, helped, complimented, or shared something with another person. Children have a strong need to feel competent (White, 1959) and finding out that he can indeed help someone will motivate a child to act that way again in the future.

Mutual helping

Children who act prosocially also tend to receive help from other children and adults, while children who do not willingly help others receive little assistance in return.

Shared work

A family or classroom is a system and there is work to do if the system is to operate smoothly. As members of these systems, children have an obligation to share in the work of the system, whether the work involves farm or ranch chores, shoveling snow, setting tables, washing paint cups, putting away trikes, or getting out math workbooks.

Pleasant, friendly, relaxing atmosphere

When children are appropriately encouraged to share, help, and cooperate, the general atmosphere of their home, classroom, or other setting is simply more inviting (Edwards, 1992).

Working with Parents. Tips for Parents: Raising a "Prosocial" Child

Here are some tips that you can give parents for encouraging kind and compassionate behavior in their child. Encourage parents to:

- **Observe children sharing and helping.** Encourage parents to watch their child closely, in school if necessary, for times when their child does share and help. Consider sitting with the parent during the observation.
- **Provide cooperative games and play materials** (Kaiser, 1995). Tell parents that these games, and not competitive games, encourage sharing, cooperation, and helping. Make children's books focusing on prosocial behavior available to parents and emphasize the value of such stories in developing sharing, helping, and cooperation.
- **Encourage children to watch television shows and movies containing prosocial content. Label examples of sharing, helping, and cooperating** (Honig & Wittmer, 1991; Rosenkoetter, 1999). Help parents understand that films provide vivid and effective models of all kinds of behavior. Plan a parent meeting or write a brief handout on how to choose appropriate videos, show clips of good videos, and give parents a list of suggested movies and videos showing prosocial behavior. Encourage parents to look for advertising that emphasizes

prosocial behavior (Stout & Mouritsen, 1988) and teach parents to make appropriate comments about the helping, sharing, and cooperation in such ads.

- **Have children participate in prosocial behaviors.** The idea here is not to force altruism but for the child just to observe and participate with a parent who shares, helps, or cooperates but does not preach. For example, at Christmastime pick a needy child's name from the tree at a local department store (you'll find such trees in a variety of stores). The **parent** buys the desired gift with his own money but takes the child along to the store to help pick out the gift. Tell parents **not** to force a child to spend his own money. That idea can bubble up later and will then be true generosity. Tell parents to make the whole process low key and tell them not to preach.
- **Give children appropriate and manageable household responsibilities.** Help parents understand how meaningful such work is in fostering sharing, helping, and cooperation. Being immersed in a family in which everybody does their **fair share** of the work is an extremely effective strategy.
- **Recognize and encourage the results of this teaching.** Bolster a parent's confidence in encouraging kind, compassionate behavior. For

example, give parents three specific ways of showing or telling their child that they recognize the child's efforts. "You were very **helpful** when we made cookies today, Amanda" or "It was kind of you to **share** your sand toys with Jess!" or "I noticed that you and the other two children worked together to build that sand castle. That's what I call **cooperation**."

Case Study Analysis: Prosocial Behavior

Each of the three children in the chapter-opener case studies, Minda, Steve, and John, have families that encourage prosocial behavior. Analyze each case study to find out how they do this.

Minda

Minda's family is helping her understand how important it is to share, help, and cooperate.

- Find evidence of this by pointing out the times when Minda was given some responsibility for specific chores, such as household tasks.
- Explain how her mother helped her understand how someone else might be feeling.

Steve

Steve's parents were good models of prosocial behavior.

- Explain how they were consistent, and were genuinely pleased about helping.
- Explain how they were nurturing and supportive models.

John

John's dad is likely to encourage John to cooperate with others, largely because Dad has a positive, authoritative caregiving style. Find evidence of this style.

- Explain how clearly Dad communicated his expectations that John would share in the work.
- Explain how he helped his son understand his point of view about the work.
- Point out the times when Dad gave specific suggestions on how John could help.

REFLECTING ON KEY CONCEPTS

1. True or false? Four-year-old Harry has new markers. He says to Tony, "Come on over here and play with the markers, Tony." Harry's behavior is true prosocial behavior—sharing his markers. Explain the reasoning behind your answer.
2. Recall an example, different from the one in the text, of a person who demonstrated true prosocial behavior. Your example can come from a

film, video, newscast, book, or real life. Justify your judgment that this was an example of true prosocial behavior by identifying the person's motivation. Do the same thing with a person who appeared to have acted in a helpful way but whose motivation was more self-centered or even selfish.

3. Describe how a very young child (up to 2½ years of age) might demonstrate prosocial behavior. Then explain how the same child will change by the time he is 10 years old so that he can exhibit true altruism.

4. Choose the one strategy that you think would be most effective in encouraging children to share, to be helpful, and to cooperate. Explain why you think that this strategy would be so effective.

5. You are the director of a child-care and development center. Explain to the assistant teachers the school policy on compassionate treatment of animals that visit or live in classrooms. List at least five positive guidelines that every classroom and teacher will follow.

APPLY YOUR KNOWLEDGE

1. **Label or discuss prosocial behavior.** All of these situations occurred in Mr. Claiborne's first-grade class. For each situation, help him generate at least one statement or question that focuses the children's attention on the prosocial nature of the activity. Emphasize the sharing, helping, or cooperating and how it affects someone else.
   - Situation: During group time, Mr. Claiborne showed a newspaper photo of rescue workers cleaning oil from a duck caught in an oil spill.
     I would say this to emphasize prosocial behavior: _____.
   - Situation: Mr. Claiborne divided his group into pairs and each pair of children planted a tomato plant in a small vegetable garden outside their school.
     I would say this to emphasize prosocial behavior: _____.
   - Situation: Moua, working with white playdough, decided to make pink by mixing in some red dough but found that Vinnie was using all the red dough. Moua asked Vinnie for some, and Vinnie said, "OK," breaking off a chunk for him. Then Vinnie got interested in the color mixing and suggested that they mix all of their dough together. Together, they pummeled and pushed the dough. Vinnie gleefully said, "Hey, Mr. Claiborne, look at our BIG ball of pink!"
     I would say this to emphasize prosocial behavior: _____.

2. **Practice prosocial behavior.** Write a lesson plan centered on one of these two activities. Each plan would help children practice sharing, helping, or cooperating. If you are working at a practicum site, seek permission to carry out the plan. Request that the teacher review, make suggestions for, and then approve the plan before you perform the activity.

Activity: Using Puppets

Present this short puppet story about helping or cooperation. One puppet, Sam, has trouble placing paper on an easel.

Amanda: "What's the matter, Sam?"
Sam: "I can't reach the clip for the paper."
Amanda: "Maybe I can reach it." (She clips the paper onto the easel.) "There, it's done."
Sam: "Thanks for helping."

Place the puppets in a learning center after this demonstration. Encourage children to practice what they observed. Encourage them to take both roles—helper and the one helped—so that each has a chance to practice helping.

Activity: Making Pudding (small-group activity)

Children work in pairs. Give one child a spoon, an empty paper cup, and a plastic container with a lid containing enough dry instant pudding mix for two children. Give the other child a measuring cup with just enough milk to mix pudding for two children, a spoon, and an empty paper cup. Emphasize **working together** and **cooperating** by noting the need to share resources if they want to make and eat pudding.

RESOURCES FOR SPECIFIC ACTIVITIES

Honig, A., & Wittmer, D. (1996). Helping children become more prosocial: Ideas for classrooms, families, schools, and communities (Part 2). *Young Children, 51* (2), 62–70. Reviews strategies and techniques to enhance prosocial development.

Kreidler, W., & Whittall, S. (1999). *Early childhood adventures in peacemaking*, 2nd Ed. Boston, MA: Work/Family Directions. Internet source: *http://www.esrnational.org* (go to link ESR Store: New Products. Then go to "Early Childhood." This book is at the early childhood link).

REFERENCES

Batson, C. D., & Shaw, L. L. (1991). Evidence for altruism: Toward a pluralism of prosocial motives. *Psychological Inquiry, 2*(2), 107–122.

Baumrind, D. (1971). Current patterns of parental authority. *Developmental Psychology Monograph, 4*(1, Pt. 2).

Bengtsson, H., & Johnson, L. (1992). Perspective taking, empathy, and prosocial behavior in late childhood. *Child Study Journal, 22*(1), 11–22.

Bohlmeyer, E. (1989, April). *Age differences in sharing as a function of children's ability to estimate time and motivational instructions.* Paper presented at the Biennial Meeting of the Society for Research in Child Development, Kansas City, MO.

Bryan, J. H. (1975). Children's cooperation and helping behaviors. In E. M. Hetherington (Ed.), *Review of child development research* (Vol. 5). Chicago: University of Chicago Press.

Bryan, J. H., & Walbek, N. H. (1970). Preaching and practicing generosity: Children's actions and reactions. *Child Development, 41,* 329–353.

Child Development Project. (1991). *Summary of Findings to Date.* Palo Alto, CA: Hewlett Foundation.

Cohn, J. F., Campbell, S. B., Matias, R., & Hopkins, J. (1990). Face-to-face interactions of postpartum depressed and nondepressed mother-infant pairs at 2 months. *Developmental Psychology, 26,* 15–23.

Edwards, C. (1992). Creating safe places for conflict resolution to happen: Beginnings. *Child Care Information Exchange, 84,* 43–45.

Eisenberg, N., Wolchik, S., Goldberg, L., & Engel, I. (1992). Parental values, reinforcement, and young children's prosocial behavior: A longitudinal study. *Journal of Genetic Psychology, 153*(1), 19–37.

Flory, R. (1999). Children's prosocial behavior: Relationships with mothers' parenting style. *Dissertation Abstracts International, 61,* No. 03B.

Greener, S. (1998). The relationship between emotional predispositions, emotional decoding, and regulation skills and children's prosocial behavior. *Dissertation Abstracts International, 59,* No. 08B.

Grusec, J. (1991). Socializing concern for others in the home. *Developmental Psychology, 27*(2), 338–342.

Hoffman, M. L. (1975). Developmental synthesis of affect and cognition and its interplay for altruistic motivation. *Developmental Psychology, 11,* 607–622.

Hoffman, M. L. (1987). The contribution of empathy to justice and moral judgment. In N. Eisenberg & J. Strayer (Eds.), *Empathy and its development* (pp. 47–80). Cambridge: Cambridge University Press.

Honig, A. (April 23, 1998). *Create a prosocial plus cognitive curriculum for young children.* Paper presented at the Early Childhood Branch of the New York Public Library, New York.

Honig, A., & Wittmer, D. (1991). *Helping children become more prosocial: Tips for teachers.* ERIC Number ED343693. Available from ERIC Document Reproduction Service.

Honig, A., & Wittmer, D. (1996). Helping children become more prosocial: Ideas for classrooms, families, schools, and communities (Part 2). *Young Children, 51*(2), 62–70.

Kaiser, J. (1995). Adult choice of toys affects children's prosocial and antisocial behavior. *Early Child Development and Care, 111,* 181–193.

Kuebli, J. (1994). Research in review: Young children's understanding of everyday emotions. *Young Children,* 36–47.

Lewis, M. (1989). Cultural differences in children's knowledge of emotional scripts. In C. Saarni & P. L. Harris (Eds.), *Children's understanding of emotion.* Cambridge, England: Cambridge University Press.

Lupinetti, L. (1999). Perspective-taking, social competence, gender, and prosocial behavior of suburban preschool children. *Dissertation Abstracts International, 61,* No. 02B.

Midlarsky, E., & Bryan, J. H. (1972). Affect expressions and children's imitative altruism. *Journal of Experimental Research in Personality, 6,* 195–203.

Naparstek, N. (1990). Children's conceptions of prosocial behavior. *Child Study Journal, 20*(4), 207–220.

Nelson, D. (1999). Social information processing patterns and prosocial behavior: A longitudinal study. *Dissertation Abstracts International, 60,* No. 11B.

Oliner, S. P., & Oliner, P. M. (1988). *The altruistic personality: Rescuers of Jews in Nazi Europe.* New York: Free Press.

Parten, M. (1932). Social participation among preschool children. *Journal of Abnormal and Social Psychology, 27,* 243–269.

Phillipsen, L., Bridges, S., McLemore, T., & Saponaro, L. (1999). Perceptions of social behavior and peer acceptance in kindergarten. *Journal of Research in Childhood Education, 14*(1), 68–77.

Radke-Yarrow, M., & Zahn-Waxler, C. (1984). Roots, motives, and patterns of children's prosocial behavior. In E. Staub, D. Bar-Tel, J. Karylowski, & J. Reykowski (Eds.) *Development and maintenance of prosocial behavior.* New York: Plenum Press.

Rheingold, H. L., & Emery, G. N. (1986). The nurturant acts of very young children. In D. Olweus, J. Block, & M. Radke-Yarrow (Eds.), *The development of anti- and prosocial behavior.* San Diego, CA: Academic Press.

Rogow, S. (1991). The dynamics of play: Including children with special needs in mainstreamed early childhood programs. *International Journal of Early Childhood, 23*(2), 50–57.

Rosenkoetter, L. (1999). The television situation comedy and children's prosocial behavior. *Journal of Applied Social Psychology, 29*(5), 979–993.

Russell, J. A. (1989). Culture, scripts, and children's understanding of emotion. In C. Saarni & P. L. Harris (Eds.), *Children's understanding of emotion.* Cambridge, England: Cambridge University Press.

Sagi, A., & Hoffman, M. L. (1976). Empathic distress in the newborn. *Developmental Psychology, 12,* 175–176.

Schenk, V., & Grusec, J. (1987). A comparison of prosocial behavior of children with and without day care experience. *Merrill-Palmer Quarterly, 33* (2), 231–240.

Sebanc, A. M. (1999). Friendship experiences among preschool children: Links with prosocial behavior and aggression. *Dissertation Abstracts International, 60,* No. 07B.

Selman, R. L. (1980). *The growth of interpersonal understanding.* New York: Academic Press.

Shaffer, D. (1993). *Developmental psychology* (3rd ed.). Pacific Grove, CA: Brooks/Cole.

Stout, D. & Mouritsen, R. (1988). Prosocial behavior in advertising aimed at children: A content analysis. *Southern Speech Communication Journal, 53*(2) 159–174.

Swanson, K. A. (1988). *Childrearing practices and the development of prosocial behavior.* ERIC Number ED299552. Available from ERIC Document Reproduction Service.

Termine, N. T., & Izard, C. E. (1988). Infants' responses to their mothers' expressions of joy and sadness. *Developmental Psychology, 24,* 223–229.

Trepanier, M., & Romatowski, J. (1981, April). *Classroom use of selected children's books to facilitate prosocial development in young children.* Paper presented at the annual meeting of the American Educational Research Association, Los Angeles.

Wiegman, O., & Van Schie, E. (1998). Video game playing and its relations with aggressive and prosocial behaviour. *British Journal of Social Psychology, 37* (3), 367–378.

White, R. W. (1959). Motivation reconsidered: The concept of competence. *Psychological Review, 66,* 297–323.

Zahn-Waxler, C., Friedman, S., & Cummings, E. M. (1983). Children's emotions and behaviors in response to infants' cries. *Child Development, 54,* 1522–1528.

Zahn-Waxler, C., Kochanska, G., Krupnick, J., & McKnew, D. (1990). Patterns of guilt in children of depressed and well mothers. *Developmental Psychology, 26,* 51–59.

Zahn-Waxler, C., Radke-Yarrow, M., Wagner, E., & Chapman, M. (1992). Development of concern for others. *Developmental Psychology, 28*(1), 126–136.

✓ CHECK OUT THE WEB SITES RELATED TO THIS CHAPTER

✓ **Educators for Social Responsibility.** Based in Cambridge, MA. Mission is to teach social responsibility in education.

http://www.esrnational.org. Home page, many good links. For example,

Link: ESR Store: New Products

Link: ESR Store: New Products. Go to "Early Childhood." Lists several good items for purchase.

✓ **National Parent Information Network (NPIN)**

http://npin.org. This is a Web site for parents that disseminates information in a variety of formats.

http://npin.org/pnews.html. Parent News, a bimonthly electronic magazine with news, information, and resources for parents and those who work with parents. Published by ERIC Clearinghouse on Elementary and Early Childhood Education.

✓ **National Association for Humane and Environmental Education.** Fostering kindness toward people, animals, and the earth.

http://www.nahee.org. The home page; has many good links.

http://www.kindnews.org/. An on-line magazine for children.

Develop an Eclectic Approach to Child Guidance

"What does this child need at this time?" In terms of guiding children, this question implies that a child's needs change over time and suggests that two children the same age might well need two different things. Early childhood professionals guide children most effectively by adopting an **eclectic** approach; they understand a wide variety of strategies, choosing the strategy that will best help **this child at this time.**

Chapter 11. Theories: Strengthening the Foundation of DAP Child Guidance. Vygotsky, Rogers, Adler—three theorists who have helped professionals develop positive constructivist guidance strategies. You will see that there are several similar threads woven into the cloth of their theories.

- Each advocates assessing what children need.
- Each takes a problem-solving approach.
- Each values adult/child discourse or discussion in solving problems.
- Each of the theories emphasizes using positive guidance strategies and avoiding punishment.

You will quickly see the similarities among these theories and will learn the specific strategies that have come from each. In some cases, you have already learned the strategies in Chapter 4 or elsewhere in this book. This chapter will help you fit these strategies into a theoretical framework or structure.

Chapter 12. Apply Your Knowledge: Use the Decision-Making Model of Child Guidance. In this last chapter, you will have come full circle; you will now use the **Decision-Making Model of child guidance,**

first described in Chapter 1. This model advocates viewing discipline encounters merely as problems to be solved and argues for making active, conscious decisions about how to solve those problems.

There are no quick fixes, no nice, easy answers to some discipline encounters. By this point in the book you should not be surprised to discover that there is no one right way to deal with any discipline encounter; there are many effective and positive approaches. You will get a chance to consider the **eclectic approach,** which draws from many theories and strategies.

Theories: Strengthening the Foundation of DAP Child Guidance

"A theory can be likened to a lens. [It] filters out certain facts and gives a pattern to those it lets in."

(Thomas, 1992, p. 4)

After reading and studying this chapter, you will be able to

❑ **Explain** how a constructivist teacher could easily use strategies from all three theories—those of Vygotsky, Rogers, and Adler—to guide young children.

❑ **Tell in your own words** how each theory advises adults to assess a child's current social abilities and competencies before deciding how to help a child in a discipline encounter.

❑ **Explain** how each theory urges adults to engage in conversations with children, conversations that help children become more competent in working and playing with others.

❑ **Identify and explain** practical strategies that come from each theory. **Practice** the strategies.

Case Studies: A Third-Grade Teacher Uses Dap
Guidance Strategies from Different Theories

Guiding Children With Strategies Based on Vygotsky's Theory

David is 8 years old and has just enrolled in the Oaklawn Elementary School, in Mr. Lee's third-grade class. He had attended kindergarten at Oaklawn but had been home-schooled for first and second grades while his parents were missionaries. Mr. Lee wanted to help David make a good transition back to Oaklawn and began by talking alone with David's parents.

David's mom told Mr. Lee that David worked very well on his own but that he had had few opportunities to work with other children in a learning environment. She said that David played with children at the mission base and got along well with them. Back home now, David also seemed to get along with other children at Sunday school, in swimming class, and at the public library's story hours. She was concerned, however, about whether he would know how to work with others in reading groups or large-group instruction.

Mr. Lee gave a copy of the daily schedule to David's parents. "I see," Mom said, looking over the schedule, "that the children have a lot of choice about what they do and when they do their work. David will certainly appreciate that."

"That's a good start," replied the teacher. "I also do large-group instruction when it seems appropriate and then I like to use small groups. The children work on projects; small groups of children just seem to come together to work on some part of the project. I will certainly do what I can to help David feel comfortable in small and large groups. I'll talk with him about the schedule when you and David come for a classroom visit."

The next afternoon after school, Mr. Lee met with David and his mom and explained the schedule to David. When the teacher asked if David had questions, David replied, "Is large group like the reading hour at the library, where children sit on the floor?"

"Yes, sometimes. Other times, the whole group goes to the gym or the children sit in chairs at their tables. It depends on the lesson." David, relaxed, nodded his understanding.

"Do you have any other questions, David?" David wanted to know how small groups were formed. The teacher explained and again David nodded.

On David's first day at Oaklawn, the children had a short math lesson in a large group. After that, each child worked on the curriculum areas that he or she had chosen for the morning. Mr. Lee planned on working on the math concept presented with groups of four children at a time. David was in the first small group. In both large and small group, the teacher has suggested where David could sit. For small group, the teacher asked Seth and David to set up the easel with a large sheet of paper and to get markers. Seth showed David where to get supplies.

Guiding Children with Strategies from Rogerian Theory

The small-group math activity was a follow-up to large group. In large group, Mr. Lee had surveyed the children for information on pets. He asked how many children had no pets and how many had a dog, a cat, a hamster, a gerbil, or fish. He asked if anyone had two different kinds of pets. In small groups, he intended to facilitate a discussion about presenting a large volume of data or information in chart or graph form.

"We sure collected a lot of information on your pets!" said the teacher. "We have to figure out a way to record the information for the whole class to see."

Rory said, "We could write sentences: Sam has a dog. Rory has a hamster. Sarah has a cat and a dog. Susan has a dog. Jim has a cat. Vanessa has a parrot. How about that?"

"That's one way to do it," replied Mr. Lee. "Then everybody would read through the sentences." Mr. Lee noticed that David was frowning. "Your face tells me that you might have a question, David."

David counted the children in the class. "Twenty-one children. One sentence about every person. It would take a long time to read all the sentences!" The other children, including Rory, agreed.

Mr. Lee told the group, "So, you all think that it would take a l-o-n-g time to read that many sentences."

All the children chimed out, "Yeah! Too l---o---n---g!"

Rory, looking like he had another idea, said, "Hey, we could count how many children have dogs. Then we could say, 'Five children have dogs,' and 'Seven children have cats,' and 'Two children have hamsters', and 'One child has a bird.' We wouldn't have so many sentences." Rory stopped and smiled, pleased with his idea.

"That's a good way to reduce the total number of sentences," said Mr. Lee, looking at the other three children in the group. "David and Nysha (pronounced Nee sha) still look like they have some questions about this, though."

Nysha, who loves math, said, "Well, how about just using a numeral to show how many children have dogs, cats, or other animals?"

Mr. Lee replied, "So, we would write 'dog' and then write the numeral that tells us how many children have dogs?"

Nysha answered, "Uh-huh. Then we wouldn't even have sentences."

Mr. Lee told her, "So it's the same information but a different way to show it."

David suggested, "Maybe we could just draw a dog and then put the number of children who have a dog next to the picture. **No** words!"

Mr. Lee looked at his mathematicians. "Now your faces tell me that you're all pleased with this idea. Is that correct? How about **one** sentence at the top that will tell others what the chart is about?" They agreed and they were off, eagerly converting all the information to an easily read chart.

Guiding Children with Strategies from Adlerian Theory

Mr. Lee and his student teacher, Sabrina, were talking about how the student's week was going, when the student said that she needed help with a problem.

"Ask away," said Mr. Lee.

"It's not the biggest problem in the world but it's making lunchtime a struggle. Lucy seems to be a real 'picky' eater when I sit at her table. We never talked about this in a class at the university and so I've been trying different things." Mr. Lee asked her to describe what she had tried.

"I coaxed her to eat lunch today and Lucy just sat there staring at me. Then I decided to use the try-a-bite strategy that my mother used with me and told her that she'd have to stay at the lunch table until she tried a bite of everything. She did stay at the table but never ate much at all and just kept staring at her plate. What am I supposed to do?"

Mr. Lee did not criticize the student teacher for using an ineffective strategy but instead asked Sabrina how she felt when she had to coax Lucy to eat.

"A little irritated. I like working with her in class but this game is wearing me down."

"Irritation surely can lead to the urge to fight with a child," said Mr. Lee. "I know the feeling. Lucy did the same thing at the beginning of the year with me. I have an idea that might work." Sabrina's nod signaled that she would welcome advice.

"I think I helped her when I simply said, 'Oh, you don't want to eat lunch today. That's OK. You can still have a good time talking with us.'"

"H-m-m. So, you didn't get into an argument with her."

Mr. Lee smiled, "Well, at first she was surprised and said, 'But, I **really** don't want to eat.' I just said, 'So, you really don't want to eat.' I think that she expected me to say something else because she looked surprised. Then, she looked at me and just blinked. She had a puzzled look on her face, as if she was trying to figure something out. The next day she started to go into her routine again. Then, to my relief, she just stopped, opened her milk carton, and picked up her sandwich."

Mr. Lee has been teaching for 16 years. He has changed his style of guiding children somewhat over the years, gradually adopting a **constructivist** approach. As a constructivist, he believes that children construct or build their own competencies and that he is their guide. Mr. Lee observes children thoroughly and often, gathering good data on which to make decisions. He knows his children well.

His third-graders, at the end of early childhood, still need to construct many ideas about getting along with other people. His students have to learn to collaborate with others in solving problems. Like all teachers, he faces a variety of discipline encounters with his group.

He uses a variety of guidance strategies, each strategy having its roots in a specific theoretical base. He made a commitment to using only **positive strategies,** which was difficult at first because he used to believe in using time-out, a form of punishment. All of his chosen strategies, whatever the theory, reflect his positive constructivist approach. He is warm and nurturing, which comes through clearly in his interactions with his class. He has created a safe and secure classroom environment. He sets and maintains limits well.

His guidance practices are positive because he believes in using positive guidance strategies, whatever the theory. He consciously rejects any practice with the potential to hurt or degrade children. Therefore, he does not believe in using punishment, such as time-out or response cost. A couple of years ago, he even rethought how he praised children, thinking at the time that he was using too much praise. He completely stopped using the phrase "Good job!" (Katz, 1993; Kohn, 2001).

Chapter 2 described how to use Piaget's theory in making decisions about guiding children. This chapter explains how to choose strategies based on three other theories. Mr. Lee has **constructed an eclectic style,** consciously selecting strategies based on Piaget's theory as well as these three other theories:

- Vygotsky's theory
- Rogerian theory
- Adlerian theory

VYGOTSKY'S THEORY AND CHILD GUIDANCE

Jean Piaget and Lev Vygotsky were both born in 1896. Vygotsky was born in Byelorussia. He graduated from Moscow University in 1917, just as the Russian revolution started. He died when he was only 37 years old.

Both Piaget and Vygotsky have had great influence on both psychology and education, although there are some central differences between their theories. Piaget lived much longer than did Vygotsky and Piaget's writing, unlike Vygotsky's, was widely disseminated. Finally, Vygotsky's work was translated, making it, along with Piaget's, available to child developmentalists and educators. Educators quickly saw the value in his views, using Vygotsky's theory to inform constructivist curriculum and instructional practice (Berk & Winsler, 1995).

Adults can also use concepts from Vygotsky's theory to help them make wise child guidance decisions. Many of the strategies that you have already learned in other sections of this textbook are based on Vygotsky's work, as you will see when you read this section.

The three concepts from Vygotsky's theory discussed in this chapter are:

- Scaffolding
- Zone of proximal development (ZPD)
- Adult/child dialogue or discourse

Scaffolding

Scaffolding: A teacher's changing support as a child develops a new competency or skill. Think of it like this: A building under construction usually has a series of scaffolds, platforms that support construction workers. They are placed where the workers need them. Likewise, a child is like a building that constructs herself. **Children are the main construction workers, constructing or building themselves;** e.g., knowledge, skills and competencies, views of morality, gender, the self, kindness and compassion. Adults help children in their construction by serving as guides, by **scaffolding** the child's learning. Other children, as well as television, influence the strength of the child's construction. A child who has a supportive social environment can forge ahead and build strong social competencies (Berk & Winsler, 1995).

Scaffolding in child guidance: how a teacher's support changes during a discipline encounter or series of interactions. For example, Mr. Lee notices that a child lacks a specific skill. He knows that the child could use support from somebody who possesses the skill (the teacher or a more skilled child). The more skilled partner provides help but tries to match the child's current level of ability.

Teachers usually offer more help when a guidance task is new. As the child gains skill in constructing the necessary knowledge, the adult can gradually step back, providing progressively less help. Scaffolding in child guidance helps children become autonomous and self-controlled. Here is an example of how Mr. Lee scaffolded Rory's understanding of how speaking thoughtless words can hurt another person's feelings.

Example. Rory had told Ellen, a skillful reader, that he did not want to be in her reading group anymore because of how she stopped to look at every picture. Ellen looked dejected and withdrew from her group, refusing to read aloud. Mr. Lee noticed and talked with Rory in an effort to scaffold Rory's understanding of the effect of degrading statements on other people's feelings.

Mr. Lee: "Telling Ellen that she slows the group down by looking at pictures was just like hitting her, Rory. How can you tell that she is probably feeling bad?"

Rory: (scrunching up one side of his mouth and looking sideways, as if feeling guilty) "I know. She closed her book and went over to her desk. I didn't hit her, though."

Mr. Lee: "I said that your words hurt her as much as hitting her would have hurt her."

Rory: (looked genuinely puzzled) "What do you mean?."

Mr. Lee: "Your words hurt her feelings."

Rory: (recognition dawned) "Uh-oh. That's not good."

Mr. Lee: "You're right. It's not good. Is there anything you can do about it?"

Rory: "You mean for me to apologize?"

Mr. Lee: "That's one thing that you could do, but only if you really mean it. I am not going to force you to apologize. You have to figure out two things: Are you ready to talk to Ellen about this? If you were ready, then you'd have to figure out how you could talk with her. I can help you if you need help. You decide what you want to do but I hope that you let Ellen know somehow that you know you hurt her feelings and that it won't happen again."

Good scaffolding assumes three things:

- Teachers (or any adults working with children) are active agents
- Problem solving is the goal in scaffolding when guiding children
- A good teacher/child relationship

Teachers are active agents

Some people believe that children, like Rory, should pick up social skills on their own. Vygotsky, however, believed that a teacher, like Mr. Lee, should intervene in a child's interaction with peers when appropriate, that teachers should be active agents in children's social development. It is appropriate to intervene when a child simply does not have the skill or knowledge that he needs to control his own behavior. It seems grossly unfair not to help the child. Mr. Lee has intervened appropriately with Rory and has helped him learn just how hurtful thoughtless comments can be.

Problem solving

Adults who scaffold children's understanding helpfully look at a discipline encounter as a problem to be solved. Vygotsky believed that problem solving was the core of all good scaffolding. Theorists in the modern era, like Vygotsky, also view problem solving as the best path to helping children construct good social skills (Kohn, 1996). Guidance strategies based on Vygotsky's theories (Figure 11.1) emphasize identifying an issue and helping a child construct the solution to the problem. Problem solving is also a central idea in child guidance based on Rogers's theories, as you will read in the next section.

This teacher is talking with Rachel about a social skill that she needs, a concept from Vygotsky's theory.

Reread the short section in which Mr. Lee and Rory talked about apologies. Mr. Lee helped Rory understand that an apology must be sincere. He also helped him to make a decision about whether to apologize. The teacher offered help (a part of scaffolding) to Rory in the event that Rory did not know how to apologize.

Good teacher/child relationships

Good adult/child relationships are the foundation for DAP child guidance in general (Elicker & Fortner-Wood, 1995; Kontos & Wilcox-Herzog, 1997). Good adult/child relationships, then, are the foundation on which scaffolding works best. In order to carry out effective problem solving with a child, a teacher must have a good relationship with her. How could you tell, in the brief example between Mr. Lee and Rory, that the teacher probably does have a good relationship with Rory?

Better social skills and understanding: the results of good scaffolding

The next example demonstrates the power of good scaffolding—Rory's greater understanding of positive social interaction.

Example. Rory thought about what Mr. Lee had said. He also remembered a PBS after-school special in which a boy figured out how to apologize to his two friends. Rory used information from his talk with his teacher and from the television show to decide on what to do. He did not consult Mr. Lee but went ahead with his plan. Later that day, Ellen found a short note in her desk. The note, taped to a library book, said:

> Dear Ellen,
>
> I am sorry that I said something mean to you. I will never do that again. Here is my new book about cats. Let's read it together, OK?
>
>   Your friend, Rory

Mr. Lee had helped Rory **construct** better ideas about dealing with other people and had helped him through well-done scaffolding.

Zone of Proximal Development (ZPD)

Basketball courts have a "free-throw" lane, the zone on the court where players toss free throws. In child development, the ZPD is the space or zone where learning and development take place (Berk & Winsler, 1995). At one end of the ZPD is a child's current ability, what he understands about some topic. At the other end of the ZPD is what the child can learn or accomplish with the help of an adult or more competent member of the culture.

In the Rory/Ellen example, Rory at first did not really understand that thoughtless words born of frustration can hurt someone's feelings (Rory's current ability). Mr. Lee gave him some help, in a warm and supportive way (the expert help). Rory later demonstrated how much he had learned as a result of the dialogue with his teacher. He demonstrated the willingness and ability to acknowledge thoughtless behavior and its effect on another person.

Adult/Child Dialogue or Discourse

Any guidance strategy based on Vygotsky's theory relies heavily on adult/child dialogues, talking about tasks that a child can accomplish with adult help. Children gradually learn how to control their own behavior when adults scaffold their understanding of social interaction. This works by inducing children to use self-directed, private speech to guide their actions.

Example. Mr. Lee and Rory talked (engaged in discourse) about the effect of Rory's words on Ellen's feelings (Mr. Lee's scaffolding through talking). When he was later alone, Rory's private speech helped him work through the problem. Essentially his private speech stated, "I said something mean to Ellen. I need to tell Ellen that I'm sorry. I will write a note and leave it in her desk. The boy in the television show attached a note to a pizza that was delivered to his friends" (a model for Rory). Rory left the book and the note in Ellen's desk (action prompted by his private speech, all resulting from scaffolding through talking with Mr. Lee).

Practical Guidance Strategies Based on Vygotsky's Theory[33]

- **Ask child to engage in problem solving.**

  "I'd like you to think of one idea that would help you remember to bring your homework."

  "I'd like you both to think about how you can both use the wagon at the same time."

- **Ask questions that prompt children to come up with solutions.**

  "I have one cracker and three children who want another cracker. How many pieces would I have to break this cracker into so that you each get one piece?"

  "You have so many good ideas, Jack. Can you think of one thing that you can do to let the other children have a chance to talk?" (Jack usually blurts out answers.)

- **Give child examples of strategies.**

  "Here's one idea. See if you think it might work. Slide over a little bit and then Sam will be able to sit next to you."

  "You can use words to tell Pippin to move. Say, 'Could you please move over a little bit, Pippin? I have to get my coat from my locker.'"

- **Model a skill.**

  Demonstrate looking around the group when sitting in group time. Say that you are looking to see if anyone wants to talk. (Models skill of paying attention to other people in the group.)

- **Set up the classroom so that:**

  Children can move around

  Children can collaborate with others

  Children can take frequent breaks from sedentary activities

---

Figure 11.1.

Rogerian Theory and Child Guidance

The work of Carl Rogers, born in 1902 in Chicago, is the basis of Rogerian theory. As an educational psychologist, Rogers counseled children and their parents at the Child Study Department of the Society for the Prevention of Cruelty to Children. Rogers was also a teacher. It was during the period from 1940 to 1963 that he developed and disseminated his views on counseling and therapy (Rogers, 1957).

If you went to a therapist trained in the Rogerian method of therapy, you would soon find out that the therapist was nondirective. A Rogerian therapist believes that you have the answers to your problems inside yourself. The therapist's role is to help you find those answers.

So it is in child guidance. Rogerian guidance strategies rest on the idea that children have the **capacity for self-direction,** that children can become increasingly able to control their own actions. Teachers and parents who use Rogerian guidance

---

[33]Source: File, N. (1993). The teacher as guide of children's competence with peers. *Child and Youth Care Forum, 22,* 351–360.

strategies believe that it is the **adult's role to support children's efforts,** to demonstrate acceptance and approval.

Notice the fundamental similarity between Vygotsky's and Roger's theories. One, both believed that children could develop or construct their own abilities and competencies. Two, both Vygotsky and Rogers also believed that children need competent, warm adult support to do their constructing.

Rogerian-based guidance, like all positive guidance, helps a child

- Become aware of all his feelings—both pleasant and unpleasant (e.g., anger or jealousy).
- Not feel shame for having unpleasant feelings.
- Perceive things accurately.
- Be much less defensive in dealing with new people, experiences, and problems.
- Think for himself.
- Trust his ability to make decisions.
- Accurately assess situations.
- Trust himself to develop good solutions to problems (Rogers, 1957).

Carl Rogers had followers, professionals educated in his theory. One of these people, Thomas Gordon, developed a program of child guidance based on Rogerian theory. The program, Parent Effectiveness Training, is best known as P.E.T (Gordon, 1978). He also developed a similar program for teachers, Teacher Effectiveness Training or T.E.T (Gordon, 1974). Gordon's objective in starting the effectiveness training programs was to teach specific guidance skills to adults. These guidance strategies are the same skills used by professional Rogerian counselors. Chapter 4 presented these skills briefly. This chapter presents three Rogerian-based guidance strategies:

- Figure out who **owns a problem,** adult or child
- **Listen actively** when a child owns a problem
- Deliver an **I-message** when the adult owns a problem

Problem Ownership

This is a central concept in Rogerian-based guidance strategies (as well as in Vygotsky's framework). Problems, issues, or conflicts arise in all relationships. The first step in solving any problem requires figuring out if a problem even exists and, if so, who owns the problem. At times, an **adult owns the problem** and at other times, the **child owns the problem.**

Decide who owns the problem by looking at whose needs are thwarted. Who is upset? Who is afraid? Who is it that cannot do something? Who is frustrated?

Example. Mr. Claiborne (the first-grade teacher) noticed Vinnie and Susan sitting on the floor, a large sheet of paper between them. They had written one sentence and seemed stuck in the middle of the second. "How is it going?" asked Mr. Claiborne. The children said that they were trying to figure out how to spell "the." This problem, the teacher quickly concluded, belonged to the children. They were the ones who were at a loss about the spelling.

Example. Mr. Lee saw that Lucy was unusually quiet on Monday, hardly speaking the whole morning. He asked Lucy if she wanted to talk and found out that her grandpa had died. Lucy owned this problem.

Example. Nellie whined, "But why do I have to wash my hands? I don't want to." Mrs. Vargas realized immediately that she, the adult, owned this problem because she was irritated about having to spend so much time dealing with Nellie's whining.

It is important to decide on problem ownership because the guidance strategies that we choose depend largely on who owns the problem. Gordon's goal was to help adults decrease the number of problems owned by both adults and children.

Deliver I-Messages When an Adult Owns a Problem

Many questions raised in workshops on guidance and discipline center on problems in relationships with children, problems owned by the adults. Children sometimes behave in ways that interrupt an adult; cost the adult time, energy, or money; interfere with adult rights; or insult adults. Some examples:

- a child consistently interrupts group times
- children assigned to clean tables do not do their job
- several girls and boys leave softball equipment strewn all over the field after recess
- a child makes too much noise with musical instruments
- a child leaves her bike in the driveway

The P.E.T and T.E.T programs urge adults to use **I-messages** when adults own a problem. The goal is to tell the child clearly that the adult has a problem with something that the child did. Another goal is to tell the child that the adult wants the child to do something to fix the problem. I-messages allow a child to make the change out of respect for the adult.

Good I-messages are simple statements of facts. A good I-message does not accuse a child of creating the adult's feeling (Gordon, 1978). Gordon says that there are three elements in a good I-message:

- Give observable data (what you saw, heard, smelled, touched).
- State the tangible effects.
- Say how you felt.

I have added a fourth element:

- Focus on change. Give some ideas about how to change things or ask questions that prompt children to come up with solutions, a guidance strategy based on Vygotsky that will encourage the child to make a necessary change (File, 1993).

Here is an example of how the first-grade teacher delivered an I-message when Ryan destroyed property (the teacher's problem).

Example. Ryan used a pencil to rip a jagged hole in a bottle of glue, not by accident. Mr. Claiborne, at first, felt very angry. He turned away, took some deep breaths to calm himself, and then turned back to Ryan. He picked up the bottle and handed a towel to Ryan. "Clean up the glue, Ryan, before it runs off the table and onto the floor." When he and Ryan had cleaned the sticky table, he took Ryan aside and calmly delivered his I-message.

- **Give data:** "I picked up the bottle of glue and saw that glue was flowing out of the hole in the bottle. I saw that you were laughing about it."
- **State tangible effects:** "You and I had to clean up all the spilled glue, which took quite a long time. I will also have to get a new bottle of glue." Ryan responded, "So?" Mr. Claiborne ignored the attempt to deflect the conversation.
- **Say how you feel:** "When I saw all the glue, I was startled and then I got angry because I saw that you were laughing about it."
- **Focus on change:** "I want you to help me figure out how to fix this problem. How will you replace the bottle of glue?" This is only the beginning of a conversation on how to replace the bottle of glue.

Practice delivering an I-message in Figure 11.2.

Practice Sending an I-Message

- **Situation.** Jessica, in Mr. Nellis's kindergarten, played in the sandbox outside along with several other children. Jessica took a hefty amount of sand and threw it in the air with both hands. She did not seem to be aiming at anyone but the other children had to dodge the sand shower. Mr. Nellis delivered this I-message:

Give data: _____

State tangible effects: _____

Say how you feel: _____

Focus on change: _____

- **Situation.** A rescue worker brought her rescue dog, Sarah, to the Mr. Nellis's K–2 class. Michael and Willis interrupted the beginning of the presentation twice by barking and then laughing. Sarah, the dog, never flinched. The presenter appeared to be upset but went on with the presentation. Mr. Nellis called Willis and Michael aside.

Give data: _____

State tangible effects: _____

Say how you feel: _____

Focus on change: _____

Figure 11.2.

Listen Actively When a Child Owns the Problem

Help a child who owns a problem by using specific communication skills that say: "You seem to have a problem. Do you need my help?" This section describes **active listening,** the P.E.T. communication skill recommended when children own a problem. (This process is quite similar to Vygotsky's idea of teacher/child discourse to solve problems.)

Use the guidelines for active listening when you want to help a child solve his own problem. In the example that follows, Jack, the child, makes a simple remark. The remark does not indicate that Jack has a problem, but Mr. Claiborne responds in a way that encourages Jack to get to the problem. Even when Jack first indicates that something is bothering him, Mr. Claiborne has no idea about what the real problem is. The teacher carefully followed the guidelines for active listening, and Jack felt safe enough to keep talking. He eventually gets to the real issue.

Example. Six-year-old Jack was playing a card game with Vinnie, who said, "I like playing cards!"

Jack chimed in, "Me too! I like playing cards!" (At this point, the teacher did not see a problem at all.)

Teacher:	"Good. I'll make sure we always have cards in the room."
Jack:	"I like playing cards at school," (emphasizing *at school*).
Mr. Claiborne:	(attending more closely now) "You like playing cards **at school.**"
Jack:	"Yeah, but not at home."
Teacher:	". . . not at home."
Jack:	"Well . . . I like to play cards with my mom."
Mr. Claiborne:	(careful not to close down the discourse or conversation) "You like to play cards with your mom at home."
Jack:	"Yep, with my mom; not with Grandpa, though."
Teacher:	"Playing cards with mom is fun but playing cards with your grandpa isn't so much fun."
Jack:	"Grandpa calls me a dummy if I count things wrong." (This is the real problem. Jack does not like it when Grandpa calls him names.)
Teacher:	"When grandpa calls you a name, you don't like it. Is that right?"
Jack:	"I **don't** like it. That's right. I don't want to play with him when he does that."

Mr. Claiborne, thinking it was time to use Vygotsky's approach, too, asked, "How can you let your Grandpa know that you don't like to be called names, Jack?" Mr. Claiborne urges Jack now to solve the problem. He does not give a solution.

Jack **owned** this problem. Active listening was an appropriate strategy. When children own a problem, they need adults to recognize and validate the feelings, but **not** to preach or tell them to feel some other way. The adult will only listen, not give a solution. The adult helps the child **construct his own solution through active listening** (see Figure 11.3).

How to Listen Actively

Remember to
- Listen carefully.
- Try to figure out what the message means.
- Listen for what the child is feeling.
- Suspend judgment (avoid judging anything about the situation).
- Let the child finish speaking. Wait one or two seconds and then speak.
- Merely reflect back your perception of the child's feelings with words or body language.

Avoid "roadblocks to communication"
- Avoid giving solutions.
- Avoid interrupting the child.
- Avoid preaching or ordering.
- Avoid giving advice.
- Avoid trying to persuade the child to feel something else.

These things close down communication. A person is not listening actively when she, for example, interrupts the child.

Figure 11.3.

Teachers are **mandated reporters of child abuse** according to their state's statutes on child abuse and neglect, and therefore must know how to act appropriately when suspecting child abuse or neglect. Abused children often make indirect allusions to problems at home, and teachers can help them by listening actively without judging or acting shocked.

Example. Joyce and her teacher were playing a board game while Joyce waited for her dad to pick her up.

Teacher: "I like playing games. Do you, Joyce?"
Joyce: "Uh-huh. Uncle Charlie likes games, too."
Teacher: "Uncle Charlie likes to play games?"
Joyce: "He likes one game the best. We play when he baby-sits."

(By this time, the teacher was worried. She knew about the indicators of sexual abuse, and it was beginning to look as if Joyce was trying to tell her something.)

Teacher: "There's one game that he really likes?"
Joyce: "Yeah. But he told me that it's a secret game and I shouldn't tell anybody else that we play it."

This teacher has listened and responded well to frightening information. She has not closed the conversation down or denied the child's feelings. She has not preached. She has not acted shocked—she has listened actively. She will record this information and date it. She will follow her state's law on the reporting of this information. The teacher makes no decisions; she merely reports her suspicions based on the information that she has received and recorded.

Case Study Analysis: Child Guidance Based on Rogerian Theory

This chapter-opening case study involved Mr. Lee and a small group of third-graders, with the children collaborating on how to present a large volume of data or information in chart or graph form.

- I think that Mr. Lee has listened actively:

Not very well   adequately   moderately well   very well   so well that he
   at all   could demonstrate it to
                                                                        others

- From my perspective, the statement that best illustrates good active listening is: _____. My reason for this choice is: _____.
- Suppose that Mr. Lee had said, when Rory suggested using sentences, "Rory, this is a math lesson, not language arts!" What is your best guess about how the rest of the conversation would have gone?

ADLERIAN THEORY AND CHILD GUIDANCE

Alfred Adler's life paralleled that of Sigmund Freud in many ways. Both were from Vienna, where Adler was born in 1870, only a few years after Freud. They both attended medical school and developed an interest in psychiatry, but they held divergent views on how the personality develops. Freud maintained that each person is primarily a biological being, while Adler believed that each person is primarily a social being.

Freud believed that biological needs drive personality development. Adler had a different view, maintaining that a person's social environment and interactions heavily influence personality development. While Freud thought that uncontrollable unconscious forces drive people, Adler's view was that people actively and consciously direct and create their own growth.

Adlerians believe that children play a large role in their own development, that their interpretation or perception of their experiences is important. Adler thought that humans are social creatures who need to attain group membership. Children go about fitting into a group by following their own interpretation of the rules for group membership (Mead, 1976).

Some children are able to achieve a sense of belonging to their group by cooperating and making useful contributions. They make accurate interpretations of the rules of group membership. Other children have a pattern of misbehavior and noncooperation because they interpret events and people's intentions inaccurately. These children have a faulty perception of how to fit into a group and use ineffective approaches to gain a place in it.

They base their behavior on their faulty perceptions of the world. To assist them, we must help them get a different perspective on things, to perceive events and people's intentions more accurately. Adlerians believe in thinking about what a child gets out of misbehavior, or what his **mistaken goal** is.

ADLERIAN THEORY: MISTAKEN GOALS—ATTENTION, POWER, REVENGE, INADEQUACY

The chapter-opener case study involving Sabrina, the student teacher, and the picky eater, Lucy, illustrated a child's faulty perception of how to fit into a group. Children like Lucy have a faulty perception or mistaken goal of how to be a group member and seek group membership through one of the following (Dreikurs, 1958):

- striving for **undue attention** from others
- seeking **power** over others
- hurting others through **revenge**
- displaying inadequacy or **incompetence**

For each of these, we will examine the child's faulty perception, what the child does, how the adult feels and usually reacts, and a better approach to the encounter. The STEP (Systematic Training for Effective Parenting) program is a way to teach Adlerian concepts and strategies to parents (Dinkmeyer & McKay, 1988).

Attention Seeking

The child's faulty perception

Everyone, including a child, has a need for and a right to attention. Some children, however, make demands for undue attention (called attention seeking) from adults. They believe, mistakenly, that they can be a member of a group by making themselves the center of attention. Getting the attention of others, then, is their mistaken goal.

What the child does

Attention seekers accomplish their mistaken goal by keeping adults busy. They are skilled in using different attention-getting techniques. Some attention seekers are active mischief makers, in trouble all the time. Other attention seekers are passive and get attention through laziness and demanding that others do things for them.

How the adult feels and usually reacts

Adults usually feel annoyed when children demand undue attention, many giving in to the child's demands. Others, clearly frustrated with the child's behavior, scold the child. Giving a child undue attention or scolding does **not** help an attention seeker. Unfortunately, it seems to strengthen the attention getting. Giving uncalled-for attention also strengthens the child faulty ideas of how to fit into the group (Mead, 1976).

A better approach

Help an attention-seeking child join a group without having to be the center of attention. Here are specific steps to take in the face of attention-seeking behavior; the basic ingredient is changing how you react to demands for undue attention.

- Ignore the impulse to give in to the attention-seeking behavior.
- Give the child attention when behavior is more appropriate.
- Encourage the child to take the perspective of others by telling him their perspective and by helping him learn to cooperate.
- Acknowledge the child's bids for help (when the child's attention seeking is laziness). Tell her kindly and firmly that it is her job, not yours. Tell her that you have confidence in her and know that she can complete the task. Discourage further attention seeking by leaving the area, allowing the child to make a new decision about finishing her work.

Example. At the beginning of the year, Mr. Claiborne noticed right away that Jessie liked to talk during any group time. Jessie always had a comment or a story to tell and Mr. Claiborne had a difficult time including other children in discussions. Jessie was an attention seeker. Mr. Claiborne was determined to help Jessie be an appropriately active participant in group activities, so he decided to try to have a talk with Jessie about how to function in a group.

He spoke quietly to Jessie after one group lesson. "I asked Moua to read what he had written but I heard you keep saying, 'I have a story.'" (Jessie said that he had

Many children make accurate interpretations about how to be a member of a group.

a good story to read.) Mr. Claiborne continued, "But I had asked Moua to read. Moua looked disappointed when he did not get a chance to read his story. So tomorrow, I will remind you to let others have a turn talking." (This is teacher/child discourse in the child's ZPD, the teacher scaffolding Jessie's understanding of group dynamics—concepts from Vygotsky's theory.)

Struggling for Power

The child's faulty perception

Some children with poor self-esteem do not think that they exert much control over things. They desperately search for control by trying to demonstrate power over others. Their faulty perception is that their personal value comes from showing others that they are in charge. For such a child, a loss of power to an adult is the same as a loss of personal value.

What the child does

Children who struggle for power develop several techniques for involving adults in power struggles, thus gaining control over them. Their techniques vary. Some power-seeking children might have tantrums. Others might be very disobedient. Still others, usually older children, might argue excessively. Some control seekers are stubbornly defiant. Some power seekers, then, are active and rebellious while others are passive, striving for power through stubbornness, forgetfulness, or even laziness.

How the adult feels and usually reacts

Adults often feel threatened or angry when confronted with a power-seeking child, just as many people are with power-hungry adults. Some adults think that a child has challenged their authority, and their first impulse is to fight back, reminding a child that the adult is in power. Adlerians believe that some children are so skillful at the power game that adults do not even realize they are in a power struggle. Some adults resort to punitive, hurtful strategies in trying to reestablish authority and overpower the child.

Engaging in a power struggle with a child makes a child's power-seeking behavior even stronger. Letting a child draw us into a power struggle does not help clarify his faulty perception of how to fit into a group. Instead, it strengthens the child's faulty perception. Mrs. Vargas, who usually quietly refuses to get into power struggles, made this mistake with Tahisha.

Example. Mrs. Vargas said, "Tahisha, you can have two more turns, and then I want you to park your trike." (An appropriate limit, stated well.) Tahisha took her two turns and then started on the third spin around the little riding track. "Tahisha, it's time to come in. Please park your trike." (An appropriate reminder, also stated well.) Tahisha rode to the shed and got off the trike, but did not put the trike inside. Instead, she walked toward the classroom. The teacher, clearly frustrated, said, "Tahisha, please put the trike inside the shed." Tahisha replied, "No!" Mrs.

Vargas, now irritated, spoke before she fully processed her feeling. "We'll see about that." She surprised herself with that response.

Even if Mrs. Vargas had made Tahisha put the trike away, Tahisha would have "won" the battle that she created. She had controlled her teacher, engaging her in a power struggle, just as soon as Mrs. Vargas said, "We'll see about that." Tahisha's power, sadly, came from starting an argument.

A better approach

Whether a child continues to play the power game depends largely on how adults react. Children like Tahisha need adults to show them positive ways of becoming group members; they do not need adults as sparring partners. Adults help power-seeking children best by changing their own way of reacting to the child's invitation to fight. Children like Tahisha need help in feeling positive power from controlling their own behavior. Here are some suggestions.

- **Resist the first impulse to fight back.** Mrs. Vargas knows how powerful an impulse it is on occasion.
- **Decide to respond differently.** Adults can make choices, so choose to avoid fighting. Say to **yourself** (private speech, a Vygotskian concept), "Looks like she wants to fight. I don't want to argue. I'd better think of something else."
- **Decline the child's invitation to argue or fight.** This will surprise a child, particularly if you have previously engaged in power struggles with him. Be helpful and label the interaction as a power struggle. Tell a child that you do not want to argue or fight and then leave. This will tell the child that you have respectfully refused to argue. It will also model an important social skill.

Example. Mrs. Vargas knew immediately that Tahisha had drawn her into a power struggle. She wanted to help Tahisha and decided to try a different, and what she knew to be a more helpful, approach. The teacher stooped and took Tahisha's hands in hers. She talked quietly with Tahisha, saying, "Oh my! It looks to me like you feel like fighting with me about the trike. I don't feel like fighting, Tahisha. I'd much rather read a story with you. I'm going to line up trikes in the shed, in their brand-new parking spaces. It would help me if you would scoot your tricycle to the shed." Mrs. Vargas patted Tahisha's hands, got up, and went to the shed.

Mrs. Vargas refused to continue to fight, clearly communicating her intention to Tahisha. When she came out of the shed, she found Tahisha's trike right near the entrance, ready for storage.

Adults usually feel irritated or even angry when dealing with a power-seeking child. Help power-seeking children by thinking through what that child needs, even in situations where a child seems bent on starting an argument. Starting arguments is usually a misguided call for help. Mrs. Vargas answered Tahisha's call for help by changing how she responded. Tahisha finally experienced power within herself; she did not need to feel power through fighting.

Trying to Get Revenge

The child's faulty perception

These children feel hurt and angry, and their goal is to get even by hurting others. Like all children, they need recognition, but these children get it in a negative way. Their revenge is hostile aggression (discussed in Chapter 9), more often seen in children at the end of the early childhood period.

Example. In Mr. Nellis's K–2 class are second-graders Willis and Michael. Willis accidentally bumped into Michael. Michael, who often assumes that people have planned to hurt him even when that is not so, glared at Willis. Later, in line for lunch, Michael stuck out his foot, tripping Willis, who was carrying a tray full of food.

Example. Mr. Lee asked Seth to put away the reading books. Seth glared at his teacher as he went about the job. He said through clenched teeth, loudly enough for Mr. Lee to hear, "Why should I have to do this stupid job? I hate this school!"

What the child does

These children expend a lot of energy convincing people that they are not likable. The child works hard at getting even with those he perceives as having hurt him. The revenge may be active, casting the child as a troublemaker, or the revenge may be passive. The passively revengeful child is quietly defiant.

How the adult feels and usually reacts

People generally feel hurt after an attack. Then they either back away from the child or retaliate against the hurtful behavior. The typical adult reaction does not help a child bent on revenge. Retaliating or backing away reinforces both the child's hurtful behavior and his faulty perception: that he is a bad, unlikable person of little value who has to hurt others to be a part of the group.

A better approach

Do the unexpected and resist the first impulse to retaliate, give sermons, or back away. Resist the urge to take the attack personally. A child seeking revenge has poor self-esteem and is sometimes very angry, as Seth is; he needs help. Adlerians believe that adults best help children like Seth by fostering authentic self-esteem and helping them deal responsibly with their anger. Seth will value others enough to refrain from hurting them only when he feels valued.

Example. Mr. Lee (using active listening from the Rogerian approach) said, "You really seem upset about putting away the books, Seth. I think that we need to talk about it." The teacher discovered, in a dialogue with Seth (one of Vygotsky's ideas) that Seth had never gotten to feed the goldfish or the hamster, something he was yearning to do. Mr. Claiborne did not realize that and reminded Seth to volunteer to feed the animals when the children chose weekly jobs. (Seth had never voiced a desire for a specific job, the other children choosing first. He was usually left with something like putting books away.)

Displaying Inadequacy or Incompetence

The child's faulty perception

These children often feel very discouraged, thinking that they are failures. They believe they have nothing to contribute to the group, so they do not even try. They want people to leave them alone.

What the child does

Often, a child who pleads inadequacy or incompetence starts a project, only to leave it unfinished, fearing failure. These children let others know how inadequate they perceive themselves to be, hoping to discourage others from expecting much from them. They quietly work out a deal with adults in which the adult leaves the child alone and does not ask much of the child, just as the child asks very little of the adult. These children tend to point out their own ineptness or incompetence.

How the adult feels and usually reacts

Adults are usually puzzled and frustrated when they interact with an intelligent child who has given up and acts like he cannot do anything, a child who has learned helplessness. They often feel at a loss about how to help such a child. Their first impulse is often to highlight the child's errors, but this compounds the problem. Many adults then perform the task for the child, which reinforces the child's faulty perception that he can be a group member only by demonstrating incompetence. For instance, a parent might do a child's math homework when the child pleads incompetence.

A better approach

Rely on your knowledge of child development. For example, if a 4-year-old should be able to zip his own coat, refrain from performing the task for him. Most important, learn how to encourage children who mistakenly believe that they have to demonstrate incompetence. Your role is to light the fire of self-confidence in the child so that he can solve problems and carry out tasks on his own.

Example. "I think you can zip your own coat. Put this part of the zipper into this part . . . good . . . now catch that little tab and pull it up. That's it . . . Z-Z-Z-ZIP!"

Example. Linda, in third grade, had just handed a paper to Mr. Lee. The children were editing their writing. Linda said, "Here's my paper, but you know that I'm a bad speller." Without even looking at the paper, Mr. Lee handed it back to her. In a kind and matter-of-fact tone he said, "You do spell some things incorrectly, but I've noticed that you don't take the time to look up the correct spelling. When you edit your own spelling, I will take your paper." Linda was surprised, having expected her teacher simply to excuse her from the editing assignment. Her display of incompetence did not work. He has been firm but kind with her.

Case Study Analysis: Child Guidance Based on Adlerian Theory

This case study involved Sabrina, the student teacher, and Lucy, the picky eater.

- I think that the student teacher's initial strategy was **in**effective because

  _____

  _____.

- Lucy's mistaken goal was: Attention Power Revenge Inadequacy
- My reason for my selection is _____

  _____.

- Take an Adlerian perspective and state why Mr. Lee's approach was more helpful to Lucy than coaxing or forcing her to try a bite.

REFLECTING ON KEY CONCEPTS

Vygotsky, Rogers, Adler—at first glance, the three theories presented in this chapter might appear to be different, with different terminology to explain the philosophy of each. In reality, there are similarities. That is why it is so easy to adopt strategies arising from each. Understand the theories most easily by concentrating on the similarities.

1. Explain how **problem solving** is a central concept in each theory.
2. Find evidence that each theory advises adults to **assess a child's current social abilities and competencies** before deciding how to deal with a discipline encounter.
3. Explain how each theory urges adults to **engage in conversations with children.** The conversations help children become more competent in working and playing with others.
4. Explain this statement: **Constructivist** teachers can easily use strategies from all three theories to help them guide children.

APPLY YOUR KNOWLEDGE

Guiding Ellie: Ellie, almost 7 years old, left the bathroom, again without washing her hands, thus not adhering to an important classroom health limit. She challenges limits and this is yet another in a string of challenges, seemingly an act of defiance, because of the sarcastic grin you observed slide across her face. You, the first-grade teacher, were clearly frustrated. Use positive strategies from all three theories in this chapter to deal with this discipline encounter.

- (Vygotsky's theory) Use **scaffolding** to help Ellie **construct** a healthier approach to dealing with limits.
- (Rogerian theory) Decide whether you or Ellie owns this problem. Then, based on who owns the problem, choose either active listening or an I-message to help Ellie. Write out the conversation for the active listening if

you choose that strategy. If you choose an I-message, write out each part of the message.

- (Adlerian theory) Identify Ellie's mistaken goal: Attention, power, revenge, incompetence. Justify your choice. Then state how an Adlerian would deal with this discipline encounter, giving Ellie a good chance of **constructing** a different idea of how to fit into the group.

REFERENCES

Berk, L., & Winsler, A. (1995). *Scaffolding children's learning: Vygotsky and early childhood education.* Washington, DC: NAEYC.

Dinkmeyer. B., & McKay, G. D. (1988). *Systematic training for effective parenting.* Circle Pines, MN: American Guidance Service.

Dreikurs, R. (1958). *The challenge of parenthood.* New York: Hawthorne Books.

Elicker, J., & Fortner-Wood, C. (1995). Research in review: Adult-child relationships in early childhood programs. *Young Children, 51*(1), 69–78.

File, N. (1993). The teacher as guide of children's competence with peers. *Child and Youth Care Forum, 22,* 351–360.

Gordon, T. (1974). *T.E.T: Teacher effectiveness training.* New York: David McKay.

Gordon, T. (1978). *P.E.T. in action.* Toronto: Bantam.

Katz, L. (1993). Self-esteem and narcissism: Implications for practice. ERIC Digest ED358973.

Kohn, A. (1996). *Beyond discipline.* Alexandria, Virginia: Association for Supervision and Curriculum Development.

Kohn, A. (2001). Five reasons to stop saying "good job." *Young Children, 56*(5), 24–28.

Kontos, S., & Wilcox-Herzog, A. (1997). Research in review: Teachers' interactions with children: Why are they so important? *Young Children, 52*(2), 4–12.

Mead, D. E. (1976). *Six approaches to child rearing.* Provo, UT: Brigham Young University Press.

Rogers, C. (1957). The necessary and sufficient conditions of therapeutic personality change. *Journal of Consulting Psychology, 21,* 95–103.

Thomas, R. (1992). *Comparing theories of child development* (3rd ed.). Belmont, CA: Wadsworth.

✓ CHECK OUT THE WEB SITE RELATED TO THIS CHAPTER

✓ **Gordon Training International.** Organization started by Thomas Gordon, who developed Parent Effectiveness Training (P.E.T.) and Teacher Effectiveness Training (T.E.T.). Based on Rogerian theory. *www.gordontraining.com.* Home page. Sign up for free tips and newsletters. Click on "Schools." Then go to "Our Classroom Philosophy" for a statement about the site's view of classroom management.

Apply Your Knowledge: Use the Decision-Making Model of Child Guidance

"Guidance is good!"

(NAEYC poster, #447)

After reading this chapter, you will be able to

❑ **Explain** what the Decision-Making Model is and identify its building blocks.

❑ **Analyze** a case study to determine how well a teacher has used the Decision-Making Model.

❑ **Summarize** the benefits of using the Decision-Making Model for both adults and children.

❑ **Apply** your knowledge of the Decision-Making Model by writing a guidance plan intended to resolve specific discipline encounters.

Case Study: What Should We Do About the Cursing?

Mr. Claiborne, as you know from other chapters, is Ryan's teacher. He is also the cooperating teacher for first-grade student teachers Cami and Carlos. They are having an end-of-the-day discussion about the day's events.

"OK," Mr. Claiborne said, "OK . . . so you've both noticed that Ryan curses."

"I suggest time-out for Ryan," responded Cami.

"His father curses, too. I've heard him curse at Ryan. Like father, like son!" added Carlos.

"Could be, but let's try to avoid blaming, because that won't help Ryan," said Mr. Claiborne. "This is a only a problem, so let's do some **decision making** and **make a guidance plan.**"

Mr. Claiborne continued, "First of all, he's 6 years old. To Ryan, *!#! is just another word, and he's imitating his dad. Our goal is not to lay blame or to be self-righteous. All I want is for Ryan to know that there are different words that he can use in school to express his feelings. So, to get us started, I want you to think about who really has a problem here—Ryan or us?"

"Ryan, of course!" sputtered Cami, giving Mr. Claiborne a look of astonishment.

"Think about that, Cami. What would the P.E.T. people say?" asked the teacher.

"Let me think . . . oh, oh, the P.E.T. people . . . oh, yeah. Figure out who owns the problem. They would probably say that **I'm the one with the problem** because when he curses **I** get upset."

"Correct," said Mr. Claiborne. "So let's help Ryan find a different way to say what he feels."

Mr. Claiborne gave each student teacher a list of guidance strategies. "Let's review some guidance strategies and make a guidance plan," he said. "Do you think that we've made it clear that cursing is not permitted here?"

"We've never really talked about it at all," responded Carlos, looking at the list. "Maybe we need to actually state a limit about cursing?"

"You might be right. Does that sound OK to you, Cami?" responded Mr. Claiborne. She nods.

"OK, **limit setting** is our first item. Now, what do you think Ryan gets from us when he curses?"

"Our attention!" said Cami. "We all laugh!"

Mr. Claiborne said, "Attention for **in**appropriate behavior. What can we do instead?"

Cami looks over the list, "Use substitution . . . let's give him a different word to use as a substitute and then encourage him for using the new word."

"Good. **Substitution and encouragement** is item number two in the plan. What if he forgets or even tests our limit and substitution?" asked Mr. Claiborne.

"Sounds like you don't want to use time-out," said Carlos.

"Right," said Mr. Claiborne. "I just don't like using punishment, and anyway, limit setting and noticing the more acceptable word will work in the long run."

Cami said, "I think that we should all just stick to the limit and the substitution and not get all upset if he forgets or tests."

Mr. Claiborne responded, "I agree, Cami! We should change ourselves a bit. **Be calm and restate substitution,** item number three on our guidance plan for the cursing. Let's stop with three ideas and review this plan that we've made."

- Set limit.
- Use substitution.
- Calmly restate the limit and substitution, if needed.

We'll evaluate it in two days at the next staff meeting. I like how we made this decision."

DECISION-MAKING MODEL OF CHILD GUIDANCE

Carlos, Cami, and Mr. Claiborne faced a typical discipline encounter and solved it with the **Decision-Making Model of Child Guidance.** You learned about the Decision-Making Model in Chapter 1 and will, in this chapter, apply your knowledge by walking through the four steps of the model. This chapter will give you an opportunity to practice making decisions just as Carlos and Cami have done with help from Mr. Claiborne. Mr. Claiborne has scaffolded their learning about child guidance decisions.

The Decision-Making Model is a way of arriving at decisions about how to handle a variety of discipline encounters with children in a developmentally appropriate way. This chapter will help you use the positive strategies described throughout this book to make developmentally appropriate guidance plans using a logical and clearheaded approach. This approach will help you avoid being caught up in emotion when faced with a discipline encounter. A guidance plan based on clear thinking and good decision making will allow you to deal effectively with a variety of discipline encounters—the typical ones as well as those that are more challenging.

The Basis of the Decision-Making Model

Making good decisions about discipline or guidance is more than just common sense. Making good decisions about guidance is not something that people do automatically. Early childhood professionals realize that they have to learn how to make good decisions about guidance, to learn and practice the strategies. Those who use the Decision-Making Model successfully:

- possess a specific knowledge base about guidance
- have specific child guidance skills
- really do respect children and families

Knowledge base about guidance

A good knowledge base helps adults use the Decision-Making Model effectively. The most essential knowledge needed is information about how children develop. Understanding what children are like at different ages helps teachers clarify their expectations of children. Adults also need information about how a child's family and culture affects her development and behavior.

Examples.

Is it reasonable to expect a 6-month-old infant to stop crying just because someone tells him to stop?

How empathic can you expect an abused toddler to be?

How difficult is it for 3-year-old children to wait in line for the next activity?

How likely is it that a 4-year-old whose dad curses will say the same words?

What effect might witnessing a drive-by shooting have on a 6-year-old?

Are kindergarten children able to understand emotions well enough to manage them responsibly on their own?

Will an aggressive preschool child outgrow his aggression by the time he is 6 or 7 years old?

How likely is it that an 8-year-old whose parents are permissive will willingly follow classroom rules and limits?

A person who can answer these and other similar developmental questions possesses one of the key elements in using the Decision-Making Model, a knowledge base.

Skills

A professional who uses the Decision-Making Model effectively also possesses specific child guidance skills. He can use any one of a variety of DAP child guidance strategies, the same ones presented in several chapters and the Appendix in this text. He has the skills to manage the layout of the classroom well, and to manage the schedule, curriculum, activities, and materials. He understands current special topics in child guidance; e.g., anger or stress, and has the skills to help children deal with these issues.

Respect for children and families

Professionals who have a deep-rooted respect for children and families are most likely to use the Decision-Making Model well. A person who does not respect children and families will have a great deal of difficulty with child guidance.

Professionals using the Decision-Making Model competently understand that they, the adults, have greater responsibility in any interaction between them and children of any age to recognize signals that children of different ages send. For

This teacher has restated a limit to Dave. This strategy was a part of her guidance plan for him.

instance, a child who loudly interrupts would undoubtedly annoy many adults, but it is up to the adult to figure out what this child needs: social skill training, limit setting, a different way of getting adult attention? The adult has to understand that it is her responsibility to ponder the problem and think it through. Here is an example from Mr. Claiborne's first-grade class.

Example. Mr. Claiborne understands that Ryan's cursing is an example of imitation but is very likely also an attempt to be recognized. Irritating? Yes. However, the teacher understands that it is up to him to recognize Ryan's attention seeking. He also knows that only he, the adult, can control how he responds to this discipline encounter. He knows that Ryan plays a big part in this interaction but that he, the adult, has the greatest share of responsibility for deciding how to handle things.

Decision making requires a great deal of active involvement. Mr. Claiborne, for example, made an active, conscious, self-responsible decision about how best to help Ryan. He did not just use the first strategy that popped into his head. He did **not** have a knee-jerk reaction; he had to work at finding a solution.

He deliberately walked the student teachers through the systematic process of choosing a strategy. He has encouraged them to recognize their responsibility for choosing the adult behavior most likely to help Ryan at this time; that is, to choose individually appropriate strategies. Choosing adult behavior also means consciously rejecting certain strategies that do **not** fit one's personal philosophy of guidance, as Mr. Claiborne rejected time-out.

Eclectic—One Strategy Does Not Fit All

Eclectic: Selecting what appears to be the best from several different methods. Mr. Claiborne, Carlos, and Cami, for example, reviewed many strategies before making their final decision. They chose the strategies that would be best for Ryan at this time. They also changed their own practices. (Tailoring a guidance plan to a specific child's needs is the hallmark of the eclectic approach to decision making.) They avoided the one-strategy-fits-all model; they did not just automatically put Ryan in time-out when he cursed. Instead, they really thought about what might be best for Ryan. They actively rejected a punishment approach because there is such great potential for harm from using such an approach (See Figure 12.1).

Different Children, Different Families Call for Different Guidance Strategies: An Eclectic Approach

This textbook is about working with real children in the real and complex world. Typical discipline encounters, such as cursing, are relatively easy to handle. We all face such encounters regardless of where we teach. Examples include children who wiggle around during group time or children who do not clean up after themselves. They also include children who grab things from others or who impulsively blurt out answers. It would be foolish to think that an adult could possibly prevent all discipline encounters. It is healthier and more productive to acknowledge that you will run up against many everyday discipline encounters and work to deal with them.

Quote

An Eclectic Approach: What Does It Mean?

An eclectic approach DOES NOT mean to "go with the flow" or "do whatever works."

An eclectic approach requires:
- understanding different theoretical approaches, not just one.
- that adults justify choices, not defensively, but in a logical fashion.
- skill with many different guidance strategies.
- a willingness to change the setting or context.

An eclectic approach implies
- that no single approach is appropriate for every child.
- a willingness to examine and change one's own practices.

Figure 12.1.

Some children, unfortunately, live under conditions that make it difficult for them to learn appropriate behavior. They present us with discipline encounters that are tougher to deal with and challenge us as we guide them. They exhibit difficult or challenging behavior. Examples are children:

- who are abused or neglected
- whose families move frequently
- whose family lives in poverty—real poverty
- who are from drug-infested areas
- whose neighborhoods ring with the noise of gunfire
- who are from permissive homes
- whose parents model anger, aggression, and lack of empathy
- whose parents are self-centered and ignore their children, in spite of having enough money and resources to care for them
- who have a diagnosable mental illness (only a qualified professional can diagnose such problems)

When you have your own classroom, you will be energized (exhausted on occasion!) by the often confusing, sometimes exasperating, wildly wonderful differences that make each child truly unique. You will meet a new group of individuals every year that you teach—children, yes, but individuals first.

Each infant to 9-year-old individual has a basic style or temperament and a rich personal history of interactions that have taught her how to exist in this large world. Children all come from different families, each with its own scripts and rules, its own communication style, its own cultural history, its own view of how children should behave, and its own style of discipline.

Some children have parents who feel secure, who understand children and children's needs. These parents know how to communicate legitimate rules and limits and how to help children live within limits. They know how to demonstrate their love and respect to their children.

Use the Decision-Making Model when guiding children of any age during early childhood.

Other children have parents who perhaps never felt cherished themselves and who cannot, as adults, meet their children's needs for nurturance and security. These parents do not understand how infants and children develop, are angry, and do not know how or refuse to take their children's perspective. They lack empathy for their children; they might well be irritable. Often, these parents have very poor and ineffective child guidance skills; for example, they do not know how to set limits effectively or how to help children accept limits. These parents do not know how to demonstrate the love that they feel for their children.

Authoritative adults realize that the children with whom they work truly are individuals. That is the best reason for adopting as flexible as possible an approach to guiding children. The Decision-Making Model is an individualized, personal model that allows you to determine the course of action most beneficial for a specific child in specific circumstances. The Decision-Making Model is **eclectic** (flexible) in that it draws from many different ideas about children and guidance. The Decision-Making Model provides the means for you to combine your knowledge and personal strengths to deal more effectively with issues facing individual children.

You will be using the Decision-Making Model in this chapter to deal with a variety of problems, including

- everyday discipline encounters
- more difficult behavior and issues
- the need to change the context or setting in some way
- the need for a teacher to examine his own practices

STEPS IN THE DECISION-MAKING MODEL

There are four major, easy-to-learn specific steps in the Decision-Making Model. The process starts with observation and proceeds to making a decision and then to acting. The process concludes with reflection. See Figure 12.2.

Use the steps in the Decision-Making Model to analyze the chapter-opening case study, "What Should We Do About the Cursing?"

Case Study Analysis: The Decision-Making Model in Action

"What Should We Do About the Cursing?"

Use Figure 12.2, the list of **steps in the Decision-Making Model,** to evaluate the Claiborne team's use of the Decision-Making Model of Child Guidance.

Describe how Mr. Claiborne, Carlos, and Cami carried out each step:

- What leads you to think that they observed Ryan's behavior?
- What evidence can you find that they viewed the issue simply as a problem to be solved? Who did and who did not—at first?
- How and when did they examine the **context** of the problem?

Explain what the group **decided** to do to help Ryan:

- They chose specific guidance strategies. Did they also decide to change the context? If yes, how?
- Did they decide to change their own practices? If yes, explain.
- When did they plan to take action and to reflect on their decisions?

Name one or two things that you might have done differently.
How likely is it, from your perspective, that the teachers will be "successful" in dealing with this typical discipline encounter? State the reasons for your view.

The purpose of the rest of this chapter is to help you practice using the Decision-Making Model of Child Guidance. You will use the model to deal with

- everyday discipline encounters
- more difficult behavior
- contextual issues
- situations in which teachers must change their own practices

USING THE DECISION-MAKING MODEL IN EVERYDAY DISCIPLINE ENCOUNTERS

Outdoor Cleanup Time

This is an example of a normal, everyday discipline encounter. It is time for your kindergartners to go inside for story, and you notice that Levi and Dave have left the trucks out on the path again instead of putting them in the spot designated for

---

Four Steps in the Decision-Making Model of Child Guidance

Observe

- **Observe the child's behavior.**[34]
- **Focus on the encounter as a problem to be solved.**
  Clearly identify the problem. Decide whether the child or the adult "owns the problem." Focus on solving the problem, not on blaming the child.
- **Examine the "context" of the problem.**
  Ask how the child's age might be affecting her behavior. Ask how the child's family, culture, or the classroom physical environment, activities, or materials have contributed to the problem. The purpose is not to place blame but simply to get a better picture of the context or setting in which the behavior evolved.

Decide

  Your observation will tell you what to change. For example, you might need to:
- **Choose a guidance strategy.**
  Use only developmentally appropriate strategies, not punishment. Consult the list of guidance strategies in the Appendix and in Chapters 4 and 11, as well as in the rest of the text. State why the chosen strategy is appropriate for this child at this time.
- **Change the context.**
  You might decide that you have to change the classroom physical environment or the time schedule. You might decide that you should choose more DAP activities, or that materials need to be better organized.
- **Change your own practices.**
  You might decide that you should change something that you are doing. For instance, you decide to talk with children about playground rules after you realize that you have never set the limits. Do you need to restate a limit? Do you need to lower your voice when talking to a child who has done something inappropriate? Do you need to ignore a child's arguing or sulking about a limit instead of getting angry and fighting with the child?

Take Action

  Take action. Carry out the guidance strategy, make the contextual change, or change the practice that you want to change.

Reflect

  Think about how things went after you made a change. Specify the things that went well. State why you think that they turned out well. Are there some things that you still need to change? Why? If you want to make another change, go through this four-step process again to refine your approach.

Figure 12.2.

trucks. You and the staff have stated the limits clearly and positively. You have done a very good job of setting things up so that it is easy for the children to park trucks; i.e., the designated parking spots are easily accessible.

Levi's parents are permissive by choice and do not set limits. Dave follows Levi's lead.

---

[34]Chapter 3 discusses observation of children's behavior.

Use the steps in the Decision-Making Model

1. Observe:
   a. What is the problem?
   b. Whose problem is it—Levi's, Dave's, Levi and Dave's, or yours? Justify your response.
   c. Examine the context of the problem. What is it about Levi's background that is probably contributing heavily to this encounter? How does Dave's personality contribute to the encounter?

2. Decide, and 3. Plan on Taking Action:

   In this case, the teachers do not have to change the context. They have set up the truck parking very well. They also do not have to change their own practices very much. This encounter calls for choosing a guidance strategy that will help both Levi and Dave. Several guidance strategies would help you deal with this encounter effectively. Here are some ideas to get you started.
   a. You have effectively stated the limit. Explain why **restating the limit** is individually appropriate, especially for Levi, who has never had to follow limits, and for Dave, who follows Levi's lead. Write the exact words you would use to restate the limit.
   b. Explain how you could use an I-message (Rogerian approach) to help Levi and Dave understand your position. Write the I-message, including all three elements (see the Appendix).
   c. Explain how you could give **helpful feedback** to encourage the boys when they do cooperate. Write out the exact statements that you would use. Kohn (2001) makes a very good case when he gives five reasons to **stop saying** "Good job!" Try to avoid mindless praise as much as possible and, instead, express genuine appreciation for their effort.
   d. Explain how you would use **scaffolding** (Vygotsky's approach) to help Levi and Dave. Write a brief statement outlining your plan for scaffolding their understanding of the need to put things away.
   e. Explain why punishment (time-out, response cost) is **not an appropriate choice** in this case.
   f. Explain why **ignoring** this problem is also not appropriate in this case.

4. Reflect:
   a. Which strategy would you feel most comfortable using?
   b. From my perspective, the most effective strategy would be ____.
   c. I deliberately chose **not** to ____ (name the rejected strategy) because ____.

USING THE DECISION-MAKING MODEL WITH DIFFICULT BEHAVIOR

Smashing Pumpkins

This is an example of how to use the Decision-Making Model when you confront what you perceive as **difficult behavior.** You are a third-grade teacher. Some of your students, including Jack and Eddie, are working on a project about pumpkins, the interest having arisen after they read a newspaper story about a farmer having grown a very large pumpkin.

Both Jack and Eddie are famous for their temper outbursts and you keep a close watch on them. They were working together writing a "newspaper story" about their decorated pumpkins when you heard them start to yell at each other. You were on your way to their work station when Eddie picked up Jack's pumpkin and slammed it to the floor, jumped on it, and smashed it to bits. Jack responded by grabbing the pumpkin that Eddie had decorated.

You said firmly but quietly, "Put the pumpkin down, Jack. Do it now."

Jack glared at you and, saying nothing, threw the pumpkin at the wall, smashing it into a slimy mess.

This is an anger-management issue. Many people would consider this difficult behavior because of the aggressive throwing of the pumpkin and glaring at the teacher, seemingly defiantly. (You might find it useful to refer to Chapter 8 when making a decision about this encounter.)

Using the steps in the Decision-Making Model

1. Observe:
   a. What is the problem?
   b. Whose problem is it: Jack's, Eddie's, Jack's **and** Eddie's, or yours?
   c. Examine the context of the problem. These are 8-year-old children whose families use harsh discipline and whose lives are chaotic. Jack is a neglected child and the human services department is working with his parents. You have been focusing on anger management with both boys but they occasionally forget your lessons, like today.

2. Decide, and 3. Plan on Taking Action:
   In this case, you will need to decide on two things. One, how will you deal with your own anger about this incident? Second, which guidance strategies will enable you to help Jack and Eddie with their anger?
   a. **You** will probably be angry immediately after this encounter. How will you get your emotions in check before dealing directly with Jack and Eddie? State exactly what you would do for yourself.
   b. You realize that this a hot time with anger flaring. It is not the time to preach or admonish. This is the time to talk with the boys **(teacher/ child discourse)** and to use **scaffolding,** both Vygotskian concepts. Before you start, decide whether you would separate them before you talk to them. Why, or why not?
   c. What will you say to each child? What will you say if one of them tries to deflect the topic by accusing the other boy? How will you get him to focus only on his own behavior and reaction to the situation?
   d. How do you think you might follow this incident up; say, the next day, when the boys have both cooled down a bit? This might be a good time to carry out another anger-management activity **(scaffolding)**. Describe at least two things that you could do.

    e. Why is it highly **in**appropriate to force the boys to apologize to each other?

    f. Why is it highly **in**appropriate to use punishment; e.g., time-out?

    g. Why is it also **in**appropriate to ignore this incident?

4. Reflect:

    a. Which strategy would you feel most comfortable using?

    b. From my perspective, the most effective strategy would be _____.

    c. I deliberately chose **not** to use _____ (name the rejected strategy) because _____.

USING THE DECISION-MAKING MODEL TO MAKE CONTEXTUAL CHANGES

A Preschool Classroom: Keep the Sand in the Pan, Please

You are the head teacher in a preschool classroom for 4-year-olds. The children are interested in writing and you provide many materials for doing so. Today, for example, in addition to all the usual writing materials, you have placed two shallow cookie sheets (with ½-inch sides) of dry sand on the table in the writing center. The table is in the carpeted area and the sand sinks into the carpet.

This was an appropriate activity with almost all the children using the sand trays to print their names or to print other letters. Nevertheless, you are getting frustrated with having to restate the limit so often, reminding the children to "Please keep the sand in the tray." The children unintentionally knocked sand out of the trays and onto the table and floor, which you have to vacuum.

Using the steps in the Decision-Making Model

1. Observe:

    a. What is the problem?

    b. Whose problem is it: the children's or yours?

    c. Examine the context of the problem, the setting. You see sand spilling out of the tray. How might a 4-year-old child's motor development affect how he uses and moves dry sand around in a large cookie-sheet–sized tray? How has your setup of this activity affected the amount of sand flipped out of the trays (trays with very low sides are on the table; the table is on the carpet).

2. Decide, and 3. Plan on Taking Action:

You have used a good guidance strategy already by stating and then restating the limit of "keeping sand in the pan." So the solution seems to lie elsewhere; i.e., you do not necessarily need to choose another guidance strategy. You could do so, of course, but there is a better solution.

Simply restating the limit, "Keep the sand in the tray, please," does not seem to be enough. Consider the benefits of changing something about the situation (the context) to be effective.

    a. You are using dry sand. How can you safely make the sand itself more stable and less prone to flying up and over the edge of the pan?

b. You decide to continue with the dry sand, fully realizing that your 4-year-olds will probably continue flipping it out of the pans. Consider changing the situation by moving the table aside for a moment and placing a large sheet under the table. Then replace the table; gently flick any sand that spills to the center, under the table. At cleanup, gather the edges of the sheet and pick up the spilled sand. How do you think that this simple change in context would affect the situation?

c. Alternatively, what can you do about the pans themselves?

d. Do you have to use the pans at all? Can you think of a different place or piece of equipment for this writing activity? What limits would you still need?

4. Reflect:
   a. Which strategy would you feel most comfortable using?
   b. The contextual change that I think would work best is _____.
   c. I do not think that ____ would be very effective. My reason is: ____.

USING THE DECISION-MAKING MODEL TO CHANGE AN ADULT'S PRACTICES

Kenny and the Math Workbook

This is an example of a situation in which a teacher needs to change her own practices. Kenny is in kindergarten and his teacher uses many developmentally inappropriate practices. For instance, she uses workbooks in three curriculum areas every day. She has set up the curriculum so that every child is doing the same workbook pages in a large group in each curriculum area. Today, for example, all the 5-year-olds are doing page 54 in the math workbook.

Kenny dreads these workbook sessions. He sat at his rectangular table with six other children, his workbook and pencil in front of him.

"Alright, everybody! Turn to page 54," called out his teacher. She waited only briefly before issuing the next command. "Pick up those pencils and put your fingers on question #1."

Kenny blinked but opened his workbook. He cautiously turned pages, all the while looking at the other children, most of whom had found the correct page. He said nothing but dipped his head a little lower.

"Kenny," called the teacher. "Pick up that pencil and get to work!"

Kenny picked up his pencil and stared at the page. He bit his lip, as he often did when under stress.

"Get to work right now, Kenny!" The teacher seemed irritated.

Kenny squeezed his pencil and looked desperately at the book belonging to the child next to him.

"Don't look at my book, Kenny," whispered the child.

Kenny turned his head back to his own, incorrect, page. He sat still, gripping his pencil, a tear forming in the corner of his eye.

Use the steps in the Decision-Making Model

1. Observe:
   a. What is the problem?
   b. Whose problem is it—Kenny's, the teacher's, or both?
   c. Examine the context of the problem. How do you think that Kenny's confusion and distress were caused by how the teacher carries out the curriculum; i.e., workbooks, whole group, all working on the same pages, for several hours each day?

2. Decide, and 3. Plan on Taking Action:

In this case, the teacher definitely does **not** need to choose a different guidance strategy. This problem has its roots in her instructional style that is utterly **in**appropriate, and which has directly caused the problem. Kenny has done nothing wrong. The teacher needs to change her own practices in order to help Kenny. Review Chapter 5 as you respond to this question.

   a. From Chapter 5, review Mr. Pelander's and Mrs. Vargas's instructional styles and how they approach curriculum. Point out two ways in which their instructional styles are different from the style of Kenny's teacher.
   b. State how you think that the teacher's method of talking with the children, especially how she issues commands, might be affecting Kenny.
   c. What does this teacher need to change about her method of talking with the children?

4. Reflect:
   a. Earlier in this chapter, you read that adults who use the Decision-Making Model of Child Guidance effectively have an abiding respect for children. What is your opinion of the teacher's degree of respect for her kindergartners? On what do you base your opinion?
   b. Suppose that this teacher goes to a workshop and learns about a more developmentally appropriate way of teaching children. On a scale of 1 to 10, how likely is it that she will adopt more appropriate practices because of attending such a workshop? "One" means that she will **not** adopt better practices; "10" means that there is a very good chance that she will change her style of instruction. State your reasons for your choice.

USING THE DECISION-MAKING MODEL TO CHANGE THE CONTEXT AND CHANGE THE TEACHER'S OWN PRACTICES

A Third-Grade Classroom: Joseph and Amanda Will Not "Sit Still" During the Last Large-Group Lesson

This example demonstrates that problems are complex and that we often need to change a couple of things, not just one. This teacher needs to change both her own practices and the context in which her students work. She has mistakenly focused on punishing Joseph and Amanda instead of looking at other factors contributing to the problem.

A third-grade teacher was upset because she had had to put Joseph and Amanda in time-out yet again during her last large-group lesson before lunch. She asked another teacher what else she could do. The friend first acknowledged the teacher's evident frustration and then asked, "Tell me what your typical morning schedule is like" (the problem always occurs in the morning). Here is the schedule:

- Opening group—30 minutes
- Reading groups—30 minutes
- Seatwork, workbook pages for different curriculum areas each day—30 minutes
- Specialist (music, guidance counselor, art, or physical education)—40 minutes (always large group)
- Large group—20 minutes (before playground time) (the trouble spot for Joseph and Amanda)

Using the steps in the Decision-Making Model

1. Observe:
   a. What is the problem?
   b. Whose problem is it: Joseph and Amanda's or the teacher's?
   c. Examine the context of the problem. How long are these third-graders spending in group work every morning? Are the teacher's instructional methods developmentally appropriate; i.e., everything done as a total group, use of workbook pages for every curriculum area, strict division of curriculum into areas? How do you think that all of this might affect Joseph and Amanda's ability to sit through yet another group lesson at the end of every morning?

2. Decide, and 3. Plan on Taking Action:

This teacher needs to changes her own practices. Time-out, a form of punishment, is an **in**appropriate strategy. Help her understand that her schedule and her instructional methods are the root of the problem. What would you say to her to make her aware of this problem? Remember to be forthright but kind when you tell her. Hearing this type of information often arouses anxiety. People get defensive if they feel attacked.

4. Reflect:
   a. If you could make only two changes in the schedule, what would they be?
   b. Time-out (punishing Joseph and Amanda) was **not** an appropriate guidance strategy. It has "backfired" and has actually had the opposite effect from what the teacher intended; it seems to have made things worse for Joseph, Amanda, and the teacher. How could this be so?

COMING FULL CIRCLE: WHAT THE DECISION-MAKING MODEL MEANS FOR CHILDREN

If you started reading this text with Chapter 1, you learned about different styles of caregiving. We will come full circle and end this book by stating what is very likely to happen if you do decide to adopt the authori**tative** style of caregiving. Authoritative parents and teachers believe that they must create a safe and secure emotional climate for children. They realize that they influence, but do not determine, a child's behavior. By using the Decision-Making Model of Child Guidance, they set the stage for many good things to happen.

Using the Decision-Making Model of Child Guidance helps children:

- feel safe and secure
- develop healthy self-esteem and a strong moral compass
- honor and respect themselves and others
- develop healthy self-control
- learn how to deal with a variety of stressors
- understand and deal effectively with a variety of feelings: anger, sadness, love, jealousy
- walk a mile in another person's shoes—or an animal's tracks—to be empathic
- be cooperative, helpful, and generous
- learn when to be assertive
- become self-responsible
- become competent partners in the dance of interaction

REFLECTING ON KEY CONCEPTS

1. Suppose that a new teacher has a lot of respect for children and families. He has studied child development and has a good knowledge base. His major deficit is in child guidance skills; he knows no strategies other than "time-out." What are the chances of this new teacher using the Decision-Making Model well? Explain your response.

2. You have learned about many positive child guidance strategies in this textbook. Suppose that somebody says to you, "Why do you need to know **so many ways** of dealing with discipline issues?" How would you answer that person?

APPLY YOUR KNOWLEDGE

Self-Test: Making Your Own Guidance Plan

Use Figure 12.2, Four Steps in the Decision-Making Model of Child Guidance, to write a guidance plan for each of the following discipline encounters. Go through the steps just as you have for the discipline encounters on which you practiced in this chapter.

- An abused toddler bites other children.
- Five-year-olds in a multiple-age grouping get younger children to do inappropriate things (e.g., swearing, throwing objects).
- Third-graders, lined up, push and shove each other while waiting for the school bus. They have been waiting for 20 minutes.
- Three- to 5-year-olds push other children while changing activities (e.g., going outdoors).
- A 4-year-old spits at other people.
- A 4-year-old, whose family consistently uses physical discipline (hitting, pinching), hits the teacher when the teacher tries to use even a positive strategy such as restating a limit.
- A 7-year-old tattles several times each day.
- Third-graders deface library books.

REFERENCES

Kohn, A. (2001). Five reasons to stop saying "Good job." *Young Children, 56*(5), 24–28.

Appendix
Review: Major Positive Discipline Strategies

This Appendix reviews the major positive discipline strategies described in this text. First, you will read a list of the major strategies. Then each strategy is presented in outline form, along with suggestions of points to remember and to avoid when using the strategy.

Every strategy outlined here is described in more detail in other chapters, mainly Chapters 4 and 11. There is a notation in parentheses next to each strategy that will tell you which chapter presents a more detailed discussion of it.

LIST OF MAJOR STRATEGIES

1. Help children save face and preserve their dignity.
2. Set limits well.
3. Teach more helpful behavior.
4. Set up practice sessions and give on-the-spot guidance.
5. Give signals or cues for newly constructed behavior.
6. Change something about a context or setting.
7. Identify problem ownership.
8. Give meaningful feedback to children.
9. Identify mistaken goals and use encouragement.
10. Ignore behavior (only when it is appropriate to do so).
11. Redirect very young children. Divert and distract.
12. Redirect older children. Use substitution.
13. Listen actively.
14. Deliver I-messages.
15. Teach conflict resolution (problem solving).
16. Recognize signs of stress, anxiety, or strong emotion; prevent overstimulation; teach calming techniques.
17. Manage strong emotions responsibly.

1. HELP CHILDREN SAVE FACE AND PRESERVE THEIR DIGNITY (CHAPTER 4)

Purpose of the strategy: To treat children respectfully no matter what positive strategy is used. Children are likely to feel embarrassed in spite of well-done positive guidance.

How can adults do this?

- Show respect for children by taking their perspective. Think about how you would want somebody to handle matters if they had just told you to calm down or that you had done something wrong.
- Once you are finished with the positive discipline strategy, let the episode become history and allow the child to get on with things. Avoid the urge to keep explaining.
- Do not flaunt your power. Avoid saying "I told you so."

- End the interaction quickly, simply, and gracefully. Quietly tell the child, especially if you've helped her calm down, "Let's go back and play now."
- Help the child deal with the root of the upset. Some children might be ready to talk about an emotion-arousing incident, but others need to wait before discussing it. Either way, schedule a time for talking about the original problem with the child. Do what is developmentally appropriate for this child at this time.

2. SET LIMITS WELL (CHAPTER 4)

Purpose of the strategy: State expectations for desired behavior. Clarify boundaries or limits.

Appropriate limits: Never arbitrary, limits focus on important matters and are developmentally appropriate.

THINGS TO REMEMBER ABOUT STATING LIMITS

- Involve children in developing some limits in a classroom or other setting.
- Tune in, help children focus on the task, and give good cues.
- Speak naturally but slowly enough so that a child hears the limit clearly.
- Use concrete words and short, natural, and normal sentences; e.g., "It's time to put the teacups away."
- Tell a child exactly what **to** do; e.g., "Take small bites of your bread."
- Be as positive as possible.
- Give choices when appropriate.
- Give short, clear, fair reasons for limits.
- Issue only one or two suggestions at a time.
- Give children enough time to carry out the limit or to complete something else before she carries out the limit.
- Restate limits appropriately. Restate limits when it is necessary to do so.

   Avoid these things when stating limits:

- Avoid giving choices when children really do not have a choice; e.g., "Do you want to go to the library?" (the whole class goes to the library).
- Avoid giving a chain of limits.
- Avoid using "cutesy" reasons; e.g., avoid saying things such as, "I think that the teacups want to be put away now." This makes a teacher sound silly.
- Avoid telling children only what **not** to do; e.g., "Don't take such big bites of your bread!"
- Avoid vague limits; e.g., "I'm not sure that you should be doing that."
- Avoid stating arbitrary or trivial limits.
- Avoid arguing or playing the "why game" about limits.
- Avoid complex or excessive reasoning about limits.

3. TEACH MORE HELPFUL BEHAVIOR (CHAPTER 4)

Purpose of the strategy: Teach helpful behaviors (e.g., using words to express anger) and deemphasize behaviors that cause problems for a child (e.g., hitting other children). Adults must pinpoint the more helpful behavior.

Method used: Several methods can be used. With young children, modeling is effective (demonstrating desired behavior, such as handwashing, table manners, social skills such as introducing oneself, using words instead of hitting to express anger).

Steps in teaching more helpful behavior:

- Observe the child to figure out what it is that he needs to know.
- Identify the behavior causing problems for the child (e.g., whining).
- Identify a skill that would be more helpful for the child (e.g., asking for things in a normal voice).
- Model more appropriate behavior (e.g., model a normal voice for the child).

4. SET UP PRACTICE SESSIONS AND GIVE ON-THE-SPOT GUIDANCE (CHAPTER 4)

Purpose of the strategy: to give the child a chance to practice a newly learned skill with expert guidance (from the adult or from a more skilled child).

How to do this:

- Teach the new skill first (e.g., using a normal voice instead of whining).
- Practice the skill with the child. Do this privately if he has just learned the skill; e.g., let him ask you for something in a normal voice.
- Give appropriate feedback; e.g., tell the child that he seems to know how to use a normal voice when asking for something, or give him hints on how to demonstrate the skill if he makes mistakes in practice.
- Observe the child as he works with other children. Be ready to give on-the-spot guidance if it is needed; e.g., Jessie starts to whine when he wants to paint and you step in to say, "Remember, Jessie, use your normal voice for asking."
- These reminders from you, the expert, are essential in helping a child strengthen a newly learned skill.

5. GIVE SIGNALS OR CUES FOR NEWLY CONSTRUCTED BEHAVIOR (CHAPTER 4)

Purpose of the strategy: To help children remember to use the appropriate behavior, really a part of good on-the-spot guidance.

Steps in giving signals or cues:

- Identify the skill for which you will use a signal or cue (e.g., asking for something in a normal voice).

- Figure out what would be a logical signal (e.g., a quiet verbal reminder: "normal voice, please," hand signal).
- Observe the child for when the appropriate skill should be used (e.g., asking to join other children).
- Whenever possible, give the signal just before the new behavior should occur and not after the child has forgotten (e.g., just before the child asks for something).

6. CHANGE SOMETHING ABOUT A CONTEXT OR SETTING (CHAPTERS 4, 12)

Purpose of the strategy: Figure out what you can do about a situation that will help a child be safe or to enable the child to use a more helpful behavior.
Ways to change something about a situation:

- Change the physical environment or time schedule.
- Increase options available to a child: prevent predictable problems, introduce new ideas, introduce new materials.
- Decrease options available to a child: limit choices, change activities.

7. IDENTIFY PROBLEM OWNERSHIP (CHAPTER 11)

Purpose of the strategy: Determine whether an adult or a child has a problem so that appropriate follow-up can be used.

- When an adult owns a problem: Use strategies focusing on self-responsible, nonaccusatory skills (e.g., I-messages, restating reasonable limits).
- When a child owns a problem: The child's needs are the ones thwarted. Use active listening when a child owns the problem.

8. GIVE MEANINGFUL FEEDBACK TO CHILDREN (CHAPTERS 1, 4, 6)

Purpose of the strategy: Give the child helpful information. Feedback is critical to constructing skills and competencies. Good feedback can also help children make changes.
Suggestions for giving meaningful feedback:

- Avoid empty praise as feedback; e.g., avoid constantly saying, "Good job!"
- Give positive feedback and suggestions for change when appropriate.
- Give **positive unconditional** feedback, positive information independent of anything the child has done; e.g., "I like being your coach."
- Express **appreciation,** meaningful positive feedback directly related to a child's effort or interest; e.g., "You remembered to use words to tell Rachel that you wanted a turn," or "Tom, Larry, and Rob designed the cover for the class photo album."

- Give feedback that **helps children construct more helpful skills.** Use your expert knowledge and skills to give information so that a child can make a better choice about how to do something; e.g., "Lauren got real angry when you hit her. Let's figure out how to use words to tell Lauren that you were upset with what she did to you."

9. IDENTIFY MISTAKEN GOALS AND USE ENCOURAGEMENT (CHAPTER 11)

Purpose of the strategy: Identify a child's faulty perception of how to fit into a group. Be aware of what a child does to accomplish a mistaken goal (seek undue attention, power, or revenge, or demonstrate inadequacy). Explain how an adult usually feels and reacts. Outline a better way to deal with a child who has any of the four mistaken goals.

Steps in changing how you react to demands for undue attention:

- Ignore the impulse to give in to the attention-seeking behavior.
- Acknowledge the child's request, but let her know that she can complete the task. Leave the area, if necessary, so that she can finish the job.
- Give the child attention at times when her behavior is more appropriate.
- Encourage a child to take the perspective of others by telling her their perspective and by helping her learn to cooperate.

Steps in changing how you react to a child who seeks power:

- Resist the impulse to fight back.
- Decide to respond differently. You do not have to be drawn into a power struggle. You can choose to respond differently.
- Decline the child's invitation to argue or fight. This will surprise a child, particularly if you have previously been locked in power struggles with her. A useful technique is to label the interaction as a power struggle.

Steps in changing how you react to a child who seeks revenge:

- Resist the impulse to retaliate or give sermons.
- Focus on helping this child change her view of herself from a person who she thinks is not valued to the view that she is a good, worthwhile person (i.e., encourage development of self-esteem, the missing ingredient).

Steps in changing how you react to a child who demonstrates inadequacy:

- Focus on what a normal child of this age should be able to do (e.g., should a 3-year-old be able to put on her own coat?).
- Refrain from performing the age-appropriate task for her.
- Encourage a child who mistakenly believes she has to act like she is incompetent (e.g., tell her that she can carry out the task, demonstrate how she can do it, encourage her to try).

10. IGNORE BEHAVIOR (ONLY WHEN IT IS APPROPRIATE TO DO SO) (CHAPTER 4)

Purpose of the strategy: To change the adult's behavior; i.e., to change the way that an adult reacts to a child; to help the adult stop paying attention to a child's unhelpful behavior.

*Do **not** ignore certain behaviors.* (I usually like to state things in a positive way but find for this issue that saying "Do not . . ." seems to be appropriate.)

- Do **not** ignore behavior that endangers anyone, including the child herself.
- Do **not** ignore behavior that damages or destroys property or that could potentially damage or destroy property.
- Do **not** ignore rude, embarrassing, intrusive, or unduly disruptive behavior.

Guidelines for ignoring behavior:

- Pinpoint the behavior that you have been paying attention to inappropriately.
- Explain briefly to the child that you will stop paying attention to the behavior.
- Be prepared. You have paid attention in the past to the behavior and it will be difficult to stop giving attention. A child will likely try even harder to get you to pay attention to the same behavior, so be prepared for a "bigger and better whine" before it decreases.
- Decide to thoroughly ignore the behavior—don't mutter to yourself under your breath, don't make eye contact, don't communicate with the child verbally or with gestures.
- Teach and encourage a more helpful skill along with the **ignore** strategy.

11. REDIRECT VERY YOUNG CHILDREN: DIVERT AND DISTRACT (CHAPTER 4)

Purpose of the strategy: To distract a very young child from a forbidden or dangerous activity and then to divert her to a different activity.

Things to keep in mind:

- Responsible caregivers understand that they perform most of an infant's or a young toddler's ego functions; e.g., remembering to keep an infant away from outlets because she does not understand the danger.
- Avoid a power struggle when stopping dangerous behavior.
- Be prepared to act quickly when working with infants and toddlers. This requires constant supervision and observation even in a baby-proofed area.

Steps in using diversion and distraction:

- Identify for yourself the things that you do not want a baby or toddler to do because the activity is dangerous (e.g., playing with an electrical outlet, even if it is covered).
- **Immediately** do something to distract an infant or toddler from the forbidden activity (e.g., roll a ball to Sari the instant you see her near the outlet).

- Decide whether to tell an infant or toddler not to do whatever it is that is dangerous (e.g., "No playing with the outlet, Sari").

12. REDIRECT OLDER CHILDREN: USE SUBSTITUTION (CHAPTER 4)

Purpose of the strategy: Form of redirection in which an adult shows a somewhat older child (over age 2½ to 3) how to perform the same activity or type of activity but in a more acceptable and safer way.

Steps in using substitutions:

- Specify the activity needing a substitution (e.g., outdoors, zigzagging through the sandbox when others are playing there).
- Develop a substitution: a similar activity or the same activity done more safely (e.g., zigzagging through a set of tires laid flat on the ground).
- Present the substitution to the child (e.g., "Looks like you want to do an obstacle course, but not in the sandbox. Try zigging and zagging through these tires").
- Be prepared for the child to test your substitution. Resist getting drawn into a fight or power struggle. Respond to testing with positive discipline; continue to make the substitution calmly and with good will (e.g., if two children run back through the sandbox, say "Tom and Jim, the obstacle course is the set of tires, not the sandbox").

13. LISTEN ACTIVELY (CHAPTERS 4, 11)

Purpose of the strategy: Careful, accurate listening to child's feelings. Use when a child owns a problem. Conveys adult's recognition and acceptance of the child and his feelings. Communicates the adult's trust in the child's ability to work through the problem.

Things to remember about active listening:

- Listen carefully.
- Wait until the child finishes speaking, without interrupting.
- Try to understand what the message means.
- Listen for what the child is feeling.
- Suspend judgment.
- Avoid preaching, giving advice, or trying to persuade the child to feel differently.
- Merely reflect back your perception of the child's feelings.

14. DELIVER I-MESSAGES (CHAPTERS 4, 11)

Purpose of the strategy: Used when the adult "owns" the problem. Give information; communicate feelings in a respectful way; give the child a chance to change her behavior (a Rogerian concept).

Steps in constructing a good I-message:

- Name the exact behavior causing the problem. Give observable data about the child's behavior—what you see, hear, touch, smell, taste (e.g., "Adam, I see that the puzzles you used are still on the table").
- Tell the child how his behavior tangibly affects you. Did it cost you time, money, effort to do the job he should have done? (". . . and that meant that I will have to put the puzzles away just before snack").
- Tell the child how you felt (remember, do not accuse the child of causing your feeling) ("I feel annoyed if I have to do somebody else's work").
- Tell the child how to change things ("I want you to do your own work and put the puzzles on the shelf").

Things to avoid in constructing I-messages:

- Avoid accusing and blaming the child.
- Do not induce guilt.
- Avoid telling the child that he caused your feeling.

15. TEACH CONFLICT RESOLUTION (PROBLEM SOLVING) (CHAPTERS 4, 11)

Purpose of the strategy: Achieve a mutually agreeable solution to a problem without resorting to the use of power. Support creative conflict resolution rather than punishing behavior accompanying conflict between children (e.g., teach children who are arguing how to resolve the conflict rather than punishing them for fighting).

Steps in using the no-lose method of conflict resolution:

- Identify and define the conflict in a nonaccusatory way (e.g., "Vinnie and Reese, you have a problem. You both want the green paint").
- Invite children to participate in fixing the problem ("Let's think of how to solve the problem").
- Generate possible solutions with the children. Accept a variety of solutions. Avoid evaluating them ("Yes, you could both use the same paint cup, . . . you could take turns").
- Examine each idea for merits and drawbacks. With the children, decide which to try. Thank the children for thinking of solutions ("You want to both use the green paint at the same time").
- Put the plan into action ("You might have to take turns dipping your brushes into the paint . . . try your idea").
- Follow up. Evaluate how well the solution worked (teacher comes back in a few minutes: "Your idea of how to solve your green paint problem really worked").

16. RECOGNIZE SIGNS OF STRESS, ANXIETY, OR STRONG EMOTION; PREVENT OVERSTIMULATION; TEACH CALMING TECHNIQUES (CHAPTERS 3, 4, 7)

Purpose of the strategy: To look beyond or under the visible behavior. To detect an underlying cause of a behavior; e.g., stress or anxiety. To get the autonomic nervous system under control.

Suggestions:

- Observe carefully (Chapter 3), noting signs of stress (Figure 3.3, Chapter 3) or anxiety.
- Decide whether to use active listening, to decrease stimulation, or to teach/carry out a calming technique (Figure 7.3, Chapter 7).
- Decide whether to change something about the classroom to decrease stress (e.g., carry out fewer or better transitions).

17. MANAGE STRONG EMOTIONS RESPONSIBLY (CHAPTER 7 FOR SPECIFIC STRATEGIES, CHAPTER 4 FOR A BRIEF DESCRIPTION)

Purpose of the strategy: To support children in recognizing and learning responsible ways to manage strong emotions such as anger. To avoid simply punishing children for behavior resulting from strong emotions.

Steps in teaching responsible anger management:

- Model responsible anger management.
- Create a safe emotional climate. Allow and encourage children to acknowledge all feelings while firmly but kindly not permitting them to hurt anybody because of those feelings.
- Help children understand their anger triggers.
- Help children understand the body's reaction to anger.
- Teach children how to deal with the stress of anger.
- State your expectations for responsible anger management.
- Help some children learn to use words to describe angry feelings, and help others to expand their feelings vocabulary.
- Use appropriate books and stories about anger management.

Author Index

Subject Index